JANET'S STORY

PART ONE

TILL DEATH DID US PART

Written By:

BURT LEFLORE

JANET'S STORY

THE STORY OF A MOTHER AND A SON
STRUGGLING TO COPE WITH ALZHEIMER'S DISEASE

BIOGRAPHY
THE LAST YEARS OF THE LIFE OF A GREAT WOMAN
AS SHE BATTLES ALZHEIMER'S WITH THE HELP OF HER
LOVING SON

THIS BOOK DEDICATED TO THE LOVING MEMORY OF
JANET OWENS LEFLORE
THE KINDEST AND MOST GENEROUS PERSON I HAVE
EVER KNOWN
DECEMBER 26, 1926 – OCTOBER 18, 2015

WRITTEN BY:
BURT. LEFLORE

ISBN: 9798606944583

LIBRARY OF CONGRESS CONTROL NUMBER:

PREFACE

JANET'S STORY is a true account of the last years of the life of Janet O. LeFlore. Janet was my mother. As her son, I witnessed how Alzheimer's and Dementia slowly stripped her of her memory; her recollections; her orientation to time and space; her independence, and her ability to perform daily routine tasks she had taken for granted the majority of her life.

Alzheimer's and Dementia also deeply affected my life in a multiplicity of ways. First it was difficult and sometimes horrifying to watch a woman who I had always admired, respected and looked up to, regressing. She had always been an amazing beacon of intelligence, light, ray of hope and love. She slowly and consistently became someone other than the woman I had known all my life. I had to sacrifice aspects of my daily routine to care for her and make sure all was well with her. It tested my patience as many days, I found myself being asked the same questions over and over about the simplest and most trivial things. There were days when she would exhibit behavior that was completely irrational and beyond comprehension, other than perhaps she no longer had the capacity to understand.

In many ways it is like taking care of a young child. However, instead of you seeing the child's growth and maturity with each passing day and finding joy in the process, you are watching an adult as their condition deteriorates with each passing day. Very often observing the onset of Alzheimer's brings feelings of desolation and helplessness. There were many difficult days trying to deal with a person who had been independent all of their life now vehemently resisting the idea or thought of people being remotely in control of their life. There are many days when you have to deal with the frustration, anger, depression, sadness, mood swings and confusion the person faces as Alzheimer's progresses and they struggle to coexist autonomously.

I decided to write this book because seeing my mother Janet LeFlore suffer from this devastating condition had such a profound effect on me. Some days it hurt me so deeply to see the things she was going through. Challenges she faced in her day to day life trying to remember and recall simple things. Challenges she underwent as she endured being misunderstood and rejected by some of her closest family members who she loved so much. Sadly and helplessly watching as she became increasingly withdrawn from the real world and isolated from society. Helpless in not being able to do anything to prevent the onset of neurological changes that occur in a person with Alzheimer's.

Similarly, there was the feeling of isolation I felt because there were not many people who I could depend on or talk to about what was going on with my mother. I found that most people find it hard to comprehend and relate to what a caretaker may be experiencing from day to day, unless they have experienced it themselves with someone in their own life. Very few people understand, so many caretakers feel alone with regard to emotional or spiritual support in their quest to care for a loved one.

By sharing and relating this story about Janet Owens LeFlore, I want to try and help more people to understand the condition called Alzheimer's. I want to give so many of the people out there who are suffering in silence or who have suffered in the past with their loves one; feeling hopeless; overly criticized; unappreciated; overworked; stressed and alone. I want to let you know you are not alone. I pray for you and your loved one. I pray you will find strength and joy in being there for them, and contentment in knowing you are blessed with the understanding that you are performing one of the noblest tasks known to man, caring for someone who cared for you.

INTRODUCTION

The Preface of this book is intended to provide the reader with the "why," giving the many reasons I decided to and needed to write this book and tell the story about the last chapters of my mother's life. The Introduction is intended to provide the reader with the "how."

The book is laid out chronologically. In deciding where to start, I had to pick a place in time. Certainly, I had to let the readers know a little about who she was and who she had been for the majority of her earthly existence. I also wanted to pick a starting point where she may have been showing very mild signs of having Alzheimer's and Dementia. A happier time, so to speak, but in many ways, it was a sad time because her husband was suffering from cancer.

JANET'S STORY is written in a narrative style. All of the subject matter and material in the book is based on my knowledge, experiences, accounts, perception, recollections, observations, perceptions and thoughts. In addition, there is a significant amount of material transcribed and copied from actual trial transcripts. There is nothing fabricated or sensationalized with regard to the content designed to make it more appealing, interesting or awe inspiring. Nothing more than the simple truth about the last chapter in my mother Janet LeFlore's life.

There were many names changed in this Biography to protect the privacy of those individuals. There was no attempt to disparage, misrepresent or to demean anyone. However, any and all statements in this book are absolutely and without a doubt true and accurate despite any disclaimers. So, if anyone feels the need to come for me, please understand I will meet you with the absolute truth. Libel is only actionable in court of law if the statements were false. However, in this case any and all statements made it this book are true beyond any shadow of a doubt and to the best of my belief.

The names of some of my deceased family members are also included in this book. I am glad those names did not have to be changed because that helps to maintain the authenticity of the work. My most sincere desire during the writing of this book was to be as authentic as possible with the story I was telling. Names of some of my living relatives have remained the same also, similarly for me it helps to maintain and preserve the originality and genuineness of the work.

Most importantly, even though I have modified some names within the lines of this narrative. I have not changed, altered, nor modified anything related to my mother's character or her life. The book is all in part a tribute to her legacy and life. Herein I have also attempted to provide a window and greater understanding of how Alzheimer's affects people and the people living with a loved one suffering from this malady. In order to tell this story, I had to discuss some things about her that were somewhat private; however, for the sake of authenticity those things had to be revealed.

There are many scenes in the book that I find to be humorous as I look back on it, even though at the time when it occurred it was alarming, disturbing or unsettling. Certainly, I want the reader to take this book seriously, but do not be afraid to laugh every once in a while. Janet is a sympathetic character because she is an elderly woman and she has Alzheimer's. Although, sometimes Janet comes hard toward people around her. She would not hesitate to tell you exactly how she felt, and it was not always in the most kind and courteous manner. Another common trait of elderly people with Alzheimer's.

There are instances when I may break off into descriptions of my perceptions and intellectual or emotional impressions regarding her idiosyncrasies and sometimes misunderstood mode of behavior or way of thought peculiar to her. However, I tried to keep it focused within the confines of what might have been happening at that point with Janet and how I may have perceived it at that point in time.

CHAPTER ONE

On this beautiful morning in Mobile, Alabama, Dr. Walker B. LeFlore is getting dressed and ready for work. He stands there in the mirror of his bathroom buttoning his shirt and tying his necktie when his wife Janet LeFlore comes into the bathroom and puts her arm around him.

"Beck hurry up, your coffee is ready," she says.

"Ok, I'm coming," he replied. "Janet, you're not even dressed yet. I thought you were going to be ready to go to the office when I left this morning. Ethel just said I had twenty patients already."

"I'll be there in about an hour," said Janet, "Just have a cup of coffee with me before you leave, and I'll be there in a few minutes. I promise."

Walker finished the loop on his necktie and goes to join Janet in the kitchen for a cup of coffee. Janet and Walker have a very fine home. The downstairs master bedroom and bath are large and ornate and comfortably furnished. The kitchen is a large and grand open area with an island bar and a stove in the middle with mahogany cabinets and granite counter tops. Janet and Walker have a fruit salad and a cup of coffee for breakfast. Janet has already placed his cup and fruit on the table as he comes into the kitchen. Walker sits down at the table and just as he gets seated and sips his cup of coffee the phone rings. Janet answered the phone.

"If that's Ethel tell her I will be there shortly," said Walker.

"Hello," sings Janet as if she is in a good mood. "Julia how is my sister doing on this beautiful morning," she said.

"Now you asked me to come and have a cup of coffee with you and you go jumping on the phone," said Walker.

"We're fine, we were just about to sit down and have a cup of coffee before Beck goes to work," she replied. "What are you doing today?" she asks in a jovial mood. "Let me call you back in a few minutes... Ok, I'll talk with you in just a second, after Beck leaves," said Janet.

Walker sits there quietly drinking his coffee looking at the newspaper and eating his fruit salad. Janet hangs up the telephone and walks over to the table. She leans over on the table and looks at

8

Walker.

"How are you feeling?" she asks.

"I don't have a lot of feeling in my fingertips, I seem to be experiencing some neuropathy in my fingers," replied Walker.

"We've got to go for your chemotherapy at 3 o'clock today don't forget," Janet said.

"I know, that's why I need to get to work so I can finish seeing all of my patients because I'm going to be tired after the treatment and I still have to go to the Hospital to make my rounds," he said.

An elderly African-American woman named Leassie can be seen seated across the kitchen in the couple's Florida room ironing a shirt. Leassie is Janet and Walker's housekeeper. She has been working for them for almost 30 years. She tells Doc that she wants to come and see him sometime this week because she needs to get her prescription for her arthritis.

Dr. LeFlore tells her he will have it for her. The telephone rings again and Janet goes over to answer.

"Hello," she sings in a playful voice. "Anna how are you doing my dear sister on this lovely morning that the Lord has made," Janet said. "Me and Beck were just sitting here having a cup of coffee, we're about to go to work in a little while."

Walker gets up from the table and starts gathering his newspaper as he is about to leave for work. She gives Beck a hug while holding the phone in her other hand. Walker heads out the door. She tells him goodbye and continues her conversation with her sister Anna.

Shortly after Walker leaves, Janet is still seated at the table with her cup of coffee. Leassie is still seated at the ironing board ironing the same shirt when her son Burton comes in the door. He is dressed in his suit and about to head for work himself. He comes over to his Mom and gives her a hug.

"Hi Baby," says Janet.

"Mom, you remember when me and Candace took that trip up to Wilmington. Well, I applied for this position teaching Business Law at the University of North Carolina and they called me and said they wanted me to take the job. "What do you think? Do you think I should take it?' Burton asked.

"Wow. You mean to tell me they offered you a position?' she

replied.

"I wasn't going to take the job, but they keep calling me and asking me to come and accept the position. I think I'm going to take it," Burton said.

"What about your job with the law firm here in Mobile?" she asked.

"Things aren't really working out for me there. The environment is so confining. The managing partner and his secretary are having an affair. She walks around all day with her ass on her shoulders like, 'You better kiss my butt because if I don't like you, you're going to get fired'," said Burton. "Her attitude and their affair just permeates the environment and I'm tired of it. I don't know, it just seems like this might just be a fresh start for us."

"Well, I think it would be a great opportunity for you baby, and you all can stay there at 1013. The house is vacant," she replied.

"If I could stay there for a few weeks until we find a place it would be a big help," he said.

"Hell, you can stay there as long as you want," said Janet.

"Mom, like I said, it would be great if we could stay there temporarily, but I'm not trying to be dealing with all these other folks, Mom. If I take this job, I want to have my peace of mind. I'm going there to work. I'm not asking for any handouts from your family," he said.

"Burton, that's my house. Me and my brother Warren built that house and if you and your family are going to Wilmington for you to take this job with the University, then I want you to stay there," she said. "Why wouldn't you? It's a completely furnished house. It's only logical that you would stay there," Janet said. "You know they still haven't paid me the rest of the $20,000 they promised me when I let them get their names on the deed," Janet said.

"Like I said Mom if we could stay there for a few days that would be great," replied Burton.

"They want me to be there on August 20th," he said.

"Congratulations. Have you told your dad yet?" she said.

"I'm going to tell him," said Burton.

"Wilmington has changed so much since I was a child," said Janet.

"You know they're making a lot of movies in Wilmington now," replied Burton.

"I heard," said Janet.

"They call it Wilmywood," Burton interjected.

"I'm going to call Bethany, Ann, and Julia and let them know we need to get the key. So, don't worry about a thing. Just get yourself ready, if that is what you want to do," Janet said.

"How do Candace and the kids feel about you guys moving to North Carolina?"

"She said I should take it, and the kids seem cool with it. The only thing is Breton is starting high school this year and he would have to start high school in a new city where none of us really knows anyone," replied Burton.

"Be sure you talk with your dad about it," said Janet.

"I got to run, Mom," he said as he kissed her goodbye. "I will go by and tell him after work."

"Bye baby. Have a nice day," Janet said.

"Bye, Miss Whitfield," said Burton as he walks out of the door.

"Bye, Burjeon," said Leassie.

Janet is still seated at the kitchen table drinking her cup of coffee. Leassie comes into the kitchen area and fixes herself a glass of water. Janet starts to rub the side of her jaw as she is experiencing some nerve pain. Janet suffers from TMJ and her nerve pain sometimes becomes excruciating. Janet looked over at Leassie and told her that her jaw was hurting. She finished her coffee and went to work with Beck. Walker's middle name is Beck. Although his first name is Walker, Janet has always called him by Beck, his middle name.

Janet is now 73 years old and Beck is 72 years old. She is a retired Chemistry teacher having taught chemistry for almost thirty years at a junior college called Bishop State Community College. She is an accomplished lady married to a very successful physician. Janet and Walker have been married for over 50 years. They met at St. Augustine's College in Raleigh, North Carolina. Janet said Walker ran into her on the yard one day knocking all her books out of her hands. She fell in love with him and they have been together ever since.

Their marriage has had its rocky points, but their love is truly a lasting union and at this era in their lives they are very close, content and happy with one another. Janet and Walker had two sons; Walker B. LeFlore Jr., and Burton R. LeFlore. Walker Jr., their oldest son, nicknamed "Champ" was 14 years older than their youngest son Burton. Walker Jr. was a graduate of the University of South Alabama and a graduate of the Tulane University College of Law. Champ was a Louisiana lawyer who loved New Orleans. He completed law school at Tulane in 1982. He took the Louisiana Bar and was admitted to practice. He stayed in New Orleans and continued his law practice from that point on. Walker "Champ" Beck LeFlore, Jr., died of an untimely death at the age of 43 on August 18, 1994. Champ was Janet and Walker's first-born son. Walker Jr.'s death was devastating to Janet, Walker, Burton and their entire family. In many ways, Champ was like the glue that held the family together. The same summer in May of 1994, Walker's mother, Teah, passed away at the age of 91. So, Walker lost his mother in May. Three months later he and Janet lost their eldest son. 1994 was a rough year for Janet and Walker.

Janet and Walker were two depression babies who both worked very hard throughout the course of their lives. They amassed financial security and a comfortable life together. Shortly after retiring from Bishop State, Janet started working with her husband in his medical practice. So much for her retirement.

However, Janet enjoys working and staying active. She enjoys the time together that she and her husband have now that she is working with him. Walker is just tickled pink to have his lovely wife working for him and to have her undivided attention to his needs and the needs of his medical practice. She does his billing and coding for the office. Walker is a good man who was devoted to his family, but his medical practice is his life, his heart, and his soul. Janet is a good woman who adores her husband and family with everything she has.

Her life at this point, in retrospect, is good. However, Walker is suffering from cancer. He has been battling cancer now for almost four years. Walker is a die-hard Doctor who keeps doing what he does, even though many days he is probably sicker than a lot of the patients he is treating. Walker has had several surgeries and several stints in the Hospital. He is also taking chemotherapy treatments which leave him feeling weak and tired. Janet, on the other hand, is in excellent health for a 73-year-old woman. Her one health issue is that she suffers from trigeminal nerve pain. There are times in her days and weeks when she feels fine and there are times and days when the pain in her jaw is almost unbearable.

She sometimes takes pain pills, but she does not like to depend on the pills because they make her feel groggy and sleepy. She is a Doctor's wife and a chemist, but she does not want to take any medication unless it is absolutely necessary. Currently, she is on no medications for any health-related issues other than an occasional pain pill for the discomfort in her jaw.

When Janet finished getting dressed, she returned her sister Julia's call to tell her that Burton is about to move to Wilmington to take a new job, and he would need to stay in the family house at 1013 South 12th Street for a while until finding a place for him and his family to stay.

Julia assured her that she did not have a problem with it, but she thought they should talk with Bethany and Anna. She hangs up with Julia and called her sister Bethany to tell her, but Bethany is not home. She leaves a message on the answering machine for her to return her call. Janet tells Leassie goodbye and leaves the house. She gets into her brand-new pearl white Cadillac Deville and heads to work.

She arrived at the office to find Walker and his staff there working on seeing his patients. He had twenty patients waiting and now an additional six patients have arrived. Janet had always admired Walker's fortitude especially since he is fighting cancer. She knows he is extremely sick himself, and when most people would have given up and stopped working if they were in the same condition, he continues to strive to help humanity and serve his patients. Janet is a dedicated wife to her husband Walker and has a deep respect for his dedication and his love for those he serves. This was a quality they both shared. She was so dedicated to her students and to helping them over her years of service as a college chemistry professor. As the day went on Dr. LeFlore and his staff managed to see all thirty-two patients who had arrived that day, and they saw all of them before 2:45 p.m., as Walker rested for a moment at his desk before he and Janet left to go to his chemotherapy treatment. Luckily, his treatments were at Mobile Infirmary Hospital which was the same Hospitals were Walker admitted his patients. The Hospitals were not located far from his office, so the two of them did not have long to drive. On their way to the hospital, Walker said, "Janet, I'm so tired."

Walker finished his chemotherapy treatment and the two of them went to the house because Walker wanted to lay down and rest for a while before going back to Mobile Infirmary to make his evening rounds. When Janet got back home, she decided to call her sister's Anna and Bethany to let them know her son Burton would need the key to the house at 1013. By the time Janet spoke with Anna, it was pretty obvious that Julia had already contacted her regarding Burton and his family's proposed stay at the house. Julia and Anna had discussed the matter and decided they did not want Burton's family staying there, not even for a few days.

"Bethany, I need you and Ann to send the key to 1013. Burton and his family are moving to Wilmington. He has a new job offer at UNC teaching Business Law," Janet said. "He and needs to stay there for a while until they get situated."

"The last time Burton and his family stayed there," said Bethany before Janet cut her off.

"The last time Burton and his family stayed there, we fixed the air conditioning unit and I paid for it, and don't believe I have received a dime from you, Julia or Ann," said Janet.

"They left the house dirty," said Bethany.

"That's a lie Burton told me he made sure the house was clean before they left," said Janet.

"I just don't think it would be a good idea. We want the house to be there for the family when we want to go there to visit," said Bethany.

"He's not going to be there that long. I think that you, Ann, and Julia need to pay me the rest of the $20,000.00 you promised to pay me when I let you put your names on the deed," replied Janet.

"Have you talked to Ann and Julia?" Bethany asked. "I will go along with whatever they decide."

"Ah, you'll go along with whatever they decide, huh?" asked Janet.

Janet ends her conversation with Bethany. Janet is noticeably angry by Bethany's response to her request for the keys to the house. Of course, they had never given Janet a key to the house since they got their names on the deed in 1998. Ever since she agreed to sell them an interest in the family homestead her three sisters just took control of the house and basically excluded Janet and all the other family members. They told her they wanted to make the house into a house for the family, but it seemed the house was just for them and their enjoyment. This had seriously disturbed Janet as they argued following Burton's visit to the house earlier that year when he got the job at UNCW. Burton advised Janet not to let them get their names on the deed when they first asked. Burton suggested to Janet that she could give them a Life Estate in the property; however, Janet being the giving, trusting, the kind-spirited and loving big sister she was, agreed to give her sisters a Feel Simple interest in the property. She hung up the phone and called her godmother, Mary Lilly Lofton, to discuss it with her.

Marry Lilly Lofton is Janet's godmother. She is 101 years old. Janet came from a family of ten (10) children. She had one sister named Evangeline, who died of appendicitis at a very young age. In chronological order, Janet had an older sister named Eldridge O. Wilson, a brother named Angle (AB) Owens, then Janet. After Janet, there was Warren Owens, Bethany O. Clark, Anna O. Lane, Carol O. Holmes, Julia O. Parrish, and Peter G. Owens. Janet's parents Angle and Mable Owens raised their large family in Wilmington, North Carolina, Mary Lilly Lofton was the family's surrogate mother. She loved all the Owens children, but she always had a special love and affection for Janet who she called her "Little Jane."

Mary Lilly was a schoolteacher in the Wilmington Public School System. She never had any children of her own. Having been married for a brief period and then divorced, she and her former husband had no children and Mary Lilly did not remarry. Marry Lilly and Janet were very close over the years.

At some point during the early seventies (1970s), Mary Lilly was about to lose her house. The house was in a state of disrepair among other things. Janet agreed to help Mary Lilly. She paid for some needed renovation work on her house and helped her with a few other expenses. In exchange, Mary Lilly agreed to give Janet a deed to her house reserving a Life Estate for herself, allowing her to remain in the house for the rest of her life and then upon her death, the house at 1006 South 12th Street would go to Janet in Fee Simple. This worked for Mary Lilly because she had no children or other living relatives. Janet and her brothers and sisters where about the only thing close to a family that Mary Lilly had. Now that Janet's mother Mable had passed away, she and her godmother developed more of a mother-daughter relationship as Janet had always been like the daughter she never had.

"Mary Lilly do you have a key to 1013?" asked Janet. "Burton is about to come to Wilmington with his family and they need to stay there for a day or two until they get settled."

"No, I had a key, but Ann and Julia took the key the last time they were down here a few months ago," replied Mary Lilly.

"Those sneaky little bitches," said Janet.

"What's the problem Janet?" asked Mary Lilly. "Have you talked with Ann, Bethany, and Julia?" asked Mary Lilly.

"Ann, Bethany, and Julia can kiss my ass," said Janet. "What they need to do is pay me the rest of my $20,000.00. They asked me to allow them to put their names on the deed and promised to pay me $20,000.00 and only paid me $7,000.00. Since then they've taken over the house. Act like nobody else matters. I'm sick of it, Mary Millie."

"I had a key, but they got it last time they were here," said Mary Lilly. "They sure did, so I don't have the key anymore. I don't see why they wouldn't want Burton and his family to stay there."

"Ok, then I'll call Ann and see if she has the key. Mary Lilly, I'll call you a little later," said Janet.

Mary Lilly and Janet end the conversation. Janet calls her sister Anna to discuss getting the key from her.

"Ann, I need you to send me the key to 1013 because Burton is moving to Wilmington to take a new job with the University of North Carolina teaching Business Law. He and his family need to stay there for a while until they get situated," Janet said. "He'll be leaving in a few days. He is supposed to start work on the 20th of August."

"Janet, Julia and I already had plans to be in Wilmington the week of the 20th and we are going to stay at 1013 ourselves, so there is no way they can stay there," said Anna.

"This is very important to Burton," said Janet.

"Julia has been planning a mother-daughter retreat for several weeks now. As many apartments and rental houses, they have in Wilmington, I'm sure Burton won't have any problem findings somewhere to stay," said Anna.

"I'm sure he won't have any problem finding somewhere to stay. That's not the issue Ann," said Janet. "He just needs somewhere to stay for a few days until he can find something; but really as far as I'm concerned, he can stay there as long as he damn well pleases. I just need you to get me the key!"

"What I'm trying to tell you is that we are already going to be there," said Anna.

"What you and Julia need to do, is pay me the rest of my money. That's what you and Julia can do," replied Janet.

Janet can hear Walker calling her from the bedroom. Janet tells Anna that Beck is calling her, and she will talk with her later. She is angry now as she hangs up the telephone with Anna. Beck is awakening from his nap and getting up out of bed. He is still wearing all his clothes as he climbs out of bed and reaches to put his feet into his shoes sitting near the edge of the bed. Beck asked her what she was in the kitchen arguing about. Janet explains that she was talking with Anna about Burton taking the job in North Carolina. Janet tells Beck to come into the kitchen and eat his dinner as she starts to fix their plates. Beck is seated on the side of the bed and rubs his head. He is so tired, and the chemotherapy is making him feel like he wanted to vomit, not to mention the sensation of numbness in his fingertips. Although he would really like to stay in bed, he has got to get up and go to the Hospital and make rounds. Beck comes into the kitchen where Janet has their dinner sitting on the table.

As Janet and Walker sit down to eat, Walker asked her again what the problem is and why she was arguing with her sister? Janet explained that they acted as if they did not want Burton and his family to stay at 1013 for a few days so that he could start his new job. Beck and Janet agree that this could be a good opportunity for their son if he could take this teaching position and get some teaching experience under his belt. Beck suggested that maybe he should see if he can find a position somewhere in the Mobile area. Of course, they both know that he planned to move to Wilmington to take the position at The University of North Carolina at Wilmington and has nowhere to stay when their family owns a fully furnished, vacant home right there in the city less than five miles from where he would be working.

However, at this point, Walker and Janet just look at each other calmly and sit down to eat their dinner. Tonight, they are having steak, baked potato, and cheese broccoli. Walker looks somberly into Janet's eyes as he takes a bite of his steak, pouring some steak sauce onto the steak. This is one of those moments where a couple of more than fifty years can talk about the things that are really on their minds and not about the things that really don't matter. Things that are related to other people, their desires, their happiness, their rules, their selfish motives, their family affiliations, their unwillingness, their inappropriateness. Sometimes a couple who has been together as long as Janet and Beck have been together can suddenly and without another word, come to an understanding. It is possible for two people to understand their family, shut it out and focus on their family and not all the extraneous outside stuff.

Janet was deeply angered and upset by her sister's unwillingness to let Burton and his family stay in the family homestead for a period until he could get adjusted and find a home in the Wilmington area. Mind you the house belonged to Janet, not the sisters. She agreed to allow them to share in the house and now they had taken the house over and wanted to exclude her and her family. Not only did they not pay her what they promised to pay her to have their names included on the Deed, now they were just behaving in a selfish manner. Their reluctance to let her son stay there was the ultimate slap in the face to Janet. Similarly, the fact that Burton had gotten the position in Wilmington teaching Business Law opened the flood gates to the whole situation and made Janet feel that she had been bamboozled by her sisters.

Ever since Janet had allowed Anna, Julia, and Bethany to put their names on the Deed in 1997, they promised Janet that they wanted to make their family homestead into a house for them to visit and have family reunions and family gatherings. Janet had not raised much of a fuss about the fact that they had not paid her all the money they promised to pay her. Until now Janet, Walker, and Burton had not really been very much concerned with the house. They furnished the house and provided it with all the comfort and amenities of any house but for the most part, it sat vacant as all of them lived in other parts of the country.

Janet being the good-hearted and trusting person she was, entered into this agreement with the sisters verbally and received nothing in writing except the Deed adding their names as owners. They paid her $7,000.00 and from that point on they neglected to pay the remainder of the money they promised to pay which was $13,000.00. They promised that they wanted to make the house into a family getaway. However, they took possession and never sent Janet a key to the house, even though they all had keys. The one time that Burton and his family took a vacation there, and he landed the position teaching Business Law at the University, there was a big issue about him and his family staying at the house. Of course, the sister's said it was going to be a family house for the entire family. However, this did not seem to be the case. Janet's sisters acted as if they really did not want Burton to visit the house. They manufactured lies that he had left the house dirty when he stayed there which was totally untrue. They also retrieved the key to the house they had left with Mary Lilly Lofton after Burton went back home. As far as Janet was concerned, this was an insult to her. She had trusted them, and now they had the audacity to turn around and want to refuse to help her son when he just needed to stay there for a few days to take a new job. Sort of like the chickens coming home to roost or poetic justice.

The time when that event occurs that helps a person to really put things in perspective. One of those times when a person realizes that something they did with joy in their heart and with the belief and misunderstanding that their actions would benefit everyone. Only to find out it seems to be benefiting everyone but you, when you should have and could have just said no to the entire deal and kept what was yours, to hell with everyone else. One of those moments when you say, hey I did this for you, and now I need you to do this for me.

CHAPTER TWO

Burton and his family did move to Wilmington at the end of the summer. Janet's sister's Anna and Julia were there two days before they arrived to make sure they did not try to stay in the family homestead. However, Burton and his wife decided to stay at Wrightsville Beach. They stayed in a very nice hotel on the beach for about two days, and then they spent about a week in a two-bedroom beach bungalow. It was much more expensive for him and his family than perhaps staying in the family house, but he and his family put that behind them as they embraced this new opportunity. Burton started his job at the University. His oldest son Breton started his freshman year at Hoggard High School. His middle boy Bryceton started preschool, and his baby boy Breaghan who was only three years old at the time was not in school. Finally, they found a three-bedroom beach cottage to rent. The beach house was located less than a block from the Atlantic Ocean. Burton loves the beach and he enjoyed his current arrangement much more than dealing with the stress of his aunts.

Anna and Julia stayed for several days to make sure Burton was not going to move into the house. Burton met with them. He and his family visited with them on several occasions. At this point, Janet was content that Burton was alright as far as his living situation was concerned; however, with her, it was still very deeply personal that the sisters blocked him from staying there. She was still quite upset about the entire state-of-affairs. Janet and Walker made plans to drive to Wilmington to visit Burton, Candace, and the kids. She was very much aware that her sisters had been spending a lot of time down in Wilmington at the family homestead. She and Walker decided that when they arrived in Wilmington they were not going to stay in the homestead with the sisters. They decided they were going to stay at the Holiday Inn Sunspree Hotel in Wrightsville Beach near where Burton and the kids were living.

Walker had to go into the Hospital for his chemotherapy treatment before they left. Janet had such a broken heart for her husband. She shed tears for him. She loved him so much. She loved him with all her heart. He was her first and only boyfriend. She had a few potential suitors before she left Wilmington for college at St.

Augustin's College. However, Janet's parents sent her to an all-girl boarding school in North Carolina for her Junior and Senior year of High School because there were so many young men trying to date her there in Wilmington. She met her husband Walker at St. Augustine's College and had been with him ever since.

Now she was with the love of her life as he underwent an enormous ordeal. He was battling cancer. Does anyone realize what chemotherapy and radiation can do to a person's body? Walker was gravely ill. He was dying and the treatments were doing little more to help him than hasten his death. Are chemotherapy and radiation a real cure for cancer? Walker was weak and his skin was discolored. He had also lost a considerable amount of weight. Despite surgery, his cancer had spread. Even though the treatment seems to do more harm than good. Nothing is more painful than trying to smile and remain positive because you know the person is physiologically changed after undergoing chemotherapy and radiation suffers with this enormous disease. There is no one who can fully understand what it is like to support a loved one through the battle of cancer. Cancer is one of the most enormous healthcare beasts. One day when medical science really finds a cure for cancer, they will look back on chemotherapy and radiation like, "OMG, what were we really doing to these people? No one knows what it is like to fight a battle with cancer unless you have actually done it. Many of the people who have fought this fight are dead. Let's just tell it like it is."

Walker was suffering from cancer and he was fighting such a horrific disease. Every year so many Americans die of cancer. There is such sorrow and sadness, unhappiness when you have a person who is already sick and now having to do and undergo all of these worthless treatments designed at eradicating the disease. Walker was Janet's husband and only love. The father of her two children. They had lived their lives and grown old together. For the most part, they had majorly succeeded in life. Janet was a chemistry instructor who retired at a state-funded Junior college. Janet had a retirement package and excellent health insurance through the State of Alabama. Beck was an accomplished Physician in Mobile. The two of them were comfortable beyond belief. Two depression babies who managed to make good despite their circumstances and meager impoverished beginnings.

Many people have had the blessings from God to have not been touched by cancer. However, Walker continued to work and stay active along with regular treatments. Most days Walker felt sicker than the patients he was treating. Beyond the devastation that this disease can do to the person suffering from cancer, it takes a tremendous toll on the people who love and care for this person.

Janet did everything she could to be understanding and loving toward her husband during this ordeal in his life. However, the sickness also took a tremendous toll on her personally. For several years, Walker and Janet decided they did not want to tell their son Burton what was going on because they did not want him to worry while he was still in law school. Burton found out the summer after he graduated law school that his dad was suffering from cancer. Walker was diagnosed in 1995 so now in 2000, he had been battling cancer for almost five years.

Burton did not find out his dad was suffering from cancer until the Summer of 1997 after he graduated from Law School. Walker and Janet attended his graduation and two days after Walker returned home from Burton's graduation, he went into the Hospital for surgery to remove a portion of his intestines with cancerous lesions. They did not tell Burton that Walker was going into the Hospital and Burton had planned to take a trip to Europe for a few days following his graduation. Burton found out when he called the house one day from France and his dad answered the phone at a time when he would not usually have been at home. Burton questioned him about the fact that he had called at a time of the day when he would not have expected to reach him because usually, he would have been at work. While Burton was traveling in the South of France, Italy, and Holland, his dad finally told him that he was in the Hospital and had undergone surgery. They explained to Burton that the calls were forwarded from the house phone to the Hospital. All of the calls Burton had made while abroad to the house had been forwarded to the Hospital, so he never knew the difference until his dad finally told him. Burton cut his trip short and returned to be by Beck's side.

However, Walker made it through but there were a few complications that he had to overcome. That summer, Walker spent almost the entire summer in the Hospital. However, he survived and went home and returned to work.

Janet was perplexed and dismayed over this entire situation. She was worried about her husband's health and now her sisters who also knew nothing about Walker's condition were really starting to bother and agitate her over the family homestead. Janet's husband Walker had already experienced his share of disappointment with his family. However, Janet had always believed her family was different, and that her family was closer and would not go through the type of problems Walker had gone through with his siblings over property and money that had belonged to their parents and family.

She and Walker planned to take a trip to Wilmington to visit Burton and his family. Janet also planned to confront her sisters about how she felt with regard to their unwillingness to allow Burton and his family to stay at the house while they made the transition into his new job and into the city of Wilmington. Janet was becoming a nervous wreck, between the Trigeminal nerve pain she suffered from in her jaw area, being worried and concerned for her husband's well-being, and now this animosity she had developed toward her sisters. Everything was starting to become quite complex and convoluted to her.

The following morning the two of them set out onto I-65 North en route to Wilmington. It was a beautiful summer morning as Walker initially took the wheel.

"Beck are you sure you don't want me to drive. My jaw is hurting me a little, but I think I can drive," said Janet.

"I got it right now, I had a good night's sleep and feel pretty good right now," replied Walker.

"We can stop in Atlanta and stay with Ward," she said.

"Pretty sure I'm not going to feel like driving any further than Atlanta today and we can continue on tomorrow," said Beck. "Let's call Ward and let him know we're coming if he's not in town well just get a hotel," he said.

"Can you believe Burton got a teaching job at such a prestigious university in my hometown?" Janet said. "I'm so proud of our son."

"He's a good kid, I think we raised him right," Beck said. "He's a tremendous father to his boys too."

"How are you feeling today?" Janet said. "I love you Beck."

"I have a tingling sensation in my fingers right now. At this point I feel rested; I don't feel tired or nauseous. No pain right now. Let's go to Wilmington and see our son and his family and enjoy ourselves," he said.

"Sounds good to me," she said.

"I remember those days when I was teaching Biology at Morehouse College and Atlanta University. I loved teaching. Hopefully, he'll gain some good experience to put on his resume," said Beck.

"Take it from someone who's been teaching for a thousand years, it's one of the most rewarding jobs I've ever had," replied Janet. "I'm glad to be retired now and working with you though."

"Working together Janet has been immensely rewarding for me too," Walker said. "You do need to start showing up on time to work though."

"Whatever," said Janet.

"I'm serious," Walker said. "I'm going to have to start docking you for coming in late."

"You go ahead and doc me, Doctor," Janet said. "I'm a retired 70-year-old woman who happens to be your wife, and I'll get there when I get good and got damn ready. You just rest assured when I show up the work is getting done."

"You got all the answers," he said. "I'm just telling you. You need to be more punctual."

"This pussy's punctual, you got any of that Viagra with you?" she said.

"Janet, Janet, Janet, Janet. You're missing the point," said Beck.

"Beck it seems to me like you're missing the point," said Janet.

"I think I get your point, but you still need to be on time," said Beck.

"I'm always on time, you didn't know?" she said.

"No, I didn't know," Beck replied.

"Well now you know," Janet said.

Janet and Beck traveled on to Atlanta and then northeast to South Carolina. It was a good drive for them because they had an opportunity to talk and to spend their time together. At this point,

Janet was driving. They stop along the road to get some gas. When they are about to turn onto Highway 74-76 which goes from Fayetteville to Lumberton and Whiteville on into Wilmington, Janet pauses for a significant period of time at the exit to the highway. She looks to the left and then to the right. Then she looks at Beck sitting there in the passenger seat. She glanced in her rear-view mirror toward the gas station they were leaving. She looked back toward Beck and in his direction and he glanced at her.

For a moment Janet feels she is suspended in nothingness. She feels and imagines that she is lost and has no idea where she is going or where she is. She felt confused and disoriented. For moment, she questions everything she perceives or does not perceive to be in her environment and point of perception. She stares over at her husband Beck. She looks again back at the road to her right and her left. At this point, Janet was in a total state of being without direction, and not knowing and understanding where she was. She was having a slight panic attack. She was driving their vehicle, yet she was not sure or certain where she was going; north, south, east or west.

For a moment she wants to ask Beck what direction they are going or for that matter where they were going. She felt embarrassed and afraid. Of course, she knew Beck was there with her, but she had never experienced this before. She felt totally disoriented. Although she was reluctant to tell him, she knew she had no other choice but to confide in Beck and let him know that she was confused.

"Beck are we going north or south?" she said.

"Janet, what do you mean are we going to north or south? We're going north," he replied.

"Mobile is south isn't it?" said Janet.

"Yes, Mobile is south, but we're going to Wilmington and Wilmington is north," Walker said. "But we have to go east on 74-76 for about an hour to get to Wilmington."

"That's right Wilmington is north. We're in North Carolina," replied Janet. "How are we going east if Wilmington is north?"

"Do you want me to drive?" he asked.

"No, I'm fine," said Janet.

"Just make a right here, 74-76 East," said Beck pointing to the right.

"How far are we from Wilmington?" she asked.

"We're almost there," he replied. "Janet you've driven this road a thousand times. What do you mean are we going North or South?"

"None of this looks familiar to me, I was just a little confused that's all," Janet said.

"If you want me to drive. I'll drive," Beck said.

"I got it. We're going north but now we got to go east for a little while to get to Wilmington. This is Fayetteville," Janet said. "Mobile is south, right?"

"Right, "replied Beck.

"Burton is going to be expecting us soon. We should be able to make some time on this highway," she said as she made a right turn onto Highway 74-76.

"We're just 84 miles from Wilmington," said Walker as they passed a road sign.

"Right we should be getting to Sawmill Road and the Owens Farm in a few miles," she said.

"Exactly," replied Beck. "Janet you really scared me for a moment there. Are you alright?" asked Beck.

"I'm fine, we're going north to Wilmington right," Janet said. "We'll let's hurry and get there. I'm tired of all this driving."

"So am I," Beck answered.

"I don't want to stay at 1013 with my sisters either," Janet said. "I want us to get a hotel. Let's just stay at Wrightsville Beach near Burton and the kids."

"That's fine with me," Beck said.

"I really don't even want to look at those heifers, much less stay with them," said Janet.

"It would be nice to stay at the beach anyway," Beck said.

"You think Burton is going to like his new job," said Janet.

"I think this is going to be a good experience for him," said Beck. "I hope he likes it. Wish he could have found a position teaching Business Law in Mobile."

"Wilmington has grown a lot over the years. You know they film a lot of movies in Wilmington now," Janet said.

Janet and Beck continued their conversation as they drove along Highway 74-76 toward Wilmington. They passed exits for Lumberton and Whiteville as they shortly arrived at Sawmill Road which intersected Highway 74-76. Janet wanted to turn and go onto her family's farmland. They made a left turn off 74-76 and drove down Sawmill Road and then made a left turn onto the little road that led down toward the farmhouse. That little two-bedroom farmhouse had been built by her father Angle B. Owens and her brothers Warren and Peter. She drove down toward the house and saw her niece Patsy Owens Mitchell's car parked in the yard. Her niece, Warren's daughter was living there at the time.

"Whose car is that?" asked Beck.

"It's probably Patsy's car, you know she's been living here for the last two years," she said as she blew the horn.

A moment later they see the face of a woman appear behind the screen door. It was Patsy. She looked out of the door, but she does not realize who is in the car at first. Janet rolls down the window and says hello.

"Hi Patsy, how are you?" said Janet.

"Is that you Aunt Janet?" Patsy replied.

"Yes, it's your Aunt Janet and Uncle Beck," she said.

"Aunt Janet!" she exclaimed as she opened the door and walked out to the car.

"Hi Patsy," said Janet.

"Hey Uncle Beck, hey Aunt Janet, what a surprise," said Patsy.

"I hope it's a good surprise," replied Janet.

"Most certainly, would you guys like to come in?" Patsy asked.

"We were just passing through. We're pretty tired from the drive," said Janet.

"Where are you staying?" she said. "You're more than welcome to stay with me if you want."

"We're tired. We're going to stay at Wrightsville Beach near where Burton and the kids are staying."

"We'll be here for a few days," Janet said. "We'll be sure and come by and see you or you can come see us before we go back."

"It's so nice to see you guys," Patsy said. "Thanks for stopping by to let me know you are going to be in town for a few days."

"How do you like being out here in the country?" asked Beck.

"I love it… It's so peaceful out here," Patsy said.

"We will see you while we're here," Janet said. "We just want to get to the hotel and rest for a little while. It's been a long drive."

"Aunt Ann and Julia and Bethany are staying at 1013," Patsy said. "You guys don't want to just stay there?"

"We're going to be just fine at the beach," said Janet as she put the car back in gear.

"Bye Uncle Walker and Aunt Janet. You guys let me know where you're staying and I'll come and visit with you while you're in town," said Patsy and she waved goodbye.

Janet and Beck pulled out of the long dirt driveway onto the highway headed on into Wilmington. A few more minutes down the road they crossed the Cape Fear Memorial Bridge over the Cape Fear River which leads into Wilmington, North Carolina. They traveled down Dawson Street toward Wrightsville Beach. As they approached 12th Street, Janet made a right turn and drove down 12th Street toward the family homestead. She noticed a car parked in the driveway near the back door toward the back yard. She glanced to the left and kept going and made a left and went to the next block and made another left which put her back onto Dawson Street and headed toward Wrightsville Beach again.

A few minutes later they were crossing Wrightsville Beach Bridge which led them on into Wrightsville Beach. They arrived in the afternoon and it was a beautiful summer afternoon. The beach was hustling and bustling like most beaches during the summer as they made their way through the pedestrians, bikers, and cars toward their hotel. Finally, they arrived at the Holiday Inn Sunspree located on the north end of the island right on the beach. Tired and weary from their drive they checked in and made it into their room. As soon as they got into the hotel room with a spacious balcony overlooking the Atlantic Ocean, they called their son Burton at work and told him they had made it into town. Burton was happy to hear they had made it in safely and indicated he would come by the hotel as soon as he got off work.

Beck and Janet settled into their room. Beck walked out onto the balcony and stood there for a moment looking out over the waves rolling into the sandy white beach and the people playing and sunbathing on the beach and the swimming pool below. Janet joined Beck on the balcony to see the view. She put her arm around him and gave him a big hug. He embraced her as the two of them hugged and snuggled for a moment on the terrace. Just being there at the beach was refreshing to both of them, and for a moment they just tried to put everything aside and enjoy each other without worrying about all the other extraneous concerns.

For a brief period, they just embraced one another and tried to forget about pain, illness, disappointment, and concern. Beck held her a little tighter. Janet felt so good inside the security of Beck's arms. Beck could feel the love his wife felt for him and had for him as she melted into his embrace. This was a moment of relief and comfort and assurance they both desperately needed. They shared one of those experiences that only a couple who has been together more than forty years can experience without saying a word. It's what you call one of those, "I got you babe," moments.

Wrightsville Beach was so incredible this time of year. The two of them felt rejuvenated and at one with one another and at peace with themselves as the beach usually has a tendency to do. The beach has that tremendous transformative power to provide that little space of freedom in a person's heart to allow someone to connect both with their inner selves and with God.

The next morning Burton came walking up to the hotel with Breaghan and Bryceton. The three of them had walked about a mile down the beach from their house to the Holiday Inn Sunspree to visit with them and have breakfast. Burton had classes on Monday, Wednesday and Friday, so it was Thursday and his day off. Burton and his family were enjoying living at the beach and they were making the leap of faith into their new home and life. Janet, on the other hand, was still basically enraged that her sisters did not want her family to stay at her house for a few days. Burton did have to borrow some money from her to house his family while he was looking for a place to stay and getting started at his new job.

Breaghan and Bryceton went up the stairs leading to the hotel and bolted toward the pool. Burton told them to sit on the side of the pool until he had a chance to call their grandparents to come down and join them for breakfast by the pool. Beck and Janet accompanied them by the pool, and they ate a tremendous breakfast of french toast, hash browns, sausage, grits, juice, and coffee. Such a wonderful day to be with family on the Atlantic Ocean by the pool. Burton and the kids were glad to see his parents. Janet and Beck were also glad to see them. They had a great breakfast on this gracious morning. They all relished their morning meal by the pool.

A little later that day, they drove down the road to Burton's new place which was a two-story beach bungalow about a half block from the beach. Burton and his family had moved into this beach cottage onto the top unit which had three bedrooms, one bathroom, a kitchen, den and living room. Out front was a large covered porch which was painted green along the pale-yellow exterior of the house. Janet and Beck visited for a while with Burton, Candace, and the kids before heading into town to visit with Janet's sisters at the family homestead.

They continued to 1013 South 12th Street were Janet's sisters Julia, Anna and Bethany were staying. Janet truthfully had some very choice words for them. However, the most choice words for them she might have had would be, "I suffer from chronic pain on a regular basis; my husband has Cancer and he is dying before my eyes and for once in my life, I needed you guys and you refused to be there for me. For once in my life, I asked you to just let me have my way and you said no. So now, as the drum major says, 'It's on!'"

They arrive at 12st Street and stop at 1006 to visit Janet's godmother, Mary Lilly Lofton. Mary Lilly greeted them at the door. They visited with Mary Lilly for a few minutes before going down to 1013 S 12th Street. Mary Lilly was every bit of 100 years old and yet she was still very healthy and vibrant. When she dressed up and did her face and hair, she was actually very attractive for her age. Even though she did not have any teeth and wore dentures. She was in a relatively good spirit and demeanor. She did a lot of walking and got around very well for a woman of her years. You would not want to go for a walk with her because she would surely out walk you and have you asking her to slow down so you could take a break.

"Hey, Little Jane," said Mary Lilly. "And how are you, Walker?"

"Hi, Mary Millie," said Janet as she hugged her neck.

"I'm fine Mary Lilly, how are you?" replied Beck.

"I'm as well as can be expected for a 100-year-old woman," replied Mary Lilly. "Life is wonderful," she smiled.

"I'm just so angry and disappointed with my sisters right now, I could scream. I could just ooooo," said Janet.

"This will all work itself out Jane," said Mary Lilly. "I know how much you love your sisters and your sisters love you, sweetheart."

"You think so?" Janet replied.

"I know so," said Mary Lilly. "No matter what. You know what Mable and Angle wanted. You know what she said in her Will. You agreed to let them change what Mable put in her Will because you have a kind heart and they will always be your sisters."

"I never thought I would live to regret the day I did that," said Janet.

"Well you did it because that was what was in your heart and that is what you wanted to do," replied Mary Lilly. "Would you and Walker like some of this fresh squeezed Lemonade I just made?"

"Mary Lilly, that's exactly what I've been trying to tell her all the way here," Walker said. "We have so much property, we hardly know what to do with it."

"Whenever I leave this world, this one is yours too," said Mary Lilly.

"Right is right and wrong is wrong," Janet said. "I never would have let them put their names on the Deed if I knew they were going to act like this. How could they be so thoughtless to not want to allow Burton and his family to stay for a few days in the house when they knew he was coming here to take a new job. That's not family."

"My little Jane, you know after all these years you are still my little Jane. Burton is fine. I've seen him, his wife and his beautiful children," Mary Lilly said. "By the grace of God, everything is going to be alright. Just have faith."

"I would like a glass of that Lemonade if you don't mind," said Walker.

"Thank you, Mary Lilly," Janet said. "Maybe I needed to hear that."

"Sometimes we all have to be reminded of the things we already know in our hearts to be true," Mary Lilly said as she poured three glasses of Lemonade.

"Mm, that's good," Walker said as he sips from the glass of cold Lemonade.

"It's good Mary Millie," said Janet as she takes a swallow of her Lemonade.

"I still remember when you used to run up and down 12th Street with your hair in ponytails. You were so small and so adorable. Such a sweet little girl, and just a tomboy to your heart," Mary Lilly laughed. "That's why even to this day, I still call you my Little Jane," she said. "I couldn't have loved you more if you had been my own child."

"I could fight too," laughed Janet.

"Walker, she was the prettiest little thing in Wilmington," said Mary Lilly.

"I know, why do you think I married her?" he said.

"I still recall that day you walked home from school crying. You told me Daisy Watkins had dipped your ponytail in the inkwell on her desk and you were afraid Mable was going to cut your hair off," Mary Lilly said. "You said please Marry Millie, please don't let Mamma cut my hair. I brought you in the house and we washed, and we washed, and we washed until just about all of the ink was out of your beautiful hair."

"I was so scared Mamma was going to tell me the only way she could get it out was to cut my hair because that's what the girls at school were telling me. I was only in the third grade," replied Janet.

"Mable just told you, you would have to go back to school and not to be afraid and face that girl if you had too. We got the ink out and she didn't cut your hair," Mary Lilly said. "You told me you wanted to beat Daisy Watkins up, and I said no Janet just say a prayer and ask God to forgive her for being mean and dipping your ponytail in the ink well. You said OK I'll ask God to forgive her."

Mary Lilly put her arm around Janet and smiled, "That's what you're going to have to do now Janet. I'm telling you the same thing right now. Just say a little prayer and ask God to please forgive them."

Janet sighs, "I'll think about it."

Beck and Janet finished their Lemonade and continued down the street to the family homestead at 1013 where her sisters Anna, Bethany, and Julia were waiting.

"One thing you need to understand is that I built this house. I never had to let them put their names on the Deed," said Janet.

"It is what it is… I'm frankly getting tired of talking about it. The writing is all over the wall," replied Beck.

"I never would have signed up for this," she said.

"But you did Janet. You did. This is exactly what you signed up for," said Beck.

"Oh no I didn't," said Janet.

"You could fool me," Beck said, "Then what would you say you signed up for then?"

"Not this," Janet said.

"Doesn't seem like it to me," said Beck.

They pull into the driveway. As they approach the door, they are greeted by the sisters. The sisters are just smiling and grinning that fake grin. Beck gets out of the car supported by his walking stick as he and Janet come inside. Anna, Bethany, and Julia notice how pale, thin and sick their brother-in-law Walker is looking. The three of them had no prior warning about Walker's condition. Walker had asked Janet not to tell anyone and she had honored his wishes. The sisters were dumbfounded when they saw his appearance. It was noticeably obvious that he was extremely ill.

"We were just having a glass of wine," said Bethany. "Would you like a glass. I believe we have some juice too."

"Hey Janet, hey Walker," said Julia.

"Hey yourself, hey is for horses," said Janet.

"Hi you guys," said Anna. "We've been looking forward to seeing you."

They are still trying to avoid staring at Walker who was once so vibrant, tall, handsome and ambitious as well as in love with their sister. Now he was starting to look like a skeleton in his own skin. They didn't know exactly what to say at this point because they were totally shocked and surprised.

"Have a seat," Julia said. "Glad y'all made it safely."

"Walker," said Anna as she hugs him.

"How is my sister and brother in law?" Bethany said.

"We're perfectly fine," said Janet.

"Walker you look like you've been on a diet," said Julia.

"I have and how does it look," Walker said as he lifted his eyebrows for emphasis.

"Looks great Chief," said Bethany.

"We got some grits, sausage, and toast left over from this morning," said Anna.

"We had a big breakfast this morning at the hotel with Burton and his boys," Janet said. "I'm not hungry."

"What about you Walker?" asked Anna.

"I'm fine," said Beck.

"We just wanted to say hello, we're going to go back out to our hotel and relax for a little while and visit with Burton," said Janet.

"Why are you all staying in a hotel, there's plenty of room here for you to stay," replied Bethany.

"I wouldn't bit more sleep in this house under this roof with you and you and you when you didn't want Burton and his family to stay here for a few days until he got situated. I would really like to take a match to this bitch and burn it down," Janet said.

Bethany and Anna approach Janet, "Janet, why are you saying that?"

"You better back off! Both of you better back off," said Janet.

"Come on now Janet, that's not what we came here for," said Beck.

"A family house, huh." Janet said, "Seems like it's only a family house when your family needs to stay here."

"Janet lets go back out to the hotel now and take a walk on the beach," Beck said. "It's such a nice day."

"I would love to go to the beach today myself," said Julia. "I bet Bethany and Ann would like to come too. We're not doing anything,"

"Can we come?" asked Anna.

"Nope," said Janet.

"All of you are more than welcome," Beck said. "Hopefully Janet will be in better spirits by then."

"So, we'll see you guys in an hour or two. We'll come out to the beach," replied Anna.

"The beach it is," said Bethany. "Maybe then we can discuss this rationally and get this worked out."

"Nah, Burton's already found a place," said Janet.

"I know we visited them out there two days ago," Anna said. "Isn't it cute. Have you seen their house? Right on the beach. They said they love it there."

"Yes, we've seen it," said Janet.

"We're going to ride back now," Beck said. "Janet's been very upset. She feels that you guys have disappointed her."

"Come on, Beck. Let's go," said Janet.

Beck and Janet returned to the Holiday Inn at Wrightsville Beach and took a walk along the shore. A picture-perfect day to be on the Atlantic seashore. The sun glistened across the ocean as the light waves rolled into the picturesque shores of Wrightsville Beach. Janet and Beck walked along the seashore as Beck put his arm around his wife and hugged her close to him. They strolled on the beach for about an hour. Neither said much. They just enjoyed the rare moment between the two of them. Janet took a long-awaited opportunity to relish the comfort she felt in her husband of so many years. Beck very much wanted to give her some solace and love.

At the end of the day, you can choose your friends, but you cannot choose your family. Beck was Janet's lifelong friend and husband and Janet was Beck's lifelong friend and wife and confidante through everything. The beach was rather busy and crowded on this day close to the end of the summer in Wrightsville. However, they were oblivious to all the other people, you would have thought they were the only ones on the shore. Janet gazed into the twilight beams of the sun as it glimmered along the north end of the North Carolina beach. It was a magnificent view and she felt so at home and at peace walking along the beach with her hubby.

They both really needed some exercise. Finally, they made it back to their hotel. Janet's sisters were there waiting for them in the lobby when they returned. At this point, it was like back to reality for the two of them. Julia and Bethany were waiting around in the lobby and out by the pool looking for Janet and Beck. They had tried to call Beck's cell phone several times and got no answer when they called the room. They were swarming around the hotel like bees in search of honey. Burton arrived right about the same time his mom and dad returned from their walk on the beach.

He noticed his aunts in the lobby near the door leading to the pool area. Burton came over and greeted them as his parents arrived back at the hotel. Janet, Beck, Burton, Anna, Julia, and Bethany boarded the elevator going up to Janet and Beck's suit. They exited the elevator and walked down the ornate corridor of the hotel toward the suite Beck and Janet were staying in with a pool and ocean view. Everyone crowded into the comfortable and not so spacious suite on the 17th floor of this incredible establishment on the Atlantic Ocean, Wrightsville Beach, North Carolina.

"You know what," Julia said. "I'm going to go back down to the pool for a minute and get some fresh air."

Burton immediately headed for the balcony to check out the view of the ocean not really realizing what was going on between his mom and her sisters. Beck went inside and took a seat in one of the lounging chairs in the suit. This left Janet surrounded by Bethany and Anna in the hallway of the suite.

"Let's go downstairs and talk Janet," said Anna.

"No, I don't want to go back downstairs now," Janet said. "You want to talk. We can talk right here. What do you want to talk about?"

"We can't really talk right here," Bethany said.

"I'm fine if you got something to say then get to talking," Janet said. "I'm listening, otherwise you might need to get to walking."

"Janet?" said Anna.

"Why are you talking to your sisters like this?" Bethany said. "What have we done to you?"

"You know what, I'm not crazy… Right is right and wrong is wrong. I'm sure the two of you know the difference," Janet said. "I know Mamma and Poppa tried to teach me the difference, and they tried to teach you all the same."

"Tell you what, just step into my office," she said as she pointed to the bathroom.

As soon as they stepped into the bathroom, Ann and Bethany approached Janet again as if they were going to tell her something or explain something to her. Janet reacted by backing away from them for a second. She reacted in a very aggressive manner toward the two of them. They just rolled up on her in the bathroom and Janet had no other alternative. They just violated her space and thought they were going to rule or regulate something. Janet felt it was imperative to put everything in the right perspective.

"Jeannie," said Bethany.

"Why would you say," said Anna.

"Say what?" said Janet.

"You know what you said," replied Anna.

"You want me to say it again," Janet responded.

"Why would you say you wanted to burn our house down?" Bethany inquired.

"Our house," said Janet.

"Yes, our house," said Anna.

"Why would you say that?" said Bethany.

"You all have no idea what the crux of the matter really is here," said Janet.

"Well tell me?" said Bethany.

"I can show you better than I can tell you," Janet said. "And we're not having show-and-tell here today."

"Janet, you need to face it. The house is ours now," said Anna as she leaned over at Janet in an intimidating manner. "We don't want Burton, Candace and their bad kids staying there."

"Really," Janet said. "Bitch, face this!"

Beck and Burton were seated outside in the hotel room outside of the bathroom door which was closed. The two of them had no idea what was brewing between Janet and her sisters inside the bathroom. Little did they know that Anna and Bethany were trying to corner Janet and more or less make her understand their point of view and Janet was not about to have it. Although, Burton and Beck did not really know why the three of them took their conversation into the bathroom. They had no idea that the tension was getting pretty thick between the three of them.

Suddenly they hear a scream coming from the bathroom. Beck's face is suddenly alarmed because probably nobody knew how angry Janet was about the situation more than him. He and Burton are startled by the unexpected scream and they were not quite sure exactly who was screaming. At that point, Janet, Ann, and Bethany emerge from the bathroom. Anna is holding the side of her face and she is bleeding.

Janet had scratched Anna on the side of her face near her ear lobe. Ann came out into the hotel room in full view of Beck and Burton and they saw the blood on her face and hand. Burton looked at Bethany to see if she was injured. She did not appear to be hurt. Beck was quite alarmed by this situation and was not exactly sure how to react. He was wondering if the struggle was going to continue now that they were out of the bathroom or was it over.

Janet stood there looking at Anna and Bethany and then Burton and Beck sitting there across the room somewhat dismayed. Bethany went back into the bathroom to get a piece of toilet tissue or washcloth to give to Anna so she could wipe the blood off her face and hand. She also wet a face towel and put it up to Anna's scratch mark like a compress to stop the bleeding. Burton looked over at his dad who at this point appeared to be a little animated in that he was in a slight bit of disbelief at what had just happened. Burton understood the look on his dad's face because he knew exactly how he felt at that point and he knew his own face was probably riddled with the same expression.

"Oh my! Here Anna," said Bethany as she reached over to pat the side of her face with the wash towel.

"Janet scratched me," Anna said as she looked over at Beck and Burton for some type of validation, reassurance or protection. Ann seemed horrified by what had just happened.

"I bet you won't jump in my face like that again," said Janet.

"Here, Ann," Bethany said as she patted the side of her face. "Let me see. It doesn't look that bad."

"Oh my God," said Anna slightly hysterical.

"What's going on Mom?" asked Burton.

"Janet!" exclaimed Beck.

There is a knock at the door. Amid the confusion in the room, it is uncertain who is knocking. It might be security or someone from the hotel staff. Burton goes over to the door and asks who it was, and he heard his mother's sister Julia outside. It's like Julia had almost instinctively left the scene and now she had returned to see if there was any need to do damage control. Burton opened the door and Julia entered the hotel suite surprised to see Anna standing there crying and holding a towel to her bloody face. Julia is surprised but not totally.

"What's going on?" exclaimed Julia.

"Walker, we better go," said Bethany.

"Ann, I want to apologize for scratching your face," Janet said. "But don't try that mess again. I'm not the one."

"I didn't do anything to you," said Anna.

"Oh yes, you did," Janet replied. "You know exactly what you did."

"Jeannie, please calm down," said Bethany.

"I'm as calm as the deep blue sea," replied Janet.

"Why are you all fighting like this?" said Julia.

"We're all family and adults here so let's act like it," replied Bethany.

"Janet, please," said Beck.

"Don't Janet me, Beck. I said I was sorry, but she had it coming," Janet replied.

"Mom, I know you're upset, but we've found a place now," Burton said. "It's not much but we're staying here on the beach and we're happy. So, let's just put it aside and move on."

"Burton, we never said we didn't want you to stay at the house," replied Julia.

"Oh yes, you did," Janet replied. "That's exactly what all of you said and you drove all the way down here to make sure he and his kids didn't go in there, not even for a night," Janet said. "Here we have a furnished house and my sisters said they wanted to make into a family house, but that's not what it is. You lied to me."

"We never lied to you," said Anna.

"You just told another lie, Ann," Janet said. "Pay me the rest of my money, that's what you can do and stop lying."

"You all have got to stop all of this arguing," Beck said. "If you keep it up were going to get put out of the hotel."

"We can still work this out," said Anna.

"You already worked it out, Ann, just like you wanted," argued Janet.

"Please, this is enough for one night," said Beck.

"Are you OK?" said Burton as he walked over toward Anna to get a closer look at her face. He puts his arm around Anna and Bethany and starts to usher them toward the door.

"It's not too bad," replied Bethany. "I think she'll be OK."

"Maybe we should just talk tomorrow. Tomorrow will be a better day," said Julia.

"Good night," said Janet.

"Good night, Jeannie," replied Julia. Then Julia, Anna, and Bethany strolled out into the hallway and onto the elevator. Burton, Janet, and Beck remained inside the hotel suite.

"Mom are you alright?" asked Burton.

"I'll be fine, baby," replied Janet.

"Lord have mercy, Janet," Beck said. "We just heard all of this screaming coming from the bathroom. We didn't know what the hell was going on."

"We just had a little meeting in the ladies' room, that's all," said Janet.

"That kind of caught us a little off guard, Mom," said Burton.

"I don't want to talk about it anymore. Burton, how do you think you're going to like your new job?" Janet asked.

The next day, Janet and Beck spent the majority of the day at Burton's new apartment with him and his family. Walker and Burton sat out on the large porch in front of their house talking. Beck enjoyed the warmth of the summer breeze blowing off the Atlantic Ocean. He sat there peacefully as Breaghan, Bryceton and Breton played nearby. Beck and Janet were preparing to go back to Mobile the following day. They could hear the people on the beach not far away as the waves washed into the shore. The warm weather and salty air had a calming and relaxing effect on them allowing them to distance themselves from the confusion that had occurred the day before with Janet's sisters.

Janet did not say much the entire day. Inwardly she was still disappointed about what her sisters had done, but she was now equally disappointed in the manner in which she handled the situation with Anna. She knew she had more diplomacy, class, and sophistication. After all, she was Janet Owens; she knew she had it in her heart to try and forgive them. She was happy for Burton and his family. Happy LeFlore he had chosen or lucked up on an opportunity to live in her hometown of Wilmington, N.C. That was certainly a new and exciting path for them to embark upon. She loved her hometown even though she had lived in Mobile, Alabama for the majority of her life.

Janet adored her grandchildren and enjoyed being in their presence on such a sunny day at the beach. She still kept pretty quiet though. She was worried about having to see her sisters again after how she had acted, and yet she knew she might very well do it again if she was put in the same or similar situation. She was wishing she could stay a few more days, but she knew Beck had to get back to work. She was also concerned that he had missed a few of his doctor's appointments to come to Wilmington with her. Beck seemed to be doing fine though. He physically looked as though the chemotherapy treatments and cancer were starting to take a toll on him. However, he seemed to be in good spirits, and he was not in any discomfort or pain.

He was enjoying being with Burton and his family at the beach just as much as she was. Julia, Anna, and Bethany did not come out to the beach today. There was no sign of the three of them. Janet and Beck did not go into town to see them either. Although, they did plan to stop by there on their way out in the morning. Janet was not looking forward to it either. She wanted to be sure and see Mary Lilly before she went back to Mobile.

The day at Wrightsville Beach was somewhat surreal for this family. It was a bonding period that families need to have sometimes. Families need to associate with each other to prevent a lack of communication. There is an old saying which says, "You cannot choose your family, but you can choose your friends," although that saying is not altogether applicable here, and yet totally applicable given the circumstances, to this situation, it is questionable and yet unquestionable. Where does it say some of us feel more comfortable and at ease with a person, we call a friend? Rather than be with someone who we grew up with who is cut from the same cloth and loin as you. However, it being altogether part of the natural order of things in the universe which drives us to the conclusion we must find a comfortable medium.

CHAPTER THREE

A year has gone by. Janet and Walker are still working in his medical practice and running back and forth to the Hospital and Ochsner Hospital in New Orleans for Beck's chemotherapy treatments. Walker has now been battling cancer for over 5 years. He has had numerous surgeries and stints in the Hospital as well as regular treatments every week. Throughout everything, he tried to stay strong and keep up the fight against this horrific disease. He continued to work and probably none of his patients were even aware that he was sick unless perhaps they noticed it in his appearance.

The chemotherapy zapped his energy and left him feeling drained and tired all the time despite his busy and hectic work schedule. Janet stayed by his side every step of the way trying to be the most loving and supportive wife she could be. She was also suffering from TMJ and had constant and regular nerve pain in her jaw. The two of them were both getting old, now in their early seventies. But these two depression babies just kept on keeping on no matter what.

Janet and Beck had been married for over 50 years. They were truly soul mates. Both of them were scientists. Both of them grew up in relatively large families in the south. Both of their fathers worked for the U. S. Postal Service as postmen. Both of their mothers were stay at home moms. Both of them grew up in medium size seaport towns. Both of them were from meager beginnings. Neither of their families struggled for the basic necessities. Neither of their families was wealthy by any measure. Both of them were born just before the Great Depression. Both of them believed in hard work and sacrifice to get what they wanted in life. They were college sweethearts and had been together on this road of life together ever since they met.

Although they were soul mates in many ways and loved each other with all their hearts; their marriage had certainly had its share of problems and ups and downs. For many years, Beck drank heavily. He had given up drinking altogether about 15 years ago. Not to mention that Beck was a very handsome and successful doctor who had a few side pieces along the way. Janet worked long hours as a chemistry professor at the local community college and was not always the best cook or homemaker. However, now at this point in their lives, they were living and enjoying the type of love and relationship and togetherness they had always wanted to have. They had traveled this journey of life together and for the most part, they had done well together.

However, at this point in their lives, they were sharing and embracing the true dedication and love they had always had for one another. They had not always had time to give to one another because they were both working so hard all the time. For many years, it just seemed like they were two people living under the same roof every day, going to bed, getting up and going back to work all over again. They were like two ships that passed in the night both carrying cargo and a crew that was on the way to a separate and unique destination. They had endured more than their share of problems and rocky roads during those many years they spent together. Beck and Janet were an American success story.

Two kids who both came from a house somewhere in the south located on a dirt road with a bunch of other brothers and sisters and two loving parents. Janet and Beck were a couple who made good both financially and romantically. The two of them might have been suffering from some aches and pains, but they were not hurting for anything material or monetary. They had a great home, nice cars, vast investments, rental property, steady and secure income. Janet and Beck had achieved financial security and were living the American Dream. The dream that every Depression Baby longed for back when they were growing up.

Today Beck was scheduled to go for an MRI. There is an old saying that doctors make some of the worst patients. This scenario was greatly played out back in 1997 when Walker had surgery on his intestines to remove a piece of his cancerous intestine. The next day Beck got out of the hospital and decided to have a nice juicy steak for dinner which caused his sutures to rupture thereby causing bile to spill out into his body cavity putting him back in the hospital for more surgery and two months of recovery following the second procedure. You would expect a doctor who has been practicing for over 40 years to know that steak is one of the most difficult things for the body to digest. Certainly, if he had been treating himself, he would have advised himself to be careful of what he ate for at least the next ten days or until his intestinal tract had healed from the surgery. He would have done that just as a matter of protocol and procedure as the party's primary physician.

So today in March of 2001, Beck is approaching his birthday on the 21st of the month. He will be turning 73 years old. Beck is about to undergo an MRI that was ordered by his Oncologist. He and Janet arrive at the MRI center about fifteen minutes early. Beck is walking with the aid of a cane. He is a relatively large big-boned man who weighed approximately 250 pounds at the time. Janet accompanies him inside the MRI center, and they check in at the front window. They are seated as he filled out the information form and treatment authorization. After waiting a few minutes, they are asked to come back into the MRI room for the exam.

"Dr. LeFlore, you can come back into the exam room now," said the nurse. She escorts him back into the MRI room. Janet follows as they go into the room with the MRI machine.

"Please take off your clothes and put this gown on," said the MRI technician.

"Thank you," said Beck.

"You need me to help you?" asked Janet.

"I'm fine, just give me a minute," as he takes off his pants and shirt and slipped into the gown. He changed into the gown and returned to the area near the MRI table.

"Just lay down here and relax. Lay down flat and when you're ready, let us know. The table is going to slide into the MRI chamber and take a few x-rays of you," said the technician.

"OK," Walker said. "About how long does it take for the MRI?" said Beck.

"Anywhere from three to five minutes," said the technician

"Three to five minutes that all," said Beck.

"Yes it's really simple. You'll be in and out of here before you know it," said the nurse.

"I guess I'm ready," said Beck as he stretched out on the table.

Beck laid down and he was soon whisked into the inner chamber of the MRI machine. The x-ray imaging beam began to travel from one end of the MRI chamber to the other in order to get a full body imaging. It was not long before the technician, the nurse, and Janet hear a banging noise coming from the inside of the MRI chamber.

They were not certain what it was at first. They heard the banging again. They hear a voice and a noise coming from inside the chamber. However, with the chamber closed for the MRI, they could not tell what was going on.

Janet is startled and knows her husband Beck is in distress. She tells the nurse and the technician that something is wrong, and they should stop the MRI. He was having a panic attack inside of that machine. Beck is demanding that they stop the MRI and let him out of this thing. He is frantic and beating on the inside of the MRI chamber to be let out. He yells that if they do not let him out of this thing, he is going to sue them. He is in major distress and continues to beat on the walls of the chamber. Finally, they reverse the imaging table.

As they stop the MRI to allow Beck to come out of the machine. He is literally kicking and screaming to get out. He is frantic. As his body is coming back out of the MRI as soon as his arms are free, he reached over and grabbed the female tech by the bottom part of her shirt. It was as if going into the MRI chamber was a terrifying experience for him. Panic was written all over his face when he emerged. He was trying to crawl off the table before it even became fully disengaged from the MRI chamber.

"Help me, please," Beck said as he sits on the side of the table quivering and hyperventilating.

"Are you alright?" the Nurse asked.

"Help me. Please, I can't breathe. I need oxygen. Do you have any oxygen?" Beck said with his hands stretched out and his head looking toward the floor. He struggled and gasped for air. Janet went over and put her arm around him.

"Beck," Janet said.

"Janet, please help me get my clothes. I need to get out of here," said Beck.

"Doctor, do you want us to try and get you to the hospital?" asked Janet. "Beck do you think you need to go to the Hospital."

"No, no, no," said Beck as he trembled and gasped for air.

"Why don't you just relax for a minute and we can go ahead and finish the MRI," said the Nurse.

"Absolutely not!" Beck snapped. "Under no circumstances am I going back in there," Beck said as if he had seen a ghost. "Give me my damn clothes. I've got to go," wheezing at this point and breathing harder at the thought of going back into the MRI compartment.

"Beck, are you going to be alright?" asked Janet.

Beck does not respond to Janet's question. The Nurse who was a little humiliated by the way Beck had talked to her, handed Janet his clothes. She puts the clothes on the table next to Beck and tries to comfort him for a second before she helped him change out of the gown into his clothes. Gradually he seems to be a little more at ease. Janet gets his pants and starts to help him put them on. She then untied the string from around his neck and helped him with his shirt.

"I'm claustrophobic," said Beck.

"Oh is that what it is," said the Nurse.

"I'm claustrophobic," he said. "I remember once my mother called herself punishing me for something and locked me in the closet when I was a child. I pretended like I had passed out when she finally came to let me out. I had to make sure she wouldn't ever try and put me in there again."

"Dr. LeFlore, what we can do is just refer you to the Open MRI Clinic," the Nurse said. "That way you can get the open MRI instead of having this type of imaging with this device."

"That would be fine," said Beck.

"I've been married to you for a thousand years and I never knew you were claustrophobic," said Janet.

"Now you know," Beck said. "I know I've told you about when Mamma locked me in that closet."

"I remember you telling me about when Teah locked you in the closet many times," she replied.

"What do you think I was talking about?" Beck said. "That's what I was talking about."

"Let's go home," said Janet.

"I've got to go and make my rounds before I go home," said Beck.

"Doctor, we've made you an appointment with the Open MRI Clinic, here is the number," said Janet.

It was Wednesday, March 21st, 2001, Beck's Seventy-Third birthday. Wednesday was usually the day during the week when Beck did not see any patients in his office. His staff still came into work on Wednesday's and so did Dr. LeFlore. He usually used his Wednesday's to catch up on his paperwork at the office. However, now that he was going to New Orleans for treatments every other week, he would usually schedule his treatments in New Orleans for Wednesday. He had a treatment scheduled for today but decided to cancel since it was his birthday. He was feeling relatively good today, somewhat better than usual as he sat at his desk writing some checks. Beck was already at work when Janet arrived.

"Well good morning Beck," Janet said. "Happy Birthday to my wonderful and hard-working husband," she said.

"Good morning, sweetheart," Beck said. "Thank you. I decided to cancel my appointment at Ochsner today. I thought maybe we could leave the office a little early this afternoon and go to the Bienville Club. Would you like that?" said Beck.

"You're the birthday boy, I would love to have dinner at the Bienville Club with you tonight," said Janet.

"Good. The Bienville Club it is," said Beck as his phone starts to beep. He picks up the line.

"Dr. LeFlore, Burton's on line one," said Ayaana.

"Put him through," Beck said. "Hello!"

"Happy Birthday Dad," said Burton.

"Thank you, Burton," he said.

"How are you feeling today?" asked Burton.

"Pretty good for an old man," replied Beck. "How about you?"

"I'm great, just got through teaching my 9 o'clock class and had a little break before my next class," Burton said. "Thought I would call and wish you a Happy Birthday. What are you planning on doing for your birthday?" said Burton.

"Working, when you get to be my age Birthdays are just another day," said Beck.

"Every birthday is a blessing," Burton said. "You should try and enjoy your day. How old are you anyway?" asked Burton.

"Old enough to be your dad," Beck said with a laugh. "We'll probably go and have dinner at the Bienville Club a little later this evening."

"That's nice, how is Mom?" said Burton.

"She's fine, she's right here if you want to speak with her," said Beck as he hands Janet the phone.

"Hi Baby," Janet said. "How are you?"

"Hey Mom, I'm doing good," Burton said. "How are you doing?"

"It's a beautiful day. Everything is OK. My jaw is hurting a little, but I'm glad to be alive," said Janet.

"I've got to run now Mom, I got about five minutes to get to class," Burton said. "Tell Dad I said goodbye. Love you guys. I'll talk with you guys a little later."

"Bye Burton, I will be sure and give him a big hug and a kiss for you," said Janet. She hung up with Burton and did exactly that. She gave Beck a big hug and kiss. The phone starts to beep again.

"Doctor, Mobile Infirmary is on line two," said Ayaana.

"Put them through," said Beck. Janet kissed him again on his forehead as she went into her office.

"Dr. LeFlore," said someone on the line.

"This is Dr. LeFlore," he said.

Later that evening, Walker and Janet arrived at the Bienville Club for Beck's Birthday dinner. The Bienville Club is a very upscale private dining club for wealthy professionals and businessmen located on the top floor of the First National Bank Building in Mobile. The Bienville Club was one of those places where the menu had no prices next to the gourmet food selections and the waiters got large tips. The staff knew Beck and Janet very well because they dined there quite frequently at the lavish club.

The Bienville Club was one of Beck's favorite places to eat. He and Janet loved the impeccable service and the wonderful food. The Bienville Club also sported an incredible view of downtown Mobile and the Mobile River. Beck and Janet had been members of the Bienville Club for many years. Dining at the club was always a unique and special experience. The main dining room was very ornately decorated with a long mahogany wood grained bar. They were greeted at the entrance by the host who was dressed in a black tuxedo suit. Beck and Janet are pleased to be greeted and seated.

"Doctor and Mrs. LeFlore," said James, the concierge.

"James, good to see you," said Beck.

"Right this way, Doctor. We have you and Mrs. LeFlore's table waiting," James said. "Happy Birthday by the way."

"Thank you," said Beck.

"Shall I have the waiter start you off with any cocktails this evening?" said James.

"None for me right now, Janet would you like something?" said Beck.

"I'll have a glass of champagne," said Janet.

"Please be seated. We'll get that glass of champagne out to you momentarily, Mrs. LeFlore," said James.

"James bring me a glass of tonic water with a lime, I can't drink like I used to," Beck said.

"Had to give that up."

"Very well, I will have the waiter bring you a glass of champagne and one tonic water," he said. "I hope you enjoy your meal tonight. It's always a pleasure to have you and Mrs. LeFlore dine with us," said James as he seated Janet and Beck at their table.

Janet and Beck looked over the menu once they were seated. Their table was right next to the large row of glass windows displaying a magnificent view of the city at night. There was soft piano music playing in the background and the room was dimly lit adding to the overall ambiance of the Bienville Club. Beck and Janet were both hungry as they looked over the menu and out onto the view of the city nighttime skyline. It wasn't long before the waiter returned with their drinks.

"Mrs. LeFlore, Dr. LeFlore it's so nice to see you tonight," said Blake the waiter. "One champagne for you Mrs. LeFlore and one tonic water with a lime for you, Doctor."

"Thank you, Blake," said Janet.

"Do you know what you'll be having for dinner tonight?" asked Blake.

"Give us a minute to look over the menu," replied Beck.

"The chef does have one special tonight I would like to tell you about," Blake said. "Duck Confit over a bed of Arugula and Roasted Rack of Lamb with Asparagus and Potatoes Au Gratin."

"Blake that sounds delectable," said Beck.

"By the way, Happy Birthday Dr. LeFlore," said Blake.

"Yea I'm getting on up there," said Beck.

"Enjoy your cocktails and let me know when you're ready to order," said Blake.

"Janet do you know how lucky I am to have the most wonderful and beautiful wife imaginable," said Beck.

"That's sweet of you Beck. Here's to you my dear on your birthday," Janet said as she raised her glass for a toast. "I've been with you now for over 56 of them," she said. "I hope we'll be together for many more to come."

"That's a lot of birthday's," chuckled Beck.

"I love you sugar," said Janet.

"I think I'm going to have the Chef's Special tonight. I have a pretty good appetite this evening. Haven't really had a good appetite in about two weeks. Probably because I didn't do the chemo today," Beck said. "Have you decided what you want?" He motions to the waiter.

"I think I'm going to have a salad and the Shrimp Scampi with Angel Hair," said Janet.

The waiter asked, "Have you decided what you and Mrs. LeFlore will be having tonight Dr. LeFlore?"

"Yes, my wife will have the Shrimp Scampi with Angel Hair, and I will have the Lamb, the Chef's Special," said Beck.

"And Blake, don't forget the birthday brownie and ice cream with the candle for my husband tonight," said Janet.

"I will take care of everything. Let me know if there is anything I can do to ensure that you have the most pleasurable dining experience," said Blake as he leaves with their order.

"I still remember in college when you used to take me to the Dairy Queen Ice Cream Stand for Ice Cream when we were at St. Augustine's," said Janet.

"What you didn't know Janet was that before I met you, I noticed that you would frequently go to the cafeteria lady and try and get her to give you more Ice Cream," Beck said. "I noticed this because I wanted to do the same thing, so I realized that you liked ice cream perhaps just as much as I liked it."

"You never told me that," Janet said. "A+ for being observant. I loved those little Ice Cream dates we used to take. Miss those days," she said. "I think one of those Ice Cream dates was when I realized I had fallen in love with you."

"I knew I was in love with you the first time I saw you," said Beck.

"I guess that's why you tackled me on the yard and knocked my books all over everywhere," said Janet.

"Glad to say it worked," Beck said. "We're still together after all these years. So, how about that?"

"Your salad Ms. LeFlore, and the Duck Confit with Arugula for you, Doctor," said Blake.

"Thank you, Sir," said Beck.

"My pleasure," Blake replied. "Let me know if you need anything."

Beck and Janet began to eat their salad as they sat there together. The piano player continued to play a soft tune on the piano. The piano player stopped his tune for a moment and announced that he wanted to wish Dr. LeFlore a very Happy Birthday. The other patrons clapped gingerly. The waiter came back over to the table and asked them if they would like to have some crushed black pepper on their salad. Blake sprinkled both of their salads with some peppercorns from the Pepper grinder. It was turning out to be a great evening for the two of them. Janet sipped her champagne. Beck savored the finely cooked duck confit which had just been placed before him. They looked into each other's eyes as they both reflected on those days at the Ice Cream Stand were they used to share ice cream together during college so many years ago, and now here they were growing old together and still in love.

"I don't know how many more birthdays I'm going to have," said Beck.

"Beck, don't talk like that, not tonight," said Janet.

"I honestly don't know how much longer I can go on feeling like this every day and going through those treatments," Beck said as he took another bite of his salad.

"Beck ever since that day at the Ice Cream stand when I realized I loved you. You have been the only man for me, and you always will be the only man for me," said Janet.

"I appreciate that Janet but I don't think you're hearing what I'm saying to you," said Beck.

"I don't think you are hearing what I'm saying to you Beck," Janet said. "You always have been and always will be the only man for me," she said. "We are both growing old but thank God we are growing old together. Sometimes my jaw hurts me so bad I just want to holler," Janet said. "I just want to say forget this," she said. "But we don't give up hope."

"Janet this disease is taking its course. I have been suffering from cancer for almost six years," Beck said. "I'm a doctor, Janet. Do you know how many people I've seen die from cancer? And now I'm dying. I can't be in denial about what is happening to me and what has happened to me over the last few years."

"Beck, you always have been and always will be the only man for me," said Janet. "Can we just celebrate your birthday tonight and not talk about dying?" Janet said. "Because as far as I'm concerned if something were to happen to you or you died, I might as well be dead too," she said. "How is your duck?"

"Good," said Beck.

"Let me have a taste," said Janet. She reached her fork across the table and retrieved a bite of the duck salad. Doctor and Mrs. LeFlore, your entrees are ready," Blake said. "We also have a little sorbet for you," he said. He served them the glass of sorbet to clear their pallets before eating their entrees. Blake pulled up with a cart of Shrimp Scampi and Lamb. He removed the glass from the plate and placed it on the table while removing their sorbet glasses. "Let me know if there is anything that I can do to improve your dining experience," he said.

"Everything looks delicious that will be fine for now Blake," said Beck.

For a moment Janet and Beck paused their conversation to taste the wonderful meal they had just been served at the Bienville Club. The waiter replenished Janet's champagne glass. She took a drink. She looked at her husband and reached out for his hand. She took his hand and placed it in hers. The two of them were really connecting at this dinner. She was certainly trying to be strong for her husband. She did not know what to say to him or what to tell him.

More than anything she wanted to tell him how much she would miss him if he passed away. She wanted to tell him that she would have no more purpose and direction in life if she was to lose him. She wanted to tell him that she loved him with all her heart. She wanted to tell him that she felt new again, just like she felt that first time in the Ice Cream Stand when she realized she loved him.

The food was good as they both seemed to be enjoying their dinner. The conversation between them had gone silent as they ate. It was not long before the staff brought out Dr. LeFlore's Birthday

Brownie with the scoop of vanilla. He and Janet were served two warm brownies with nuts, ice cream, and whipped cream. The brownie was warm having just come out of the oven and was smothered with caramel and had a candle stuck in the scoop of ice cream. The dessert was quite tasty as one would feel compelled to eat fast before the ice cream melted into the warmth of the delicious brownie. The staff sang a warm and heartfelt Happy Birthday to Dr. LeFlore as he blew out the candle. He and Janet ate their dessert. One thing that Beck was saying to his wife Janet that evening regarding his health and physical condition was very true. He was getting worse and his cancer was starting to spread. He was getting weaker and sicker with each day and each treatment. There was no real sign of improvement after several years he had been battling this disease and undergoing rigorous treatment. It seemed the disease and the chemotherapy was starting to get the best of him. He wanted to be positive about the outlook but in reality, there was not a lot to be positive about.

He was often very weak and lethargic, and his appetite was not always good. There were many days when he really did not feel like eating at all, or he would try and force himself to eat because he knew he had to eat. He also suffered spells of vomiting. He had lost a lot of weight. He did not experience the extreme hair loss that many chemo patients suffer from. His skin color was darker, and he had started to look as if he had a permanent suntan. His clothes fit him a lot more loosely which gave him the appearance of being emaciated.

Janet was very much in denial about Walker's prognosis. She knew Beck was an extremely sick man, but in her heart, she was not ready to accept the idea of losing him. She accompanied him to all his appointments and treatments. She was witnessing his illness firsthand but she still hung onto the ray of hope that a miracle might occur and the cancer would go into remission or simply that he was still with her, so she could just continue to hang onto him.

Certainly, like most women, she understood the concept that many women outlive their husbands for whatever reason. However, truthfully Beck had been in her life for so long, she could not fathom what she would do without him in her life. All she knew was that she loved him immensely. The last few years of their marriage had been some of the best years. They had experienced a great deal of togetherness and closeness especially since she had retired and started working with him in his office. They were literally together all day every day and they both liked the newfound togetherness they had tremendously. They were both still working in their Seventies.

Despite everything that was going on with Walker regarding his health, his work was what really kept him going. His work and patients were of primary importance to him. It is what motivated him to keep trying even though many days he just felt like lying in bed and dying. At the end of the day, he knew if anything happened to him his wife and family would be comfortable. However, the thing that really kept him motivated and wanting to live was his work. Beck truly lived for and embodied an inner truth that he possessed, and that was his ability to heal people. Now he was sick and unable to heal himself. His other inner truth was his undying love for his wife Janet. Beck once told Burton a few years ago that he wished that he would go before his wife Janet because, if she went before him, he would probably start drinking again.

Beck's drinking was an entire other topic of discussion. For several years, Beck drank heavily. His drinking took a considerable toll on his marriage and his medical practice. However, Janet still hung in there with him during the ups and downs. Although, Beck always remained one of the busiest and most sought-after Physicians in town. He saw and treated a lot of patients. He worked long hours and was under an excessive amount of stress. The drinking was hard on his family. Janet had weathered many storms with him, his busy schedule, his stress, and his drinking.

Although, Beck had stopped drinking completely for a while now, for over fifteen years to be exact. Beck had been sober, and it had made such a difference in his life and the happiness between him and his wife. Not to mention the fact that he learned how to deal with the stress of his busy medical practice in more productive ways. His practice started to grow even more. So, when he said to his son Burton, he hoped he would go before his wife because if she went before him, he would probably start drinking again, Burton knew exactly what he meant by his powerful statement.

On the following Wednesday, Walker had to travel again to New

Orleans for his regularly scheduled appointment. Usually, Beck would drive on the way to New Orleans and Janet would drive home. Sometimes they would spend the night at the patient hotel accommodations and travel back to Mobile the next morning. After undergoing his treatment, he would undoubtedly be zapped of energy and want to sleep most of the way back to Mobile.

Today the skies were overcast, and they periodically drove into patches of rain along the way. The rain was light though and did not pose a major impediment to driving safely. Mostly the skies were just cloudy and gray on the Mississippi Gulf Coast along Interstate 10 into New Orleans, Louisiana. The two of them had been driving to New Orleans for Beck's treatments for almost a year and a half. Twice a month Beck took his treatments at Ochsner Hospital.

Ochsner Hospital was the same hospital in New Orleans where Janet and Beck's oldest son Champ died of Aids back in 1994. It was August 18th, 1994 to be exact. So now just as she had once stood by in the same hospital and watched her son die at a very young age, she was now accompanying her husband through yet another horrifying and painful experience.

"Champ loved New Orleans," Janet said. "Beck I miss our son so much. Every time I come here, I just feel him and sense him and think of him. He loved this place called New Orleans, Louisiana."

"Our son did love this city," said Beck.

"Every time I go into that hospital, it's hard to go in there sometimes because I just think about him and how he died. It's hard sometimes to go in there. The other day while you were doing your treatment, I went upstairs to the room where our son left us. There was somebody in there, so I came back downstairs, and I just sat there and cried," she said. "And I think about you, and I wonder how it must feel for you to have to come here and undergo those treatments," said Janet.

"Janet, I miss him too," Beck said. "My namesake and I don't even want to start to describe what I feel like having to go into that hospital where our son died and know that I'm dying," he said. "A son is supposed to bury his father, not the other way around."

"Don't say that to me," said Janet.

"I still remember coming here for his graduation from Tulane Law School," said Beck. "So proud of him, he was such a brilliant young man and on his way to a promising career as an Attorney."

"Remember how we tried to get him to come back to Mobile and he said no. I am going to be a Louisiana Lawyer," said Janet.

"A Louisiana Lawyer he was," said Beck. "I do wish he had come back to Mobile and practiced."

"He could have gone anywhere and practiced Beck," Janet said. "He said New Orleans was his niche. He said he felt like this city suited him and his personality. He had developed a spiritual connection with New Orleans," she said. "That's why he always weighs heavy on my mind when we come here."

"New Orleans is a spiritual kind of place, just look at all of the voodoo stores on Bourbon Street," replied Beck.

"Hold on," Janet grabbed the side of her face in severe pain. "It hurts, hurts," as she reached out her hand to grasp her husband's arm. "Hurts!"

"Janet, what is it?" asked Beck.

"Hurts, it hurts!' she said.

"Do you want to pull over?" he said.

"No, it hurts," she said pointing at her jaw and the area around her cheek.

"We're going to have to get you in to see a specialist," said Beck.

"Mmmhhhh," Janet moaned in pain.

"If you feel better after my appointment, would you like to go to City Park?" asked Beck.

About that time Beck and Janet arrived at Ochsner Hospital where Beck was scheduled for his treatment. Janet looked a little sad as they went into the waiting room. Her thoughts remained on her eldest son who predeceased her and now her husband was suffering from this devastating disease. Although, she usually looked forward to the ride back and forth to New Orleans because it allowed the two of them to spend some time together away from work.

However, she always felt sad when she finally got to New Orleans because she would always think about her first-born Walker Junior. Going to Ochsner always brought back memories of him during his last days when he was sick at that hospital. Now the new memories of Beck having to undergo these repeated treatments that inadvertently did not seem to be doing him much good. She would try and think back to happier days with her son and her husband in

New Orleans because they did have many happy days together there visiting Champ. Beck and Janet had even seen Muhammad Ali and Leon Spinks fight in New Orleans many years ago, but unfortunately going to this hospital with her husband just made her feel nothing but abjection and barrenness. It did nothing but bring back the same sorrow and emptiness that she felt when her son had died in that room on the 5th floor of the same hospital on August 18, 1994. She could not ever deny; however, that Ochsner provided a level of superior care to her son and her husband but sometimes sickness and pain hurts and makes a person feel some type of way..

Beck was called in to undergo his treatment. Janet waited for him there in the waiting room. She sat there alone sad and gazing in front of her, trying to cope with her feelings and find some sort of happy place. Janet was an eternal optimist. However, it is not easy for a mother to make peace with losing her child. Certainly, it is a pain that many mothers in this world have had to live with, but it is a pain that usually never goes away in a mother's lifetime. She just sat there and stared into space almost as though she was in a despondent and dejected trance. The images of her son dying in that hospital room and the feeling of helplessness that she felt knowing there was nothing she could do for him except for sit and watch him suffer.

She wanted to find a corner somewhere and wrap herself in a ball and just cry some real tears. The emotions just overcame her all over again and again as she went there to be with Beck who was now afflicted and in just as much anguish as her son who had gone before him. There did not seem to be anything she could do to make the situation better. All she could do was just pray and wait on what seemed to be inevitable. That was extremely difficult for someone like Janet who liked to be a catalyst for improvement and change.

When Beck completed his treatment and returned to the waiting area where Janet was seated, he could see the mournful look on her face. He felt much of what Janet was feeling himself; however, he was also dealing with his own fear of dying. He was dealing with the realization that he and Champ may be reunited soon. Although, he already knew how difficult it was for his wife to lose him and how hard it may have been on her trying to help him through his illness. She perked up a little when she saw Beck. She tried to look more self-assured, but Beck was aware of her expression and her conversation about what she was feeling. At that point, he wanted to try and get out of his own melancholy and concern for his current condition and try and comfort her.

He was exhausted from his therapy, but he wondered if he could muster enough energy to go for a short walk in City Park. He did not really feel like going anywhere but to bed; although, he wondered if it might help Janet to clear her mind a little. They left the Hospital and went out to the car. Beck took the wheel as he drove them in the direction of the park. They still had plenty of time to pick up a bite to eat and have their lunch in the park before they would have to drive back to Mobile. They went to Magazine Street and stopped at a Po Boy shop and ordered sandwiches to take to the park with them.

They took Carrolton Avenue to City Park Avenue as they turned into the picturesque and tranquil New Orleans park. Beck spotted a bench not far from the street, so he pulled over and parked so they could walk over to the park bench and had a seat.

"Janet, not a day goes by that I don't think about our son Champ. He was a brilliant and dynamic young man," Beck said. "The two of us were blessed to be his parents," he said. "Walker Beck LeFlore, Jr., yes, I remember the day he was born. The first time I saw a child of ours in the flesh. I can never forget the love I felt in my heart for you and our newborn son. That moment changed our lives forever, for the better. You and I became a family, a real family," said Beck.

"Why aren't you eating your sandwich?" asked Janet.

"Are you listening to me?" asked Beck.

"Yes, I'm listening to you. I'm listening to every word you said," replied Janet. "I was just wondering why you weren't eating your food," she said. "It's good. Here. Take a bite of mine. Taste it" Janet said. "Try and put something on your stomach Beck. Here you go."

"I don't really have much of an appetite right now, to be truthful. The chemo seems to take my appetite and energy," said Beck. "Now what was I saying?" he asked.

"You were saying when Champ was born, we became a family," said Janet.

"We'll always be a family and we have to find strength in God and each other," Beck said. "The two of us have so much to be thankful for as we should also be thankful for having had such a wonderful son," he said.

"We still have one more wonderful son," said Janet.

"Yes, we do," he said. "You and I created and raised some great men and for that, we should be nothing but thankful," said Beck.

"It's just that when we go into the hospital, it's almost like reliving that whole experience all over again," Janet said. "I know he is gone and I'm trying so hard to accept it. Every day it seems to get a little better and a little easier to let him go. But I would like to forget having had to see him suffer like that. I would just like to forget the way it made me feel to watch my child dying of Aids. I wish I could forget it, just put it out of my mind forever."

"I'll take a bite of that sandwich now," said Beck as he put his arm around his wife.

"Sometimes I have dreams that he's still living here in New Orleans in some obscure house and for some reason he just doesn't call us much or come to see us, but in my dream he is still living and alive," said Janet as she reached her hand with the sandwich in it towards Beck's mouth so he could take a bite.

"He was my oldest son and I admired him very much as a young man," Beck said. "I think he was a pretty good big brother to Burton too."

"I think Burton took his brother's death pretty hard," said Janet.

"I know Champ's death was difficult for Burton," replied Beck. "Do you remember when Burton came down here from New York for his funeral. He was so upset he forgot to bring his shoes and borrowed some dress sandal type shoes from Champ's friend Anthony and ended up with that fungus on his feet. I think he must have gotten that fungus on his feet from the funeral home," said Beck.

"A fungus on his feet?" said Janet.

"Yes, he didn't tell you," Beck said. "He got some kind of fungus on his feet, and I had to give him some antifungal cream to get rid of it," said Beck.

"Janet we as a husband and wife, we as a mother and father, we as a family can overcome anything," said Beck. "We just have to put our faith in God."

"You never told me Burton had a fungus on his feet," said Janet.

"It was pretty bad," Beck said.

"We probably need to be heading back it's getting late," Janet said.

"You feel like driving now," Beck said. "I'm a little tired. Don't really feel like driving right now."

Janet and Beck proceeded to leave New Orleans City Park and head back to Mobile. They wanted to try and make it to Mobile before dark. They drove down Chef Menteur to Morrison Road and exited onto Interstate 10 East headed back to the Port City. It was not long before they passed through Slidell and over the Lake Pontchatrain Bridge. It wasn't long before they crossed over into Mississippi. The sun was starting to set in the west as they made their way east through Mississippi toward Mobile.

"Beck I'm glad we became a family," Janet said. "There is no other man on this earth that I would want to be my husband and the father of my children, our children."

"Janet, I thank God every day that we became a family," Beck said. "There is no other woman I would rather be my wife and the mother of our children."

"Do you mean that?" said Janet.

"I wouldn't have said it if I didn't mean it," Beck said. "Did you mean it?"

"With everything that is my being and my soul," replied Janet.

"What are we looking like on gas right now?" he said.

"We're getting low," Janet replied. "We probably need to go ahead and stop and get some."

"Looks like we've got a few more miles to the next exit. We can stop in Gulfport," said Beck.

"Beck when are you going to take me to the casino?" asked Janet.

"When do we have time to go the casino?" said Beck.

"We'll just have to make some time," replied Janet. "I would really like that."

"We'll see," Beck said. "Slow down Janet we're coming up on the next exit."

"I see it," said Janet.

They pull into the nearest gas station off the highway in Gulfport. Beck gives Janet his credit card and asked her to go inside and pay for the gas while he pumped. She took the card and went into the gas station and paid the cashier for the gas. She glanced out of the window as Walker stood there by the pump waiting for the attendant to turn it on. Their Cadillac Seville only took Premium Unleaded. The digital reading on the pump went to zero and he began to fuel the car. Janet returned and sat back in the driver's seat as they waited to finish refueling the car. He finished fueling and returned the nozzle to the pump. Beck proceeded to get back into the car.

Now they had gas and they were on their way to Mobile. As they got to where the east and west exit ramps where located leading onto Interstate 10 Janet paused for a minute. She felt slightly disoriented.

"That says east and the other sign says west," Janet said. "Beck are we going east or west?" "This one says New Orleans and the other one says Biloxi. I thought we were going to Mobile?"

"Janet, what are you talking about? We're going to Mobile," said Beck.

"Where's the sign for Mobile? I don't see any sign for Mobile," she said.

"We have to go through Biloxi before we start seeing signs to Mobile," Beck said. "You know that. As many times as we've driven this highway from Mobile to New Orleans."

"I know, I was just looking for a sign for Mobile because I knew we weren't going to Biloxi," said Janet.

"We have to pass through Biloxi to get to Mobile," said Beck.

"Right, because we just left New Orleans," said Janet.

"Yes, Janet we just left New Orleans," Beck replied. "Now we're on the way to Mobile."

"Right, we're going east! Now I remember," said Janet.

"Janet, are you serious?" Beck said.

"What do you mean am I serious?" Janet said. "I'm perfectly serious."

"Janet, I'm a little worried about you," said Beck.

"It's almost dark out here, I'm just trying to get my bearings," said Janet.

"We're going east," said Beck as he adjusted his seat to a reclining position. "Do you want me to drive?" he said.

"No. I'm fine, you just get some rest Beck. I know you're tired," said Janet.

"Are you sure?" asked Beck.

"Yes. I'm sure," said Janet.

"And why would you be worried about me?" asked Janet.

"Because this is starting to become a pattern of yours," Beck said. "This is the second time we were on a familiar stretch of highway and you acted as if you were confused or disoriented. I hope you're not starting to suffer from Dementia."

"No, Beck. I'm not suffering from Dementia," Janet said. "I'm trying to make sure we're going the right way and we don't get lost out here on the highway," she said. "Is there something wrong with that? Honestly, you try and make the smallest things into something huge."

"Janet, I'm so exhausted," said Beck. "We're going east to Biloxi and then to Mobile. We're going to make a right, right here. Right here, I 10 East."

"You don't have to talk to me like I'm stupid," she said.

"I'm not trying to talk to you like you're stupid. Janet, I'm not trying to argue with you about this, I would just like to get back to Mobile so I can lay down and get some rest," Beck said. "I'm exhausted. Every time I take one of those treatments it makes me feel like I'm dead and I'm not dead yet. I don't know what's worse, this disease or the bullshit chemotherapy, which doesn't seem to be doing me a damn bit of good. If I'm going to die, I just hope it's not out here on this highway."

"So we're going East to the right, right here." Janet said, "That's all I wanted to know."

"Yes. New Orleans is west, and we are going East to Mobile," said Beck.

"That's all I wanted to know," she said, "Thank you. Thank you."

Janet and Beck merged onto the east exit back onto Interstate 10. Walker stretched out in the passenger seat and tried to take a nap as they traveled along 10 East back to Mobile. Janet drove the rest of the drive back to Mobile as Beck rested. There was little or no conversation between them for the remainder of the trip back to Mobile.

It was not long before they were pulling up at their residence located on Rue de LeFlore. Not sure if it was fully explained, Beck and Janet lived on a street that they had built and named, Rue de LeFlore which means the Street of LeFlore in French. Beck and

Janet were a very accomplished couple. Their home was a modest mansion nestled back in the cul de sac of their own street. Back in the day they acquired a relatively large parcel of land, located right in the heart of Mobile and built their dream home and subdivided the remaining property and sold off approximately eight other lots to third parties.

Janet and Beck made a tremendous deal on their investment and got their house paid off relatively quickly. Janet and Beck were a smart and tremendously industrious couple who had acquired a substantial amount of real estate and money in their lifetime. Beck and Janet were a powerhouse couple. They were both extremely successful people in their own right. Both of them together were completely motivated and unstoppable. As Janet drove them into the back yard of their home, Beck was just waking up from his somber rest. He was so glad to see his back yard and back door. Now if he could just make it inside to the bed to get some sleep. They went inside and went straight to bed in their downstairs suite, they were both tired and exhausted.

Meanwhile, in Wilmington, Burton was applying for a full-time position with the University of North Carolina at Wilmington. The University had invited him there as an adjunct professor and offered him an opportunity and a one-year contract to get some teaching experience in the area of Business Law. They promised him that if he did a good job, they would consider him for the full-time tenure track position. As the year winded down to a close, Burton had done a tremendous job. All the Business majors wanted to take his class after the first semester. Burton enjoyed his position as a professor, but he worried about his dad. He knew his dad was sick and not in the best of health. However, he had faith that he and his mom were doing the best they could to manage.

He hoped they would hire him for the full-time tenured position. He applied and he interviewed even though they told him from the beginning there would be other candidates considered. Burton had done a tremendous job delivering the subject of Business Law to his students. Deep down inside, even though Burton enjoyed his position at UNCW he longed to get back to Mobile. Wilmington and Mobile are two cities that are very similar in that they are both small quaint southern towns on the water.

While living in Wilmington, Burton started to realize one of the things about his mom and dad that made them more compatible. The two of them both came from relatively large families; both of them were children of a postmen; both of them came from homes where their mothers were housewives; both of them grew up in similar communities; both of them were Depression Babies who had survived more than their share of adversity and poverty; both of them were extremely motivated to succeed.

However, one day during late April, Burton's wife Candace called him at work. He indicated to her that he was about to go and teach his next class and that he could not talk right now. He dismissed the conversation as she had called him at work. Shortly after he hung up the phone and left to go and teach his one o'clock class. She called again and again and again. Burton was now downstairs in his classroom teaching his second section of BL and the phone in his office continued to ring.

Burton's office mate finally answered the phone. Candace asked for Burton and she indicated that he had gone to teach his class. She also reprimanded Candace, indicating that she had just overheard her conversation with Burton, and she knew he told her he was about to go teach is class. His coworker wanted to know why she continued to call after he already told her he needed to go and would call her back when he got out of class? Furthermore, she was interrupting her work.

Burton's coworker abruptly ended the conversation by hanging up on Candace. She felt that Candace had disrespected her and Burton on their job. She had heard the conversation and heard Burton tell her that he was about to go and teach his class. However, after he hung up the phone and left the office, she just continued to call his line. Burton's coworker was trying to finish her lesson plan and get ready to give her students their final exams and she did not understand why this woman continued to call the line after Burton clearly said he was about to go and teach his next class.

Candace was infuriated that his coworker had confronted her in such a manner. She was angry and her hormones were raging. She was pregnant with their fourth child. She and Burton had gotten pregnant again. Her continuing to call after Burton had terminated the conversation was certainly nothing new. At this point when she was confronted by Burton's office mate, Candace was totally insulted and embarrassed. Candace was about one month into her fourth pregnancy. However, there was no excuse for her continuing to call Burton's office and interrupting his coworker. Especially after Burton had spoken with her briefly and told her that he would have to go because his next class was in a few minutes.

Furthermore, Candace knew that Burton was applying for the full-time tenure track position with the University. His one-year adjunct professorship was about to be up, and he wanted to be hired permanently. So, it is somewhat incomprehensible why Burton's wife would show up on his job a week later and confront and assault his coworker. That is exactly what Candace did. She went onto campus the following Saturday while Burton was there preparing his lectures and exams for the upcoming week. As finals were approaching, his office mate was also there doing some preparation for the upcoming week.

All of this was right during the time when the review board was making their selection on how they were going to fill the permanent position teaching Business Law that Burton hoped would be awarded to him. He had done such a tremendous job this year. Enrollment in his class literally doubled the second semester because the students liked and respected him and his teaching methods. On that bright Saturday morning, Candace entered the School of Business at the University of North Carolina at Wilmington and assaulted and harassed his coworker simply for asking her to please stop calling their office repeatedly and disturbing her while she was trying to do her work. Burton was not present when the altercation occurred.

The campus police were subsequently called. Candace was arrested temporarily and detained at the Campus police headquarters. They spoke with Burton's coworker and with his wife. Burton was not questioned because he was not a witness to the incident and was not around when it occurred. Candace was banned from coming onto the campus. She was informed by the campus police that if she was caught trespassing on the university grounds that she would be subject to arrest.

It is fair to say that a reasonable person under the same or similar circumstances would not have continued to call her husband's work phone repeatedly after they had just spoken, and he said he had to go and teach his next class. Similarly, it seems rational to surmise that any woman who supported her husband and knew that a great job could help him to support her and their children would not show up at his job and have any type of confrontation with a coworker for any reason or any purpose.

In addition, Burton and Candace were no longer living at Wrightsville Beach. They had moved into a house located in downtown Wilmington. Two months prior, Burton had become embroiled in a dispute with his former landlord because the college kids who lived beneath him repeatedly harassed him and his family and the landlord would not try and smooth out the situation.

Basically, what happened was, the girl's downstairs were having a wild party one Friday night. At some point, Candace called the police to shut the party down because she said the party was keeping her and the kids awake. From that point on, the students who lived on the lower level of Burton and his family started calling the police to his door for any and every reason they could possibly think of. Literally, every time he and his family had a knock at the door it was the police. This was their retaliation for Candace having called the police to subdue their party.

Burton complained about what was happening and asked the landlord to try and deal with the situation between them and the downstairs neighbors. The landlord refused to get involved. Burton became upset because the landlord would not ask his tenants on the lower level of their house to stop calling the police to their apartment on a daily basis for no reason. He subsequently refused to pay rent and the landlord immediately sought to evict them from the house. About a month later they were evicted from the beach house.

From Wrightsville Beach, Burton and his family moved to a historic house located in Downtown Wilmington on Nunn Street. The beach property they were leasing was a furnished unit, so they had not moved any of their furniture to Wilmington yet. When they moved into the new house, they had little furniture in the house other than their beds and a table and a few chairs. The house they moved into was a large historic two-story dwelling located less than a block from Front Street in Wilmington.

Burton was on the verge of getting the full-time position with a significant pay increase, health insurance package and more job security. He had clearly demonstrated that he was a worthy candidate for the job. The staff liked him. The students found him to be a motivating professor. It was about to be an overall win-win situation for Burton and his family. However, Candace, his wife, came onto campus on that Saturday and harassed, confronted and assaulted his female coworker for asking her to please not call the office so frequently, especially after she had just spoken with her husband in her presence. She heard him make a reasonable and honest request to call her back when he finished teaching his class. Here Burton's wife had shown up and wrecked Burton's chances of ever getting that offer to teach there permanently and they were expecting their fourth child.

Needless to say, the following week after the incident Burton was informed the review board was no longer considering him for the promotion. He knew from the very beginning they were interviewing other candidates. He knew there was no guarantee that he was going to get the tenure track position; however, before the incident between Candace and his coworker he had been practically awarded the position. The faculty head had not made the announcement because they were planning to make the final decision and announce it at the end of the semester. They wanted to review Burton's evaluations before making the final recommendation that he be offered a new contract. Now all hopes of that ever happening had been shattered. Burton's ridiculous wife had completely managed to take that option completely off the table.

Burton had been prepared to accept possibly being passed over for someone else, but he had never dreamed he would not be offered the position because his wife came on to campus and attacked his office mate who was very happily married and much older than Burton. There is no way Candace could have thought anything was going on between them. Certainly, there was nothing between them other than they shared an office and a cordial working relationship. They were rarely even in the office at the same time. It was completely unfathomable why Candace would have done such a thing when she knew how much it meant to him that he be awarded the full time BL position. At this point, Burton had little more to do than to finish out the semester.

That evening Burton was a little distraught and upset. He went home and said very little to Candace or the kids. He felt like he had no idea what he was going to do. He really enjoyed teaching Business Law and had sincerely hoped he was going to get asked to fill the full-time professorship. He was right there. He had been practically certain they were going to offer him the job. He went out into the back yard and sat down by himself. He did like Wilmington, but he often missed Mobile. He was worried about his dad because he knew his health was getting worse.

He was trying to let it sink in that he and Candace had another child on the way. Burton felt so much anger toward her right then for sabotaging his potential opportunity. An opportunity now shot to hell. Burton was in a whirlwind of thought at this point about everything that was going on. He decided he would call his mom. Whenever Burton needed someone to talk to, he would call Janet. She was always there for her son.

"Hi Mom," said Burton.

"Hey Burton, how are you?" said Janet as she placed the phone between her shoulder and head while she finished washing her hands.

"They said they weren't considering me for the full-time position anymore," Burton said. "You'll never believe…. Candace went on my job and assaulted my coworker."

"Whaaaaaaat," said Janet.

"Yea so today they told me they weren't considering me for the position I was trying to get," Burton said. "How is Daddy doing?"

"He's, he's fine," Janet said. "Oh, Burton I'm sorry to hear that. Why would she do something like that? Does she think you're involved with this woman?"

"No, Mom, there is no way she could think that," Burton said. "Candace called the office the other day and I was about to head into my next class so we spoke for a brief second, and I told her that I would call her back. I went to teach my class and apparently, she kept calling and calling the office. Nancy eventually answered the phone and asked why she kept calling the office when I was not there. She told Candace that she was trying to get her work done and the repeated phone calls were disturbing her."

"From that point I guess she and Candace got into it," he said. "When I got back from teaching my class Nancy told me that Candace had gotten an attitude with her when she asked her to stop calling so much."

"My goodness," said Janet.

"Later that day when I went home Candace was saying that my coworker had been rude to her and hung up the phone in her face," Burton said. "So, I was like well Candace if I had just talked to you and told you I was about to go and teach my class why would you keep calling the office anyway. So, then she started calling my coworker a bitch and got an attitude with me. But I never thought she would go to my job and basically try and fight the woman."

"I can't believe what I'm hearing," said Janet.

"Well you heard it right here," he said.

"She actually tried to fight the lady, your co-worker?" said Janet.

"Mom, she came to my job and jumped on Nancy for absolutely no reason. The campus police had to get involved and everything. I mean why would she even go on my job in the first place." said Burton.

"Oh, Burton," said Janet. "Do you like it in Wilmington?" she asked.

"It's OK, I kind of like Wilmington but I miss Mobile," he said.

"Are you thinking about coming back down here?" she asked. "Or do you think you might want to stay there?"

"Mom I mean do you realize how embarrassing it is to have your wife show up to your place of employment and assault your coworker for absolutely no reason?" asked Burton. "I do miss home Mom, but if the money was going to be right here, then I'd stay here in Wilmington."

"I did tell you that I taught at Williston High School many years ago," said Janet.

"Yes, Mom. I know you taught at Williston," replied Burton. "You know Breton is going to high school there now."

"How's Breton and Bryceton and Breaghan doing?" she asked.

"They're all doing fine Mom," said Burton.

"I miss my grandchildren and your dad misses them too," she said.

"Well perhaps you'll be happy to hear you and Dad are expecting another grandchild," said Burton.

"What are you talking about Burton?" said Janet.

"Candace is pregnant," said Burton.

"Candace is pregnant!" exclaimed Janet. "Again," she said.

"Yes. It looks like we're going to be having another baby," he said as a small smile appeared on his face.

"Another baby," Janet said.

"Yea, another baby," he said. "I don't know if I told you but I'm about to start a Real Estate Broker's class. Here in the state of North Carolina, if you have experience or advanced education you can complete the Real Estate Broker's course and sit for the exam. I've always wanted to get into the Real Estate business."

"You're taking a Real Estate Broker's course," she said. "So, you already completed the other course you were taking, the real estate course you told me about?" she asked.

"Yes. I completed the preliminary real estate agent course." Burton said, "You know I already took that course before I went to Law School and completed the licensing exam and got my license, but it lapsed while I was in Law School."

"I remember you telling me about that," Janet said.

"You know they're making a lot of movies in Wilmington," Burton said. "Wilmington is becoming a little film mecca," he said.

"Burton, I know you have a lot going on right now, but it would be great if you could come home just to visit maybe you could bring the kids," said Janet.

"Mom, I'm going to see if I can make it, the summer's coming up. Basically, at this point I'm planning to move back to Mobile," Burton said. "It's going to take me the rest of the summer to complete my Brokers course and to take the state exam and then basically I'm going to be moving home and apply for my reciprocal license there," Burton said.

"Are you sure that's what you want to do?" said Janet.

"I want to get into the Real Estate business, yes," Burton said.

"You still don't have any real interest in practicing law?" said Janet.

"Not really. I've been enjoying teaching Business Law and I was really hoping they were going to offer me the full-time position,"

Burton said. "There's a lot of lawyers out there, Mom. Sometimes you got to zig while everybody else is zagging," he said. "I'm not saying that I have absolutely no interest in practicing law, it's just that I've wanted to get my Real Estate Broker's license for a while, and I think I will enjoy being in this business, and I have an opportunity to do it now."

"And Candace is having another baby," Janet said. "My goodness gracious. Have you talked to Daddy?" Janet said. "He will certainly be surprised to hear that."

"Not in a few days," Burton said. "Is he home now?"

"Not right now," Janet replied. "He should be back soon. He's at the hospital making his rounds. I can have him call you or maybe you can call back a little later and talk with him. Let him know what your plans are."

"Sure, I will, I need to talk with him anyway," said Burton.

"Burton you hang in there and just remember to take one day at a time," Janet said. "Everything will work itself out," she said

"I will, Mom," said Burton.

"No, arguing with Candace," Janet said. "There's no excusing her coming to your job and having any sort of confrontation with your coworker. But don't be around there arguing about it."

"Mom, I'll call back in a little while and see if I can catch Daddy," said Burton.

He and Janet hang up as Janet goes back to nibbling on a piece of cheese and straightening up the kitchen. She is waiting for Beck to arrive as she is heating some food for his dinner. She paused briefly as she took a bite of the Red Rhine cheese which she often used to make her Macaroni. Janet loved Macaroni and Cheese and she had prepared some for their dinner tonight along with some Chicken wings and Broccoli.

She held her hand up to the side of her face. Her jaw is hurting this evening, and she did not want to take any pain killers to help with the pain because she did not like the way the pain pills made her feel drowsy. She sat down at the table for a moment and just cringed in pain as the nerve endings in her face pulsated. She hoped that Beck would be making it home shortly. It was not long before she saw the lights of his car shining through the glass door of their house as he pulled into the back yard. Janet greeted him as he came into the house.

"Beck, your dinner is ready. Sit down and eat before it gets cold," said Janet.

"I'm so tired. I'm not that hungry but I'll try and eat a little something," said Beck.

"I just talked with Burton," said Janet.

"How's he doing?" Beck asked, "Has he heard anything about the position he applied for?"

"He said they told him today they were no longer considering him for it," Janet said. "It appears that Candace went onto his job and assaulted his coworker."

"She did what!?" said Beck.

"She came to his office on campus and got into a confrontation with the lady he shares the office with," said Janet. "And he says they are no longer considering him for the position he had hoped to get."

"That doesn't surprise me one bit," Beck said. "Every time Burton is doing good; she somehow manages to derail his progress. It never fails." Beck continued, "As much as I hate to say it, I wish he would divorce her. She's been nothing but an Albatross around his neck ever since he met her."

"Beck, don't say that. Burton loves his little family so much and he seems to be doing everything he can to keep his family together," said Janet.

"I wish it wasn't true, but it is," said Beck.

"He loves his family Beck, and I believe he wants to keep his family together," replied Janet.

"It would be nice if he got some help from his wife," replied Beck. "So, this incident between her and the coworker is going to go into his personnel file and when he applies for another job they're going to say, hey by the way."

"Beck, sit down and eat something," she said. "How's your appetite?"

"I haven't eaten much today, and I know I need to eat but I don't have much of an appetite and what you just related to me has just taken away what little appetite I had," Beck said. "Whatever happened to a wife supporting her husband and both working together to accomplish their goals?"

"She's so insecure," replied Janet.

"I don't know what her problem is, but it's destroying our son," said Beck. "All Burton has been talking about for the last few weeks is how much he hoped they were going to give him the full-time tenure track position. He was really hoping that was going to work in his favor, and that would have done nothing but benefited his wife and children. How does she expect him to support them? She's not working?"

"He was telling me that he wants to move back to Mobile." Janet said, "He is taking a Real Estate Broker's course and wants to get his Broker's License and go into the real estate business."

"I would like to see him move back home, but I know how important this was to him," said Beck.

"Burton said Candace is pregnant again," Janet said. "We're going to have another grandbaby."

"You've got to be joking?" Beck said as he shook his head.

"I'm not joking. I'm just as serious as a heart attack," said Janet.

"That's all the more reason why she might not want to cause problems for him at his job," said Beck.

"I agree," replied Janet.

"Now let me just make sure I heard you correctly," said Beck.

"You heard me correctly," said Janet. "Candace is pregnant with baby number four."

"Candace is pregnant," Beck said. "Are you sure about that?"

"That's what he told me," Janet said. "Why don't you call him."

"I will," said Beck as he let out a big yawn. He sat there and bowed his forehead into his hand as he sat in the thinking man's position for a moment. "I'm just so tired right now. Let me catch my breath for a second."

Beck went into the bedroom and started to change his clothes. He put on his bathrobe and sat on the side of the bed for a moment. He wanted to go and try to eat his dinner, but he was so tired. He just felt like if he laid down, he would probably fall asleep as soon as his head hit the pillow. Now Janet had just given him the news that there was a new grandchild on the way and Burton had lost his job. He wondered to himself if he would even live to see his expected grandchild born. He sat there quietly as he rotated his neck and just tried to contemplate everything he had discussed with his wife regarding Burton.

He wanted to call Burton and talk to him. He felt exhausted and he was not exactly sure what he would say to Burton right now. Truthfully, he was happy to hear the news of the possibility that he and Janet had another grandchild on the way. He and Janet loved their grandchildren dearly. He was even glad to hear that Burton might be moving back to Mobile. However, he was somewhat disappointed to hear about Candace's behavior at Burton's place of employment. He tried to muster enough energy to go back into the kitchen and take a few bites of his dinner before he went to bed. The phone rang. Janet answered and it was Burton.

"Hi, Mom. Did Dad make it home yet," Burton asked.

"Yes. He's here. Hold on a second," Janet said. "I'll get him."

"Hello," said Beck as he picked up the phone in their bedroom.

"Hi Dad, how are you doing?" asked Burton.

"Tired Burton, just tired," Beck said. "How are you son?"

"I got a lot going on right now, Dad," said Burton.

"Your Mom was telling me," Beck said. "So, you and Candace are expecting another child?"

"Yep," said Burton.

"That's nice," Beck said. "That's what you want?"

"I don't have a problem with it," Burton said. "I have a major problem with Candace right about now, but I don't have a problem with us having another child."

"Seems to me like you and Candace keep having problems in your relationship and yet the babies continue coming. If you want to have a stable life and stable family, you've got to make sure your wife understands she mustn't do anything to jeopardize your lively hood," Beck said. "Frankly speaking, if you ask me, that's exactly what she seems to do repeatedly. Your wife, the mother of your children is supposed to be in your corner helping you, and working with you, not against you," he said.

"Dad, you think I don't know that," said Burton.

"I don't know what to say, Burton," replied Beck.

"I was really hoping the promotion was going to pan out for me, especially in the wake of the news that we're having another child,"

Burton said. "Teaching here has been an incredible experience for me."

"It would be nice if you would try and get down here to visit us." Beck said, "I would like to see you and my grandchildren."

"I will Dad, but I'm taking this real estate broker's class, and I'm going to be tied up with that most of the summer. I want to go ahead and get it out of the way and take the exam. Basically, from that point I'm planning to apply for my license in Alabama and move back to Mobile," he said.

"Please try and bring the kids to see us when you can Burton," Beck said. "It's been a while since we've seen them."

Burton soon finished giving his final exams and left his position with the University. He worked diligently for the next few weeks on his real estate Broker's course. As the summer progressed, Beck and Janet went through the motions of work and chemotherapy treatments. The cancer which Beck had been fighting for over 5 years was doing nothing but progressing. It did not seem to be getting any better and Beck just seemed to continue to lose weight and suffer side effects from the chemo.

His clothes were starting to fit his frail body very loosely. His fingernails had gotten dark. His hair was thinning. His skin looked like he had sat in a tanning bed too long. However, he continued to see his patients and continued to try and maintain a positive outlook on life. Certainly, Walker was a doctor himself and he knew he was dying, but he was a fighter and he was determined to fight this thing until the bitter end.

Janet did everything she could to be a supportive and loving wife. Sometimes Janet would just wonder to herself what she would do if her husband passed away. Unfortunately, it was not something that she was prepared for and she did not know how she was going to handle it if it happened. She knew Beck's condition was getting worse, but it was easier and more comfortable for her to remain in a state of semi-denial. As long as he was still with her, she had hope.

She hoped that some miracle would happen and suddenly, his cancer would go into remission. Certainly, there were instances where this occurred, so it was not totally unreasonable to have some degree of a sanguine expectation that maybe he would show some improvement or recover altogether. She prayed to herself that somehow her husband would manage to make it through this illness he had been suffering from for some time now. Often it is not easy to let go, and certainly, at this point, she had no reason to feel that she should let go. Beck was not giving up, so why should she. The two of them had defied the odds all their lives. Why should she have a negative perception now?

She was certain of one thing, no matter what, she was going to be with her husband Beck every step of the way. She would not focus on the outcome, but on the day to day process of being there for Beck no matter what. She and Beck had been together for over 50 years and she was going to do whatever it took to help her husband through this ordeal.

CHAPTER FOUR

During the month of August, Beck was admitted to the hospital again. Janet contacted Burton to let him know that his dad was in the hospital and asked if he could come to Mobile. Burton had just completed his Broker's course and had taken the state exam and passed it. He decided to drop everything and head to Mobile to visit with his mom and dad. He was extremely concerned about his dad's condition and had been worried about him all Summer.

Luckily, he had achieved the goal he had been working on and it was a good time for him to go and be by his father's side. He could hear it in Janet's voice that she was noticeably stressed and worried. Burton jumped on the highway and traveled to Mobile. He did not bring his family with him. He had asked Candace to come but she did not seem to have a lot of interest in traveling to Mobile at the time. He traveled by himself and got there as fast as he could.

When Burton arrived in Mobile, he literally got off the highway and went straight to the hospital to visit with his dad. He found Beck in the hospital room accompanied by his mother who had been staying with him in the hospital. Beck was happy to see Burton as he came in and kissed his dad and hugged his mom. He did not know what to think of this current situation, other than he felt that his mom and dad needed him. Beck and Janet were some of the most self-sufficient people you would ever want to meet.

Certainly, Burton had always felt that he was wanted by his parents, but he had rarely felt that he was needed by Beck and Janet. This was probably the first time in his life that he honestly felt that both of his parents desperately needed him. Beck was extremely ill, and Janet was consumed with indecision about what to do and how to handle what was happening to Beck. Burton encouraged his mom to go home for a while and get some rest and he assured her that he would stay there with his dad.

Janet reluctantly agreed to go to the house for a little while, as she had been there at the hospital with Beck for several days. She was glad to see Burton and welcomed a little relief. However, she did not want to leave her husband's side. She was relieved that Burton had finally arrived and could give her some assistance with all that was going on in their lives. She had just about reached her breaking point and she did not know what to do. There was not much she could do other than pray and keep trying to be strong for herself and for Beck.

Beck asked if the boys had come to Mobile with him. He told his Dad that he had not brought the kids on this trip. Beck was very disappointed. He longed for his grandchildren and desperately wanted to see them. He knew it would not be long before he might be one of the dearly departed. He wanted to have what little relationship he could with his offspring before he died. He suggested that he felt it was Candace's fault the kids had not come with him. Burton assured him that he would bring the kids to see him before they went back to school. As they had decided, due to Candace's pregnancy they would wait until December or January before they moved back to Mobile.

However, Burton knew his dad wanted to see the boys, but he was low on money and just had to get down to Mobile by whatever means necessary. It had been two months since he left his job at UNCW. He was concerned about his dad and his health and just felt the need to get to Mobile to see him. Bringing the children was not his primary concern at this point.

"They said they think I have a blood clot," said Beck.

"Really, are they giving you any blood thinners?" said Burton.

"They're supposed to be bringing an x-ray machine here to the room so they can do an x-ray and try to find out where the blood clot is," Beck replied. "But it's been several hours since they ordered the x-ray and they haven't come to do it yet," he said.

"Do you want me to go and ask what the holdup is?" said Burton.

"Actually, I would," said Beck.

"Sure Dad," Burton said. "I'll be right back."

Burton left his father's side and went down to the nursing station on his floor and asked if they would be coming by his dad's room to take the x-rays they were supposed to be taking. The nurse looked up from her chart at Burton and told him that she was aware the doctor had ordered an x-ray. She stated that to the best of her knowledge they should be coming to his room any moment. Burton explained to her that his father was worried because they recognized the blood clot several hours ago and he had been waiting for the x-ray. He asked the nurse if she would please check to see what was taking so long. She assured Burton that she would check with the Radiology department. Burton left the nurses station and returned to Beck's side.

"What did they say?" asked Beck.

"She said she would call and see what the holdup was," said Burton.

"It doesn't make any sense for it to take this long for them just to do a simple x-ray," replied Beck.

"She's checking on it, so let's give them a few more minutes," Burton said.

"Come here, son," said Beck as he reached out his arms to hug Burton.

"Love you, Dad," Burton said as he leaned over to hug him.

"I want to ask you something," said Beck.

"What's that," Burton said trying to remain upbeat and positive.

"Have I been a good father to you?" asked Beck.

"Yea, you've been a pretty good father to me. I wouldn't trade you for the world," Burton said. "Why do you ask me that?"

"I just want you to know I love you very much, and I'm very proud of you," said Beck.

"Guess what? I got my Broker's license," said Burton.

"Congratulations," replied Beck.

"I passed my state exam two days ago before I left to come down here," said Burton.

"That doesn't mean that you have no intentions of practicing law does it?" asked Beck.

"No, Dad, but I'm excited about getting my Broker's license because I love the real estate business, and I'm planning to open my own company when I get back here to Mobile," Burton said.

"But right now, my primary focus and concern is getting you better and out of this hospital," he said. "Burton, I want you to promise me that if anything happens to me you will take care of your mother," Beck said. "I really worry about her sometimes."

"Dad, you're talking about you worry about Mom. But you're the one in the hospital and you're the one we need to get better right now," said Burton.

"Burton, I mean what I'm saying to you, promise me that you will take care of your mom if anything happens to me. It's important that you understand what I'm saying to you, and that you will give me your word son that you will be there for your mom," said Beck.

"Dad you can rest assured that as long as my heart is beating and there is blood flowing through my veins, I will take care of my mom," replied Burton.

"I love your mom more than anything in this world," said Beck.

"Dad so do I, I love you and Mom both and that goes without saying," Burton said.

"Can you believe they still haven't come by my room to take the x-ray," Beck said. "Of course, they want to take the x-ray to make sure I do have a clot before they give me anything to reduce the thrombosis. Can you believe it's been almost five hours now?"

"The nurse said she was going to get them up here, just relax Dad," said Burton.

"This is not acceptable, it shouldn't take that long for them just to do a simple x-ray," Beck said. "I've tried my best to be a good father to you son. I just hope I haven't let you down."

"Dad I hope I haven't let you down as a son," Burton said. "You have been a good dad, a very good dad, perhaps not perfect as no one is perfect, but a very good dad none the less," he said. "And I have tried my best to be a good son."

"You are a wonderful son Burton," Beck said. "There is something I need to tell you and I hope you'll understand," said Beck.

"What's that?" asked Burton.

"I want you to know that I didn't leave you anything in my Will," Beck paused as he spoke. "It's nothing personal. You haven't done anything to offend me, and it certainly isn't that I don't feel you deserve anything in the event of my demise," he said. "In all truthfulness, it's just that I have to be honest. I don't like your wife, and I feel that you and Candace will eventually be getting a divorce. I don't want her to have anything that I ever worked for," said Beck.

"I don't really know what to say," Burton said. "Dad I didn't come here to discuss your Will. I don't want anything from you. I want you to get better. Get out of this Hospital and come home."

"Burton as your father I feel that it's necessary I tell you while I'm still alive and here to explain," Beck said. "I would hate to leave this earth and you read my Will and wonder why, and have no explanation. I owe you an explanation son, and I hope that you will understand. I feel that I'm doing this to a certain extent to protect you, in the event you and your wife divorce, which I personally believe is inevitable. I don't wish that for you; although, I do wish for you to be happy. Your mom would give you her right arm if you asked for it, and I'm sure that if you ever need for anything, if she has it, she will help you. You may not want to have this conversation, but it needs to be had," he said.

"Dad that's fine," Burton said. "The gift of you; the gift of having you as my father in my life; the gift of your love, and your guidance is the greatest gift that you could ever have bestowed on me," said Burton.

"I appreciate you saying that," said Beck.

"I mean it, and I don't want to discuss your Will anymore." Burton said. "You're far from dead man."

"I have a tumor on my neck, and it seems to be growing," said Beck.

"Where?" asked Burton.

"It's right here," said Beck as he turned in the bed and pointed to the growth at the base of his neck.

"Is it something they can surgically remove?" asked Burton.

"I'm not opting for anymore surgery," Beck said.

"I see it," replied Burton as he touched it with his fingers.

"They still haven't come to take that x-ray either," said Beck.

"I will go back down to the desk and ask them again what the holdup is," replied Burton.

"That's OK, if I am going to die, there is no need for me to stay here and die," Beck said. "I can go home and do that. Will you look in the closet and see if you can find my clothes?"

"Dad what are you talking about?" asked Burton.

"I'm lying here with a blood clot in my circulatory system." Beck said. "That hematoma could lodge itself in my heart, lungs or brain at any moment and they're just taking their sweet time getting here to do that x-ray," he said.

"Dad let me call the nurse down here and see what's going on," said Burton.

"Burton, I said that's OK. I need to get out of here. I'm in a hospital, my condition is critical, and I don't seem to be able to get the care I need. I might as well go home," said Beck.

"Dad seriously," Burton stated as he reached out to and placed his hands on his dad's shoulders to try and calm him down.

"Burton can you get my stuff and help me out of here," Beck said. "I'll be damned if I'm going to lay here and be neglected in a hospital when I can just go home and die," he said.

Dr. LeFlore started climbing out of his hospital bed. Burton picked up the intercom and called for the nurse to come to the room. A few seconds later the nurse on duty popped her head into the door and saw him struggling to get out of the bed with IV's in tow. He started to take the IV's loose. Burton was not quite sure how to stop him. The nurse ran back out of the door and down the hall to the nursing station. By now he was sitting up on the side of the bed and started taking out the IV's. It was not long before the nurse returned with about six or seven additional personnel.

"Dr. LeFlore, please we need you to stop removing the IV's and get back into bed," said one of the on-duty nurses.

"Dad, come on now, don't do that," said Burton.

"Burton can you get my stuff, I said I'm going home. I'm not staying here," said Beck.

"Doctor we need you to cooperate with us," said one of the male nurses on duty as he and one of the female nurses gently tried to restrain him and prevent him from taking out the IV's.

"I may be dying, but I'm not going to die in this hospital today," Beck said. "I'm out of here."

The two nurses forcefully jerked Dr. LeFlore back into the bed as the other staff gathered around his bed and they all began trying to restrain him. Dr. LeFlore started kicking and jerking back and forth as he fought them. He turned to his left and bit the female nurse on the arm as she was trying to restrain him. The nurse jumped back as her arm was bleeding from the bite. At that point, the staff started more aggressively trying to restrain him. As the

83

nurse to his right backed away from his bed to tend to her bite mark, another one of the staff grabbed him by the shoulder and continued to try and subdue him.

Dr. LeFlore fought them with everything his sick, weak and frail body could muster. Burton was standing there astonished at what was happening and not really knowing whether to help them or to tell them to get away from his dad. He could clearly see Beck was in distress and everything was happening so fast at this point. Burton was still holding his dad's hand. At that instant, his hand grew cold. Burton could feel the change in the temperature of Beck's hand as he held it tightly. Beck held his son's hand with everything he had. The nurses were trying to come between him and his dad as he tried to stay there by Beck's bedside. His dad looked him in his eyes as his eyes seemed to roll back into his head.

"Burton, I'm dying!" Beck shouted. "Burton, I'm your father," he said. "Please don't let them do this to me! Please help me Burton! I'm your father. Don't let them do this to me."

Burton did not reply. He knew something was wrong because he could feel how cold Beck's hand and arm had become. The staff grabbed him around his wrists and were attempting to put his wrists into the wrist restraints. Burton stood there helplessly not knowing what to do at this point as he heard them saying something about intubating him. The nurses now worked quickly to restrain Dr. LeFlore as they began to intubate him. Why they had decided to intubate him at this point is unknown. Why they all of a sudden went from doing absolutely nothing, as Beck sat and complained they would not come and do the x-ray that was ordered several hours ago, to now this extremely aggressive behavior toward him as he attempted and stated that he was leaving the hospital was beyond Burton's comprehension.

He just stood there wondering what he should do as his dad cried out for his help and asked him not to allow them to treat him in this manner. The entire scene was terrifying for Burton. For all of Burton's life, his father had been a beacon of strength and determination. For the first time, he saw his dad as vulnerable. As the disease progressed and took its course, Beck was getting sicker and weaker. He had rarely seen his father as being helpless and susceptible before, and similarly Burton had never felt so helpless in not being able to do anything to comfort him. Most of his life Burton had perceived his dad as being very much in control of everything around him.

This time, Beck was clearly not in control. However, he fought with all the will and determination he could manage to exude. It took eight people to hold him down. Burton decided that he would not attempt to stop this intervention. He felt the numb coldness of his hand which had been previously warm as a human should be. Burton knew something was going wrong and Beck had verified it when he stated that he was dying. At the moment Beck said, he was dying, Burton felt the temperature of Beck's skin drop. Even though the Hospital staff was just doing what they do, little did they know that Dr. LeFlore had probably saved his own life.

"Please take it easy, with my dad," Burton finally said. "Why are you guys doing this to him?"

"I think he's having a psychotic episode," said one of the nurses.

"He's not having a psychotic episode," replied Burton. "He was wondering why nobody had come by to take his x-rays or to give him any blood thinners since he might have a blood clot."

"He can't leave the hospital," said another nurse.

"Obviously," Burton said. "You don't have to be so rough with him. Please treat my dad with some dignity and respect," said Burton.

"He just bit the nurse," said one nurse. "Can you step back a little," said one of the male nurses as he stepped between Burton and Dr. LeFlore who was still struggling and fighting.

"Be careful," Burton said. "This is inhumane."

"Are you OK, Celeste?" asked another female nurse.

"He bit me pretty hard," replied Celeste.

"Can you step back some more," said another one of the nurses.

"This is my dad," said Burton.

"We're doing everything we can to help your dad," the nurse replied.

"Burton!" yelled Beck before they started to run the tube down his throat to connect him to a ventilator.

Meanwhile Janet was back at the house. She had taken a bath, changed her clothes, and was standing before the mirror combing her hair. She stared blankly into the mirror at her reflection as she did not know exactly how to feel at the present. She was a nervous wreck. She was so exhausted and worried about Beck. She had been staying at the hospital with Beck around the clock. This was the first moment she had to herself in days. She was glad to have a second of relief but did not feel comfortable being away from her husband's side since she felt that he needed and wanted her there.

Janet gazed into the mirror almost as though it were some sort of magic mirror or crystal ball that was going to give her the answer to the questions she had going through her mind. Although, the mirror gave her no reply as she already knew most of the answers to her questions. However, hearing and accepting the difficult truth was much too painful for her to bear. For a moment, she allowed herself to drift back into her comfort zone of eternal optimism and faith. All she could do at this point was hang on to her hope that somehow Beck would get through this and they could continue to grow old together.

She went into the refrigerator and took out a bowl of Potato Salad and fixed herself a small portion in a saucer sized plate. She then poured herself a small glass of Pepsi. She wanted to eat a little something and have a sip of Pepsi because she had not eaten much in two days. Janet never really ate much though. She always had been a very small eater. Usually she did not like to eat out of a large plate, but preferred to eat her meals out of saucers and small sized dishes. Today was certainly no different as she sat there and nibbled at her saucer of Potato Salad, trying to somehow regain her desire to eat and stop worrying.

Janet felt completely alone there by herself at their mansion size home. She wondered what it would be like for her there alone if anything happened to Beck. At this point, she was not aware they were waiting on an x-ray for Beck because they had detected a blood clot in his circulatory system. She had no idea about what had happened in the recent minutes since she left the hospital. She had not heard anything from Burton or the hospital at this point regarding Beck.

After eating the Potato Salad, she started to piddle around the kitchen. She rinsed off her plate and wiped off the countertop. The telephone rang. It was Ethel, one of Beck's nurses and office assistant. Ethel asked Janet if she had any idea how long it would be before Dr. LeFlore got out of the hospital. Ethel said that Dr. LeFlore's patients where calling and trying to set up appointments to see him and she did not know what to tell them. She knew that she was supposed to refer them to one of the other Doctors that was filling in for Dr. LeFlore, but some of his patients had said they did not want to go to any other doctors. Several of his patients had said they did not want to be referred to other doctors and they would wait until Dr. LeFlore was feeling better. So, they ultimately wanted to know how long it would be before he got out of the hospital and returned to work.

Janet told Ethel that she was not certain how long he would be in the hospital or if he would be able to return to work right away, even when he was released from the hospital. Janet suggested to Ethel that she should tell them if they have an emergency, they should call one of the other doctors or go to the hospital. Janet said to tell the patients who only wanted to set up their routine doctor's appointment for a routine checkup that you will contact them to set up an appointment when he is back in the office.

Janet also stated to Ethel that she would call their payroll service and make sure the office staff got their checks on Friday. And she would try and stop by the office to check on them. Ethel further inquired about Dr. LeFlore and expressed her and the rest of the staff's concern for Dr. LeFlore's health and well-being. Janet tried to speak confidently that Beck would be back at work in a few days, and that everything was going to be alright.

Ethel spoke again of how Dr. LeFlore's patients missed him and expressed their concern for him as well. Beck had hundreds of devoted patients who loved him dearly as a physician. Beck was one of the most successful and sought-after doctors in the city of Mobile. Janet also knew that she was going to have to find time to go into the office and do Dr. LeFlore's billing. Billing and coding were her jobs in the office. Since she had retired from teaching. Ever since she had been doing his coding and billing work.

Although they had money in the bank, she knew that it had been almost a week and a half since she had submitted any of his bills. She was way behind and had no idea how she was going to get caught up on her work. All she could think of was her husband in the hospital. She embraced her feelings of loneliness and tried to simply feel grateful for their life together, their happiness and their success. As she tried to figure out how and when she would find time and energy to get into the office and submit his paperwork, she knew it would not be any time in the immediate future.

However, now that Burton was there, she knew she would probably be able to get to work sometime soon without feeling like she had abandoned Beck at the hospital. For several days straight she had been at the hospital with Beck round the clock. Janet had been experiencing a great deal of anxiety and stress. She desperately needed this quiet moment to herself.

Burton still there at the hospital with his dad. By now Beck's hands had been restrained and he had been placed on life support. He was heavily sedated and unconscious now. Burton sat there by his side watching over him. He did not want to worry his mother with the news since he felt she would become frantic and rush back to the hospital. He knew she planned to come back and decided not to bother her right away, as he felt that she might need a moment to herself. Burton was worried about his dad.

He hoped he had done the right thing to allow the staff to intubate Beck. Burton did not like having to see them treat his dad in such a manner and he was feeling conflicted. His desire to protect his father at a vulnerable state coupled with his desire for whatever was medically necessary to achieve the goal of getting his dad better and out of the hospital. Presently what had been done had been done, and here Burton had just arrived in town and walked in on all of this.

Burton watched his dad as he took breaths through the ventilator. He took his hand and placed it on Beck's head as he said a prayer for his father. He prayed for his dad and to help him to help both his mom and dad during this time. Burton prayed that God would give him guidance in helping to make any decision as a family member and son that he would have to make on his parents' behalf and well-being. Burton was overcome with a feeling of compassion for Beck as he wondered how long his dad was going to live. He knew Beck had been suffering from cancer for many years, and it was obvious that the disease was starting to get the best of him.

Here he had come to the hospital where his father had engaged him in a conversation concerning his Will which he had not anticipated. Obviously, it was clear to him that Beck was now contemplating his own death. Beck had always been straight forward about everything going on in their lives, ever since Burton could remember. As he had related to Beck earlier, he was not concerned about his Will. After all Burton was their last surviving child and his Mother Janet was a generous woman.

He appreciated the candidness with which Beck had handled that discussion; however, upon this juncture it appeared he had not been fully informed about everything that was going on with his dad. He felt that he needed to talk with his doctors and find out for himself what was really going on. It was time for him to have some equally candid conversations with some of the people caring for Beck at the hospital about his prognosis. Burton contacted the nurse and asked her to request a consult with all of Dr. LeFlore's doctors. Dr. LeFlore's nurse on duty stated she would contact his doctors and ask them to contact him or come to his room to speak with him about his dad.

The nurse informed Burton that she would let his doctors know that he wanted to talk with them but that it would probably be tomorrow morning before he would be able to talk with them. Dr. Sewanee walked into Beck's room as he was there to make sure the settings on his vent were correct. The nurse introduced Burton to Dr. Sewanee. The doctor was busy checking the stats on the machine as the nurse introduced them.

"Dr. Sewanee this is Dr. LeFlore's son Burton," said the nurse.

"Oh hello, how are you," replied Dr. Sewanee.

"Do you think it's necessary to have his hands in those restraints?" asked Burton.

"We want to make sure he doesn't try and pull the tube out of his throat?' he said.

"It just seems cruel," Burton said. "He's chained to the bed."

"I'm also a little concerned about the recent psychotic episode he just had," replied Dr. Sewanee. "Has he ever had an episode like this before that you know of?"

"No this wasn't a psychotic episode," Burton said. "He clearly stated that he was concerned that it had been determined he had a blood clot, and there was an x-ray ordered for him and it had been several hours and no x-ray. He wasn't psychotic he just said he would rather go home than wait here at the Hospital and be neglected."

"Dr. LeFlore is getting the best care possible," Dr. Sewanee said. "Rest assured he's not being neglected."

"Why has he been put on a ventilator when he was breathing just fine before," Burton asked.

"I'm giving him some Heparin. It's a blood thinner to stop the coagulation of his blood tissue," said Dr. Sewanee. "We should be able to get him off the vent in a few days."

"There's a lot going on with your dad at this point, and I'm not his primary physician, perhaps you should talk with Dr. English, I believe he's his primary physician."

"Yea Dr. English," he replied. "Can you let all of his other doctors know that I would like to speak with them?" asked Burton.

"Sure," replied Dr. Sewanee.

"This is the only dad I've got Dr. Sewanee," said Burton.

"He should be fine at least as far as him being on the respirator goes," said the doctor.

"I still don't like him being restrained like that," said Burton.

"He shouldn't be restrained long, and he probably won't be on the vent very long," Dr. Sewanee said. "That's a precautionary measure to make sure he doesn't harm himself."

"Thank you," said Burton.

"If you have any further concerns just ask the nurse to page me," said Dr. Sewanee.

"Will you just be sure and let his other doctors know I need to talk with them," Burton said. "I would like to know what is going on him."

"Have a good evening," said Dr. Sewanee.

Janet was still at the house trying to calm her nerves. Burton had not called her yet or notified her as to what was going on at the hospital with Beck. Suddenly she sensed a feeling of urgency to get in the car and drive back to the hospital. She had an uneasy feeling that something was not right with Beck. She could have simply picked up the phone and called the hospital and asked Burton. However, her inner chemical bond with this man was disturbed. She had an uncomfortable feeling inside. She knew she needed to return to Beck's room at the hospital as soon as possible.

Somewhere in Janet's psyche she was acutely and fully aware that her husband needed her. Before she could get her purse and head back, the telephone rang. It was Burton on the other end.

"Mom are you alright?" said Burton.

"I'm fine," she said. "How's Beck?" asked Janet.

"He had an episode," Burton said. "He's on life support."

"An episode, on life support, Oh God," Janet said. "What kind of episode?" She asked, "Why did they put him on life support?"

"It all happened so fast, one minute we were here talking, and he said something about waiting for them to come and do an ex-ray because he had an embolism. Then after about an hour went by, he started saying he wasn't going to lay here in the hospital and be neglected and he wanted to go home." Burton said, "Right about that time, as he was getting out of bed saying he was going to leave," he said. "About eight people from the hospital staff came in here restrained him and intubated him."

"I knew I shouldn't have left him," said Janet.

"Mom you can't take on the entire world on your shoulders by yourself," Burton said. "I'm here and I can give you some relief. You need some relief Mom," said Burton.

"I was about to come back anyway," Janet said. "I've been feeling uneasy about Beck ever since I got home," said Janet.

"Mom you don't have to rush back here," Burton said. "I'm here with him."

"I know Burton, but I've gotten my things together and I can come back there now," Janet said. "You've had a long drive today. You need to get some rest. I'll see you in a minute."

"Mom I know you're worried about Dad. I promise you. I don't mind staying here with him for a little while longer," said Burton.

"That's fine," Janet said. "I don't want to be away from him now. He needs me."

"There's not a lot either one of us can do for him right now Mom," said Burton."

"Your dad and I have been married for over 50 years," said Janet.

"I know Mom and I know this must be hard on you," replied Burton.

"It may be hard on me, but I must be there for him," Janet said. "Your dad hasn't been doing very well Burton. I'm worried about him."

"I'm worried about both of you Mom." Burton said, "Dad is laying here sedated hooked up to a ventilator and you act like you're a nervous wreck," Burton said.

"Fifty years is a long time to be with a person," Janet said. "After you've been with someone that long, they start to become a bit like the air you breathe. You kinda start to feel like it would be impossible to live without them." she said. "Nervous wreck or not, I would be more comfortable there at the hospital with Beck. I have had a chance to take a bath, regroup and get my things together. So, I'll see you shortly."

"I love you Mom," said Burton.

"I love you too Baby," said Janet.

It was not long before Janet had arrived back at Beck's bedside. He was now resting as the respirator assisted his breathing. Burton was standing there next to the bed holding his dad's hand. Janet had a cot posted next to the window where she placed a bag of her belongings from home. A respiratory therapist was in the room checking the settings on Beck's respirator. Beck lay there still and somewhat comatose as the machine assisted with his breathing. He was breathing on his own for all practical purposes. As the therapist left the room Burton walked over to his Mom and embraced her for a moment. It was a simple hug for reassurance as they stood there looking at Beck suffering and hooked to a breathing machine with a tube down his throat. One of those moments in time when you find yourself coming to grips with the reality that your loved one may not be with you longer. Not only by his thoughts and word but by the obvious and noticeable condition of his humanity and humility.

A few days later they extubated Beck and removed the restraints. He lay there cleaning his mouth with a swab. He was in a great deal of pain. Beck cleaned his mouth thoroughly. Burton was there at his bedside. The sun was shining through his hospital room window. It was nearing the end of August and it seemed that Beck was going to be discharged from the hospital and would be able to return home. Janet had gone into the office to do Dr. LeFlore's billing and payroll for the office staff.

A new day had arrived, and it appeared Beck was doing somewhat better after that serious scare. The next day Beck was discharged. He returned home accompanied by Janet and Burton. Beck got out of the wheelchair at the hospital discharge ramp and took a seat in the car. They all drove to the house where they helped Beck inside. Burton was glad to see his dad coming home because he needed to get back to North Carolina. His son Breaghan's birthday was quickly approaching and he needed to get to NC because he needed to finish finalizing his business there. It was his plan and intention to move back to Mobile. His wife was pregnant with their fourth child. Burton had been gone for over a week. On the way home, Beck said that he missed his grandchildren and did not understand why he did not bring them to visit him.

Burton assured Beck he was going to get the children down to see him. Beck was adamant about the fact that he wanted to see his grandchildren. Burton wanted so bad to bring his boys to Mobile to see their grandfather. He and Candace would have probably moved before the new school year, but they decided to wait until after the baby was born. They were not sure if their newborn would be a girl or a boy. All they knew was they were about to have another child and so far, they had three boys. Candace said she did not want to know the sex of the child. So, from that point they were just waiting, hoping and praying for a healthy baby.

Burton left Mobile not long after he got his dad back home and comfortable in bed. Burton was trying to come to grips with the inevitable fact that his dad was dying of cancer. Certainly, his father, the infamous Dr. LeFlore, had treated many cancer patients during his years in the practice of medicine. Beck knew he was dying. Here Burton was facing his father's diagnosis and at the same time looking toward his son's birthday on the 28th of August and the birth of his next child. Meanwhile, he was expecting another surrogate, another vessel to his legacy. He and his wife were expecting their fourth child. It did not really matter the sex of the child. They were losing an icon and welcoming a mystery. The LeFlore family was at a crossroads. They were losing and winning all at the same time. The wheel of life was in full effect.

Burton made it back to Wilmington in time to spend Breaghan's birthday with him. Breaghan was turning three years old. As Burton arrived back home, he could see that Breaghan had been waiting and wondering if he was going to make it back for his birthday. Burton had brought some presents for him. Later that day they went out to a place in Wilmington that was a restaurant and large game room to celebrate Breaghan's birthday. They played games and had ice cream and cake. Breaghan loves sweets. Breaghan and the other kids all had a good time together.

However, Burton could not get his mind off his dad. Beck was hanging heavy on Burton's heart. His father was sick, and his Mom seemed to be crumbling under the pressure of everything going on with her husband. By now his wife Candace was starting to show signs of being pregnant as she was expected to deliver the baby in December. Burton was glad that he had been able to make it back in time for his son's birthday and that he was able to see his dad home from the hospital before he left to return to Wilmington.

Beck had started to complain that he was having difficulty hearing because of the tumor that was growing on his spine. He also claimed the tumor was affecting his balance and making it difficult for him to walk. Burton called and tried to talk with him, but Beck kept saying that he was having a hard time hearing what he was saying. Burton was very concerned about his dad and wanted desperately to communicate with him. As the days passed it seemed the tumor was starting to affect him more as his hearing got worse and it became more difficult for him to walk.

Janet was doing everything she could to take care of him. Janet was consumed with her husband's needs as his health appeared to be getting worse. Although Beck still wanted to go into work, Janet encouraged him to stay home and get some rest. It was amazing how Beck had the desire to continue working and refused to give up. Janet drove him to the office so that he could check in with everybody. She needed to do some billing and they also needed to do payroll again.

Beck looked so frail and his skin was discolored and drooped off his bones. He struggled to walk with the aid of a cane as he went from the car to his office. The girls in the office were glad to see Dr. LeFlore and they welcomed him as they tried hard to not appear shocked by the way he looked at the time. Beck had a few patients waiting to see him. He did attend to those patients even though he was much sicker than all of them combined. As they spoke to him, he struggled to hear what they were saying. But just kept asking them to speak up so he could hear them.

Janet and Beck worked at the office for several hours that day as he finished with his patients and she worked on getting his bills out and payroll for the staff. The mood at the office was somewhat melancholy that day. Dr. LeFlore sat down in his seat at his desk and just closed his eyes and leaned back. He was feeling a great deal of neuropathy in his fingertips and hands. He was tired and ready to go but he wanted to give Janet a chance to finish what she was doing. Beck dozed off for a moment in the comfort of his chair. He felt so lethargic he could hardly keep his eyes open. Janet worked in her office at the computer as she heard Becks phone buzz as Ethel was attempting to transfer a call to Dr. LeFlore.

He did not respond, and Ethel buzzed him again. Still there was no response. Janet went into Beck's office and found him there in his chair asleep. Janet told Ethel to take a message for Dr. LeFlore and he would call them back. Janet completed her work and the staff locked he front door as they went home for the evening. Janet turned off the lights at the office. Beck set the alarm and locked the back door as they went home for the evening. Janet helped Beck into their Cadillac Deville and Janet drove him home.

On the morning of Tuesday September 11, 2001; America and the world watched and listened as the World Trade Centers in New York City and the Pentagon in Washington D.C., where attacked by terrorist. Janet and Beck watched on television as the events unfolded. They watched as two airplanes flew into the World Trade Centers and the two buildings collapsed to the ground killing thousands of people. They also heard the stories of an airplane that crashed as a group of passengers fought with terrorists who had hijacked a plane flying over Pennsylvania. They were both astonished as they witnessed the current events unfolding live on the news.

Later that day, Janet and Beck still had not gone out. Janet had busied herself around the kitchen with their maid Leassee. Beck lay in bed watching the news as it continued to be reported about the terrorist attacks on the World Trade Center. Janet's sister Julia called and the two of them chatted for a minute about the recent news regarding the World Trade Center bombings. After Janet got off the phone with Julia her sister Anna called, and they talked for a brief while about the recent news. Shortly after she concluded her conversation with Ann, Burton called.

"Mom," Burton said. "Have you been watching the news?"

"Yes, I've been watching," Janet said. "So sad."

"How's Dad doing?" Burton asked.

"He's about the same, he's resting right now," said Janet.

"Can I talk with him for a minute?" asked Burton.

"Sure," said Janet as she went into the room to tell Beck to pick up the phone. "Beck, Burton wants to speak with you."

"Hey Dad," said Burton.

"Hello," said Beck.

"How are you doing man?" asked Burton.

"Ha, what did you say Burton? Speak up, I can hardly hear you," said Beck.

"I said how are you feeling!" said Burton as he spoke a little louder.

"I don't know son," Beck said. "I'm having difficulty walking and I can hardly hear a thing," he said. "Burton how am I going to practice medicine like this? How am I going to practice medicine like this?" he asked.

"Dad you got to hang in there," said Burton.

"What did you say?" said Beck.

"I said you got to hang in there Dad," Burton said. "I love you man."

"Love you son," Beck said. "I'm going to put your Mom back on the phone. I can hardly hear you. Janet!"

"OK Dad, I'll talk with you later," said Burton.

"Baby," Janet said as she picked up the phone.

"Yea Mom, Dad is saying he is having difficulty hearing?" asked Burton.

"His doctor said the tumor on his neck and spine is growing rapidly and it's causing him to have more difficulty hearing and he is having some difficulty walking," Janet said.

"They can't surgically remove them?" Burton asked.

"I think they're going to try radiation," Janet said. "He's to go for the radiation treatment in a few days."

"I'm going to try and get back down there as soon as I can," said Burton.

The next day Beck was ambulating from the bedroom into the kitchen area and he fell in the doorway of the bedroom. Janet heard Beck fall as he hit the floor. She rushed to where he had fallen and tried to help him up. Beck was a large man and he was having difficulty getting up off the floor. Janet quickly realized that she could not lift him by herself. Janet tried and tried to help Beck off the floor. She was frantic and she had no idea what to do to help her husband.

She was afraid that he may have had some broken bones because he fell so hard. Walker had collapsed on the floor much like the World Trade Center had collapsed the day before. Janet felt so helpless as she struggled to figure out how she was going to get Beck off the floor. Janet called Burton on the telephone and she was hysterical.

"Burton, your dad fell on the floor and I can't lift him!" Janet said, "I don't know what to do, what should I do?" she asked.

"He fell?" said Burton.

"Yes, he's fallen in the doorway and I can't get him up," said Janet.

"Mom call the paramedics," Burton said. "They can help you get him up."

"Paramedics," said Janet.

"Call the paramedics right now, just dial 911 and tell them Dad fell and he is unable to get up and you can't lift him, they'll come out and help you." Burton said. "Hang up and call them right now, and I'll call you back in a few minutes."

"OK I'm going to call them right now," said Janet. Janet dialed the emergency number. "My husband Dr. LeFlore has fallen on the floor and I can't get him up!" she exclaimed.

"Mam please calm down," the emergency dispatcher said. "We'll try and get somebody out there as soon as we can to help," replied the dispatcher.

"Please hurry," said Janet.

"Is your husband alert?" asked the dispatcher.

"Yes, he's alert but he's unable to get off the floor and I can't lift him," said Janet.

"I understand, we've got an ambulance coming out to your house right now. They're on their way," said the dispatcher.

It was not long before the ambulance arrived. Janet let the EMT's into the house. They arrived with a stretcher and maneuvered it into the hallway leading to the doorway where Dr. LeFlore had fallen. There were three EMT's and they were able to pick Beck up off the floor and get him onto the stretcher.

After checking him out for a brief moment they suggested that they would like to take him to the hospital for further treatment. Beck was taken by ambulance to the hospital. He had only been out of the hospital for about two weeks and now this incident had him back in the Hospital again. He was presented to the Emergency room at Mobile Infirmary Hospital and was admitted by one of the Emergency Room doctors. Beck's doctor indicated that they were running some tests and it would probably be tomorrow before the test results were back.

Meanwhile they scheduled him for radiation treatment the next morning. After Beck was admitted and taken up to his room, Janet went home to pack her bag so that she could stay at the hospital with Beck. Janet felt as if her entire world was crashing in as she walked to the car. She wanted to call Burton because she was certain that he was worried. As she drove down the street toward home, Janet felt as though this could not be real and she wondered for a moment if she was going to wake up and realize that this was just a bad dream that she had been having.

"Burton I just called because I wanted to let you know they put your dad back in the hospital today," said Janet.

"Oh boy, I figured that," said Burton. "I'm going to pack and try and get back down there. I'll try and get out of here day after tomorrow, and I'll be there. OK? How are you holding up?"

"I'm not holding up too well, Burton. I'm worried sick about your father," she replied.

"I understand," said Burton.

"And my jaw is killing me, it hurts, it hurts," said Janet.

"Are you taking anything to help with the pain?" asked Burton.

"You know I don't like to take pain pills," replied Janet.

"Maybe tonight would be a good time to take one Mom, and you have got to get some rest. You sounded hysterical on the phone when you called earlier," Burton said. "I thought you were about to tell me that Dad had passed away or something."

"No, thank goodness it wasn't anything like that," Janet said. "I couldn't get him off the floor by myself. I'm about to go back over to the hospital to be with him. I just wanted to let you know that everything is alright now. He's off the floor and they decided to admit him to the hospital."

"Do you have any idea how long they're going to keep him?" asked Burton.

"I'm not sure, Burton," replied Janet.

"I'll be there in a few days, I promise," said Burton.

Burton approached his wife Candace and explained to her that his dad was not doing very well and that he wanted to take the kids to Mobile to visit him. Burton said that his dad really wanted to see his grandchildren and he was adamant that he wanted the kids to come down to Mobile to visit him. Burton and Candace decided that Burton would go ahead and leave. She would depart for Mobile on Saturday. Burton left for Mobile on Thursday and Candace and the kids left the following Saturday all headed to Mobile.

Janet sat there in the hospital room with Beck as he slept. The room was dimly lit, and the television further illuminated the room as she reclined onto the cot next to his bed. She got up and checked on Beck, watching him while he slept peacefully. She kissed him on his cheek and gave him a hug. Beck reached out to her and hugged her. He awoke just briefly and looked in her direction. He then put his head back on the pillow and went back to sleep. She returned to the cot and lay down next to him. It all seemed surreal to her. Beck's doctors had come by the room earlier and spoke with Janet about what her plans were for Dr. LeFlore. They indicated to her that it would not be long before Beck passed away. They stated they did not intend to keep him in the hospital much longer because there was little more they could do for him.

Beck was in the end stages of his disease and they told her that they could only initiate comfort measures at this point, since they would no longer be treating the cancer. The cancer had metastasized and spread. They suggested that Janet should decide whether she wanted to place him in hospice care at the hospital or she could take him home. Janet hoped that Burton would soon arrive so that she could help her decide what she should do. She felt so alone and confused as she tried to internalize what Beck's doctors were saying to her. She had been asked to come up with a course of action and neither decision seemed plausible because they both equaled the same result. She felt trapped between a rock and no place to turn, only wondering how long it would be before her son Burton would be there.

It was not long before Burton made it back to Mobile. His mother did not tell him what the doctors had said. She could not bring herself to tell him. She told him that he needed to talk with Beck's doctors which is exactly what Burton wanted to do and intended to do. Janet wanted to tell him herself, but she could not bring herself to utter the words. She did not want to hear herself say to Burton that the doctors had said there was nothing more they could do for Beck. She was so afraid for Beck and equally fearful for herself because she could not imagine what life would be like without her husband of more than 50 years.

Burton went to the hospital that evening when he got into town, but he was not able to speak with his doctors that evening. Burton found his Mother frantic and distraught. She did not know what to do and made it perfectly evident that she wanted Burton to make whatever decisions needed to be made. Although she did not disclose any information about what the doctors had already told her before he arrived.

Burton had never seen his mom like this before. Usually Janet was a very assertive woman and extremely intelligent. She was a woman who was always ready to come up with a plan and make a way to reach her designated goal or objective. Janet was also someone who had no problem verbalizing how she might have decided she was going to go about reaching her thought out point of view. This time Burton found his mom to be indecisive and unwilling to communicate. She was vulnerable, frail and saddened by their recent experiences. She wanted to hold on to her husband even more now than ever before.

However, at the same time she knew he was suffering. They say you never come to the full understanding of how much you love someone until you realize that you are about to lose them. Janet was in such emotional pain as she watched Beck fighting for his life. Or was he fighting for his life? It is possible that he had given up. It is possible that his circumstances gave him no choice but to succumb to the disease he had been battling for over six years now. At least that is what his doctors were saying.

Burton attempted to comfort his mom. He was tired himself from having driven over twelve hours from Wilmington to Mobile nonstop. Burton contacted the nurses station and asked if he could speak with his dad's doctors. They told him it would probably be the following morning before he would be able to speak with anyone. Janet was also concerned how her son would handle the news regarding Beck's prognosis. She knew it would most likely tear him apart as it was ravishing her soul now. She could not figure out a way to tell him what the doctors had said. She kept asking him if he had talked to any of Beck's doctors. He explained to her that he had tried but they said it would probably be tomorrow before he could talk with anyone.

After speaking briefly with his dad, Burton decided he would go home to his house and get some rest. He would come back to the hospital tomorrow and consult with his attending physicians and find out what was going on with Beck. Burton indicated to Beck that the kids   should be on the way down to Mobile to visit him. Beck seemed pleased to hear his grandchildren were also on their way. Burton encouraged Janet to go home and get some sleep, but she said she wanted to stay at the hospital with Beck. Janet said there was no way she would leave Beck and encouraged Burton to go on to his house and relax for a little while. Burton assured Janet that he would return as soon as he had a chance to get some rest. Beck and Janet both told Burton they were happy to see him, and they would be looking forward to seeing him in a few hours. They also indicated they were glad that his children were coming because they both wanted to see them. Burton went to the house, leaving Janet there with Beck.

The following day Burton's kids arrived in Mobile with Candace. Burton took the kids over to see his dad. The kids visited with Beck briefly. Beck was glad to see them. The visit from the grandchildren lifted Beck's spirits considerably. Janet was equally happy to see the kids. It had been almost a year since they had seen them. Beck perked up and tried to pretend like he was not in such pain as he greeted them. Breton, Bryceton and Breaghan all sat on the hospital bed with Beck. Bryceton picked up the remote control and started to press the buttons. Before anyone had realized, he had inadvertently called the nurses station. The nurse responded but Beck quietly and patiently told the nurse everything was alright. The sight of the boys brought a smile to Beck's face as it seemed that it had been a while. The boys had just got in off the road and they were hungry. Burton said he was going to take them to get something to eat and then he would be back.

Burton took Candace and the boys to a nearby restaurant to get them some food. They rode around for a few minutes after picking up the food and then he went to drop them off at the house. Burton still maintained his house in Mobile and it was still fully furnished. When they moved to Wilmington a year ago, they basically left all their furniture. They did not move a lot of things to Wilmington initially. When they returned to town, they had all the comforts of home as they knew it before they moved. The kids were a little rambunctious as they were still hungry and had also completed the considerable ride on the highway to get to Mobile. Burton was in a hurry to eat and get back to the hospital because he expected to meet with one of Beck's doctors regarding his dad. Once Burton got the kids back to the house and settled in, he rushed back to the hospital in hopes that he would not miss his scheduled conference with his doctor.

Burton arrived back at the hospital. He found Janet still there sitting there with Beck as he watched television. Right about the time he arrived, Beck's doctor presented himself for their conference. Janet continued to be seated and did not say much while the doctor was in the room. She did not come over to be a part of the consultation. She just sat there in her chair and watched as the doctor examined Beck. He then walked away from Beck's bedside toward the far corner of the room as he prepared to speak with Burton.

"So, what's going on with my dad? How is he doing?" asked Burton.

"He has a tumor that has developed on his spine and the base of his neck, and the tumor is causing him to have difficulty hearing. He said he's been having some difficulty walking," Dr. Roth said. "It also appears that he's started aspirating," said the doctor.

102

"Aspirating?" said Burton.

"Yes. It means that materials such as pharyngeal secretions, food or drink or stomach contents from the Oropharynx or Gastrointestinal tract might empty into his lungs," Dr. Roth said. "He took a radiation treatment, but it doesn't seem to have reduced the tumor."

"Mom, do you want to come over here and talk with him?" Burton asked.

"I'm right here, you go ahead and speak with him. I'm going to sit over here with your daddy," said Janet.

"Burton at this point we are no longer treating your dad's cancer. There isn't much more we can do for him," Dr. Roth said. "All we're doing at this juncture is comfort measures. He may have another six weeks if that. You might want to discuss with your mom weather or not you want to put him in hospice care here at the hospital," said Dr. Roth.

"Hospice care?" said Burton.

"Yes, we can admit him to hospice care here at the hospital," said Dr. Roth.

"There's nothing more you can do for him here at the hospital," interjected Burton as he glanced over at Janet who was sitting there watching and listening to every word.

"I guess if there is nothing else you can do for him here then we better take him home," said Burton. "Mom I guess we need to make plans to take Daddy home with us."

"Is that what you think is best Baby, then that's what we'll do," Janet replied.

"We can arrange that as well," Dr. Roth replied. "We can have hospice care come out to the house."

"Well we'll just take him home then," Burton said. "Thank you, Doctor."

"Have a good evening," said Dr. Roth.

Janet was still sitting there next to Beck with a bewildered expression on her face as Burton walked over and gave her a hug. Finally, Burton knew what she did not want to tell him herself. She embraced her son as he tried to come to grips with what he had just discussed with Dr. Roth. Beck was dying and his overall prognosis was not good. Burton sensed that it was time for him to take the

103

lead and help his mom as she was completely overwhelmed with their current situation. Burton was overcome with a serious realization that both of his parents desperately needed him right now. Janet needed him and she made it perfectly clear as it was obvious that his dad needed him.

"Mom, we're going to take him home," said Burton.

"That's fine," said Janet.

"Everything is going to be alright," said Burton.

"You think so," replied Janet.

"We'll just have to work through this," said Burton.

"I love your dad so much," Janet said. "Do you know I have been with this man for over fifty years," she said.

"I know Mom," said Burton.

"No, I don't think you know," said Janet as she shed a tear. "I don't think you can begin to know, and I hope you won't ever have to know" replied Janet.

"I love Daddy too Mom," Burton said. "Why didn't you tell me?"

"I couldn't," Janet said. "I just couldn't. I couldn't tell you. I just found out myself."

"We just got to do what's best to keep him comfortable," said Burton.

"Did he say when we could bring him home?" asked Janet.

"I'm not sure," Burton said. "He didn't say, probably in a day or two."

"I don't know if I can do it Burton," said Janet.

"Mom we can do this," Burton said. "I'll just have to stay down here and not go back to Wilmington right now until we get everything situated."

"Burton I can't ask you to stay," Janet said. "You've got your family and Candace is pregnant."

"Mom we're moving back here anyway," Burton said. "We're just going to wait until after Candace has the baby and let Breton finish the semester in school. It won't hurt for me to stay here with Dad for a few days. Everything will be fine; we just need to focus on taking care of him right now."

"Your dad was so happy to see the boys," Janet said. "You never realize how the smallest and simplest gestures of love and kindness may mean so much to someone who is aging and sick. They lifted his spirits and mine too. Just seeing them. They sure have grown."

"Yep they're growing up, and as you can see, I got another one on the way," Burton said. "Dad are you awake?" said Burton as he nudged Beck's shoulder. "Dad we're going home"

Beck opened his eyes and looked at Burton as he nodded his head and said, "Uh hu."

"We'll be getting out of here very soon," Burton said. "Mom I'm going to go to the house and check on the kids, and tomorrow we'll need to start getting things in order so that we can bring him home."

"OK Baby," said Janet.

"Why don't you go home and get some sleep," said Burton.

"No, I'm going to stay here with Beck," said Janet.

"I'll be back in the morning so we can start making arrangements to bring him home," said Burton.

"Love you," said Janet.

"Good night Dad, good night Mom," Burton said as he exited the hospital room.

Janet continued to sit there with Beck. She sat there on the side of his bed holding his hand and watching television as he slept. She really wanted to sink into the bed alongside him and hold him in her arms. She loved Beck with every fiber she had in her soul. She was inspired that Burton had decided to bring Beck home, and she started getting herself mentally ready for the task of caring for her husband in the comfort of their home. She felt a renewed strength in the wake of this adversity she was facing now that her son had arrived. Janet realized that she had become so consumed with everything going on in her life that it might help to have an objective opinion. Burton was her ray of hope and help. Janet wiped tears away from her face and squeezed Beck's hand and showed him more love.

Burton was devastated as he left the hospital, having been told his dad would not have very long to live. He wondered what he would do now that he needed to try and help take care of his father in Mobile, and his family was living in North Carolina. He had a child on the way. Burton was not currently working. He was making plans to move back to Mobile. Now confronted with the inevitable truth that his dad may not even live until the end of this year or the first of next year. What does one do when they are forced to face the uncomfortable truth that their parent is dying?

Burton was filled with sorrow in his heart, soul and mind as he slowly interpreted what was clear and obvious. He thought about his wife carrying the unborn fetus that would be their fourth child. He thought about his three boys, Breaghan, Bryceton and Breton. He thought about his mom and dad. He wondered what life would be like without his dad around. Mostly he was empty as though he were a vessel not certain what to hold inside. He looked forward to finding some type of comfort in being with his family when he arrived back at the house.

Burton got back to the house and found the kids sitting around the television. He did not say much when he returned. He just walked into the den and passed by Candace and the boys. He went into the living room and sat down in one of their living room chairs facing the front window of the house. He did not say anything as he sat there staring blankly out of the window.

He did not know exactly how he was going to tell his family the news. He did not know exactly how he was going to accept the news himself. For now, he just sat there pondering to himself. He could not believe what he had just been told at the hospital about Beck's condition. It hurt him so much to see the pain that his mother was going through. Although, he had to deal with what was going on with his own sorrow. He had to deal with everything going on in his mind at the time and was uncertain how he would do it.

"Can I ask you a question?" Candace said. "Why would your mother come in here and hang my picture on the wall. Nobody asked her to hang any pictures here."

"What picture?" asked Burton.

"Right there, my mom and dad's picture," Candace said. "Nobody told her to hang that picture on the wall."

"Are you serious?" replied Burton.

"This is our house, but she comes in here whenever she wants and hangs pictures," said Candace.

"I just left the hospital and they told me my dad is dying, but all you want to talk about is a damn picture," said Burton.

"Why would she come in here and hang my picture on the wall when I don't want it there," Candace said. "It's not her picture."

"Maybe you didn't hear what I just said?" he asked.

"Tell your mother not to bother my stuff. I don't want her hanging pictures," said Candace.

"I'll tell you what," said Burton as he stood up, reached over and took the picture off the wall and let it drop to the floor breaking it. "You don't want the picture on the wall and now it's not there anymore. Happy!" said Burton.

As soon as the picture hit the floor, Burton heard footsteps coming from the den area. It was his teenage son Breton, who had run out of the den and into the living room area where Burton was standing there arguing with Candace. The picture was shattered all over the floor. Breton charged Burton like a football player charges his opponent as if he were trying to tackle him. He made contact with Burton and knocked him back. Burton grabbed him and pushed him back. Almost simultaneously Breton ran into Burton's study and made a phone call.

Burton could not hear exactly what he said to the dispatcher as Burton was still standing there simply dumfounded. Breton hung up the phone and charged at his dad again. By now Burton's two younger boys had come into the dining room area to see what was going on. As Breton charged him, Burton grabbed him and dumped him on the floor. A brief struggle ensued between the two of them. It was not long before Burton had pinned his son down and restrained him and told him to back off. It also was not long before the police arrived at the house.

When the police arrived, Candace and Breton rushed to the door. The cops asked what happened and Candace lied to them and stated that Burton had pushed her to the ground and was trying to stomp her and she was five months pregnant. She pointed to a mark on Breton's arm and told them that Breton tried to defend her from his father's attack against her. She invited the police officer into the house to look around. He saw the picture broken on the floor and somehow were convinced that Candace was telling the truth. Even though Candace had blatantly lied about what happened, there was not much Burton could say. He had broken the picture and there did appear to have been some sort of altercation in the house. He could not deny that he broke the picture; although, he had not put a hand on his pregnant wife.

Furthermore, he only attempted to defend himself against his teenage son's aggression toward him. At any rate, it was not long before the officer handcuffed Burton and asked him to sit in the back of the patrol car. He could not believe all of this was actually happening. There really was not much he could do or say to change what was about to happen as it appeared that two witnesses were presenting the cop with a story. One was pregnant and one was a child. Burton just sat there in the back of the car as the officer concluded his investigation which would ultimately result in Burton being taken to jail.

As the officer pulled away from the house with Burton in the back of his cruiser, Burton just thought to himself that he was in a state of absolute disbelief. Here he had just been told that his dad only had a few weeks to live. He goes home sorrowful with absolutely no intention of starting any kind of fight or argument with Candace and certainly not any of his kids. He just really hoped that he might have been able to get some love and comfort from his wife and family; however, he got none of that from his wife.

He had been attacked by his oldest son, at a moment when he realized he was about to lose his father. He was thinking about how he was a father and how important his father's role was in his life, and that he wanted to play an important role in his son's lives. He had been attacked by his oldest son and had gotten into a fight with him. In all his years, he would have never attacked his own father, the way his son had attacked him. The idea of having a physical altercation with his son was beyond his comprehension and he wondered why all of this was happening.

Burton spent the night in jail. While there it began to dawn on him that he was all alone in this world. He was no longer a little boy. He was no longer a child. He was a man. He was a grown man who no longer had his daddy to call when he got into a bind or a tight. There was no one to come and bail him out. There was no way he was going to call Beck and ask for help. His dad was sick and if anything, Beck needed his help. He could not bother his mom with his current circumstance. How could he call either of his parents and even bother them with this, as if they werenot already dealing with enough. And he certainly was not going to call his so-called wife who was instrumental in landing him there with her lies about what had occurred. Furthermore, Burton believed that Candace had instigated the altercation between him and Breton as his younger boys Bryceton and Breaghan watched helplessly.

Suddenly, Burton realized that he was a man on his own in this cruel and heartless world. As he sat there feeling forlorn and forsaken by practically everything he had heard at the hospital about his father and everything that had occurred at his home that evening; he started to come to a realization. All he wanted was just to get a little love and support from his wife as he tried to sort through what was going on in his mind. The spoiled brat blanket of security and belief that his parents would be there to help him through any situation or adversity was now gone. It was now shattered just like the picture he had broken all over the living room floor. He felt his entire world crumbling before his very eyes. Not to mention the fact that he was in jail charged with something he did not do. It also dawned on him that he could not and would not leave Mobile. He was going to stay.

The doctor just told him his dad did not have long to live. His wife was a total bitch and showed zero sympathy or understanding toward him or his feelings. His oldest son had attacked him without provocation. Now he was in jail. What a day.

However, there is one thing certain that came out of this series of events. Burton realized that he was basically alone in this world. He realized he had truly become a man. As most boys do not truly become men until they lose their father. Of course, Burton had not lost Beck yet, but it was inevitable. Conversely, he felt that he was failing as a father. The one thing that he wanted so desperately to embrace at this point in time, was being a father himself. Slowly the realization sunk in his head that he no longer had anybody to call for help.

He no longer had his father who had been his rock all his life. He would no longer have his dad who always told him that he would not support him if he was wrong but would support him to the end if he was right. He no longer had someone to call to help him get out of this mess, it was just him. That was it, just him. Burton just sat there thinking as eventually he dozed off for a little while on the hard metal bench. The next morning, he was released. Burton asked the bail bondsmen if he would give him a ride back to his house as once again, he really had no one to call to come and get him and did not want to worry his parents. When he arrived at home, Candace and the two younger boys were gone. He found his teenage son Breton there lying in bed. He met his son at the doorway to his bedroom. He could tell that his son was a little worried and probably felt bad about what had happened the night before. Burton confronted him in the hallway of their house.

"Let me tell you something," Burton said as he reached out his hand and placed it around his son's throat. "I am going to tell you this and I don't ever plan to repeat myself again," he said as he stood there with his hand around his throat. Burton did not try to choke him. He just had his hand placed on his throat as his arm was extended.

"What?" said Breton.

"Son, if you ever try some shit like that again, I will kill you. Do you understand?" Burton said. "If I'm going to go to jail, it'll be for something I actually did. You attacked me. I didn't do anything to you or your mom. She said she didn't want the picture on the wall, and I removed the picture. I'm your father. My father, your grandfather, is in the hospital right now and he may not have long to live. With everything that is going on right now, you mean to tell me I've got to fight my own child. Not acceptable under any circumstances," said Burton as his son Breton stood there and listened.

"Well, Dad," said Breton.

"No 'well Dad' nothing, if you ever try and step like that to me again, I mean what I said," Burton said. "I love you dearly son, but make no mistake. And I'm not going to continue this conversation with you because I said what I had to say. There's really nothing you can say to me at this point that's not going to piss me off even more," Burton said. "A month ago, you rammed your mom's head into the wall, and now you're going to attack me. I don't know what is going on with you, but you better get yourself together because this type of behavior will not be tolerated," as he removed his hand from his son's throat.

Breton was a well-behaved kid at school, but Burton and Candace had been having some problems at home. He never got in any disciplinary or academic trouble in school, but he was very withdrawn and had few friends. They had their share of problems with him at home. Lately he had been acting out at home and exhibiting disturbing behavior. On one instance prior to his assault on his dad he had pushed his mom's head into the sheet rock along the stairway of their house in Wilmington. Burton reprimanded him about that incident; however, it seemed the behavior had now been directed at him.

Burton had to regroup and focus on the situation at hand regarding Beck. He went into his room and took a shower. He laid down in his bed for a few minutes and then got up and put his clothes on so that he could go back to the hospital. Basically, at this point, he had very little to say to Candace and he wished they would just leave and go back to Wilmington. Burton had one focus and objective in mind. He needed to get his dad home and he needed to give his mom any and all support necessary to help her through this time. He was so sick and tired of the drama between him and Candace. Now his son had started to act out in response. This was something that was not going to be solved or resolved in the immediate future. The immediate future entailed Burton facing what he would have to face in the next few days and weeks as Beck's terminal condition progressed.

Candace did not bother to bring the children by the hospital again to see their granddad before she left town after causing all this unnecessary turmoil and confusion. Burton was at the hospital with Beck when they left, and he and Candace did not have many words before they departed. The one time he needed her to be there for him, she was emotionally unavailable. Burton was certain at this point the he was not going to leave Beck. He knew his dad needed him and he was not going back to Wilmington right away. He busied himself at the hospital making plans with the hospice care people to bring his dad home so he and Janet could care for him.

The following day Beck was release from the hospital. As the ambulance pulled in front of the house, they opened their back door and removed Beck on the stretcher. Beck appeared confused and bewildered. However, he knew he was coming home. It appeared obvious to Burton that his dad was worried about something. He did not want to be placed in the back bedroom. Janet and Beck slept on the bottom floor of their house and they had two bedrooms on the bottom wing.

The front bedroom was theirs and there was another bedroom in the back. Beck did not want to be put in the back bedroom. He wanted to be in their bedroom with his wife Janet. When Burton arrived at the house with his Dad, his Dad never said it to him, but it was clearly evident Beck did not want to be in the back bedroom. He wanted to be in the bedroom with Janet even though he knew they would not be in the same bed, since the Hospice people had delivered and installed a Hospital bed for him. The bed was installed in their bedroom. It was clear that Beck breathed a sigh of relief when he finally realized that he would be in the bedroom with his wife.

Burton accompanied the paramedics into the bedroom with his dad and made sure they were able to move him from the stretcher to the bed. Beck was a large man. He weighed approximately 260 pounds. Moving him was not an easy task. As Janet, Burton and the hospice nurses would soon realize. Moving and positioning Beck did not come without some degree of effort. The EMS workers were able to move him from the stretcher to the bed and get him positioned. Shortly thereafter they continued on their way. Burton remained there with his Beck as he tried to get him situated and comfortable. Beck was ailing and in a considerable amount of pain.

Burton thought about the many times in the past when he had been sick or ailing and his dad, his doctor came to his rescue and did something to help make him well again. There had been many times when he had been in distress and in need and his doctor had been there to take care of him. Now his doctor was in distress and in need. His dad was sick, and it was his turn to return the many gestures of healing and comfort that his father had given to him. Once Burton got him into the room and situated Beck looked at Burton and said:

"Hey Burton, can a guy get a beer around here?" asked Beck.

"Dad, you know you can't have any beer or any liquid for that matter," Burton said.

"Come on just one beer," Beck said.

"Dad, do you want me to adjust the bed at all. I can move it up or I can move it down a little," Burton said. "Is this adjustment comfortable for you?" asked Burton.

Beck did not reply. He laid there and watched his son as he slowly drifted to sleep. Burton covered him and gave him a hug and kiss. He took Beck's hand and held it for a moment as he watched his dad resting.

CHAPTER FIVE

As the days went by Janet and Burton cared for Beck at home. Beck was unable to get out of bed. Beck's terminal illness was coming to terms as his body succumbed to the advanced stage of his condition. He was placed on a feeding tube and was unable to move out of his bed. Beck was still a relatively large and heavy man. Moving him was difficult and helping to reposition him in bed was a bit of a task. He was catheterized and had become incontinent. Besides being conscious and awake at times he was relatively nonresponsive and did not communicate much verbally. hospice care came by every day to bathe him and assist in Beck's care. The only form of medical treatment he was receiving at this point was measures to make him comfortable and as free of pain as possible. Janet and her son Burton settled into a routine of round the clock care for Beck as he slipped further and further into oblivion.

Janet retreated into herself for a moment as she lay there in bed one night watching over her husband. She thought about when she first met him at St. Augustine's College in Raleigh, North Carolina and how handsome he was as a young man. She reflected on their first date at the ice cream parlor and how they would study together in the library. She thought about the first time they ever kissed and the first time she made love to him when they were in college. She reminisced about the first time she took him home to Wilmington to visit Poppa, Mama and her sisters and brothers. Similarly, the first time, he brought her home to Mobile to meet Teah, John and his sisters and brothers. How she tried Gumbo for the first time and got sick on the stomach because the soup looked like dishwater, according to Janet.

She remembered the birth of their first child Walker B. LeFlore, Jr. The days they struggled financially while they worked at various teaching jobs, and when Beck went to Atlanta so he could do his Master's in Biology. He got a position teaching Biology at Morehouse College. She taught in the Atlanta school system where she taught and befriended a young lady named Gladys Knight who often babysat their son Champ, who had not got his nickname yet.

Beck applied to and was accepted to medical school. Afterward, they moved and spent their days in Nashville while he studied medicine at Meharry Medical School, and she worked on her master's and got paid for doing research at Fisk University.

She pondered on their lives together, their careers and their accomplishments. For a moment she felt happy. She had not experienced this in a while. She was not happy that Beck was dying. She was just thankful to have had such a wonderful and blessed life with the man of her dreams. She went back in her mind to when Beck graduated from medical school and they moved to Philadelphia so that he could do his residency at Albert Einstien.

Janet secured a top paying position at Smith Kline and French as a chemist doing research in the field of Electron Microscopy. Janet thought about how and when she became pregnant with Burton, and how badly she and Beck wanted another child. She was afraid that she might not be able to have any more children after having had two ectopic pregnancies. Then finally she and Beck were expecting another child. They wanted him to be born in Mobile, so she resigned from her job as Beck finished his residency, and they left Philadelphia to settle in Mobile, Alabama before their next child was born. She reminisced about how she and Beck decided to name him Burton, after her Gynecologist Dr. Burton Walenback.

She liked the name Burton and became stuck on that name for her son. Initially, they planned to name him Burton Walenbach LeFlore until Champ suggested they should not give him the middle name Walenbach. Once back in Mobile, Beck set up his medical practice and she accepted a full-time position teaching chemistry at Bishop State Community College. Janet and Beck embarked on a new era in their lives as they finally had achieved some degree of financial security. They welcomed their second child into the world on a cold, overcast and joyous day in November during 1965 at Martin Deporis Hospital. At that time, Martin Deporis was the segregated hospital for black people in Mobile. They established themselves in the Mobile community as they raised their two boys. Beck's father John LeFlore was a major activist in the civil rights movement and there were a lot of things going on in Mobile, Alabama and the south in general. Meanwhile, during the late sixties, Janet lost her father Angle

B. Owens and Mamma were left alone living out there in Northwest on the Owen's family farmland in Brunswick County, North Carolina. Their son Champ encountered racial problems as Most Pure Heart of Mary Catholic High School which he attended was dismantled and he entered the formerly segregated McGill Toolen High School as one of the pioneer African American students to attend the Jesuit High School for Boys and Girls in the city.

Beck and Janet worked hard to achieve the level of success they had always dreamed of having. She and Beck lived in a house owned by Beck's Aunt Lovie for many years when they first moved back to Mobile. The two of them had their share of problems along the road to success. Beck started working long hours as his medical practice placed more and more demands on him. She endured the years where Beck started drinking heavily.

She recalled the years when Beck cheated on her and produced a set of twins with another woman. She recalled the many fights they used to have while Beck would be in a drunken rage and the few occasions where he had beat her once breaking her arm and once fracturing her rib. She survived those rough years as she and Beck reconciled, and she forgave him for how she felt he had mistreated her. Beck turned his life around and started acting like the model husband and father she always wanted and believed he could be. She recollected when Beck lost his father John in 1976. When her father-in-law, John as she called him, died in the bathtub. She wanted to be the best possible wife she could be because she truly loved her husband. She believed they were soul mates. They readjusted to their busy schedules and newfound stress in their lives and grew. She and Beck matured into real adults and a real married couple. They modified lifestyles and reorganized their lives.

Finally, after many years of working and saving their money during the mid-nineteen-seventies, when they were both in their late forties, Janet and Beck built their first home. They bought a tract of land and subdivided it into several lots. Janet and Beck designed and constructed their dream home and built it in a cul-de-sac and named the street Rue de LeFlore. They were able to sell off the lots and this helped to pay for their new home. By then Janet had become a tenured chemistry professor and Beck was one of the most successful and sought-after physicians in town.

Janet remembered how she and Burton visited Mamma in Wilmington and her legs were swollen. Janet decided that she would have to take Mable to the hospital even though Mable said she did not want to go. Mable, Janet's mom said she just wanted to die at home. Janet refused to listen and took her to the New Hanover Medical Center for medical treatment. As Mamma got worse the rest of the family showed up. Mamma stayed in the hospital for almost two weeks before she passed. She remembered the sorrow and despair she and her siblings faced then and now here she was facing it again.

She decided to bring her sister Eldridge home with her and care for her after Mamma passed. Beck did not like it and he did not necessarily want her sister El living there in their house, but he accepted Janet's decision and agreed to it. Janet continued contemplating on their lives together as she sat there with her husband holding his hand and trying to accept that he was dying. He would no longer be there with her. It is almost as though their entire marriage was flashing before her eyes and she knew she was quickly approaching something she had always feared and dreaded. She tried to turn back the hands of time in her mind, but she stood helplessly caught in the present reality of their lives together. She contemplated about how it must have felt for Mamma when she lost Papa and how she tried to be there with Mamma every step of the way through her grief and pain. As well as, how she and her brother Warren and A.B., fronted the money to rebuild the house in Wilmington so that Mamma could move back into town and not be out there in the middle of nowhere.

She wanted Mamma to be able to return to 1013 which had become so run down and in a state of disrepair that it had become uninhabitable. She and her brother Warren rebuilt the house for Mamma. And her sisters managed to get their names on the Deed and take it over, excluding her and her family. She had been the rock for Mamma and Papa. She had been one of the solutions to the many of the problems Mamma and Papa had over the years and she had taken care of all her younger sisters and brothers.

She thought about how their son Champ completed his master's at The University of South Alabama and applied to Tulane Law School and was accepted. She recollected on how their younger son

Burton graduated high school from John L. LeFlore High School which was named after Beck's father John who had worked so tirelessly as a civil rights activist and political figure for so many years before he passed away. Then Burton later graduating from law school at Florida State. She reflected on when she retired from Bishop State and started working with Beck in his office. Although she gained so much in terms of her personal fulfillment as a chemistry teacher, she so enjoyed being a part of Beck's practice. The closeness between them increased two-fold when she started working with Beck. The two of them became inseparable and he seemed to appreciate her so much more. Beck loved being able to have her undivided attention and having her at his, "Beck and call." Janet loved being there with and for her husband Beck throughout the day at work and then at home in the evenings. Overall their lives together had been so tremendous she felt blessed to be Beck's wife. She felt thankful for the life they had shared together as she fought back her overwhelming sorrow. She wanted to focus on the joy of their life and marriage. She kept trying to focus on their happiness, but her despair kept knocking her back into reality.

She sat there holding her husband's hand as he lay there dying. Janet tried not to focus on her pain but on the pain and suffering that Beck may have been experiencing. She fought back the tendency to want to be consumed with what she was going through at the time and focus on what Beck might be undergoing as his sickness continued to progress closer toward the end of his life. She was hurting but she was not dying; although, she felt completely dead inside. She wondered how much longer they would both have to endure this outrageous suffering. Was there no compassion? Was there no mercy for old people who had worked their entire lives only to have to face the inevitable? Only to face sorrow after all the happiness. Only to face pain after all the heartache. Only to face uncertainty in the light of absolute certainty. Only to endure torture after having to face the adversities of survival.

"Mom," said Burton as he walked up behind her and put his arm around her shoulder.

"Burton," she replied as he had startled her so deep in thought.

"How's he doing?" asked Burton.

"About the same," she replied.

"I'm sorry I didn't mean to startle you," said Burton.

"I was just thinking," said Janet.

"About what?" Burton asked.

"About your dad," Janet said. "I love him so much. Me and that man have been together for a long time."

"Dad," Burton said. "Has he said anything to you today?"

"No not much," replied Janet.

"Is there anything you need me to do?" asked Burton.

"No, not right now," she said. "You can talk to me for a minute."

Burton began to change Beck's nutrition bag as he clamped off the line to his feeding tube and detached the part leading to his stomach from the part which connected to the bag. The doorbell rang. Janet went to answer the door. It was the hospice nurse Peggy who had arrived to see about Beck. Once Burton completed the change of Beck's feeding tube, the nurse came in and bathed him. She made sure he was changed. It took all three of them to turn and maneuver Beck in the bed.

Beck lay there with his eyes open just gazing into space. Beck's eyesight was not very good, and he was not wearing his glasses. By this point, Beck also could not hear very well so if you spoke to him, he would usually respond by indicating that he could not hear what you were saying. Beck was taking Morphine and the Morphine seemed to keep him sedated most of the time.

About the time Janet, Burton, and the Hospice Nurse finished working with Beck, the telephone rang. Beck and Burton's cousin Ray LeFlore was on the phone. Ray was an Attorney who lived in New York City. Ray was Beck's father's brother's son. Their branch of the LeFlore family had left Mobile when Ray's father George and his mother Marcella moved to Schenectady, New York where George started a business as a courier for the United States Postal Service. Burton and Ray were very close. Burton visited Ray quite frequently in New York over the years. Ray visited Mobile on several occasions. He was a wealthy New York Attorney and true New Yorker. He was fascinated by Mobile, Alabama because Mobile was the place of his birth. He and Burton were great friends and kept in touch regularly. On this day Ray called with concerns about Beck since he heard Beck was very sick.

"Burton, I hear your dad's not doing very well and I was thinking about coming down to Mobile to see him," said Ray.

"Well Ray truth be told, he is not doing so well," Burton said. "As much as I would hate for you to come down here and have to turn around and fly back to New York and come back in a week for a funeral. If you want to see him alive you might want to come on now," said Burton.

"I am going to make a reservation and come on down to Mobile," said Ray.

"How is your Mom?" Ray asked.

"She's hanging in there," Burton said. "So, if you come, when do you think you would be flying in?"

"I'll call the airline and see if I can get a flight in on Friday," said Ray.

"Ray that would be awesome if you could come down and see Dad," said Burton.

"It's done, I'll call the airline and make my reservation and call you back and let you know when I will be arriving," said Ray.

"Thanks, Ray. I would love to see you, man. Call me back and let me know when to meet you at the airport," said Burton as he hung up with Ray.

"Mom, guess what? Ray is coming. He said he wanted to see Dad, and he'll probably be flying in on Friday. He's going to call me back in a few minutes after he makes his reservation," said Burton.

"That's nice of him," Janet said. "Ray is such a sweet person."

"Ray has been almost like a brother to me ever since Champ passed," said Burton.

"He has, he really has. Maybe that will lift your dad's spirits a little to see him," said Janet.

"I hope so," Burton said. "I know it will lift my spirits."

"Leassie, can you go upstairs and help me straighten up the guest bedroom, we may be having a guest," said Janet.

"Actually, Mom what we'll probably do is go over to my house and spend the night," Burton said. "You got enough going on here Mom. I don't want to inconvenience you, and I know Ray wouldn't want to inconvenience you either."

"It's no inconvenience," Janet said.

"We'll just be over here and go over there to sleep for the night," Burton said.

The phone rang and Burton thought it might be Ray calling back. He answered the phone expecting to hear Ray's voice, but it was Janet's sister Bethany. Burton and Bethany spoke briefly before he gave the phone to Janet. Bethany wanted to know how Walker was doing. Janet spoke with her for a few minutes. They discussed Beck and then exchanged small talk for a while. Shortly afterward Janet's sister Julia called.

The conversation with Julia was pretty much the same as the conversation with Bethany. Julia wanted to know how Walker was doing. Janet appreciated her sister's calls, but she didn't feel much like talking. She was consumed with her husband and everything that was going on with Beck. She was a nervous wreck and did not exactly want to express her despair over the phone to her sisters. She would have liked to have heard one of them say they were on their way to Mobile like Ray had just told Burton. However, neither of them said anything about coming to Mobile. It is not certain if they even fully understood the seriousness of Beck's condition at the time. Janet never really told them the entire story concerning Beck's health because he did not want anyone to know. Even in one of her darkest hours, Janet still managed to play the big sister in control.

Another phone call came in shortly after Janet got off the phone with Julia. Burton answered once again thinking it was Ray. However, it was not Ray, it was Mattie LeFlore and Chris. Mattie was Walker's oldest brother John's ex-wife. Mattie lived in Los Angeles with her son Chris who was Walker's nephew. Mattie and John LeFlore Jr., had three children, Lamont, Butch, and Chris. Mattie spoke with Burton about her concern for his dad. She told Burton that she was praying for Walker and him and Janet. Mom. She indicated that she might want to attend his services in the event he passed away. She asked Burton to keep her posted on his condition because she and Chris would likely want to travel to Mobile for the funeral. Burton asked Mattie if she wanted to speak to Janet. Mattie said she would be checking up on both of them periodically to see how they were doing. Burton assured her that he would let her know if there were any developments with his Dad so she could make whatever arrangements they needed in the event

Back did pass away. Burton thanked Mattie for her concern and concluded the call.

When Burton arrived at the airport on Friday evening to pick Ray up, he was met by members of the Army National Guard was posted at the airport. The military presence at the airport was a result of the recent tragedy of the bombing of the World Trade Center in New York on September 11, 2001. Less than a month following this horrific event, the nation's airports were on a high alert peak security status. Burton was approached by an armed guard as he entered the airport parking lot as he drove toward the terminal. The guard stopped him and asked for his identification. Burton explained to the man that he was not a terrorist. Burton told him before presenting his identification that he was here to pick up a family member and that he was an American and local resident of Mobile, not a Muslim terrorist. He showed the guard his identification and could proceed to the terminal area to pick up Ray. He saw Ray inside the terminal following his arrival immaculately dressed in his Brooks Brother's suit and tie as usual. Burton was indeed happy to see his cousin. He got Ray's luggage and got him to the car, and they headed back to the house.

Burton and Ray returned to the house and found Janet there caring for Walker. Janet gave Ray a hug as he entered the house. Beck was, for the most part, not communicating. Although he would stare and look at people as they came into the room. Ray went in to speak with Beck. When he saw Ray, he tried very hard to muster up a smile as Ray extended his hand and shook Beck's hand. Beck sort of sank back into his pillow as if that simple smile and handshake had taken a lot of energy on his part. You could tell that Beck recognized Ray as he tried very hard to sound upbeat and positive when he was talking to Beck. Even though Ray understood his cousin was in ill health, he was still somewhat shocked when he finally saw him. Burton stood there with his dad as Ray spoke with Beck. It was one of those somewhat awkward moments as another family member had come to the understanding and realization that Beck was in his final days.

Shortly after Ray arrived, some of Beck and Janet's best friends Percy and Gladys Johnson stopped by the house. Gladys and Percy lived up the street and had been friends of Beck and Janet for many years. Percy was a local businessman and in recent years he had become a minister and had started to pastor a church in addition to running his business. Janet greeted them at the door. They came inside and she took them back into the bedroom so they could see Beck.

Ray and Burton were still there visiting with him. Percy came in and greeted his longtime friend followed by Gladys. Beck extended his had to shake Percy's and tried once again to concoct a pleasant look on his face. Janet introduced the two of them to Ray LeFlore. Everyone stood there around Beck's bed. Janet, Burton, Ray, Percy, and Gladys all held hands. Everyone stood around the bed with their heads bowed as Percy began to pray. Beck was semi-alert and coherent but the Morphine he was taking had him somewhat despondent as it was obvious that he was in extreme pain.

"Dear God, place your healing hand upon your servant Walker, as he has healed so many in his lifetime. My very close and dear friend Walker. God give him comfort and peace as he is a good man deserving of such. Oh Lord, we send this prayer up to you in my friend Walker's name. Lord whatever is your plan whatever is your will, have mercy on Walker and give his family strength and guidance during this time. In Jesus Christ name we pray unto you oh Lord. Show Walker your kindness and your tender mercy dear God. We are praying out of our love and concern for this nobleman and his devoted family. We lift this prayer up to you Oh Lord. Amen," said Percy as he ended his prayer.

Janet went into the kitchen as Percy, Gladys, Ray, and Burton all sat around the island table. They began to talk as Janet asked if anyone wanted anything to eat or a glass of champagne.
Burton gave Ray a beer out of the refrigerator and got one for himself. Percy jokingly laughed that he no longer drank any alcohol or beer, but he would take a glass of water. Janet poured a glass of champagne for her friend Gladys and herself. They all left Walker there in the room by himself, but he and Janet's room was located on the hallway right off from the kitchen. Beck lay there silently but he could barely hear the others conversing in the kitchen as he drifted off to sleep. It was one of those moments where everyone tried to avoid discussing what was really on everyone's mind. There are times when families and friends must come together and basically

not discuss the central issue most prevalent and foremost in their thoughts. The central and prevalent thought and issue on everyone's mind was Walker.

"Ray LeFlore, I have heard so much about you," Percy said. "It's very nice to meet you."

"It's nice to meet you and your lovely wife as well Percy," replied Ray.

"How long will you be in town?" Percy asked.

"Just for the weekend," Ray said. "I flew in to check on Walker and to see Burton and Janet."

"Ray I want you to know how much I appreciate you coming to see Beck," said Janet. "I know it means a great deal to Burton."

"Janet, don't even mention it," Ray said. "After talking with Burton, the other day, I decided that I would come. You know this guy is my tight man."

"I can't begin to tell you home much that means to me Ray," said Burton.

"You live in New York. Don't you?" asked Gladys.

"Yes, I live in Manhattan," replied Ray.

"I have a brother who lives in New York," Gladys said. "He is a professor at Columbia University."

"Really, what does he teach at Columbia?" asked Ray.

"He is a History professor," she said.

"Percy and Gladys have been friends with me and Beck for years," said Janet.

"Many years is quite an understatement," said Gladys.

"Let me tell you something, me and my buddy Walker have been friends for a long time," Percy said. "Me and that guy there, boy I could tell you some stories."

Suddenly Janet felt her jaw starting to hurt and throb. A sharp pain struck her just like a bolt of lightning. It was almost as though everything became a blur as she stopped focusing on the conversation at the table as she was overcome with a piercing sensation on the side of her face. She did not want to say anything to her company about it because there was already enough going on without her interjecting anything about the pain she was feeling. As if everyone there did not already know she was in pain, not necessarily the pain she was currently experiencing. The pain made the side of her face numb as she paused with her head down momentarily. No one at the table really noticed as they continued the conversation. Everything was absolutely overwhelming for her. Being there with Beck and watching him suffer was taking every ounce of energy she had. Trying so hard to fight back her feelings of sorrow and hopelessness. She was working so hard to support her husband during his time of need. She wanted to be a cordial host to her guests. A line of sharp pain from her chin to almost midway between her face up by her ear hurt so bad it's almost like she could feel the pain ringing in her ear. She just tried her best to grin and bear it as she attempted to regain her focus on their conversation.

Later that night Gladys and Percy returned home. Ray and Burton prepared to go over to Burton's house for the night. Janet urged them to stay with her, but Burton said he would prefer to go back to his house and hang out with Ray for a little while before they went to bed. Janet's TMJ was causing her such excruciating pain that she could have cared less what they did, she just wanted to take something for her pain and lay down in her bed near her husband and pray until she went to sleep. Burton finally left with Ray and she was now alone with Beck. Janet was in so much physical and emotional pain and anguish that she felt like she was having an out of body experience. She was sorrowful because she knew her husband was suffering. Her jaw was pounding. Her spirit was mortified. She went over to Beck's bed and checked on him. He seemed to be resting. She was glad that he was sleeping so she could try and sleep some herself not really knowing what tomorrow would bring. She had a headache.

She poured herself another glass of champagne and got under the covers. She wished so bad she could feel her husband's arms around her, holding her as she lay there.

She could hear Beck near her in his bed. She listened to him breathe as he slept. She had listened to him breathe and snore while he slept for so many years. Beck even almost sang a song for you when he was sleeping. His breathing sounded congested and labored. She was thankful, especially for Burton that Ray had come to visit. She knew how much Burton loved and admired Ray and how much it must have lifted Burton's spirits to see him. However, she missed having Burton there with her at the house to help her with Beck. She remained focused on the sound of Beck breathing in his sleep. She was extremely tired. She hoped that maybe if she could get some rest, she would feel better and be able to work with Beck in the morning.

Sunday morning October 14th, 2001, Janet woke up feeling a little better. The pain in her jaw had subsided. She changed Beck's depend and replaced the bag leading to Beck's feeding tube and made herself a cup of coffee. Janet said good morning to her husband. He lay there with his eyes open but did not respond. He seemed to be gazing into nothingness. Beck appeared vulnerable and helpless. The gaze on his face was becoming more and more in despair. Janet noticed that his breathing continued to be labored. As she adjusted his cover, Beck grabbed her arm. Although it startled her a bit, she was glad to feel his embrace. She repositioned her arm and placed her hand in his hand. He held her hand firmly as he placed his other hand on her arm just above her wrist and pulls her close to him. She reaches around his back and puts her arm around him. Janet gave Beck a loving hug and holds him close to her. She walks around to the other side of the bed. She got into his bed right next to him and put his arm around her as she held him and embraced him. Tears started to roll down her face.

Beck appeared to enjoy having his wife laying there next to him and holding him. For the moment Janet found such comfort there holding her husband Beck. She kissed him and told him that she loved him. She tried to make sure she did not get her arm tangled in his feeding tube. She reached between his legs and took his penis in her hand. She tried not to disturb the catheter that was running down the shaft of his private. The catheter made him feel less flaccid and erect. She got an idea and decided to pull the catheter out. She had seen it done a few times since Beck had been home. She pulled the catheter out and got on top of her husband. She placed him inside of her as he lay there. For the first time in many days, she heard him utter a word, and that word was, "Janet." She had not heard him call her name in a while. "Yes, Beck my dear, I love you," she replied. Janet made love to her husband for the last time. She held him and laid there with him until she felt his body grow cold.

Janet thought she needed to call Burton and Dr. Daniels. There was no doubt in her mind that Beck was dead. She called Burton who answered the phone as if he was in total and complete denial. She also contacted Dr. Daniels who was one of Beck's good friends and his personal physician. She explained to Daniels that she was worried about Beck and asked if he could come over to the house and check on him. Dr. Daniels said that if she would give him a few minutes to get ready, he would be right over.

Janet called Burton again and urged him to get to the house as soon as he could. She knew Beck was dead, but she could not utter the words to tell her son. She just asked him to please come as soon as he could. Burton assured her that he would be there as soon as he and Ray got something to eat. She thought to herself that Burton did not seem to realize the sense of urgency she was trying to express to him. She wondered how long it would be before Daniels arrived. Although, at the same time she knew it was inevitable that he would eventually get there and be forced to come to the realization that his Dad was gone.

"Burton, where are you?" Janet asked.

"We're still at the house Mom, I am going to take Ray out to have some lunch and we'll be right over," said Burton.

"Please hurry Burton, it's your dad," said Janet.

"Mom I promise you as soon as we get something to eat, we'll be there," Burton said. "I'm hungry and I'm going to grab something and be right there," he said.

"OK.... We'll be here waiting on you," said Janet.

"I'm going to take Ray to Justine's and get some brunch," Burton said. "Mom is everything alright. I mean if you need me to come right now I will."

"Just go ahead and eat and get here as quickly as you can," Janet said. "I'm worried about your Dad."

"Alright Mom, I will be there in about an hour," said Burton. "We're going to have lunch and I'll be right there."

"Hurry up please," said Janet.

"I'm on the way," said Burton.

"I'm worried," said Janet.

"What, what did you say?' asked Burton.

"I'm worried about your dad," said Janet.

"I'll be right there, call you back in a few minutes," said Burton.

"I'm waiting on you," said Janet as she heard a beep on the other line. "Hold on, I think that's Dr. Daniels."

"Mom we'll be there in a few minutes," said Burton.

"Hello," said Janet as she clicked over to the other call.

"Janet, I'm in route to your house, how is he doing?" said Dr. Daniels.

"I think he's dead," said Janet.

"Oh, Janet are you sure," said Dr. Daniels.

"He's so cold," Janet said. "He's so cold. I know he's dead. Will you please get here as soon as you can?"

"Just stay calm Janet, I'm on the way," Dr. Daniels said. "Although I want to let you know there isn't much I can do if Walker's passed away."

"I will see you when you get here," said Janet.

It wasn't long before Dr. Daniels arrived at the house. She called Burton again. Burton indicated that he and Ray were finished having lunch and they would be heading to the house right away. Daniels examined Beck and concluded that he was dead. He gave Janet the prognosis. She was not surprised.

"Janet, I think Walker is gone," said Dr. Daniels.

"Please, please say it isn't so," replied Janet as she burst into tears again.

"There's no heartbeat, no pulse, and no respiration, "Dr. Daniels said as he puts his arm around Janet.

"Oh no, no, no, no!" Janet exclaimed. "Not my Beck, my precious Beck. How am I going to tell Burton?"

"There isn't going to be any easy way to tell him, Janet," Dr. Daniels said. "I will tell him if you want."

"Do you know how long me and this man have been together," Janet said. "Forever, forever, my God, how will I live without him," she said as she wiped the tears from her face.

"You'll just have to take one day at a time," Daniels said. "He was extremely ill; he is no longer suffering. He is at peace." Burton and Ray could be heard coming into the house.

"Mom, I'm here," Burton said. "Whose car is that parked outside?"

"We're back here with Beck," Janet said. "Dr. Daniels is here."

Burton went into the bedroom. He saw his dad laying in his bed and Dr. Daniels standing there next to the bed with Janet. When Burton entered the room, Janet turned and walked away, leaving Dr. Daniels standing there with Beck. Janet went into the kitchen where Ray was. Burton felt as if everything was moving in slow motion as he approached his dad's bedside. He kept his gaze on his dad and Dr. Daniels as he moved closer.

Dr. Daniels looked Burton in the eyes as if to say I have something to tell you; however, he never said a word. Burton came over and shook Dr. Daniels hand as they greeted one another. Once Dr. Daniels had established that he had Burton's full attention, he shifted his view to Beck. Burton took his dad's hand in his own hand and it felt cold. Beck's hand felt like he had been soaking it in ice water. Burton took a long look at Beck and back at Dr. Daniels.

"He's dead, isn't he?" said Burton.

"Yes," replied Dr. Daniels. "He wasn't only a patient; he was my friend and colleague. I had a tremendous amount of respect and love for him. I'm sure this must be difficult for you and your mom. Let me know if there is anything I can do?"

"Thank you, Dr. Daniels," replied Burton.

"I'd better be going," said Dr. Daniels. "If there is anything you need. Feel free to call me."

"Thank you," Burton said. "Talk with you later."

Burton could feel the sadness starting to increase inside his being as he realized his father was dead. He stood there silently with his dfather as he tried to wrap his mind around this current situation. He knew it was coming and he had tried to prepare himself for it; however, it felt like he had been hit with a ton of bricks. Janet walked Dr. Daniels to the door and did not come back into the room with Burton right away. Janet wanted to give Burton a chance to process this for himself without imposing her sadness on him at the same time. She spoke with Dr. Daniels briefly as he left and then remained in the kitchen with Ray. She urged Ray to go into the room with Burton.

"Burton, I'm so sorry," said Ray.

"Yea, I am too," replied Burton.

"Walker was a great man and his legacy will live on through you and your kids," said Ray.

"Got another one on the way," said Burton.

"I know," said Ray.

"I knew this was going to happen, I told you," Burton said. "When we talked last week, and I said I would hate for you to have to fly down here and have to fly back to New York and turn around and come back for a funeral. I knew it. Do you think you will be able to come back for the funeral?"

"Yes, I will have to clear some things on my schedule during the latter part of this week, but I will be there," replied Ray. "As soon as you know which funeral home is going to be handling everything, let me know and I will call and make my reservation. Hopefully, I can get one of those bereavement fares, regardless, I will be here."

"Thanks, Ray, you don't know how much that would mean to me man," said Burton.

"Burton you needn't say another word," replied Ray.

"Mom, where are you?" said Burton.

"I'm in here," said Janet.

"I can't believe my dad is gone," Burton said as he went into the kitchen. When he saw his Mom sitting there, he embraced her in his arms. "I love you, Mom."

"I love you too, Baby," replied Janet.

"I'm going to be here with you every step of the way," Burton said. "We're going to get through this."

"Janet, do you know who you would want to handle the service?" said Ray.

"Allen and Johnson, they handled Teah, John, and Lovie," Janet said. "Allen and Johnson were founded by Lovie's father in law, C. First Johnson," she said. "We will take Beck there."

"We'd better call an ambulance," said Burton.

It was not long before the ambulance arrived to transport Beck to the mortuary. Burton let them into the house as Janet sat there and watched with a blank expression on her face. Some of the neighbors stopped by to see what was going on, when they saw the ambulance. They all knew Dr. LeFlore was sick. The EMS workers struggled to remove Beck from the bed and to place him onto their gurney. Beck was still a relatively large big-boned man. Finally, they managed to move him so that he could be transported. As they wheeled Beck's body down the hallway toward the door. Burton watched them as they were taking his dad out of the house.

It dawned on Burton that his father was never going to return home. Burton was overcome with emotion. He started crying uncontrollably. He saw them as they took Beck's body out the door. He gasped and cried as he started to recall the back in the day when Beck's Dad John LeFlore passed away. Burton remembered that day when he was riding back to Teah and John's house after his grandfather died. Beck stopped there in the middle of the street on his way there and just broke down crying. Beck screamed my daddy is dead, as he cried. Burton had probably only seen his dad cry one other time in his life. Now here he was crying and coming to the realization that now his dad was dead. He was only facing what other men have met, but it hurt like hell. He had witnessed his own father face it and now he was facing it. Burton was thoroughly immersed in his sorrow and personal grief.

All the years in his life he had spent patiently awaiting his father's return home from work or wherever he might have been. Burton was confronted with the reality his dad was never coming back home again. Beck had gone home to meet his maker. Janet tried to comfort Burton, but he was about to hyperventilate. Burton cried, he cried, and he cried. He was immensely sorrowful as he witnessed them load Beck's lifeless body into the ambulance. He stood there wiping the tears off his face and trying to compose himself.

Janet tried her best to console her son. Janet wanted to drop down to her knees and scream, but she knew she might be even more messed up since she had broken her knee several years ago. She was beyond the pain, beyond the sorrow, beyond anything imaginable. She was simply numb as she tried to help her son cope with the loss he must have been feeling. She needed to subjugate her feelings and come to Burton's rescue. Since clearly, she was unable to rescue herself.

The ambulance drove away with Beck's body. Janet and Burton both knew this was the end of life as they once knew it. Dr. Walker Beck LeFlore, Sr., was about to say his last goodbye. Janet had a lot of planning to do and work to get done to arrange her husband's funeral. She hoped her son would be helpful. Ray indicated that he needed to be getting to the airport soon because he had to fly back home to New York. The ambulance carrying Beck's body made a right turn on the way to the funeral home. The three of them watched helplessly waiting for a moment to say cut, end this endless menagerie of wishing and wanting a miracle to something you know will never come to fruition. And then it comes around full force. It comes with more thrust and more velocity than ever before. Reality makes waves and disappoints the hopes for a miracle and then you realize this is the only blessing you could have possibly hoped for.

The hopes and dreams of the strangers that come on the shoulders and backs of the wanton wanderers. The belief of the solitary ones, and those who know, those who would rather not understand, those who are knowledgeable and those who really don't want to know. Those who are without a clue as to what is going on. Those who are dead and the ones that are alive. As life takes its course, we will all face death no matter how we deal with it. We will always be welcoming life, supporting our survival and the progeny of others or burying those we love, hate or have indifference toward. Life is an endless wheel where people drop off and emerge. Life is like a windmill circling amid the ever-evanescent sunrise and sunset which is the constant by which we live and accept our mortality.

Everyone who lives must die. Every person on earth has an endless ebb and flow which will end when it is time for them to come or to go. They say a baby comes into the world crying and everyone around is standing around smiling. Similarly, when someone dies, they say everyone is standing around crying and yet the person is smiling because they have found peace in the Lord our God. Isn't this an incredible irony? A person comes into the world crying while those around are usually happy and jubilant. Meanwhile, when someone leaves this earth, they are surrounded by sadness and sorrow, yet they are happy to be free of the pain and suffering in this world of yesterday, today and tomorrow. Janet and her son Burton were standing at the crossroads of their new life and existence as a family, as mother and son. There is no one on earth who she could imagine would be feeling her sorrow more than her son Burton following the loss of Beck. She tried to figure out how she could remain strong for him. She hardly knew how she would remain strong for herself.

CHAPTER SIX

"He's gone! Beck is gone!" Janet said to her sister over the phone.

"Walker is dead?' replied Anna. "Oh, Janet I'm so sorry.

"He's gone, he's gone, he's gone, Beck is gone!" cried Janet.

"Janet I'm going to go and pack my bag right now," Anna said. "I'll get Bethany and Julia and we are going to get on the road as soon as possible and drive to Mobile," she said. "Do you hear me sister?"

"Please come as soon as you can," said Janet.

"How are you holding up Janet?" said Anna.

"I'm not," Janet replied.

"I'm so so sorry Janet," said Ann. "Let me get myself together and I promise you we're on the way."

Janet hung up the phone with Anna. She sat down at the kitchen table and continued to cry. Burton tried to console her. He put his arm around her and gave her another hug. Janet cried and cried and cried. Burton realized it was best to say nothing and just let her get it all out. He shed tears now not only for his dad, but for how he saw it was tearing his mom apart. He had never seen his Mom like this before. Janet was heartbroken as she sat there mourning the loss of her husband Beck. The telephone rang. Burton went over to answer the phone. It was Janet's sister Julia.

"Hi Burton, how are you darling?" asked Julia.

"I've had better days Aunt Julia," he replied.

"Ann just called and told me that Walker had passed," said Julia.

"Yea," Burton said. "Hold on, let me let you speak with my mom." He handed the phone to Janet.

"Julia," said Janet.

"Yes, Janet. It's Julia," she replied. "Ann just called and told me Beck passed away. I want to let you know my heart is heavy. I'm praying for you and Burton."

"Thank you, that means so much to me, Julia I don't

know what to do." She said, "Julia he's dead, he's dead."

"We are going to get our ducks in a row and get down there as soon as we can," said Julia. "We'll try and leave tomorrow."

"OK," said Janet.

"I'll call you back a little later and check on you guys," said Julia.

Janet returned to her seat at the kitchen table and resumed her sobbing. She felt like her entire world was falling in. Now once again her jaw had started to hurt. She was in such serious emotional pain at the moment she could hardly connect with the physical pain from her jaw. She paused and yawned placing her hand over her mouth and back to her forehead. She buried her face in the palm of her hand and continued to wail and call her husband Beck's name. Burton remained close by as if his mere presence might give her some comfort, but it did not seem to be doing much good. He tried to think of a way to console his mom. Janet was so sorrowful, and it dawned on him that he would have to be strong for his mom and help her through this. That was about all he could do, since he could not come up with any magical solution to take her tears away or his own for that matter. The phone rang again.

"Burton, this is your Aunt Bethany," said Bethany. "Ann just called, is it really true?"

"It's true," Burton said. "My dad passed away earlier today."

"Where is Jeannie, how is she doing?" Bethany asked.

"She's not doing too good right now," Burton said. "Hold on, let me let you speak with her. Mom its Aunt Bethany," he said.

"Hello," said Janet.

"Jeannie," Bethany said. "How are you? I just got off the phone with Ann. Just want to let you know we are making plans to come down there. We hope to leave as early as tomorrow. We are going to get there to you as quickly as possible," said Bethany.

"Bethany," said Janet.

"Jeannie, I know this is a difficult time for you and we are going to make you feel like the loved sister that you are and help you with anything we can. That I can promise," said Bethany.

"Hold on Bethany, I got a call on the other end," said Janet as she clicked over on the two way. "Hello, oh hi Cabbie, hold on a second Carol, I was on the phone with Bethany." Janet clicked over again. "Bethany, this is Cabbie on the phone, I'll call you back in a minute," she said.

"Ok Jeannie, I'll talk with you a little later, and we are on our way," said Bethany.

"By Bethany see you guys when you get here," Janet said as she clicked over again to her other sister Carol holding on the other line. "Cabbie are you there?"

"Hey Jeannie, I'm so sorry to hear about Walker," her sister Carol said. "You know we all loved Walker since the day you brought him home from St. Augustine's."

"I don't know what I will do without him," said Janet.

"You will just have to take life one day at a time Janet, one day at a time," Carol said. "At first it will seem unbearable, especially if you truly loved him like I know you did."

"I loved him with all my heart, I feel like a piece of me is missing, and it hurts like that piece was snatched off my body," said Janet.

"All you can do is take it one day at a time, sooner or later it will get better and be easier for you to bare," Carol said. "It's been almost 25 years since Fred died and not a day goes by that I don't miss him or think about him, and I haven't remarried so you already know," said Carol.

"Who are you telling, you were here in Mobile with me at my house during Thanksgiving when we got the news that Fred had died, I will never forget it," Janet said. "It was just like yesterday when me and Burton got on that plane with you to fly back to Washington DC and found poor little Cheryl there at the hospital fighting for her life and Fred was dead," said Janet.

"I remember it like it was yesterday too, who knows if I had not been at your house, I might have been in the car with them when the accident occurred," said Carol. "Despite everything that me and Fred had been through, you know I loved him more than anything and when he died it ripped me apart, it ripped our family apart and we have never been the same," she said.

"You know your sister Janet was there with you every step of the way Cabbie and I know how much it devastated you," Janet said. "Now I finally know what you must have felt."

"I know what you must be feeling right now Jeannie," said Carol.

"Are you going to come for the funeral?" asked Janet.

"I'm not sure Janet, you know I don't have any money." Carol said, "And Ann, Bethany and Julia are supposed to be driving there but they probably won't come and get me to ride with them. What if I come down to Mobile after the funeral and spend a few days with you?" Carol said. "How about that?"

"Cabbie that would be fine and if you don't have the money, I will buy you a ticket," said Janet.

Janet poured herself a glass of champagne. She tried to regain her composure as she wiped her face with a paper towel. The phone continued to ring throughout the evening as various family members and friends called to give Janet their condolences and ask if there was anything they could do to help.

Janet welcomed the concern; however, she really just wanted to be left alone. She wanted to ball herself up on the sofa with her glass of champagne and cry some more. She felt so vulnerable and alone. Even though her son was there, and her family was calling to check on her, she felt completely alone without Beck. She could not believe Beck was dead. She still did not want to believe it or accept it, even though she knew in her mind that it was absolutely true. Janet wondered how she could even get up tomorrow morning and face the day without her husband in her life.

The next morning Burton and Janet went down to Allen and Johnson to get started with the arrangements for Beck's funeral. They were met by Ms. Mack who spoke with them in her office for a moment about when they would like to have the funeral and other matters pertaining to Beck's services. From Ms. Mack's office, they went into the casket room to look around. As soon as they walked in the door, they saw this beautiful metallic brown looking box sitting right there in the middle of the room. Just like the shiniest and fastest car displayed in the middle of the showroom floor at an auto dealership, this casket was the first thing they saw when they entered.

Janet and Burton went over to take a closer look at it. They looked at the other caskets on display and came back to the metallic brown looking box they saw when they first walked in. Burton told Janet that he liked that one and asked her what she thought. She said she liked it as well. Burton asked Ms. Mack how much they wanted for it and she said Eight Thousand Dollars. Janet and Burton both looked at her in amazement and disbelief that she actually said the casket was Eight Thousand Dollars. They moved on and looked around some more and inquired about a few more which were more reasonably priced. As they concluded their meeting with Ms. Mack, Janet had a renewed spirit. Through her grief and sadness, she suddenly felt needed again by Beck. She suddenly realized her sense of purpose. Beck was not altogether gone. He was still here, and he needed her to handle their business. She had her son with her as well and she knew he was going to help her with the important decisions she would have to make during the next few days. She was expecting her grandchildren; her sisters; brothers and other family as well as many friends. There were so many things that had to be done in a very short amount of time. She would have to busy herself and work toward giving her husband a beautiful funeral.

"Mom I really like that casket for Daddy, but eight thousand dollars is ridiculous," said Burton.

"Who are you telling?" she said.

"I really would like to get that for Dad but there is no way we're going to pay no eight thousand dollars for it," Burton said.

"We need to call the church and see when we can meet with them to discuss the funeral arrangements," said Janet.

"Who do we need to call?" asked Burton.

"We should call Kris right away and let her know that Beck has passed," said Janet.

"Do you have her number?" Burton asked.

"I think so, I'll have to look for it in my rolodex," Janet said. "When is Candace going to be here with the boys?"

"They should be here by Wednesday or Thursday," replied Burton.

"We have got to get the house cleaned up, Ann, Julia and Bethany said they will be here tomorrow," said Janet.

"I talked to Rita and she said she was going to bring Uncle Warren," Burton said. "What about Uncle Peter, is he coming?"

"I'm not sure. He said he might not be able to make it. You know he has real bad back pain, and it makes it hard for him to travel or sit for long periods of time," Janet said.

"Mom that's bullshit, if Uncle Peter wanted to come, he would come," Burton said. "But that's your baby brother, he can do no wrong."

"What does my baby brother have to do with it. I wish he would come, but I'm not sure if he's coming, and I can't make him come," said Janet.

"Well at least most of your family is coming and that's all that matters," said Burton.

"Burton funerals are times when families bond together and show up for one another," Janet said. "We need to call Ellen. Now that Beck is gone, Ellen is John and Teah's last surviving child."

"Why do you think Dad and Ellen didn't communicate much over the last few years?" said Burton.

"It seems like when Teah needed to be cared for in her later years, Ellen put herself on disconnect," said Janet.

"I spoke with Horace and he will tell her, I don't have

her number," Burton said.

"I'm pretty sure we have her number, we will call her," Janet said. "After all what kind of sister wouldn't come to her own brother's funeral if there was any possible way she could be there."

"I will do the obituary and get it in to the newspaper," said Burton.

"We need to select some pictures," said Janet.

"Mom I love you," said Burton. "I can't believe Daddy is gone."

"I love you too Baby," Janet replied.

"I think we're going to plan a wonderful going home ceremony for Daddy," said Burton.

"Remind me to call this lady about doing the programs," said Janet.

"Just give me the number and I will call them right now, before we both forget," said Burton.

"I think we can get this done if you will hang in there with me," said Janet.

"Mom it's you and me together forever," replied Burton.

"Let's make this a wonderful service for Beck," Janet said.

"Mom we've got a lot to do," said Burton.

"There's nothing we can do except to do it," said Janet.

As the hours rolled by, Janet and Burton worked collectively to get Beck's funeral arrangements together. It wasn't long before Julia, Ann and Bethany arrived in Mobile. Shortly afterward, Burton's wife Candace arrived with Breton, Bryceton and Breaghan. Burton had called Mattie and Chris LeFlore out in Los Angeles. They indicated to Burton they would not be able to come but shortly afterward Mattie's son Lamont LeFlore called Burton and said he wanted to attend his uncle's funeral. Lamont asked Burton if he could stay at the house with the family. Burton was shocked that he had called Mattie and Chris only to find out they had no intentions of coming for the funeral. Now here Lamont was calling and saying he wanted to be in the place. It was all good, the only problem was Beck despised Lamont. Similarly, Lamont had an extreme disliked for his Uncle Walker even more. The two of them had numerous conflicts and differences throughout the years. The most severe dispute was when Lamont stayed with his grandmother and stole Ten Thousand Dollars out of Teah's savings account.

The Feds came to Beck looking for him. Instead of turning him in, he gave Lamont, who was his oldest Brother John's son, an ultimatum. Leave town or else. Walker disliked Lamont with a passion. He felt that his nephew Lamont was a con man who was always out for the inevitable encounter with his twisted and distorted ways. Walker once told Lamont that if he did not stop using Cocaine, he would likely find himself unable to urinate. Walker said this to him during one of their many confrontations. Lamont was now on Dialysis and needed to make arrangements for his appointments before he could stay.

And now, Mattie and Chris said they would not be able to be in attendance, but Lamont was going to show up as their proxy. Although Burton was aware of the differences his Dad had with Lamont, he did not share the same extreme indifference to Lamont as his Dad. Certainly, this was not the time to be holding grudges, especially since he had no grudge against Lamont. He told Lamont that he was welcome to come stay at the house if he wanted to attend his Dad's funeral.

Janet's sisters where there and her grandchildren had all arrived. There were many more expected over the next few days as the funeral approached. Janet's heart was cold and barren as she processed the sadness of losing her husband; however, she felt the warmth and love of her family around her. The support was greatly appreciated and needed. Janet came from a huge family, having grown up as one of ten children. Her brother Warren was expected to be flying in with his daughter Rita very soon. Warren was two years younger than Janet. The two of them were very close growing up and remained close throughout their lives.

Warren lived in Hampton, Virginia with his wife Bercenia and his three children.

Warren looked strikingly like her husband Walker, only Walker was taller than Warren. Janet anxiously awaited Warren's arrival as she knew it was not altogether easy for him to travel at this point in his life. Unlike her younger brother Peter, who had said he would not be able to make the funeral. Warren was going to be there for his sister no matter what, if there was any way he could. That was just the type of man Warren was. Janet had an older brother named Angle Benjamin but, A.B., as he was commonly called, had died a few years prior. All her brothers lived in Hampton, Virginia.

Just having her family around her in the house made such a difference. Even though she knew it would not be long before the funeral was over, and she would find herself back there at home all by herself and alone. Left only with the memory of her husband of over fifty years and the life they had together that was no longer. There are stages of grieving that most people go through and she started to understand that she was going through those stages herself.

First, there is the initial grief and then there is what I will call the funeral stage. The stage where you're busy trying to get a lot of things done in a few days leading up to the funeral. It's the stage where your loved one is still technically there and still in need of your assistance to get their funeral done so they can have a proper burial. Usually a person is surrounded by family and friends who give them support and comfort. This helps to ease the pain.

Janet postponed the extreme grief she was undergoing. Janet realized it would be a good opportunity to put her sorrow aside and just savor being around her family. She was inundated with making the arrangements for Beck's funeral and now she had some help. However, the help was nice, but her sisters needed to understand that Beck was her husband, and things were going to be done the way she and Beck wanted. As long as Ann, Bethany and Julia understood this simple fact, and provided assistance without trying to take over the show it was all good. Inwardly Janet was happy her family was there with her, but she experienced sensations of guilt for remotely being happy during this time of sadness.

However, a funeral is meant to be a celebration. A celebration of life and love someone shared with their family, friends and the world. Who ever said a funeral had to be sad? That is one of the things about death and funerals. Sometimes people don't know how to feel. It is such a sad occasion, but it's not altogether wrong to be in a celebratory state of mind. Different people handle death in many ways as people deal with and process their grief and express it or a lack thereof. Some come with the endless fake tears and screaming while others may remain stone faced and smile while deep in their heart they are feeling cut to the core. By no means am I saying tears are fake or stoned faced smiles are masked sorrow. It's just that people handle, approach and look at death in different ways. There is no one way to grieve, handle death or to express one's emotions when it comes to the loss of a loved one.

"Mom, it's almost time for Uncle Warren and Rita's flight to be coming in," Burton said. "I'm going to head out to the airport and pick them up."

"What time are they supposed to come in?" asked Janet.

"Their flight arrives at 2:35," replied Burton.

"You'll need at least 30 minutes to get to the airport and it's 1:45 now," said Janet.

"Jeannie someone's at the door," said Julia.

"Can you answer it for me Julia," Janet said. "Here's my key to the front door."

"Janet, I found these pictures in the photo album," Anna said. "We should use some of these to make a photo collage for the funeral program."

"If anyone wants some Tuna fish, its ready," said Bethany.

"Grandma Janet, come here I want to show you something," said Bryceton.

"What Bryceton?" asked Janet as she took him by the

hand. "What do you want to show grandma?"

"I drew a picture Grandma, it's a picture of Granddaddy," said Bryceton.

"Bryce that is a nice picture of Granddaddy," said Janet as she looked at the picture.

"That's Granddaddy?" asked Breaghan.

"Yes, that's Granddaddy Breaghan, I drew a picture of him see," replied Bryceton.

"I love it Bryceton, thank you so much," Janet said. "Can I have it?"

"I drew it for you Grandma," Bryceton said. "It's yours."

"Janet it was the florist at the door, it looks like Patsy sent you some flowers," said Julia.

"That was nice of her," Janet said. "Where did you put them?"

"I placed them in the foyer with the rest of the flowers," replied Julia.

"That's fine," said Janet.

"Janet do you want me to make you a Tuna fish sandwich?" asked Bethany.

"No Bethany I'm full, I just got through eating some Potato salad," Janet said. "I'm full."

"It's good, it will be right here if you want some, I am going to sit my ass down for a minute," said Bethany as she laughed.

"Grandma can I have a cookie?" asked Breaghan.

"Why of course you can Breaghan, that's what cookies are for, my precious Grandbabies," Janet said. "You and Bryceton give grandma a hug and I will give you another cookie."

"Love you Grandma," said Breaghan.

"Bryceton come over here and give Grandma a hug," Janet said. "That is a very nice picture of Granddaddy."

"Janet we are going to need to call the lady who is doing the programs in a little while, she said she will need everything no later than tomorrow at 5," said Ann.

Later that afternoon Burton decided to take his boys to the store and buy them a suit so they could be presentable when they attended their Grandad's funeral. Certainly, Burton knew his Dad would have done the same. Burton also knew his Dad would want his Grandchildren to look nice. Beck had hundreds of suits. He wore a suit and tie practically every day of his adult life. As he fought his feelings of loss with regard to his Dad, Burton realized the really big and huge picture.

This picture being the fact that he was a Dad. He was the father of three wonderful sons, and he had another child on the way. He started to realize comfort in coming into his own as a man and as a father himself. Yes, he was laboring with the pains of his loss. He reached the understanding that it was his unavoidable destiny. Burton wondered if there was any truth to what the Hindus believe in reincarnation. He wondered if there was any truth to the idea that souls live, die and return to earth. He wondered if the child he was expecting with his wife had now become a vessel for the wayward soul of his father. One thing is for sure, no one can prove with reasonable certainty or deny with the ascertainable accuracy the truth or falsehood of exactly what happens to the human soul when someone dies.

What exactly happens when someone dies? Is it just completely the end? Certainly, it is the end for their body and physical being. However, what about the soul? What happens to the essence of every human life, that something we call the spirit? Does it transcend into total nothingness; does it ascend into angels and heaven; or some dismal corridor of demons. Does our soul become like the animals and the plants that we consume to survive? Does a human soul actively seek another human container to continue its journey in this world or does it float like air in the universe for eternity?

We understand what to do with the remains as they are buried, burned and cast away throughout the world. Or is there a collective human existence that is me, that is you? This is the single question that has puzzled mankind throughout the ages. This is the single question that man cannot truly and effectively answer with reasonable certainty. The type of certainty that can be proved with any ascertainable data. So, we say its God, and just put it in God's hands, if you believe in God. In a world where there are so many different points of view about this topic. As for me, I believe in God. I believe in a higher power that is far greater than myself. I believe in the wheel of life, evolution and reincarnation.

    Janet was back at the house. Warren had arrived and she was trying to get the back bedroom straight for him. Naturally now that Poopie was in the house, as they affectionately called him, it was on and poppin. She needed to change the sheets on the bed in the alternate downstairs bedroom to make sure her brother Warren would be comfortable. Her sister's Bethany, Ann and Julia busied themselves around the house, helping Janet straighten up the kitchen. Her two youngest grandchildren played around the house. There was a lot of life and chatter in the house which made Janet a little less heavy hearted.

    Her oldest grandson Breton was sullen and quiet. He was very close with his Granddad and also, he was worried that his Dad was upset with him because of the fight they had a few weeks ago before they went back to North Carolina. He felt bad about what had happened, and he wondered if his Dad would ever forgive him. Breton and his Dad had not said much since they arrived in Mobile. Burton was still very angry with him, but there was so much going on in the house at the time. Burton had taken him out with the other two brothers to find them something to wear to the funeral; however, they had not talked much about anything other than what size suit he needed.

    Breton sat there and tried to think of a way to bridge the gap between him and his Dad since it did not appear his Dad was trying. He knew his Dad must have been feeling some type of way since Beck had passed, and it appeared that his behavior had compounded the situation and made things worse. Breton wondered if his Dad hated him now.

    Meanwhile the following morning Burton was on the

phone with another funeral director at a different funeral home. This gentleman named Dan Boltman had contacted Burton, to see if he could convince Burton to bring his father to his funeral home instead of Allen and Johnson. Burton did not really understand why he would have contacted him about this in the first place, but they did talk briefly. Burton explained to him that another funeral home was handling the arrangements and it would not make any sense to change funeral homes in midstream.

Even though he did own a legitimate funeral home, Burton felt distrustful of him because it seemed to Burton who had never actually planned a funeral that it was somewhat unethical for a funeral director to solicit business in this manner. Burton did explain to Mr. Boltman that he was unsatisfied about one thing, which was the fact that he wanted a casket for his Dad which he felt the funeral home was charging too much for. Burton explained they wanted Eight Thousand Dollars for the casket, and he wanted it but was reluctant to pay that amount for it.

After Mr. Boltman explained that he could go right over to Allen and Johnson and pick his Dad up today if he wanted, he explained that he could also help him find the casket at wholesale. He explained to Burton that he could have the same casket delivered to the funeral home in the event he decided not to remove his Dad from Allen and Johnson. Burton was not going to entertain the idea of having his Dad moved, but he did want to find out how much he could purchase the casket he wanted for his Dad. Burton described the casket to him and gave him as much information as he could about the box. Boltman told Burton to give him a few minutes to look it up.

Mr. Boltman called Burton back shortly and indicated he had found it and that it could be purchased wholesale for Thirty-Five Hundred Dollars. The price that Boltman gave Burton probably had an upcharge for his services in finding it, but that was not discussed. Burton was quite pleased to hear that he could purchase the casket for significantly cheaper than what Allen and Johnson were trying to sell it for. Boltman explained that he could have the casket delivered from New Orleans and it would only take about two days to get it here. That would be in time for the services that were scheduled for his Dad.

He told Burton he could have it delivered there to Allen and Johnson and there was nothing they could do but accept delivery and work with your requested wishes. Burton had never been involved in arranging a burial. He had always thought that you were more or less obligated to use the products offered by the funeral home you chose to handle your loved one's arrangements.

Boltman assured Burton he was not in any way obligated to purchase one of their caskets. He could buy a casket anywhere he chose, and the funeral home would have to work with him either way. Although Burton questioned Boltman's business practices and had no intention of getting entangled with him; Boltman was giving him valuable information about how the funeral home business works and just how cutthroat it can be. As he started to feel that Allen and Johnson were being a little cutthroat themselves for trying to overcharge them some much for that Bronze casket.

Burton told Boltman that he would need a few hours to think about what they had discussed. He also indicated that he was going to contact Allen and Johnson to discuss it with them. Boltman assured Burton that he could make whatever he wanted to happen. Burton thanked him and they concluded their conversation. Burton sat and thought about their conversation for a minute. He wanted that casket for his Dad and he really didn't want to do any business with Boltman, so he needed to contact the mortuary.

"Hi, is this Ms. Mack?" asked Burton.

"Mr. LeFlore, good morning," Ms. Mack said. "Yes, this is Ms. Mack. I recognized your voice. How are you doing today?" she said.

"I'm hanging in there, just trying to get everything in order," said Burton.

"I still remember those days when you used to do the

obituaries for the Mobile Press," said Ms. Mack.

"Yes Ms. Mack I remember you," said Burton. "I'm the guy who used to do your obituaries at the Press."

"Your Dad was a great man in this community, and we are proud to be working with your family," said Ms. Mack.

"We will be taking everything over to Ruth for the programs today," said Burton.

"Have you prepared his Obituary yet, things are a little different since when you were at the Mobile Register," said Ms. Mack.

"What do you mean?" asked Burton.

"You only get five lines, anything beyond that you have to pay for," she replied.

"Wow we didn't even charge for them when I was a copy clerk," he said.

"They do now, so we need to get it and take a look at what you have," said Ms. Mack.

"I'll bring it over later this afternoon," Burton said.

"Have you decided what you would like for us to dress Dr. LeFlore in," said Ms. Mack.

"The sooner you can get that over here the better," said Ms. Mack.

"We are also waiting to hear from the church about Saturday," Burton said. "Saturday is the day we are shooting for at this point for the funeral."

"Do you have a number for the church that you can provide me with just in case we need to talk with them?" said Ms. Mack.

"I will get that for you as well," said Burton.

"I wanted to talk with you also about that Bronze casket," Burton said. "I really want to get that for my Dad."

"That is fine, I think you have made a good choice," said Ms. Mack.

"Since you guys want Eight Thousand for it, I think I'm just going to buy it elsewhere and have it delivered there," said Burton.

"Mr. LeFlore if you purchase a casket and have it delivered here, we would be utterly offended," replied Ms.

Mack.

"Say what?" replied Burton.

"In all of my many years as a funeral director, I have never seen anyone going around shopping for caskets," said Ms. Mack.

"What's wrong with trying to get a bargain on a box that is going straight in the ground?" said Burton.

"Oh, my goodness, I bet your father is back there rolling over in the morgue right now," said Ms. Mack. "All of the times I worked with Dr. LeFlore to plan some of your other family members funerals, there was never anything like this."

"Ms. Mack we're just talking about the price of a casket," said Burton.

"Mr. LeFlore we would be offended if you bought a casket from those people and had it delivered here," said Ms. Mack.

"I'll be over there a little later to bring you the things we discussed," said Burton.

Later that day Burton went over to the funeral home with his mom and her sisters to take some clothes for Dr. LeFlore and to discuss other particulars. Burton was still adamant about the price of the bronze casket that he wanted for his dad. He spoke with Ms. Mack in the presence of Janet, Ann, Julia and Bethany regarding the matter. Finally, Ms. Mack agreed to reduce the price of the casket to Four Thousand Dollars. This was still expensive, and he still felt like they were being overcharged, but at least he could avoid dealing with Boltman. The end result was Allen and Johnson came down on the price and he was able to get what he wanted for his dad. Burton was satisfied at this juncture. They concluded the meeting.

Beck's funeral was quickly approaching. The wake was scheduled for Friday. The local television stations and newspapers aired stories about Dr. Walker B. LeFlore's having passed away. The stories generally read local physician and son of local civil rights leader John L. LeFlore passes. The family stood around and watched as the news story aired. Similarly, news articles as well as his obituary appeared in some of the local newspapers. Many people who were not yet aware that Beck had passed, had now become aware.

The next day everyone busied themselves doing something. Julia and Bethany were working in the kitchen cooking some grits and Conecuh Sausage. Burton always found it fascinating how his relatives from up north ran to the store to purchase Conecuh Sausage as soon as they got south of Virginia. Conecuh Sausage is manufactured in Conecuh County, Alabama and apparently, they don't sell it north of the North Carolina and Virginia state line. Janet's sisters who all lived in Virginia and Philadelphia would go to the grocery store as soon as they got far enough south and would always buy Conecuh Sausage. It always fascinated Burton how they liked the sausage so much which people in Alabama buy faithfully but for the most part take for granted.

It was kind of like how Burton usually ate cheesesteaks every day when he would visit Philadelphia. As Burton watched Janet's sister Julia cooking the sausage, he started thinking about Philadelphia cheesesteaks which he probably craved regularly, as much as they craved the infamous Conecuh Sausage. Burton also reflected for a moment on one of the occasions that he was visiting Philadelphia as a child. Ann's husband Mike promised Burton that they would go and get some bar-b-que at this place in Germantown. Mike said to Burton repeatedly for almost two days that they were going to have some of the best bar-b-que in Philadelphia.

Finally, they went to get the bar-b-que that his uncle had him anticipating. Burton recalled the evening when they went to the little hole in the wall located on Germantown Avenue. They placed their order. The owner of the restaurant was there in the back cooking. Somehow Burton ended up meeting the owner of the establishment, only to find out he was from Mobile, Alabama. Burton found it humorous that the guy who made the best ribs in

Philadelphia was from Mobile.

Janet was seated at the kitchen table and she seemed to be in a fairly good mood today. Most of the arrangements and preparation for Beck's funeral had been completed. All she had to do was to go over to the church and let them know what readings she wanted from the Bible and get that over to the printer so she could complete the programs for the funeral. All of the photographs had been selected. Burton had completed his dad's obituary and gotten Janet's approval on it. The last thing she needed to do today was to meet with Kris at Good Shepherd Church and hammer out the church service for Beck's funeral and it was practically done.

It was a bit of a relief as she was still in the honeymoon stage of her grief and she had a house full of family there with her giving her love and support. Janet's two younger grandchildren where seated at the bar building Legos and her oldest grandson Breton was in the den watching television with his mom. Burton noticed Anna seated at the glass table in the Florida room at the typewriter. She was typing something on the typewriter. Janet did not really pay much attention to her, but Burton was curious to know what she was typing, since basically the obituary had been completed and there really wasn't much that needed to be typed at this point.

As he thought about it for a moment, he became even more concerned because it dawned on him that she might be trying to make changes to the Obituary that he had written. He had it the way he wanted it and had allowed his mother to review it and she approved what he had written. So why would she be making any changes to the document. He approached her and asked what she was typing.

"Aunt Ann, what are you so busy typing?" said Burton.

"Huh," said Anna.

"I said you sure are busy typing something on that typewriter," Burton said. "What are you typing?"

"Typing a letter, come over here and take a look," said Ann.

"A letter?" said Burton.

"I'm writing a letter to Walker's patients letting them know that he passed away," Anna said. "I'm almost finished with it, give me just a second and I'll let you take a look."

"A letter to my dad's patients?" said Burton.

"Yea, it's just a notification to them making them aware of Dr. LeFlore's passing," said Anna.

"That's nice but did my mom ask you to do that?" asked Burton.

"No," she replied.

"We don't need you to do that right now Aunt Ann," said Burton.

"I'm just trying to be helpful. His patients need to know he's dead so they can go and find another doctor," said Anna.

"I understand but several news stories just aired yesterday and today," said Burton.

"I'm almost finished with it," Ann said. "You and Janet take a look at it and decide what you want to do."

"If it needs to be done, either I will do it or my Mom will do it," Burton said. "We may decide to try and sell his entire practice to another doctor or group of physicians." Burton said, "We really don't know what we're going to do at this point or which direction we are going to go with that. So, you drafting a letter to his patients is a bit premature."

"I'm sorry, I was just trying to be helpful," said Anna.

"And there's certainly a lot of things we need help with, but that's not one of them," said Burton.

"Mom do you think we should send out a letter to dad's patients at this point?" said Burton.

"What do you think?" said Janet.

"I don't think its necessary right now," said Burton.

"Then I don't think its necessary right now either," said Janet.

"I'm just trying to be helpful," said Anna.

"That's fine, but we don't need you to worry about that when there are so many more pressing matters facing us," said Burton.

Janet busied herself getting the last-minute details arranged. Time was ticking down closer and closer to Beck's funeral. They practically had everything in order with the funeral home and the church. The wake was scheduled for Friday evening and the funeral was scheduled for Saturday at Good Shepherd Episcopal Church at Eleven O'clock in the morning. Ray LeFlore flew in on Friday morning as he had promised he would. Lamont LeFlore also arrived in town. Lamont was living somewhere in Georgia at the time. Many of Janet's siblings were in town for the funeral except her brother Peter and her sister Carol. Janet's sister Julia, Bethany, Anna, Warren and her niece Rita had traveled to Mobile to attend Beck's funeral. Burton's wife and his three children were also there. Janet had not heard from Beck's sister Ellen since she called to give her condolences right after she heard Beck had passed. Janet had a full house as she welcomed the company and the comfort that everyone tried to give her and Burton.

Later that evening they all went over to Allen and Johnson to attend Beck's wake. There were about thirty or forty people seated in the chapel as well as a few who just came in to pay their respects and leave. Burton was already there when Janet arrived with her sisters. Burton had been there for a while, for the most part he just stood there by his dad's casket viewing him as he lay resting in the eternal sarcophagus trying to internalize the fact that his father was actually dead.

Janet was accompanied by her brother Warren, Rita, Julia, Anna and Bethany. Ray was also there. Lamont however did not make it by the funeral home for the wake. He indicated to Burton that he needed to go and arrange for his dialysis treatments. Burton felt that Lamont had ample time to schedule his dialysis and make it to the funeral home that evening, but he did not say anything to Lamont about it. Burton's family was also there. They did not see Beck's sister Ellen.

There were a number of Walker's fraternity brothers who

had shown up to perform their fraternal funeral ritual to honor their fraternity brother who had died. Burton found this interesting since his dad had not been the most active with his fraternity over the years. However, he found the ritual at Beck's funeral service to be interesting and he learned something.

Janet's brother Warren was seated in the front row and he had a clear view of Walker's body. Warren was in the early stages of Alzheimer's and suffered from some memory loss. Although, he was still relatively alert and oriented. Warren sat there for a period of time as the look on his face became somewhat distressed. Burton watched Warren closely, and he noticed that Warren had not broken his gaze away from the casket where Walker was laid to rest. He did not look away and he did not look around. Warren must have sat there for about 5 minutes just staring at Walker. Burton sat next to Warren on the front row. He was not sure what was on Warren's mind, and he knew he had not gone to sleep because his eyes were blinking. Burton turned his head toward Warren as if to get his attention. Warren did not look his way, he continued to stare at his brother-in-law.

"Uncle Warren," said Burton.

"Who is that?" Warren said as he slowly turned his head toward Burton and pointed toward Walker.

"You don't know who that is?" asked Burton. "That's my dad, your brother-in-law, Walker," said Burton.

"Walker," Warren said with a dazed and confused look on his face. "Walker!? Walker's dead?" he said almost as though he was surprised and relieved at the same time.

"Who did you think that was?" asked Burton.

Warren hesitated for a second before he spoke, "I thought that was me," he said.

"You, no that's not you," Burton said. "That's Walker, you remember Walker don't you," said Burton.

"Yea I remember Walker," Warren said. "Janet's husband Walker. Your daddy."

"That's right," said Burton.

"I'm sorry to hear that," said Warren.

This was about the point where two of Dr. LeFlore's nurses walked into the funeral chapel and literally became hysterical when they saw Dr. LeFlore. Ethel and Ayanna both broke into a cry of shock and disbelief. Perhaps for them it was more-so coming to grips with the fact that they may be out of a job soon. Janet and the others turned around as they could hear Ayanna and Ethel in the aisle of the funeral chapel cutting up. Ethel and Ayanna eventually found a seat and quieted down a little. About that time, Walker's fraternity brothers assembled around the chapel and began their ritual service paying tribute to their departed fraternity brother. The crowd became quiet as the Alpha's joined hands and went through their ritual.

As for Janet this was a day leading up to a day that she had always known would probably come. The only other day that would possibly have come was her wake and upcoming funeral. She truly believed that her marriage to Beck was until death did them part. So here she was facing what she knew she might have to face, but not wanting to believe it still. As the Alpha's finished their ritual, they came over and shook her hand and embraced her as they extended their condolences to her. Some of them she knew, and some of them she had never seen before. She hugged them and shook hands with them as they all walked by the front row toward their seats.

Janet continued to feel hollow and numb as she greeted his fraternity brothers. This was the day before the day she had always dreaded. She appreciated her family being there with her through this time. She decided she would have to ride this wave because it was the wave that had been dealt to her. There was nothing more she could do.

It was not long before they went back to the house following the wake. Burton stayed as long as he could. He went back and stood by the casket and stayed with his dad as long as he could. Eventually, Ray and Beck's friend Percy joined him and suggested that Burton should leave with everyone else. Burton could have just stayed there with his dad. He wanted desperately to spend whatever final moments he could spend with his father's flesh, even though he knew his dad's soul had gone on to glory. Burton agreed to head out with them after pausing there for another moment in silence with his father. Janet proceeded to the car with Warren and her sisters. Candace, Rita and the kids rode together. Ray rode with Burton back to the house.

"Jeannie, are you alright?" said Bethany. "Is there a store around here were we can stop and get some wine?"

"There's a Delchamps not too far from here," Janet replied.

"We got some wine at home," said Julia.

"If you're talking about the wine we had last night, it's gone," said Anna.

"We can stop by the store, it's not far," Janet said. "Just make a left."

"What street is this?" said Anna.

"Broad Street," Janet said. "Make a left."

They all went to the store and purchased a few snacks and some wine. Following the grocery store, they proceeded to the house. Janet and the others settled in for the evening. Two bottles of Barefoot wine on the table and some potato salad, tuna fish, fried chicken, mac and cheese were all at the house having been brought over by some of Janet's neighbors and friends. Janet was nibbling at the food as Anna came into the kitchen wearing her night gown. Rita, Warren, Bethany, Ray and Candace were already seated at the bar or standing around in the kitchen area talking.

Anna popped the first bottle of Barefoot wine and started pouring herself a glass. Janet got a glass for herself and the others at the bar. Ray poured himself a glass of Vodka, and Warren indicated that he also wanted a shot of the Vodka. Ray poured Warren a shot. Burton got a beer out of the refrigerator. He fixed himself a cup of ice and poured the beer over the ice. Everyone gathered around preparing helpings of food and having drinks.

"Jeannie, how are you holding up sister?" asked Bethany.

"As well as can be expected," she sighed. "It's so nice to

have all of you, my family here."

"Janet we would not have missed our brother-in-law's funeral for anything," Anna said. "This is what we do. We are your sisters, your family." she said as she hugged Janet.

"We know this is a tough time for you sweetheart," Julia said. "Jeannie its times like these, when family has to show up for one another."

"Here let me pour you a glass of wine," said Anna.

"I would really prefer a glass of champagne," replied Janet.

"Champagne it is sister," said Anna.

"I can't begin to tell you how much it means to me," Janet said. "And Ray thank you so much for turning around and coming back," said Janet.

"Janet, don't even mention it," Ray said. "I'm honored to be here to celebrate Walker's life."

"Ray was here last weekend when Beck passed, and he found it in his heart to fly back to Mobile from New York again for Beck's funeral," said Janet.

"Ray you were here last weekend when Beck passed?" said Bethany.

"Yes, after talking with Burton I decided to come down," replied Ray.

"What part of New York do you live in?" asked Rita.

"I live in Manhattan, on the lower east side, 31st between Second and Third." said Ray.

"I come up there occasionally to visit my two sons." Rita said, "Two of my boys live in Brooklyn."

"I'll give you my number, give us a call sometimes when you're in town," replied Ray.

"Janet," said Warren.

"Yes Poopie, what is it?" replied Janet.

"I'm a little hungry, what you got to eat?" asked Warren.

"We got plenty of food Poopie, what do you want?" Janet asked. "We got potato salad, fried chicken?"

"Daddy what do you want, I got it Aunt Janet," said Rita.

"Here Warren eat a little of this mac and cheese, it's delicious," said Julia.

"I'll take a piece of chicken and some of that," said Warren.

"The plates are in that cabinet right there," Janet said. "Right there," she said as she pointed toward the kitchen cabinet in the left-hand corner.

"There is some Gumbo in the refrigerator if anyone wants some," Burton said. "I had a friend of mine make me some, and it is excellent. You won't find any better Gumbo than hers."

"Burton why don't you put it on the stove and heat it up," said Janet.

Burton took the pot of Gumbo out of the refrigerator and placed it on the stove. He turned the heat on medium low so that it would heat up some. He also took a container of rice and placed it on the table. After taking out the Gumbo and rice, Burton left the crowd and went outside to his car. As he walked to the car by himself, he was thinking about his son Breton. The two of them had hardly said a word to each other since Candace and the kids had arrived in Mobile.

Burton had for the most part ignored Breton and it was relatively easy to do so with everything going on and all the people in the house. Burton was still quite upset and angry with his son, following the fight they had a few weeks earlier. Burton was hurting so bad inside and he wondered if his son was hurting too. Here he was about to bury his father tomorrow and he and his own son were not on good terms. Burton did not know exactly how he was going to smooth things out with Breton, and all the same make him understand that he was not going to tolerate the way he had behaved. Burton opened the door to the car. He could see his son Breton coming out behind him.

"Hey," Breton said. "Hey Dad."

"Hay is for horses as your granddad always used to say," Burton said. "How are you?"

"I'm alright," said Breton. "How about you Dad?"

"I've had better days," said Burton.

"I just find it hard to believe Granddaddy is dead," said Breton.

"Yep it's difficult for me to believe it myself," replied Burton. "I'm going to miss him a lot."

"Yea, me too," said Breton.

"You sure look nice," said Burton.

"Yea thanks for the suit," said Breton.

"It looks good on you," Burton said. "You look like a rather dignified young man."

"Dad I don't know what I would do if you died," said Breton.

"Well Breton we're all going to die one day and that is about the only thing that's absolutely certain in life, and that is why sons shouldn't attack their dad's and why a father never wants to fight his own child. Because someone could die." Burton said, "I would never have stepped to that man, my father, the way you stepped to me. But if you step to me like that again, I got something for you."

"I'm sorry, Dad! I'm so sorry," Breton said as he started to cry. "I'm sorry Dad."

Burton saw the tears streaming from his son's eyes as he reached out and embraced him. Tears came to his eyes, "Come here son, it's gonna be alright. Everything's going to be alright."

"I just made everything worse, and now Granddaddy is gone!" Breton said. "Granddaddy always used to try so hard to help everybody and make sure everything was alright for everybody."

"I know," Burton said as he hugged his son. A teardrop streamed down Burton's face.

"I loved Granddaddy," said Breton.

"I loved him too, and I love you son," Burton said. "We got to stay strong for him."

"I love you, Dad," said Breton. "I'm so sorry," he said.

"Son you don't know how much I love you and how much it means to hear that from you right now," Burton said. "These last few days and weeks haven't been easy. One thing is for sure, I may have lost my pops, but I'm a dad and I know your grandfather would want me to try and be the best father I can be to my kids."

"Dad, I'm going to try and be the best son I can be," said Breton.

"And at the end of the day, that is all we can do, try to be the best we can be toward all and one another," said Burton. "Come on let's go inside," said Burton as he and Breton went into the house.

The night continued on as the family sat around with Janet drinking wine and snacking. Burton was so relieved that he and Breton had patched things up between them. Here he was about to bury his father tomorrow and he and his own son were not getting along. Burton was glad that he did not have to face what he had to face on Saturday while holding a grudge against his own child. The crowd seemed to be growing tired as Warren had already eaten, had his shot of liquor and gone to bed. Janet saw Burton walk into the house with Breton. She did not recognize any noticeable tension between the two of them. She hoped in her heart that Burton had found a way to forgive his son for the altercation between them. Janet took another sip of her champagne.

She looked around at her sisters, Julia, Anna and Bethany; her niece Rita, and Beck's cousin Ray to make sure they were all comfortable. Janet glanced over at her daughter in law who was pregnant and plump as she could be, overflowing with new life that would soon come into the LeFlore family. Candace said she did not want to know the sex of the child but somehow, they all knew it was a boy. Candace was standing there at the end of the table, she did not say much. She was about seven months pregnant at the time. Janet thought to herself, what an irony it was, a life had departed and yet here another life was on the way. Janet found herself as many people have, on top of an enormous abyss of sorrow. With family and friends around her, holding her hand preventing her from falling into that abyss even though she is hanging right over the middle of it, as if suspended in air. She knew soon this gathering would be over and she would have to face the demons of her loneliness, sadness, heartache and sorrow. It was not long before everyone had gone to bed.

The next morning, the limousines from the funeral home showed up at approximately 10:00 am. There were two limousines waiting in front of Janet and Beck's house as the family arrived and got into the cars to be transported to the Good Shepherd Church for Beck's Funeral service. The church was not far from the house. It was a quiet and somber ride to the church. There was not a lot of conversation or chatter on the way as they arrived at the church.

Janet disembarked the limo accompanied by her sisters. Her husband was waiting for her at the church. Almost exactly as it was when a couple marries, he was waiting for her at the altar. Although, this time it was not a celebration of their marriage or future together. It was a celebration of all the days and years they had shared together. It was the end, not the beginning. It was the, "Till death did us part." The culmination of all the happiness and heartache. It was the resolution of all the beginnings and endings and all the days and nights together. Here was the man she had met over fifty years ago, waiting to say his final goodbye. This was her final goodbye. How was she going to handle being without him? How was she going to endure going into this church and praying to God when her heart was so heavy, distraught and dejected? She felt like a piece of her was missing and gone forever. Janet was about to walk into this house of God, this church and fixate herself on a coffin that contained her husband's remains.

Janet was stepping into the beginning of the end. As she thanked God for the many great and wonderful days she spent with her husband Dr. Walker (Beck) LeFlore, she also thought about the tough days and the difficult moments she spent with Beck. She knew in her soul, that she would not have traded a single day of life with Beck. She and Beck were soul mates and they had maintained their lives together and succeeded beyond belief.

Janet, Burton, Candace and his kids made their way into the church followed by the rest of the family. Beck's casket was placed there before the altar at the front of the church. It was a sad and somber moment. The funeral began and lasted for a little over an hour. Almost the entire experience was a blur for Janet. It had to be one of the saddest days of her life. She stared at the casket sitting there before her and she kept thinking to herself that her husband was inside of that thing. She thought to herself that she would never see him again, at least until she was one day laid to rest in one of those boxes. The priest read some passages from the scripture that she had selected earlier in the week. Beck's best friend, the now Reverend Percy Johnson, delivered the eulogy. Percy delivered an impassioned and energetic eulogy which probably came very easy for him.

The two of them had been very close friends over the years. Janet listened to Percy deliver the Eulogy. She thought it was beautiful, the way Percy spoke about his friend Walker. It dawned on Janet that for all the years that they had been friends and all of the time they spent together enjoying each other's company and companionship, she never imagined it would be Percy standing here in the church delivering a eulogy on Beck's behalf. She thought to herself, that Percy was not even a pastor when he and Beck first met.

At any rate, she and Burton had agreed there was no person better to give the eulogy, than Beck's old drinking buddy. The two of them had certainly had some good times together. Janet found it hard to focus on everything he said, because she kept staring at the casket where Beck's body lay. It seemed like some weird music continued to play in her head but there was nothing playing, not even in the church at the time. She could not make any sense of the music or the words that were being said. Although, she heard every word, the words just seemed to go into one ear and out of the other as she could not manage to take her eyes off the casket positioned there in front of her. The church was practically full. People all around; however, for a moment there she felt all alone as if she was the only one sitting there with that dearly departed box in front of her. That unapologetic thing that is usually the last way you see them before they truly become a part of your soul and your recollections.

Janet felt her sister Julia put her arm around her as she handed her a handkerchief to wipe the tears from her face. Following the eulogy, her sister Anna took herself up to the pulpit and said a few words. Anna spoke about the first time that Janet brought Walker home with her to meet Mamma, Poppa and the Owens family. Anna said that she remembered how handsome Walker was and how all of her sisters fell in love with Walker when they first met him so many years ago. Janet went back in her mind to that day, as Anna spoke. She wished that she could step back in time to that day and start their lives all over again. Although that day had long since passed and she was caught in the reality of this day.

Burton went to the pulpit and thanked everyone for attending. Janet could hear the sadness in his voice as he spoke, and she could see the mournful expression on his face as he briefly addressed the crowd. Janet knew this must have been a difficult time for her son Burton. She wished like most mothers that there was something she could do to change what he was going through. However, she knew they were both at the point of no return. Their lives would forever be changed.

Her husband, his father was gone and there was nothing they could do to change it. Burton had tried his best to be there every step of the way since Beck's need for care had intensified shortly before his death. Janet greatly appreciated Burton being there for her and Beck. After Burton made his statements, the funeral service was concluded, and they left the church in route to Magnolia Cemetery.

Following the interment ceremony and prayer, everyone was dismissed and told it was alright to go home. After everyone had basically left Burton stayed behind. Burton did something that was a little strange. Burton asked the funeral director for the key to Beck's casket. He requested that it be opened. The funeral director complied with Burton's wishes, even though he thought it was a little odd for him to ask such a thing. Burton opened the casket and saw his father's lifeless body inside. He paused for a moment and took a last look, before closing it back and locking it, Burton wanted to make sure that his dad was inside that box, since he had not seen it opened before the funeral. Burton told the limousine to wait for him or they could go to the house and take some of the others and come back and get him. The driver who was a very attractive German woman, stated that she would go to their house and drop off the family members in her car and come back for him. Burton's wife Candace remained there with Burton.

Burton asked how long it was going to be before the bulldozer would be around to complete the burial. In a distance they could see the bulldozer and it appeared to be headed in their direction toward the cemetery plot. Burton wanted to stay until the burial was completed. Burton was used to the old school way people were buried, when they actually interred the body in the ground and covered the vault before the family left the graveside. Recently funeral directors started ending the services while the body was still above ground. Everyone promptly leaves and they have no idea what happens to their loved one after they are gone.

Given the controversy and dispute, Burton had with the funeral home concerning the casket he purchased for his dad, he wanted to make sure it went into the ground with him. He knew the funeral home was not happy with the price they got for the box and he was going to make sure he got what he had paid for, with no monkey business.

The bulldozer eventually made it over to the grave site and lowered the top of the vault onto the casket. Burton stood there watching as this process took place. Candace took a seat on the grass on the opposite side of the plot and watched along with him. He watched as they committed his parent to the earth and his eternal resting place. Simply leaving after the interment ceremony did not give Burton the closure he needed. He often wondered how other families found it so easy to walk away and jump into their cars without knowing their loved one was properly buried. Burton certainly felt that he would rest better knowing he had stayed and made sure. It was simply how Burton felt. And he certainly was not going to let the funeral home pull a fast one on him. It was not long before the burial was complete. Burton felt assured that he would not be wondering if the funeral home had switched his dad's box because they did not get the price they wanted for it. The driver returned to pick them up and they went on back to the church with the rest of the family.

By the time Burton got back to the church for the repass it was just about over. Everyone had made it back to the house and by now, just about everyone had changed clothes and gotten comfortable and were sitting around the table talking or watching television. Several families from the church also stopped by to fraternize following the funeral. The doorbell started ringing and before long the house was filled with guests, friends and family. Janet was surrounded by a lot of love and support as people dropped off more dishes and stopped by to visit with her and the family.

She decided she better try and enjoy this time and moment because it would not be long before everyone would be gone, and she would be there alone and empty without her wonderful Beck who she had loved so much for so many years.

Bethany invited Sabina, the sexy german limousine driver over to the house after the funeral. When she brought Burton and Candace back to the house, she parked the car, turned it off and accompanied them into the house. When they arrived back at the house, Bethany greeted them at the front door and again invited Sabina to come in. Sabina accepted the invitation and came along to hang out with the rest of the family. Naturally this was a social family gathering, and it was only inevitable that there would be some drama as long as Candace was involved. As soon as Candace realized Bethany had invited this pretty lady to join the family at the house, she started asking Burton why his

Aunt Bethany had invited the driver from the funeral home to socialize with their family. Burton immediately stated that he had no idea why she invited her and asked why it mattered anyway. Burton had just buried his dad and he was emotionally into his feelings at this point and was in no way concerned with the limo driver. As far as Burton was concerned, they were still celebrating his father's life. The more the merrier. Candace started to become agitated at the idea of Sabina being there at the house.

Candace started to follow Burton around the house as he was trying to unwind from everything that had just transpired. She questioned him again about the lady Bethany had asked to come and socialize with them at the residence following the funeral. Burton could not believe it, here he had just buried his father and now his wife Candace was hassling him about some woman that he did not know, who had been asked to hang out at the house by his aunt. On the other hand, Burton could believe it. This was the nightmare he had been living for many years. If it was not Sabina, it would have been something else.

This was a funeral which had now culminated into an after burial social function. There had to be some sort of conflict going on. Certainly, his dad had passed, and he had just buried him, but there was not about to be extended any sort of comfort zone for him to relax and collect his thoughts without being harassed by Candace.

The situation was about to go down, and it would not be long before she became involved in a confrontation with the unsuspecting Sabina. Candace was going to confront her for nothing, and then play the innocent pregnant one. Certainly, some would say, it was only because she was pregnant, but Burton knew it did not make a bit of difference if she was pregnant or not. Candace was going to cause some issues and there was going to be some sort of confrontation. It is the only way a control freak can desperately attempt to control the situation or circumstances over which they have no control. She stated to Burton that his aunt was trying to cause problems between them by asking this woman to come and socialize with the family.

Burton stated to Candace that it only had to be a problem if she made it one. He clearly indicated to his wife that he loved her and was so happy that they were about to have another baby together. He told Candace if she had any love and compassion for him, she would kindly leave him alone and stop bothering him. It did not matter to her if he had just buried his father, plain and simple it was about to go down. Candace had identified her target and she was ready.

If Burton was not going to put Sabina out of the house, she was going to make sure that she was put out all the same. Burton was not going to ask her to leave because he had no reason to do so. She was cute and she seemed like a nice person to him. Burton was not concerned with her presence. He was more concerned with why his wife could not see that he needed her understanding, comfort and love. Burton understood one thing after all the years with her, he was not about to get it. Very much like he did not get it the night doctors told Burton that Beck was dying and he and his son got into a fight.

Inevitably, Candace stopped talking with Burton about her disapproval of Sabina being there at the house. She approached this woman and confronted her for no reason and started to antagonize her. She started an argument with her. She made it perfectly clear that she disapproved of Bethany's decision to invite her to the house and was therefore willing to go to war with Bethany as well if her plan to harass Sabina and get her put out got foiled. Candace is a crazed woman who will go to any and all lengths to win a petty confrontation initiated by her.

Of course, Candace would ultimately and later argue that she had no choice but to stand her ground against this evil and vindictive woman who she had never met in her life. Surely, she would be a sympathetic character since she was pregnant and obviously grieving the death of her father-in-law. Somehow Candace always had a way of making it all about her. She always had a way of starting something out of absolutely nothing and now was going to be no exception.

After Sabina had been chased off by Candace, Burton wondered what would be next. He understood fully there was going to be no holiday or vacation from the toxicity and the venom that he lived with on a daily basis with this woman. There would be no, I realized your dad passed and it would be appropriate and kind to give you the respect of knowing you might be hurting inside. None of that was about to happen. Not today, it was going to be all about her and that was for sure.

The rest of the ladies at the house including Janet quickly tried to neutralize the situation and make sure that Candace understood this evening was not about to be about her and her feelings. The women in the house agreed to allow Savina to be escorted to the door basically for her protection; however, they made it perfectly clear to Candace that she would need to go and sit herself down somewhere because there would be no more conversation or debate about her predicament or concerns.

Burton drifted further into his own world. He disliked seeing Sabina mistreated in his home for no reason. Even most importantly, he once again had to internalize that even on the day of his father's funeral, his wife could not suppress turmoil and drama into the situation and just be at peace. Burton wanted so bad to try and come to terms with himself and the loss of his father. Even on one of the worst days of his life, she somehow had to make it even worse and try to play the victim afterward.

Everyone liked Sabina and had no problem with her congregating with the family, so needless to say some were upset that she had basically been forced to leave. According to Candace, all of those women knew what Bethany had done, and what they were doing. They were against her. Burton just looked at her in total disbelief. He really could have cared less if she was there or not. He simply wondered if now he could be left alone to work through his emotions and try to deal with his loss without being badgered constantly by his pregnant wife. As a matter of fact, he was absolutely not going to continue any type of conversation with her that did not center around how he was going to somehow deal with his mind body and spirit following the loss of his father.

As far as Burton was concerned, once again, Sabina had nothing to do with his problem with his wife. He did not even know the woman. The primary issue was, why did Candace want to make such a fuss about Sabina when Burton did not even know her. Burton could not understand why his wife could not have maintained her focus on them; on him and helping him get through this ordeal. Here she was pregnant with baby number four. Why would she want to cause a commotion at the house following the funeral for no reason? For what would she want to put her husband through that unnecessarily when there was absolutely no cause for her to be concerned about Sabina in anyway.

The evening following the funeral proceeded on into the night as friends stopped by to visit with Janet to offer their condolences. Janet invited her company into the living room of the house, and they all sat around and talked and shared stories. There was a steady stream of people between the living room and the kitchen. There were a number of dishes in the house from people who had brought food by the house. In addition, her sisters had prepared a few dishes also. She and Walker's nephew Lamont was there, he sequestered himself in front of the television.

Lamont had not attended his uncle's funeral or his wake. Janet thought it odd that Lamont had rushed to Mobile saying that he wanted to go to Beck's funeral and then ended up not going. However, she was too caught up in everything else going on to be worried about him. As Janet sat in the living room chatting with her family and friends, she could not stop thinking about her husband who had been laid to rest in the cemetery today. Today was his first night of eternal rest. She wondered how she would be able to handle never seeing him again.

The next morning, Janet was awakened by her sister

Anna. She was still tired and not quite ready to get up yet. Janet wondered how Anna had managed to awaken so early since they had been up very late the night before. She really wished that her sister had not bothered her, but she was sure that she meant well.

"How are you doing this morning?" asked Anna.

"Still sleepy," Janet replied. "What time is it anyway? You're up early."

"It's about 7 a.m., How did you sleep last night?" asked Anna.

"I've had better nights," Janet said. "I tossed and turned most of the night even though I was utterly exhausted. Just really fell asleep about two hours ago."

"I didn't sleep well last night either," Anna said.

"I used to sleep on the other side of the bed. This was Beck's side of the bed," Janet said. "An old lady once told me that if you ever lost your husband, you should start sleeping on his side of the bed. It's a way that you can stay closer to your husband even though he might be gone. I don't think I'm ever going to change these sheets either. These were the last sheets he slept on."

"I can't say I've ever heard that old wives' tale," said Anna.

"I would try anything right about now," Janet said. "If it weren't for Burton, I probably would have just let them bury me right along with him. I loved that man so much," said Janet.

"I know how much you loved Walker," Anna said. "I know how much you must be hurting inside right now, Janet," said Ann.

"I wouldn't wish this on my worst enemy," she said.

"Thought I would come and see if you wanted to have a cup of coffee with me?" Anna said. "I started a pot and it should be ready in a few minutes."

"A cup of coffee would be nice," said Janet as she struggled to smile.

"I can fix us some breakfast if you're hungry," said Anna.

"I ate so much last night, I'm about to pop," Janet said. "I can wait a little while until the others wake up."

"Have you read Walker's Will yet?" asked Anna.

"Yes, I was there with him when he had it prepared," Janet said. "He left everything to me."

"He didn't leave Burton anything?" asked Anna.

"No but it doesn't really matter. He is going to get it all when I pass away, and he can have whatever he wants. I don't care. It's his anyway," Janet said as she sat up on the side of the bed.

"I didn't know Walker had issues with Burton like that," said Anna.

"Beck didn't have any issues with Burton," Janet said. "Beck loved the ground that Burton walks on. He did however have some issues with his wife. Beck wasn't a big fan of Candace."

"Whaaat?" said Anna.

"Oh yea," Janet replied.

"I'm sure Walker had his reasons and he knew what he was doing," said Anna.

"Candace had the audacity to stand right there in that kitchen one night and said to Beck, 'When you die, I am going to get everything you have.' "Janet said, "Beck was heartbroken. A few days later Beck went and had his Will redrafted and he took Burton out of it."

"I just don't see how you're going to be able to do it all Janet," Ann said.

"One thing is for sure, Beck left me comfortably and I have my retirement and social security coming in," Janet said. "I don't have to worry about money."

"Well if you," Anna said before Janet cut her off.

"Beck left me $500,000.00 in life insurance benefits and he has close to $1,200,000.00 in his retirement 401 K," said Janet.

"Walker certainly provided well for you Jeannie," Anna said. "If there is," she said.

"And they could have it all, every dime of it, if I could just have my Beck back, happy and healthy and with me again."

"There's one thing for sure," Anna said. "That's not going to happen. Walker's not coming back and you've got to decide what you're going to do with that money."

"I'll probably give most of it to Burton," Janet replied. "He has a family and they have another baby on the way," she said. "Isn't that something, they have another baby on the way."

"Candace walking around here just as plump as a Thanksgiving Turkey," said Anna.

"She said she didn't know if it was going to be a boy or a girl," said Janet.

"Sister, if there is anything I can help you with let me know," Anna said. "I mean that, if you need anything don't hesitate to call me."

"Thank you, Ann, I appreciate that.," said Janet.

"What are Burton's plans, he's planning to stay in Wilmington isn't he?" asked Anna.

"No, I don't think so," Janet said. "He's been taking a Real Estate Broker's course the last few months, and he has passed his exam. I believe he is planning to come back here to Mobile with his family and get into the real estate business."

"He doesn't really have much interest in practicing law, does he?" asked Anna.

"Not really, it doesn't seem like it," Janet said. "If he does come back here, I'm going to let him take over managing all of me and Beck's property." Janet said, "You know before Burton was born, I was starting to think I wasn't going to be able to have any more children, and when he came into this world it was such a blessing for me and Beck."

"I remember Jeannie," said Anna.

"He is still one of the biggest blessings in my life, and his little family is so adorable," Janet said. "I love my grand babies so much." She said, "And he has another one on the way."

"Well Jeannie like I said, if there is anything I can do to

help you in any way just let me know," Anna said. "I'm just a phone call away."

"I'll keep that in mind Ann," said Janet.

"That coffee should be ready by now," Anna said. "Let me fix you a cup."

"Thank you and good morning to you too," said Janet.

It wasn't long before the rest of the family had awakened and gathered around the kitchen table. Anna and Bethany prepared a quick breakfast of grits, Conecuh Sausage and melon. Everyone sat around eating their breakfast and drinking coffee and juice. As Janet sat there nibbling at her breakfast it dawned on her that this was the first day of the rest of her life alone without her husband Beck.

She looked around at Burton and his children; her sisters and brother Warren; Ray, her niece Rita and her nephew Lamont. She felt a brief wave of desperation as she tried so hard to enjoy this moment with her family around. She knew in a few days they would all be gone. She would probably be sitting there at that same table by herself missing her husband like never before. The phone rang and it was her sister Carol.

"Hey Cabbie," said Janet.

"Jeannie, how are you doing this morning," said Carol.

"Is that Carol on the phone?" asked Julia.

"You doing alright today Jeannie?" asked Carol. "I know these last few days have been hard for you. So, what are y'all up to this morning?"

"Just sitting around eating breakfast right now," said Janet.

"Tell Cabbie I said, hey sister," said Anna.

"Ann said hello," said Janet.

"Tell everyone I said hello," said Carol.

"She said hello to everybody," said Janet.

"Jeannie make sure she is going to be able to come down here in a couple days," Bethany said. "We don't want you to be by yourself right now."

"Bethany wants to know if you are still going to come down here and spend a few days with me?" Janet asked.

"Janet, what did I tell you," Carol said. "I'm going to be there for you, sister."

"I'm going to call and make you a reservation today," Janet said. "I promise."

"Why don't you bring Cheryl?" said Anna.

"No, I think Cheryl is going to stay here in Hampton," Carol said. "I'm going to come down there and spend some one on one time with you."

"OK then some one on one time it is," said Janet.

"Tell Cabbie we miss her down here?" said Julia.

"Did you hear that? Julia said to tell you we miss you," said Janet.

"I miss you guys too," said Carol. "Jeannie I just wanted to check on you this morning and make sure you were alright. I'll let you get back to breakfast and plan to see you later in the week."

"OK Cabbie, I'll give you a call later tonight before you go to bed," said Janet.

"Give everybody a big hug and kiss for me Jeannie, talk with you later," Carol said. "Love you and see you in a few days."

Later in the afternoon on that picturesque and warm southern Sunday in October they went outside and sat on the lawn chairs and just talked and laughed. Burton cooked some hamburgers and hot dogs on the grill. It was not long before Ray LeFlore had to get to the airport to fly back to New York. He said his goodbyes to everyone. He and Burton left so that he could get to the airport in time for his flight. Everyone else just sat out there in Janet's huge back yard until it was almost dark talking.

Janet's sisters had planned to head back home themselves on Tuesday morning. Her brother Warren and his daughter Rita flew out of Mobile on Monday to go back to Hampton, Virginia. Monday was pretty much like Sunday. Everyone started their morning in the kitchen with coffee and breakfast and then moved out to the back yard to enjoy the great October weather in sunny Mobile, Alabama. Burton's wife and kids left heading back to North Carolina;

however, Burton remained in Mobile to help his mother with her affairs. It was his plan to remain in Mobile until right around the time his new baby was expected. They were going to let Breton finish out the semester in school. Burton had no plans to go back to Wilmington other than to pack up their belongings and move them back to Mobile.

There was a house that he and Candace had looked at before they moved to Wilmington right around the corner from his mom. Burton had found out the house was still on the market, so he and Candace had discussed making an offer on the house. Burton decided that as soon as he had a chance, he was going to go back and take another look at the house and make an offer on it. Basically, his plan was to help his Janet and be there with her, while making arrangements to move his family back to Mobile. He was excited about starting his real estate business there and looking forward to the future. Burton missed his father, but he decided to focus on being a dad himself. He felt like the more time and energy he spent with his kids the less time he would have to sit around feeling depressed. Burton knew deep down inside that is what his father would want him to do anyway. He was soon to be the father of four children, and it was time for him to get it together for his family and for his mom who now also needed him more than ever.

Janet's nephew Lamont LeFlore was still there at her house. He had been very quiet for the last few days. He was sleeping in the den on Janet's sofa, and had not said much at all to anyone for the last few days. Lamont pretty much stayed out of the way and kept to himself. He did not attend his uncle's funeral or wake. He asked his Aunt Janet if he could stay with her for a few days because he related to her that he was interested in moving back to Mobile himself. Janet agreed to let him stay there with her for a few more days, even after the rest of the family went back home. Janet did not necessarily want to be bothered with Lamont, but she did not want to be alone either, so she agreed.

As soon as Burton realized Lamont was going to be staying at the house for a few more days following the funeral he made sure that he took anything pertaining to his father's personal or financial affairs out of the house and over to the office. He was now skeptical of Lamont's motives for having wanted to come. Burton knew his mom was vulnerable and he felt it necessary to make sure there was nothing at the house that he could get his hands on. Burton knew how trusting Janet was, and he was not about to allow Lamont to take advantage of her in any way. Certainly not the way he had taken advantage of their Grandmother while she was living, when he stole over Ten Thousand Dollars from her.

Burton also knew how his dad felt about Lamont and how Lamont felt about his dad. The two of them did not like each other one bit. Beck never forgave him for stealing all of that money from Teah. Burton started to wonder if Lamont was just lying in wait until he had the opportunity to find out whatever he could about his uncle's estate and either steal or try and talk Janet into giving him some money. Burton had also noticed the Three hundred dollars he had hidden in a box under his bed was gone. He was not going to accuse Lamont or anyone, because there had been a lot of people in the house over the last few days.

However, he felt there was a strong possibility that Lamont might have taken the money. Lamont was about the only person who had been at the house by himself for any period of time. Tuesday morning Janet's sisters Bethany, and Julia were preparing to depart and head back to their respective homes in North Carolina, Virginia and Pennsylvania. They brought their bags down and placed them near the doorway as they said their goodbyes to Janet. Burton got the key to Ann's Mercedes and loaded the bags into the car for them.

"Jeannie as much as we hate to go, we must go my dear," Julia said. "We love you sister."

"I wish you guys could stay with me a little longer," said Janet.

"It's so sad," Anna said. "I wish we could stay a few more days too."

"Jeannie, you know if you need me, just call me," said Bethany.

"Thank you, guys, so much, I don't know what I would have done if y'all hadn't been there," replied Janet.

"Jeannie you needn't say a word," Anna said. "That is what family is for and time's like this when family just has to show up."

"And you guys certainly showed up and I thank you so much," said Janet.

"Jeannie do you mind if I take this Peace Lilly back home with me?" Bethany asked. "I think I have a place for it, somewhere at the house where I would like to put it, if you don't mind."

"Sure, Burton will you put that in the car for Bethany," said Janet.

"Are you talking about that one Aunt Bethany," Burton said as he pointed at the Peace Lilly sitting in the corner near the back door.

"Yes, Burton that's the one, if you wouldn't mind putting it in the car for Aunt Bethany, I would appreciate it," said Bethany.

"Janet I'll be calling you every day to make sure you are doing OK," Julia said. "You can expect that phone call from me every day at least for the next few weeks. I'm gonna be checking on you sister."

"And we won't hesitate to come back down here if you need us Jeannie," said Anna.

"We'll see about that," replied Janet.

"Who's got the camera?" said Julia.

"Yea let's take a few pictures before we leave," said Ann.

"Hold on, I think I have it here in my purse," said Bethany reaching into her purse.

"I've got my camera right here," Burton said. "Everybody, get together a little closer and let me take a few photos so we can remember this moment in time."

"How is that?" asked Anna as she put her arms around her sisters and posed.

"Fine, got it." Burton said, "Let me take a few more."

"Take a few with my camera too Burton," said Bethany.

"Ok everyone smile," Burton said. "Give me the other camera."

"Smile Jeannie," Julia said. "Everybody smile."

"Jeannie, we got to get on the road," said Ann.

"Please drive safely and no speeding ," Janet said.

"You know Ann will put the pedal to the medal in a minute," said Bethany.

"We'll all take turns driving, we got a long drive back," said Julia.

"If you guys will just call me every once in a while, and say hey sister, how you doing?" Janet said. "That would make all the difference in the world."

"Have a safe trip," Burton said. "Thanks for coming."

"Bye," they all said as they drove out of the driveway and down the street.

CHAPTER SEVEN

Not long after her sister left Janet started to feel the loneliness and sorrow, she had been dreading for days. Her jaw started hurting her again. It was throbbing and pulsating so bad that she had to go to her room almost immediately to lay down for a minute. Burton asked her if she was alright and she explained that her jaw was hurting. When she made it to her bedroom to lay down, she laid on Beck's side of the bed and took her pillow between her arms. She thought about Beck and wished that he was there holding her in his arms. She wondered how she was going to sleep at night without him beside her, and how she was going to go through the days to come without him in her life.

She cried quietly there in her bed. She did not want Burton to hear her crying. She just wanted to be there in that spot where Beck used to lay his head. Her jaw was hurting her so much she almost wanted to scream. Her heart and soul were in such pain she wondered how she could take it. Janet laid there for a moment and said a prayer asking God to give her the strength to get through this and to please ease the pain in her jaw. She wanted to take a pain killer but decided to just endure the pain because she felt it was too early in the day, and she did not want to be groggy. Janet wondered what she was going to do with herself, now that her other half of more than fifty years was gone.

Burton started going into Beck's office to work on getting his real estate company started and to tending to the matters pertaining to his father's estate. He and Janet had agreed that he would serve as executor. Burton was honored that his mom had asked him to serve as executor of his father's estate, and he set out to make sure he expedited everything that needed to be done to get the ball rolling. Every day he would go into the office and spend about half of the day, implementing the start of his new business and he would spend the other half of the day tending to his Mom and Dad's affairs. He wanted to prove to his Mom that things were going to be done properly and that she could feel secure in knowing it was being taken care of. Burton created the new signs for his company. He met with his parents' tenants to let them know they would need to contact him if they had any problems and that he was going to be managing their property. He also worked with Beck's staff to wind up some of the affairs related to Beck's medical practice.

As the days went by Janet felt hollow inside, but she continued to persevere. Janet sent her sister Carol a plane ticket and she came to visit as she had promised. Beck's nephew Lamont was also still there staying with her. Meanwhile, Burton stayed between his house and Janet's house. For the most part, he was staying there with his Mom, but some nights he would go to his house and stay. He was spending a lot of time at the office working. Janet was glad to have Carol's company.

Carol was very understanding about what Janet may have been going through. Carol had lost her husband many years before. For now, she and Janet were the only two widows in the family. She was patient and understanding with her sister as she knew she was going through a difficult time. Janet was even happy to have Lamont there with her. Lamont had now come out of his shell and had resumed being his gregarious, verbose and overly talkative self. Since Janet said it was alright for him to stay, Burton did not protest. However, he did feel Lamont was up to something and took every step possible to make sure he would not get away with it. Burton and Lamont talked, and he was not rude to Lamont. In a way, it was almost like Lamont was acting as a surrogate for Champ who would have been about the same age as Lamont if he was still living. Janet was, for now, taking depression and life one day, one step at a time.

"Aunt Janet, I appreciate you letting me stay here with you for a minute," Lamont said. "I've been thinking about moving back to Mobile for a while. I'm up in Athens, Georgia right now and I'm just getting tired of it," he said. "It's a little slower pace town than I'm used to. I'm on Dialysis now and I need to be somewhere near a decent facility where I can get my treatments three times a week."

"You've got to go three times a week to dialysis," said Janet.

"Yes, I got to go Monday, Wednesday and Friday or Tuesday, Thursday and Saturday," Lamont said. "At least three times a week. My life depends on it. I had kidney failure, its either that or get a kidney transplant."

"How is Mattie doing?" asked Janet.

"Mom is fine, mom's fine." Lamont said, "Her and Chris moved from Mississippi back to LA. They live just outside of Long Beach now."

"I want to call her sometime soon and thank her for the flowers she sent," Janet said. "That was sweet of her."

"Yea, yea, yea we can call her," Lamont said. "She would love to hear from you, Aunt Janet."

"What are you planning on doing today?" asked Janet.

"I don't have to Dialyze today so I thought I would get out and see if I can find a little place to stay," said Lamont.

"Lamont, you're more than welcome to stay here for a few days while you weigh your options?" said Janet.

"Aunt Janet do you think I could borrow about Fifty Dollars until my check comes," Lamont said. "Ever since I've been on dialysis, I get a disability check, so I can pay you back."

"Sure, Lamont I'll loan you Fifty Dollars as long as you don't tell Burton," she said.

"For sure," Lamont grinned. "I won't tell him a thing."

"Let me see if I have that much in my purse," said Janet.

"Don't worry Aunt Janet I will pay you back as soon as I get my check," said Lamont. "I'm sure Uncle Walker left you and Burton in pretty good shape. My dad didn't leave us anything. Not a thing. Nothing. Whatever he might have tried to leave us, his wife and nursemaid Veronica saw to it we didn't get it," he said.

"He may not have had anything to leave you, Lamont," Janet said. "The greatest thing he left you was his life and his legacy."

"That's easy for you to say, Aunt Janet," Lamont said. "I know Uncle Walker left you well."

"He did and I'm thankful, but your uncle and I have both worked hard all our lives," Janet said. "So, a lot of what he, quote-unquote left me, was already mine. It was ours, we worked for it."

"All the same, I wish somebody would leave me something for a change," Lamont said. "My dad could have looked out for us; he just chose not to."

"I don't know Lamont, I just don't know," Janet said. "I can't speak for John. Your father was a good man."

"He didn't leave me, Chris or Butch anything Aunt Janet," Lamont said. "Nothing, I'm sure Uncle Walker left Burton something."

"Lamont you may not know what you think you know," said Janet.

"I'm just saying Aunt Janet," said Lamont.

"Here, here's Fifty Dollars," said Janet.

"Thanks, Aunt Janet," said Lamont.

"No problem," Janet said. "Just don't tell Burton."

"Janet," her sister Carol said as Lamont was leaving. "Janet!" Carol called out as she came into the kitchen where Janet was seated.

"I'm right here Cabbie," Janet said. "Come on and have a cup of Coffee with me."

"Jeannie you know I can't drink a lot of Coffee," Carol said. "It makes me sick on the stomach."

"Well then have some juice, sit down," said Janet.

"What were you and LA in here talking about?" asked Carol.

"Nothing much," said Janet.

"He was asking you for money, wasn't he?" said Carol.

"He asked me if he could borrow Fifty Dollars," said Janet.

"Jeannie LA is a grown ass man," Carol said. "He shouldn't be around here asking you for money."

"Cabbie it's fine," said Janet.

"How long is he planning on staying here?" said Carol. "He's been here since Beck's funeral."

"Yes, he came for the funeral," said Janet.

"And he hasn't gone home yet," said Carol.

"He asked if he could stay for a few days and I said it was alright," said Janet.

"You can say what you want Jeannie," Carol said. "I know Walker would not like him being around here asking you for money."

"Beck disliked Lamont with a passion," said Janet.

"Then why are you letting him stay here?" Carol said. "He came for the funeral and now he can take his ass home."

"Cabbie," Janet replied. "There's no point in stressing yourself out over nothing."

"I'm not stressing myself out," Carol replied. "If you don't mind him being here then I'm fine with it, sister."

"It's just a few days, I don't mind." Janet said, "He's family."

"Don't let him take advantage of you Jeannie," Carol replied. "That's all I'm saying."

"I'm not," Janet said. "Don't worry."

"He just asked you for money and you gave it to him," Carol continued. "Grown ass, grown ass man. Seriously, Janet, I don't trust him."

"He'll only be here for a few more days," Janet said. "What is life worth if you can't help other people sometimes."

"Jeannie if you're not worried about it," Carol said. "I'm not worried about it. Just be careful. I don't care what you say, I don't trust him. He needs to take his ass home where he came from."

"He said he wants to move down here," said Janet.

"Yea, he probably wants to move down here and live with you, if he could," said Carol.

"That's not going to happen," Janet said. "He's not so bad Cabbie," Janet responded. "Everyone needs a helping hand sometimes."

"Jeannie, if LA is OK with you, he's cool with me," said Carol.

"It's only for a few days," Janet said. "I can use the company when he starts getting on my nerves, I will send him on his way if he hasn't already left."

"Alright sister," said Carol.

"Alright then, how are you today," Janet said. "It's so good to see you, Cabbie. I so much appreciate you coming to spend a few days with me."

Janet and Carol continued their conversation as Leassie arrives at work. Janet lets Leassie into the house. Leassie, Janet and her sister Carol exchange pleasantries as Leassie comes in and starts to prepare for work. It's not like Leassie did much or could do much anymore. She was now in her eighties and had severe arthritis in her hands. Janet and Walker pretty much allowed her to stay on at work with them because she had been working for them for so many years. Leassie was like a part of the family. Leassie did keep Janet's bed made and the kitchen cleaned, but mostly she liked to sit at the ironing board and iron clothes. Apparently holding the iron and applying light pressure against the ironing board gave her some relief from her Arthritis. So, for a while now Janet and Beck had some of the freshest pressed clothes in town. Leassie would spend at least three hours out of her workday with the ironing board in the Florida room ironing clothes. She didn't really want to, or probably could not do much more than what she did. Leassie had been a patient of Dr. LeFlore for every bit of 40 years and had been a devoted housekeeper to Janet and Beck for over 30 years.

Later that day Burton returned home from the office. He had a few things he wanted to discuss with his Mom regarding his father's estate. He noticed Lamont's car was still parked in the yard. He was concerned that his cousin had not left yet. It also bothered him that his Mom seemed to be fine with him being there. Of course, his Mom's attitude bothered him slightly, but he expected this type of behavior from Janet. Burton understood that Janet was not the type of person who was going to stress herself out about Lamomt. In addition, he knew his Mother to be a very trusting and non-assuming person. Burton wondered to himself if Lamont would only be the first of a number of vultures trying to pray on his Mother's kindness.

What bothered Burton most, was that Lamont was still in Mobile at the house, and he felt it was reasonably certain he was trying to see what he could get from his Mom. Burton had noticed as well that Lamont had moved from the sofa into the upstairs bedroom. The only consolation Burton really had was, he realized and knew that Lamont was less treacherous in his older years since he had suffered kidney failure and gone on Dialysis.

He also had some money coming in the form of a Disability check. Burton surmised that Lamont probably had to lay off the Cocaine since he had problems with his kidneys now. He knew that his Dad would not be happy that he had even allowed him to come and stay at the house in the first place; however, what was he supposed to say to his cousin when he humbly asked to attend his Uncle's funeral.

Burton figured that he could rest at night knowing that he had removed anything from the house that Lamont might have been able to get his hands on in the form of checks or anything remotely related to his Dad's finances. There was very little financial information at the house anyway, since they always kept all of that type of material at the office. He entered the house and found Janet standing there at the bar in the kitchen chatting with her sister and Lamont. He spoke to everyone as he walked through the kitchen and upstairs to his bedroom. Later that evening when he noticed his Mom was by herself, he pulled her to the side and spoke with her about it.

"Mom there are a few things I want to discuss with you," Burton said. "Do you have a minute?"

"Yes, Baby. What is it?" asked Janet.

"I have some documents I want you to review and sign," Burton said. "I'm trying to get the ball rolling with the Probate of Dad's estate."

"What do you need me to sign?" said Janet.

"First of all, do you mind if I serve as Executor of Daddy estate?" asked Burton.

"We already agreed you would serve as executor," said Janet.

"Just double checking," Burton said. "This form here states that you are waiving your right to serve as executor since Dad originally named you as Executor. I will need this to file the Petition to Probate his Will. We won't be able to do much in the form of handling any of his affairs until we Probate his Estate and get Letters Testamentary from the Court."

"Letters Testamentary, what is that?" asked Janet.

"It's an Order from the Court granting us the right to manage Dad's affairs since he has passed away," Burton said. "We cannot transact any business on his behalf or our behalf until this is done. We have to Probate his Will and get the Letters Testamentary from the Probate Court before we can do anything."

"I want you to serve as executor Burton, and if you could help me with that, I would be greatly appreciative," said Janet.

"Mom you know I would be honored to serve as executor of my father's Estate," Burton replied. "I'm here for you Mom and I am going to help you in any way I possibly can."

"I know you will sweetheart," said Janet.

"Take a minute to read over this before you sign it," Burton said. "Let me know if you have any questions."

"Where are my glasses?" asked Janet.

"Right here," replied Burton as he handed her the glasses along with the document. "It's a fairly cut and dried form, you're giving me the authority to serve as executor."

"I see, no problem," she said as skimmed over the page and signed the document.

"Now I can Petition the Court to Probate his Will and request they name me as executor," Burton said. "I have an original copy of Dad's Will and a copy of the Death Certificate." Burton said, "All I need to do now is finish the Petition and include this document and we'll be good to go."

"OK," replied Janet.

"I've also started putting together a timber deal for our land up in Clarke County. We have several hundred acres of standing timber up there and I think we need to see what we can get for it," said Burton.

"I think that would be a good idea," Janet said. "Did you contact Columbus Life about Beck's insurance policy?"

"Yes, I did contact them," Burton said. "I sent them a copy of his Death Certificate and we should be hearing from them in a few days."

"Very good, thank you, Baby, so much for helping me with all of this," said Janet.

"Mom I told you, you don't have to worry about a thing," Burton said. "I got you. I also contacted the Social Security Administration about paying you a Death Benefit, but it's not very much."

"Social Security doesn't pay much of a death benefit at all," Janet said. "I don't see how they expect anyone to be able to bury their loved ones for what they pay."

"I did contact them for what it's worth," said Burton.

"Good," Janet said. "You seem to be on top of things Baby, just keep me posted with what's going on."

"Mom, what's the deal with Lamont?" Burton asked.

"What do you mean?" replied Janet.

"He's still here," Burton said. "The funeral was over a week ago. Why hasn't he gone back to Georgia?"

"He asked if he could stay here for a few days," Janet said.

"The funeral is over," Burton responded. "What is the point of him still being here? Everybody else went home already."

"It's alright Burton. He said he was thinking about moving down here to Mobile," said Janet.

"All of a sudden, he wants to move to Mobile," said Burton.

"I don't have anything to do with that Burton," Janet said. "He asked if he could stay a few more days, and I told him it would be OK. I don't mind. Do you have a problem with him staying for a couple of days?"

"Mom it's just that he said he wanted to go to Dad's funeral and that is why he was coming, but then he didn't attend the wake or the funeral. Now he has conveniently decided to stay for more time because all of a sudden, he wants to move to Mobile," Burton said. "It's not so much that I have a problem with him staying here for a few days or moving here if that's what he wants to do. It's just that I feel he's up to something."

"Well he is your cousin, Beck's nephew," said Janet.

"Yea and Daddy couldn't stand him, and I really don't think he cared much for Dad either," said Burton.

"Do you dislike him that much?" asked Janet.

"It's not that I dislike him so much," Burton said. "I feel that he is an opportunist and he's trying to hang around for the wrong reasons and for that I do dislike him."

"It's only for a few days," Janet said. "I've actually been enjoying his company."

"What do you call a few days Mom?" Burton asked. "You and I have a lot of things to get done in a short period of time before Candace has the baby. I don't see how we have time to be dealing with LA right now."

"If you want me to ask him to leave," Janet said. "I'll ask him to leave. But he's family, and there is no harm in trying to help family when you can."

"Alright Mom a couple of days," said Burton. "I don't want him trying to get any money from you. I tell you what, why don't you give me your checkbook and I'll take it over to the office," he said. "At least we don't have to worry about him trying to forge checks on your account like he did Grandma Teah."

"I'll give you the checkbook if that will make you feel better," Janet replied. "I personally don't think there is any reason for that, but if it will make you feel better."

"Personally, it would make me feel a lot better Mom," Burton said. "Is there anything else you and Dad might have had around the house that I might have overlooked that we might need to take over to the office?"

"Probably just the checkbook, but I will make sure there's nothing else," Janet said. "We keep just about everything related to our finances at the office anyway."

"I'm trying to protect you," Burton said. "LA is my cousin as you said. He and I have had some good times together, but if he tries to steal anything from you, I'm going to hurt him."

"I don't think you have to worry about that," said Janet.

"I did stay with them for a minute while I was in California," said Burton.

"Just like I told Cabbie earlier today," Janet said. "If he starts to get on my nerves, I'll tell him to leave."

"Anyway, Mom I'm going to go ahead and get this stuff filed tomorrow with the court," Burton said. "And if you want to harbor this fugitive for a little longer, I'll leave it alone."

"I didn't think you would mind," Janet said. "I'm not going to give him any money, I promise."

After Burton and Janet finished discussing the few matters of business they needed to discuss, Burton left and went over to his house for a minute. Burton noticed a message on the answering machine, so he pressed the button to listen. He had not been living there and did not get a lot of phone calls at his home number so he was curious as to who it might have been. He heard the voice of a female speaking on the line and thought that it might have been a message for his wife Candace; however, the person indicated the message was for him. Burton listened further as the caller identified herself as Charlotte. There was only one person that he knew of named Charlotte and this was a phone call that he had possibly been expecting since his Dad had passed.

Charlotte asked if Burton would return her phone call and left a phone number where she could be reached. Burton stood there for a moment looking at the message machine trying to decide if he should return the call or not. He played back the message and wrote down the number she left as her return phone number. Burton then stood there staring at the piece of paper where he had written the name and number.

While he was standing there looking at the piece of paper, he had a flashback to his childhood when his family was living in their old house on Davis Avenue. Burton remembered some mail coming in the mailbox addressed to his Mom. He was there with Janet when she opened the mail. Inside the envelope was a picture of Beck seated at a table with two little girls in his lap.

The girls appeared to be twins. He was only about Eight years old at the time and did not fully understand, but he had enough sense to know that someone sending mail to his Mom with a picture of his Dad holding two little girls was probably not a good thing. He remembered Janet being very upset after seeing the photograph. Later that night when Beck got home from work, Janet confronted him about the photograph. Burton could remember lying in bed and hearing his parents arguing. He listened closely but could not hear much of what was being said. Janet was very upset, and Beck became somewhat defensive. They argued for a period of time, but all Burton could really make out was Beck's voice saying to his mom, "I am going to take care of you." Burton did not really know what his Dad meant by that statement. The arguing went on every day for almost a week and then he never heard another word about the picture, etc.

Later in life during High School, there were instances when kids he went to school with would come up to Burton and say that he had a sister. They would ask him if he knew his sister or something along those lines. Burton would think back to that photograph that came in the mail and to those arguments between his parents. He figured the two girls in the picture must have been the alleged sister or sister's that he was supposed to have. He distinctly remembered two little girls in the picture, but now the kids in school who mentioned this to him said sister in the singular and not the plural.

Burton never asked his dad about the rumors he heard, and he never discussed it with Janet. He figured there must have been a strong chance the rumors were true. However, he decided if Beck wanted to discuss it with him, he would have done so. Burton remembered how flabbergasted Janet was when she received the picture in the mail, and he dared not ask his mother about it for fear it would hurt her again. Burton worried it would bother his mom that kids were telling him this in school and would open up a whole new can of worms, like the one he remembered many years ago. Burton decided to dismiss the rumors. It only happened on two or three occasions and it mostly came from a young lady, whose mother was a nurse. Burton had a crush on the young lady and he never asked her to elaborate on what she had said about him having a sister.

Finally, when Burton got married to Candace and moved her to Mobile, soon Candace came back to him stating that she had heard Dr. LeFlore had another child out of wedlock. Candace told Burton his sister's name was Charlotte. For many years, Candace would constantly throw it up in Burton's face that his father had another child by another woman. As if Burton had any control over what his dad may or may not have done. However, even though Burton endured years of abuse from his wife regarding the allegations that his dad had another child by a woman not his mother. Burton never discussed it with either of them.

Finally, after Burton finished Law School and moved back to Mobile, his wife came home one day stating she had met his sister Charlotte. She stated that she thought Charlotte was a very nice person and she had said she wanted to meet Burton. Candace talked about their meeting at length and how Charlotte had spoken very fondly of him and referred to him as her brother, expressing repeatedly her desire to meet him in person because the two of them had never met.

Candace indicated the two of them had exchanged telephone numbers and that Candace had asked her to contact their house so that she and Burton could meet. Burton felt that Candace was being sincere about having met her and about her opinion that she was a nice person. It was comforting to hear the things Candace said about having met Charlotte. She gave Burton her phone number and encouraged him to contact her. Although, Burton appreciated Candace's willingness to encourage him to meet his alleged sister. Burton gave it considerable thought following their conversation and he decided that he did not want to meet her. He still refrained from bringing any of this to his parents. Not even with his Dad, during the last days of his life when Beck wanted to engage in those real heart to heart conversations.

Burton reached the conclusion that Beck was dead now. He was curious about statements from people throughout his life that he had a sister. He finally wanted to meet her. Burton had heard about her many times over the years, and it was about two years prior when he got the affirmative news that she wanted to meet him. He had been clearly informed that, as far as she was concerned, he was her brother. He had flat out declined to call her or entertain a phone call from her before. It was not long after this, Burton and Candace moved to North Carolina. Burton thought to himself, he needed to know. After all these years he needed to know for himself. Now was the perfect opportunity.

Candace was in North Carolina, so he could meet her without having Candace around trying to monitor the situation and attempting to control the outcome. His father was gone, so he did not have to engage in a question and answer session with his father that might have put his father on the spot. Janet was spending a lot of time with her sister Carol and so he could meet with her, without worrying his Mom might get involved or feel some type of way about it. Finally, and perhaps least importantly, yes, his dad had passed, and he felt it was a good idea to find out where her head was at, as far as whether his Dad had left her anything in his Will. He picked up the telephone and dialed the number he had written on the sheet of paper. The phone rang as Burton listened with anticipation.

"Hello," said Charlotte's voice on the other end of the receiver.

"Hi is this Charlotte?" asked Burton.

"Yes, this is Charlotte," she replied.

"I got a message from you and I was returning your call, this is Burton," he said. "Are you doing anything tomorrow evening? If not, could you meet me at Justine's downtown for dinner?"

"I guess, tomorrow about what time?" asked Charlotte.

"Sure," Burton replied. "I'll see you tomorrow about 7:30 at Justine's."

Meanwhile, Janet was back at the house talking with her sister Carol and Lamont. They were all having a relatively pleasant conversation as the evening drew later and later.

"Aunt Janet, I'm going to have to go to bed in a minute," Lamont said. "I have to go to Dialysis in the morning. I really shouldn't be drinking this beer, but I can have a little every once and a while."

"If you shouldn't be drinking Lamont," Carol replied. "Then don't drink."

"Seriously Lamont, let's not have any emergencies tonight," said Janet.

"I can drink a little beer every once in a while," Lamont said. "It will be alright since I have to go to dialysis in the morning if I drink too much it will make me really sick."

"How long have you been on dialysis now anyway?" asked Janet.

"A little over three years now," Lamont replied.

"I have a friend in Hampton who is on dialysis and he says it's not easy to have to take those dialysis treatments three and four times a week," said Carol.

"My life depends on it," Lamont said. "You see this?" He said pointing to an enlarged vein in his arm. "This is a shunt."

"A shunt?" said Janet.

"Yes, this large vein is where they hook me up to the dialysis machine so the machine can filter my blood," Lamont said. "The dialysis machine basically performs the same function as the kidneys."

"I was wondering what that was," Janet replied. "I just thought you had an enlarged vein; I didn't realize that was for your dialysis."

"Yea my friend Doug has one of those too," said Carol.

"Since my kidneys failed, I have had to make a lot of changes in my lifestyle if I want to live or avoid getting sick," said Lamont.

"How old are you LA?" asked Carol.

"I'm Fifty-Nine," he replied with a chuckle.

"Is it painful to take the dialysis?" asked Janet.

"Not really, it's more painful when your body has to tolerate more and more waste and toxins which build up in your system when you can't release them through the ordinary course of excretion," replied Lamont.

"I see," Janet said. "Beck used to treat some patients who suffered from kidney failure."

"To be truthful Aunt Janet, I'm getting a little tired," Lamont said. "I guess I'll go ahead and get to bed. I generally like to go to bed early and wake up early."

"I'm getting a little tired myself Jeannie," Carol said. "But if you want to stay up for a little while and talk, I will try and stay up with you."

"I wasn't quite ready to go to bed," Janet replied.

"I'm going to turn in myself," Lamont stated. "I will see you in the morning, Aunt Janet."

"Goodnight," said Janet.

"Goodnight LA," said Carol.

"Goodnight," said Lamont as he dismissed himself from the table and went upstairs.

"Janet where is Burton?" Carol asked. "Where did he go?"

"I think he said he was going over to his house for a little while," said Janet.

"I was wondering," Carol said. "He walked in earlier and I hadn't seen him since."

"He may stay over there tonight," Janet said. "He's been spending the night over here sometimes and then he will stay over there every once in a while. Do you want to ride over there?"

"Not necessarily," Carol said. "I was just wondering where he was. I hadn't seen him in a while."

"He'll probably be back in a minute," Janet said. "One thing I can say is he's tried to stay close by my side through much of what has been going on lately. I appreciate him for that."

"He's a good son Janet," Carol replied. "He's a good person."

"Who are you telling," said Janet. "Seems like he's all I have now that Beck is gone and my little adorable grandchildren."

"And you mean to tell me Candace got one more on the way," said Carol.

"Yes, she does," Janet said. "She's pregnant with number four."

"Is it going to be a girl or a boy Jeannie?" said Carol.

"I don't know, it would be nice if Burton would finally have a little girl," Janet said. "At the rate, he's been going so far it will probably be another boy."

"Jeannie that is such a blessing," replied Carol.

"Yes, it is," said Janet.

"And so, tell me, how are you doing sister?" asked Carol.

"Thankful you came to see me, and you're here with me Cabbie," Janet said. "Thank you for not letting me be alone right now."

"Thanks for sending me a ticket so I could get here," said Carol.

"Thank you for coming," said Janet.

"Jeannie, I know what it was like for me when Fred passed," Carol said. "Even though we were having a lot of problems at the time I know what it was like."

"Cabbie I'm certainly not the first woman to lose her husband, and I most certainly will not be the last, but I feel like a piece of me is missing. I feel like a part of me is gone. This seems like what it would be like to lose my leg or my arm." Janet said, "Like something that has been a part of my life, my heart, my soul, has been taken away."

"Beck will always be with you Jeannie," Carol said. "You just have to learn how to find him. You may not understand what I mean by that now, but trust me, you will."

"I loved him so much, and we have been together ever since I can remember," Janet said. "He was the love of my life."

"Ever since I can remember that's for sure, Walker and Janet, Janet and Walker," Carol said. "We all used to be so jealous because Walker treated you like his Princess. He treated you like a Queen," she said. "He was so good to you."

"Yea he was alright," replied Janet as she smiled. "There were some rough times in our marriage."

"Every couple is going to go through rough times," Carol said. "But you guys managed to work it out and you stayed together." She said, "You have so much to be thankful for Janet."

"I do have a lot to be thankful for," said Janet.

"Till death did you part," said Carol.

"You and Walker spent your lives together and you guys had a good life. Not just because you guys had money, but because you guys truly loved each other."

"Fifty-five years Cabbie, and no we didn't always have money, but we did have a lot of love for each other," Janet said. "Truthfully it seemed like when we first started to get a little money thing seemed to get worse. Beck started drinking a lot and running around."

"Jeannie you and Walker survived all that, you and Walker overcame all that mostly in part because you loved him and he loved you, Jeannie," said Carol.

"I did love him with all my heart, I still do," Janet said. "I loved that man, it always seemed like me and him were just meant to be together."

Meanwhile, Burton was seated at a table awaiting the arrival of his alleged half-sister Charlotte. There were a lot of things running through his mind at the time. He had pretty much decided that he was going to make the call that night. Meaning he was going to make a decision right then once he met her, based on their meeting on this particular evening whether or not he believed her to be his sister or not. Although there were many thoughts racing through his brain as he sat there waiting for her, he was certain about one thing. He was going to reach a conclusion and then he was going to act or react based on that conclusion. If after meeting her, he did not think she was his sister, he planned to notify her of the same. On the other hand, if after meeting her, he concluded she was his sister, then he was prepared to accept it graciously and move forward from there.

Burton sat there sipping his Sprite and looking over the menu. He was hungry and he hoped she would hurry and arrive because he did not want to be rude and go ahead and order before she got there. He glanced around the room just to make sure she had not already arrived and sat at another table not noticing him there. He then realized he had no idea who he was looking for. He had never met her, and he had no idea what she looked like. Burton realized that much of what he would have to rely on in making his judgment call about her legitimacy as his father's child would be her appearance. What if she didn't look anything like his dad, but then again, he had no idea what her mother looked like either. Burton glanced back down at the menu trying to decide what he wanted to order.

A lady walked up to the table. She pulled the chair across from him back and took a seat. Burton looked across the table at her and he was speechless for a moment. Burton fought to keep his mouth from dropping wide open. He practically fell out of his chair. He could not believe his eyes. He took off his glasses and rubbed his eyes and put his glasses back on and took another look at Charlotte.

She looked just like his dad. Charlotte was the spitting image of his father. He felt like he was looking at a female version of Beck which he had never seen before; however, if there was a female version of his father, Burton knew he was looking at it right then and there. He had never seen a female version of his dad because he did not have a sister. At least he didn't think he had a sister until now.

"Hi Burton, how are you?" said Charlotte.

"Yes, I'm Burton, you must be Charlotte?" replied Burton.

"I'm Charlotte, it's nice to finally meet you after all these years," said Charlotte.

"It's nice to meet you too," Burton said as he extended his hand to shake hers. "Very nice to meet you." Burton paused for a moment as he held her hand in his. "I'm, I'm speechless."

"Why do you say that?" asked Charlotte.

"Amazing," said Burton.

"What? What's Amazing?" asked Charlotte.

"You look like, you look just like, umm, uhhh, my dad," Burton said.

"Thank you, I guess I'll take that as a compliment," said Charlotte.

"You look just like him," Burton said. "Wow…. I'm, I'm sorry are you hungry. I'm starving. The food here is great. Have you been here before?"

"No, I've never been here, what's good?" said Charlotte.

"Practically everything," Burton said. "If you see something you like, you probably won't be disappointed. I think I'm going to get the Rack of Lamb."

"Mediterranean chicken looks like it might be good," replied Charlotte.

"It's probably delicious," Burton said. "Why don't you try it. Whatever you want, it's on me."

"Have you guys decided what you'd like?" asked the waitress as she came over to the table.

"I think I'll have the Turtle Soup and the Rack of Lamb," Burton said. "And she will have, you want the Mediterranean Chicken?"

"Yes," said Charlotte.

"She will have the Mediterranean Chicken," said Burton.

"Would either of you like a salad with your meal?" asked the waitress.

"I would like one, thank you," replied Charlotte.

"Could I have a small one with some Bleu Cheese dressing," said Burton.

"You will love our Bleu Cheese dressing, we make it in house and it's fabulous," said the waitress. "And how about you Mam?"

"The Bleu Cheese will be fine," said Charlotte.

"Would you like a glass of wine or something?" asked Burton.

"Just a glass of water for now," Charlotte said. "I may take you up on the glass of wine in a little while, but just water for right now."

"I'll get that order in and get some water for her," the waitress said. "Would you like some more Sprite?"

"I'm good for now, thank you," he replied. "This is a great restaurant; I know the owners and they are really cool."

"It's nice, thank you for inviting me here," said Charlotte.

"I want to ask you something," said Burton.

"Go ahead ask?" replied Charlotte.

"Do you have another sister?" asked Burton.

"I had a sister, a twin sister," said Charlotte.

"You were a twin," replied Burton.

"Yes," said Charlotte.

"What was her name?" asked Burton. "When did she die?"

"Her name was Claudia," Charlotte said. "She died when we were Five."

"How did she die?" asked Burton.

"She was always very sickly," said Charlotte. "She died of Pneumonia."

"Sorry to hear that," said Burton.

"I came to the funeral, but I don't think you saw me," said Charlotte.

"No, I didn't see you," said Burton.

"I was there," Charlotte said. "I parked across the street from the cemetery during the burial. Then I visited Claudia's grave site afterward. She's buried in the same cemetery not far from where my dad is buried."

"Why did you park across the street?" Burton said. "You didn't have to park across the street."

"Hey, I'm an illegitimate child," Charlotte said. "I always have been. It is what it is."

"You certainly look more like him that I do, that's for sure," said Burton. "Your lips, your teeth, your eyes, your forehead, your cheekbones, even your complexion. OMG," said Burton.

"It's really nice to finally meet you, Burton," Charlotte said. "I have known of you for all my life and I used to see you around. I've seen you tons of times, but you didn't know who I was and probably wouldn't have recognized me anyway."

"Here's your Turtle Soup Mr. LeFlore and your Salad mam," said the waitress as she returned.

Burton and Charlotte had a nice dinner. The food was good, and it seemed they were getting along with one another. Burton realized he had little choice other than to accept that she was his half-sister and he felt comfortable with that since she looked so much like his dad. He found out that she was married and had three children. She had two boys and a girl. One of her son's had the same name as one of his son's. He also saw that his wife Candace was correct in that she seemed to be a very sweet person. After talking with her for a considerable amount of time over dinner, he also realized that she did not seem to want anything from him other than for him to acknowledge that she was, in fact, his sister.

Following dinner, she and Burton sat at the bar and had a drink. Burton introduced her to the owner of the restaurant and his wife. After they had drinks, Burton invited her back to his house so they could continue their conversation. Burton felt comfortable with Charlotte and he was enjoying their conversation so far. He was inwardly happy that he had finally decided to meet her. For the present, Burton felt like he was doing some real discovery about who his father really was. He was discovering a side of his Dad, that was at this point, somewhat painful and revealing and yet comforting at the same time. He was discovering that he had a half-sister who actually happened to be pretty cool.

Charlotte trailed Burton back to his house, and they went inside and continued talking. Burton offered her a beer. They must have conversed for a least another hour there at the house. By now it was starting to get late. Burton walked her to the door, and they stood out on the front porch and talked for at least another half hour. She made her way to her car and Burton walked her outside where they talked a little longer. They talked just like two people who had a lot of catching up to do. And indeed, they did have a lot of catching up to do. At this point, Charlotte was seated in her car with the engine running. Burton looked up and saw Janet's car traveling down Robbins Street toward his street. He could see Janet behind the wheel and Carol riding in the passenger seat of her Pearl White Deville that Beck had bought her about a year before he passed.

For a second there, Burton wondered how he was going to handle this situation. He was not sure if he should introduce Charlotte to his mom or just try and play it off like she was just a friend passing through. Burton looked at Charlotte and looked over his shoulder at the white Cadillac as it came to a stop at the stop sign and signaled left. Janet was about to turn onto his street. He wondered if Charlotte would feel uncomfortable meeting his mother. With all the uncertainty looming in Burton's head about how a possible introduction between his mom and Charlotte would turn out on that night; he knew his mom was hurting inside and it might not be the right time to spring this on her. However, he knew inside that she was already aware of it. All the same, she didn't have to be aware they were out there talking that night.

This was their first meeting and so far, it had gone well. He did not want to put Charlotte on the spot and he did not want to cause Janet any more unnecessary heartache or concern. Janet passed by him as he stood out there on the side of Charlotte's car. She slowed down and Burton thought she was going to stop right there by the car. However, she continued around in front of the car and parked in front of the house. Burton thanked Charlotte for joining him for dinner and coming by the house to talk. She pulled away. Burton said goodbye to Charlotte and walked over to where his mom's car was parked.

"Hey Mom, hey Aunt Carol," said Burton.

"Who was that?" asked Janet.

"What, who?" said Burton.

"The person in that car," Janet said. "Who was that?"

"Just a friend," Burton said. "She was just leaving."

"Burton you know you have a baby on the way," said Janet.

"Yes, I do," Burton said.

"I hope you're not out here entertaining females," said Janet.

"No Mom, just talking," replied Burton.

"Hey Burton," said Carol.

"Hi Aunt Carol," Burton said. "It's late, I thought you guys would have been in bed by now."

"No, we were still up and decided to ride by here and check on you," said Janet.

"I'm fine," replied Burton.

"Are you coming by the house tonight, or are you going to stay over here?" asked Janet.

"I'll probably come on out to the house," said Burton.

"Just wanted to make sure you were alright Baby," said Janet.

"Yea I'm alright," Burton said. "I tell you what, it's getting late. I think I'll go and turn out the lights and lock up and head to your house for the night."

"OK we'll see you in a few," said Janet.

Janet pulled away in her car as Burton went inside to close the house up. He felt that he had done the right thing by not introducing them or telling his mom he had been talking with his half-sister. It was not necessary right now, nor would it probably ever be necessary. He was glad that he had gotten to finally meet her, and he felt that he wanted to stay in touch with her. For now, he figured, as far as Janet was concerned it was a non-issue. Burton remained at the house for a little while to finish his beer, before he locked the house and drove around to Janet's house.

The next day Burton approached Janet and indicated that he needs to talk with her. He made sure that his aunt nor his cousin were around because he wanted to talk with Janet in private. When he arrived home he found, his aunt seated in the chair by the door in the Florida room and Lamont was not there. Leassie was seated in the Florida room near Carol ironing one of Janet's blouses. Janet was in the kitchen piddling around. Burton asked his Mom to come into the Living room so they could talk. He had met with the Real Estate Agents who had the house listed that he and Candace liked. He wanted to know if Janet would ride around with him and look at it.

"What is it Burton?" asked Janet.

"Mom I met with the real estate agents who are selling the house over on Oak Knoll," Burton said. "I went and talked with Earnestine at the bank and she said she could probably get me approved for a loan. The only problem is, I don't have the money for the down payment."

"About how much is the down payment?" asked Janet.

"It's going to be somewhere between Ten and Twenty Thousand Dollars," Burton said. "Would you come and look at the house? You and Daddy considered buying the same house before you guys brought this land over here."

"Sure, I would love to look at it," said Janet.

"Let me call the agents and see if they will come back out to the house and meet us," said Burton.

"Call them," said Janet.

An hour or two later, Janet and Burton were back at the house on Oak Knoll meeting with the agents. The house was a relatively large home that sat back a distance off the street. It had a brick walkway across the front yard that led up to two mahogany twelve-foot double doors. The house is an older house with a very contemporary design. The agents were out front waiting for Burton as he arrived with his mom.

"So, you want to buy a house on Pill Hill," said Janet.

"Pill Hill?" said Burton.

"Yes, this neighborhood is called Pill Hill," Janet said. "Very close proximity from the Infirmary Hospital. Back in the day doctors owned all the homes back here."

"You're telling me something new," Burton said. "I didn't know they called this area Pill Hill."

"Mom this is Jim and Nancy," Burton said. "This is my mother Mrs. LeFlore."

"Very nice to meet you, Mrs. LeFlore," Nancy said. "This is my partner Jim. And yes, Burton this neighborhood is nicknamed Pill Hill."

"Nice to meet you as well," said Janet.

"Come on inside," Burton said. "Do you remember when you and Daddy started to buy this house back in the Seventies?"

"Yes, I remember," said Janet. "I also remember when we were looking at the lot down the street shortly after looking at this house and they removed the sign from the property the next day," said Janet.

"Mom this is 2001 not the 1970's anymore," Burton said. "This house is fabulous. I never forgot about the bomb shelter in this house. Do you remember the bomb shelter in this house? When have you ever seen a house with a bomb shelter?" said Burton.

"Burton, I know you've already seen this, but Mrs. LeFlore this is the living room and small foyer," Jim said. "Up this small flight of stairs to the family room and Kitchen area."

"I've seen it before myself, many years ago," Janet said. "But I don't mind looking again. I really liked this house back then. Even though I'm glad me and Beck decided against it and moved where we moved."

"This is the dining room," Nancy said. "Kitchen here as we now step into the family room."

"How do you like it Mom?" said Burton.

"It's nice," said Janet.

"We'll be right around the corner from you," Burton explained. "We're already right around the corner from you but, Mom if I could buy this house and get the two extra bedrooms."

"It does appear you could use some additional bedrooms," Janet said. "How much are they asking for the house?" said Janet.

"They're asking Three Hundred Thousand," said Nancy.

"It's been on the market now for almost two years," Burton said. He pulled his mom over for a sidebar between them and said, "I think this seller will take a lot less than what they're asking. It has been on the market now for two years. I hear the guy who owned this house was a doctor at USA, apparently, he has moved to Atlanta and I'm sure he bought another house by now. I'll bet if I make an offer, he will be willing to sell this house for way less than Three Hundred Thousand."

"Did you see the courtyard out here," Burton said. "Isn't that nice?"

"Yes, it's a beautiful courtyard," said Jim.

"There's also another patio on the side of the house," Nancy said. "Would you like to see it Mrs. LeFlore?"

"How about we look at the bedrooms and then go out back and then work our way toward the front of the house again," said Burton.

"The bedrooms are this way," said Jim.

"This is bedroom number one," Burton said. "A full bath and bedroom number two."

"This is a lot of house," said Janet.

"There is also a full bathroom on the other side of the hall," said Nancy.

"Here's bedroom number three," Burton said. "Up the hall is bedroom number four and through here is the master bedroom."

"I love those high ceilings, and the ceiling fan," Janet said. "And there's a fireplace."

"Here's the master bathroom, and walk-in closet," Jim said. "Isn't it grand?"

"And those doors go into the same courtyard that we saw from the family room," Janet said.

"Yes, Mom those doors lead into that same courtyard," Burton said. "Let me show you the garage and back yard," he said as he took Janet by the arm. "Watch your step."

"So, what do you think so far Mrs. LeFlore?" said Nancy.

"It's a beautiful house," Janet said. "Ultimately it will be Burton's decision though. You know my husband and I started to buy this house about 25 years ago, I can't believe Burton is thinking about buying this same house all over again."

"Yes, he told us you and your husband thought about buying this house," said Jim.

"It's almost kind of surreal that I'm looking at this house all over again so many years later," Burton said. "This is the garage and there you can see out into the back yard," Burton replied. "It doesn't have a very big back yard."

"What do you think they would take for it?" asked Janet.

"Way less than Three Hundred Thousand," said Burton.

"Are you going to make them an offer?" asked Janet.

"Yes," Burton said. "I want to make them an offer. Come on, let's finish looking around and we can discuss this a little later. I want to know what you think about the house right now."

"It's wonderful and if you think you can get it for a better price than make them an offer," Janet said.

"I want to make them an offer," Burton said. "I don't have enough for the down payment though."

"Don't worry about that," Janet replied. "If you want to buy this house. I will help you with the down payment."

"Mom, they're saying I got to pay off both of my CD loans and come up with some cash for the down payment," said Burton.

"How much?" asked Janet.

"If you all need some more time to discuss this we can wait outside," said Jim.

"No, there's no need for that," said Burton. "We'll just finish up this discussion at home. Let's finish looking at the house."

"I just love those front doors," Janet said. "I certainly remember those exquisite front doors, they are gorgeous."

"Jim and Nancy, thank you once again for coming out and meeting me again," Burton said.

"Burton, just give us a call and let us know what you want to do," said Nancy.

Janet and Burton concluded their meeting with the agents regarding the house at Oak Knoll. Burton escorted Janet down the long walkway back to the car as the agents locked the door and returned to their car. Burton opened the door for his mother as she seated herself on the passenger side and he walked around and got into the car himself. They waved goodbye to Nancy and Jim as they drove off.

They stopped once more on the street to take another look at the house from the street. The house appeared huge as it sat atop the hill with those oversized windows and large mahogany front doors.

"What do you think?" asked Burton.

"I like it," Janet said. "What do you think?"

"It's a great house," said Burton.

"What do you think they would take for it?" asked Janet.

"I think they will take a lot less than what they're asking for this house," said Burton.

"Burton if you want me to help you with the down payment I will," said Janet.

"I love this house, mom, and I know for sure Candace likes this house, but I think I should look at a few more houses before making a final decision," said Burton.

"You should look at a few more before you make a final decision," Janet replied. "I'll go with you if you want to go and look around some."

"Maybe we can arrange to see a few houses tomorrow then," replied Burton.

The next day Burton went through a local publication that was advertising homes for sale. Burton saw a few properties that he was interested in and he contacted the agents to see if they would arrange to meet with him to show the houses. He and Janet rode out to West Mobile and they looked around at several houses in that area. They met with two or three agents and subsequently looked at about seven houses total. Janet and Burton spent most of the day going from property to property. After viewing the houses and discussing numbers Burton said to his mom that he still liked the house they saw yesterday on Oak Knoll and it was much closer to her.

Janet's sister Carol was still there with her; however, she was starting to say that she thought she would need to return home. Carol wanted to stay a few more days, but her daughter Cheryl kept calling and saying that she wanted her to come on back home. Cheryl and Candace shared a home together in Hampton. Janet was enjoying having her sister Carol there with her. Carol wanted to be with her sister as much as she could because she felt her sister needed her. However, Cheryl kept calling with one problem after another. Carol started to become a little agitated and worried so she told Janet; although she wanted to stay a few more days, she would need to return to see what was going on with her daughter. The following day Janet and Burton took Carol back to the airport and she flew back to Hampton.

Carol was quite a comfort for Janet. Her presence was good for Janet as she was being very understanding and helpful during these days following Beck's death. She and Carol had spent a lot of time together talking and appreciating each other's company. They had cried together, and they had laughed together while she was there. Her sister had shown her a great deal of kindness and cooperation. Carol had been very attentive to Janet over the last few days while she was there. Janet started to feel a bit lonely now as she and Burton drove back to the house. Janet had really enjoyed her sister's company, and that was exactly what she needed during this time.

As the days wound down to the birth of Burton's next child, Burton had been working hard getting things situated where his new business venture was concerned. He also devoted his time to getting affairs together with regard to his father's estate and winding down his dad's medical practice. He had someone working on a design for his company signage and they had almost reached a final proof of his new real estate signs. He filed his articles of incorporation and purchased a business license. Burton also registered his licenses with the Real Estate Commission. He probated his father's estate and was working on a timber deal for some property they owned up the country.

Janet's nephew Lamont was still there, and it was starting to bother Burton. At this point, Lamont had been there over a month and Burton was about ready for him to leave. Burton felt that Lamont had long overstayed his welcome. Janet did not really mind Lamont because he was talkative and had been keeping her company over the last few weeks. Although Janet wondered why Lamont had not gone home yet, she did not want to be alone. Her fear of being alone with her sorrow and longing for her departed husband was greater than her need to be rid of her nephew. Burton felt Janet had been more than hospitable toward him, giving him more than enough time to do whatever it is he wanted to do. As far as Burton was concerned, all he wanted to do was try and figure out how he was going to con Janet out of some money.

Secretly Burton had been alright with him staying for a while. However, at this point, he knew that the time was coming closer and closer for Carol to be giving birth to his newborn. Burton knew he would need to leave and travel back to Wilmington. He also planned to take Janet with him. He did not want his mom to be left alone and he felt that she would like to go to Wilmington. Certainly, if he hoped it would uplift her mood to share in the new life their family was about to gain as it had just lost their icon.

He needed to get Lamont out of the house so he could make arrangements since he was relatively certain their baby would be coming any day. It would be better to get Lamont on his way so that in the event of an emergency, they could leave and lock up the house, without it suddenly becoming convenient for them to leave him there while they were called out of town. Furthermore, they had been more than gracious to him despite everything they might have been going through.

Janet had given Lamont Five Hundred Dollars and Burton managed to find out about this when Janet mentioned it to him. Burton was angry that Janet had given him some money; however, at this point, he had known it was inevitable. Burton knew full well that Lamont was out to con his Mom from day one. He never intended to attend his Uncle Walker's funeral. He could not stand his uncle. They had numerous negative encounters over the years. Janet had surprisingly accepted his company and did not mind giving him a few hundred dollars. She was not concerned about it in the least. She had decided what she was going to give him, and she did it.

Burton was not surprised. Burton's main objective was to make sure that he made some other arrangements because he felt he was taking advantage of his mom's hospitality. Needless to say, he knew he would be needing to get back to his family in North Carolina soon. He also needed his mom's attention to some very important matters. He was tired of Lamont being around trying to snoop in his mom's business. Burton hated it had to come to the point where he was going to have to straight put Lamont out. LA knew full well he was exploiting the situation, and he was ready to roll with it as long as Janet was in agreement. The only problem was Burton had decided it was time for Lamont to go. Burton was standing outside when Lamont's car pulled into the yard.

"LA, I need to talk with you for a minute," said Burton.

"What's up, Cuz?" said Lamont.

"Nothing much man," Burton said. "Can I talk to you for a second."

"Yea what's up?" asked Lamont.

"L.A., the funeral is over," Burton said. "The funeral is over, and everyone has gone home except you and I'm kind of wondering like why you haven't gone home too. Feel me."

"Yea I feel you Cuz," said Lamont.

"Naw I don't really think you're feeling me, man," Burton said. "Mom's has got a lot going on right now. She just lost her husband, and this is a rough time for us. You know what I'm saying."

"Aunt Janet said it was OK if I stayed for a few days," Lamont said. "She said it wasn't a problem. I've been trying to see if I could relocate down here."

"Lamont if I was going to move to California and I wanted to stay with Aunt Mattie for a while so I could look around," Burton interjected. "I would call her and say, Aunt Mattie, I want to move to Cali do you think I could come and stay with you for a few weeks," according to Burton. "I wouldn't just show up at the house under the pretext of attending a funeral and then impose myself upon her."

"I understand," said Lamont.

"I don't think you do, for real," said Burton.

"Hey man I'll try to make arrangements," said Lamont.

"If you want to relocate down here that would be wonderful," Burton said. "I would love for you to move down here. That's great. It's a whole city out here ready for you to relocate in."

"I've been looking around for a place," said Lamont.

"Let me put it like this," Burton explained. "I don't know what you're going to do or where you're going to do it, but it's not going to be at my Mom's house after tomorrow."

"The fuck you mean, man," said Lamont.

"Just what I said," replied Burton.

"Let me discuss this with Aunt Janet," Lamont replied. "I have no problem working this out with her."

"There's nothing to be worked out LA," Burton said. "You been here long enough, I need you out of here tomorrow."

"If that's what Aunt Janet wants then fine," said Lamont.

"That's what she wants and that is what I want," Burton said. "It's not even about that, why do I even have to have this conversation with you. You been here damn near a month and a half. The funerals over." He said, "Time to go home. There's nothing to discuss with her. I'm telling you right now."

"Cool, whatever," replied Lamont.

"Tell you what," Burton said. "Get back in your car and follow me to the gas station. Just follow me up to the service station right now."

"For what?" asked Lamont.

"I got a Hundred Dollar bill on me!" exclaimed Burton. "This Hundred Dollars is yours. I'm going to fill your tank up with gas and give you this Hundred Dollars and wherever you decide to go tomorrow is on you, just as long as you know coming back to my mom's house is not an option."

"Hey, Burton I appreciate that," Lamont replied. "I'll pay you back."

"No I don't need you to pay me back," Burton said. "You're not going to pay me back so don't even say that. You just need to make some other arrangements as of tomorrow. As a matter of fact, come on let's go up to the gas station right now," Burton said. "Get in your car and you can just follow me up there. We'll go up there now."

Burton got into his car. Lamont got into his car. Lamont followed Burton to the gas station about a mile away from his house. When they arrived at the gas station, Burton took the nozzle of Lamont's car and pumped a tank full of gas into his car. The total amount of gas was Forty Dollars and some change. Burton gave him the Hundred Dollar bill and basically reinforced what he had already said earlier which was that as of tomorrow he was going to go somewhere besides his mom's house. He assured Lamont that in no uncertain terms was he to deviate in any way from the prescribed course of action or the two of them were going to have some problems. Burton then told Lamont to follow him around to a vacant house that his mom owned on Martin Luther King. They both got into their respective vehicles and drove to the house on Martin Luther King and parked in the driveway. Burton got out of his car and Lamont got out of his car. They met in the middle of the driveway and continued their conversation.

"LA this house is vacant," Burton said. "If you want to rent the house, I would be glad to rent it to you or if you want to buy the house, I would consider selling it to you. I will rent it to you for Six Hundred Dollars a month," he said.

"Well yea, sure I'll think about it," replied Lamont.

"The house needs a little work and it could take few days to get the work done," Burton said. "But if I rent it to you, I need my money and if you don't pay, I'm going to evict you, just as simple as that."

"It's a nice thought, but it's just me," Lamont said. "I don't really need that much house, it's only me," said Lamont.

"I also talked with your cousin Bill Frazier," Burton

said. "You got a whole nother side of your family of your mom's here in Mobile. Your mom and dad were both from Mobile. You got tons of cousins and relatives here. It's not like Mom is the only family you have or the only person you know down here," explained Burton.

"That's true, my mom, we have a lot of family here on her side," replied Lamont.

"Bill said you could come and stay with him for a few days if you like," said Burton.

"Oh, nah nah man I don't want to go and stay with him," said Lamont.

"Why not?" Burton said. "What's the difference. He might even be able to give you a job down there working at his club."

"Maybe I can talk to him about the gig at his club, but I don't want to stay with him," said Lamont.

"He said it was cool and he didn't mind," Burton said. "I just don't want to make you think I put you out with no options. Bill is a grown man about the same age as you. Seems like you and he would have much more in common than you and my mom."

"I'm just saying," Lamont said. "Burton I'll be fine."

"You don't have any problem staying with my mom, but you don't want to stay with Bill," Burton continued. "Oh, so what you're saying is that after a day or two Bill is going to be like he's a grown ass man who works every day and you need to be the same or be on your way," said Burton.

"Burton, I appreciate you loaning me the Hundred Dollars," Lamont said. "I promise I'll pay you back."

"You're not going to pay me back," Burton said. "It's a gift from me to you. If you don't want to stay with Bill fine. If you want to rent the house fine, but after today, Mom's house is not an option."

The next morning Lamont got his things and left. Burton was not sure at first if he had decided to go back to wherever he was in Georgia or if he was going to stay around Mobile for a little longer. He really did not care. He knew that his wife was expecting a baby, his Mom was mourning her husband and he needed to do what was in the best interest of his immediate family at the time and unfortunately, Lamont was in no way a part of the equation.

He would later find that Lamont had not gone back to Georgia and had in fact decided to remain in and around Mobile. However, he made no effort to contact his cousin Bill about lodging or employment. Burton was not sure exactly where he went or where he was staying at that point, but he knew he was not at Janet's house anymore, and that was all that mattered. Burton could have possibly allowed him to stay at his house; however, he would have been facing the same problem.

The objective was to get rid of Lamont and let Lamont do his own thing in his own space, home, apartment, room or place. Who comes to town saying they want to pay their last respects to their dearly departed and stays indefinitely? Janet and Burton had pressing issues going on in their lives and Lamont hanging around had only become a major distraction that could not possibly be benefiting anyone but him.

With Lamont now gone, Janet could get focused on some of the other important business matters that Burton needed to discuss with her. For several weeks, he felt that he could not talk with his mom or had to dip around corners and whisper to his mom about certain business-related issues because he was concerned that Lamont was hanging around trying to snoop into he and Janet's affairs. They were also able to start making arrangements and preparation to go to Wilmington. The days were ticking down and it was only a matter of time before Candace gave birth to their fourth child. Burton wanted to utilize his time as best he could while he was still in Mobile, but he also wanted to be able to get to Wilmington as soon as he heard his child was on the way. Although Janet now felt even more lonely than before, Lamont being gone was a bit of a relief for her. She was tired of him too and deep down inside, she knew what he was trying to do. She just did not want to make him leave and feel guilty about it. He was just a nephew around running his mouth about insignificant, trivial and ridiculous topics, keeping her mind away from the looming sorrow. Janet had been ready for Lamont to leave; she just didn't want to start to feel the loneliness inside that she kept dreading.

Burton and Candace agreed with their landlord in Wilmington, they were going to move out at the end of November. Candace's mother had been with her assisting her in North Carolina while Burton remained in Mobile. Burton arranged for Candace, her mother and the kids to stay in a condo at Wrightsville Beach for the month of December. Burton and Janet were going to join them in Wilmington at the condo. The plan was to welcome the new baby into the world, spend Christmas at the beachfront condo and move back to Mobile the day after New Year's. Moving was not very difficult because they did not have a lot of furniture in Wilmington.

They would put a few things in storage and then rent a U-Haul truck and transport everything back to Mobile the first of the year. Candace relocated to the beachfront condo with her mother and the kids as the clock started ticking on the birth of their new baby. Burton did everything he could to try and make it a smooth transition for them as they had the baby and prepared to relocate back to Mobile. However, with each passing day in the month of December, the birth of the new baby became more and more imminent.

On the 8th of December, Burton received a call from his mother-in-law Louise that Candace had gone into labor. He purchased a ticket and he left Mobile on the next plane smoking to Wilmington, North Carolina. Janet would follow a few days later.

CHAPTER EIGHT

Burton arrived back in Wilmington, rented a car and went immediately from the airport to New Hanover Memorial Hospital where he found his wife and their beautiful healthy bouncing baby boy. Candace had given birth to another baby boy and Burton could not have been prouder or pleased to look into the eyes of his newborn son. The little boy did not have a name yet. Burton had a few names in mind and Candace had a few names in mind, but they had not decided on anything or agreed on a name for their son. Here he was standing there holding his newborn son, witnessing a new life before him. His own flesh and blood staring back at him, looking right into his eyes.

After having laid his father to rest a little over two months ago, for a brief second he flashed back to the image of his father's dead and lifeless body after he had departed this earth. Now he was gazing into the face and the image of an infant child having just made it into this world. Burton felt a contentment that he had not felt in a long time. He felt a new vitality that he had not experienced for a while. Burton said a small prayer to himself and for his newborn and his family. Burton felt that God had taken someone away from him and had now replaced him with this beautiful baby and this wonderful new life. He still grieved for his dad, but he now had so much to be happy and joyous about. He hugged his wife who was still in a bit of pain and somewhat cranky. You did it, he told her. We did it. He's a handsome little guy, Burton said to his wife.

Burton realized he was witnessing the wheel of life right before his very own eyes. He hugged the little baby as firmly as he could without hurting him. He could not believe it. Finally, he felt the goodness of God working in his life. He believed that he was witnessing the miracle of life as it worked according to the natural order of things. He checked the baby's hands and feet and looked him over from head to toe real good. He was perfect and had received a good bill of health from the doctors at the hospital. For all intents and purposes, their newborn baby was happy and healthy. Burton had so much to be thankful for, it was now hard to continue to feel sorry for himself as he had for so many days prior to this day. What a gift from God Burton thought to himself as he held his newborn son in his arms.

Burton took one of the little baby bottles that Candace had sitting on the nightstand next to her bed. He checked to see if the baby was hungry and wanted to feed. After all this was certainly not his first rodeo with a baby. He placed the bottle gently inside of his mouth and he took the bottle and started feeding. This was the first time Burton had fed his newborn and it felt so good to experience this. He was delighted to say the least. He looked forward to his mother Janet coming to Wilmington. Burton hoped seeing this new bundle of life that had just entered their family would brighten her spirits as it had lifted his.

Burton asked Candace what she thought about the name Blake. However, she did not reply to his question. She had dozed off for a moment and apparently did not hear what he had said. Burton remained there at the hospital with Candace and the baby for a few hours, before leaving to go out to the beach to check on the other kids. The other boys were at Wrightsville Beach with Candace's mother. He was not certain exactly where they were staying, so he knew it would take a moment to find the condo. Burton felt a renewed strength and faith in life as he drove out to Wrightsville Beach to settle in.

The next day Candace was discharged from the hospital. Burton met them at the hospital to bring her and the baby back home to the condo where they were staying. They had a small crib in their bedroom at the condo for the baby as the other boys shared an adjoining room. Candace's mother was sleeping on the sofa. With Candace back at their spot on the beach, Louise started making plans to return to Michigan. She had been there in North Carolina with Candace and the boys practically ever since they had returned to North Carolina from Beck's funeral. Burton appreciated his mother-in-law coming to help out. It had made things much easier with him having been in Mobile and not there in Wilmington.

And so, his mother-in-law prepared to fly back home, and his Mother Janet would be arriving there in a few days. Janet had stayed back to get herself together, and they could receive a better bargain on an advanced purchased ticket. Burton had to pay top dollar to leave for Wilmington on such short notice. He also knew he would have to fly back to Mobile and return to Wilmington again before Christmas. He had practically finalized the arrangements to purchase the house on Oak Knoll before leaving. In a few days he would have to fly back and finalize the purchase. He wanted to get it done before the New Year, so when they returned to Mobile, they would be the proud new owners of that house.

Soon Burton took his mother-in-law to the airport and it wasn't long after when Janet arrived there in Wilmington. Burton had been worried about his mom back in Mobile by herself. He was worried that his cousin Lamont might be still be trying to pray on her in his absence. However, he had made Janet promise she would not allow him back into the house for any reason before she left town. Burton asked Janet to promise him that she would not tell Lamont of her plans to go out of town or even that Burton had left town. Although he was not sure how that went, he did make sure that Lamont was not staying there in her house when she left to go to Wilmington.

When Janet's flight arrived in Wilmington it was a cold dreary overcast December day in North Carolina. Burton was pleased to see Janet since he had been worried about her mental well-being. This was the first time she had been totally alone with herself since his father had passed. He was glad to have her in Wilmington. He hoped more than anything seeing the new baby who still did not have a name would brighten her horizons some.

Burton also thought a change of scenery and being back in her hometown would make her feel better as well. It was cold on the beach as they arrived that evening. The wind blew off the Atlantic Ocean causing a wind chill effect and making it feel even colder. Since it was the off season at Wrightsville Beach, Burton was able to rent the waterfront condo at a very reasonable price. It was furnished and there was no problem with them staying there for only one month.

As Janet settled into the condominium, she was greeted by her grandchildren Breton, Bryceton and Breaghan before Candace cordially said hello and showed her the new baby. Janet's eyes lit up as she saw the new baby for the first time. For the first time in months of Sundays it appeared Janet actually had displayed a sincere smile on her face. Burton had not seen her smile in so long. He knew that his mother had been through a lot these last few months and he somehow wanted to help lift her burden. Burton wanted so bad to help to ease the pain he knew she was feeling inside. She took the baby in her arms and asked Burton and Candace what they had decided to name him. They both shrugged their shoulders indicated they had not. They were still going back and forth about his name.

Janet, Burton, Candace, the kids and the baby all settled in for the next few weeks there on the beach as Christmas approached. Burton purchased a little Christmas tree for them to have at the condo. He also had some gifts for the kids which he hid over at Janet's godmother Mary Lilly's house. It was rather quiet and uneventful as the days went by. Janet was glad to be there with Burton and his family. Seeing the new baby and being with her grandchildren did make her feel a little less sorrowful. Janet also was glad to be spending time there in her hometown of Wilmington on the beach in winter. Janet reminisced about many Christmases over the course of her lifetime there in Wilmington.

She remembered some of the Christmases she had traveled there from Mobile or wherever she may have been living at the time. She also thought back further to Christmases she had spent there at 1013 South 12th Street with her brothers, sisters, her parents as a child. She did not have the strength or energy to back down that road with her sisters about the house which still sat there vacant and furnished. However, here she was staying on the beach with her family. She welcomed the chance to just relish this time with her family.

The coziness of the quaint beachfront condominium with Burton, her grandchildren and his wife was comforting to her. She did not wish to drudge up or bring up the issue about staying in the house. Burton had made the arrangements and he had not brought it up. Janet knew she was in no position to handle any unnecessary drama in her life. She wanted to be into herself, her thoughts, her feelings, her life and her family. Janet found herself in a good place as far as her state of mind was concerned. She was glad that Burton was back with his family also. She had wanted Burton there with her in Mobile, but had been concerned that his family needed him too, especially with Candace having been pregnant.

Even though she was still grieving deeply for her husband, she was glad not to be alone. It was easier when she was not alone. The kids and the baby kept her plenty of company. Candace was kind to her and showed appreciation for any help and assistance she could give while she recovered herself following the delivery. She was finally able to spread a little happiness and contentment over her sorrow and relished this time together with Burton and his family.

Burton returned to Mobile for two days prior to Christmas. He finalized everything and closed on their new house on Oak Knoll. He also went to court on the matter surrounding the incident with his son. The charges against him where dismissed. He handled the rest of his business in Mobile and returned to Wilmington to be with his family for Christmas.

They all spent a quiet Christmas there on the beach. For the most part Christmas was joyous. The baby was doing well. The kids were happy. They were all starting to get a little cabin fever though, as they looked forward to the new year and the trip to Mobile. On New Year's Eve Janet took a walk on the beach. It was chilly that night. She listened to the waves and gazed at the many stars in the sky on this cold and clear night.

There on the beach gazing into the nighttime sky she felt more spiritual and connected to God. She thought about Beck and wondered how long it would be before she would die and be with him in Heaven. She wondered if his soul were out there in the sky somewhere watching her as she walked along the beach, or was he just gone with no logical explanation.

Before leaving they went by and listed their son's name as Burton Bridge LeFlore II on his Birth Certificate. Afterward they got on the highway and headed back to Mobile. Burton and his family liked Wilmington; however, Burton felt it was best they move back. He bought the house to give his family the security of knowing they were coming back to something better than when they left Mobile.

CHAPTER NINE

It was January 2002, Janet, Burton, his children and his wife Candace had completed the relocation process back to Mobile. They enrolled the kids in school in Mobile and decided they would stay at the house with Janet until they completed a few minor repairs and renovations to their new home on Oak Knoll. The agents dropped by Janet's house and gave Burton the keys to their new house. They were all excited. Burton and Candace figured it would only take a week or two to get the house ready for them to move in, so they opted to stay with Janet instead of going to their old house to stay. Janet appreciated having her grandchildren and the new baby in the house with her.

One afternoon while Burton was at the office working and Janet was at home with Candace and the grandchildren, a man stopped by the house to visit with Janet. The gentleman's name was Mr. George Wilson and he had heard about Dr. LeFlore passing away. He wanted to talk with Janet and give her his condolences. The doorbell rang and Janet went to the door to answer. Janet was delighted when she realized who it was and opened the door. Burton's wife Candace also heard the door and went to see who it was.

"Ms. LeFlore, I'm so glad I caught you here at home," said George.

"How are you George?" Janet replied. "It's so nice to see you."

"I'm fine Ms. LeFlore," George said. "How are you?"

"Not bad for an old lady George," said Janet as Candace walked up behind them with the baby in her arm.

"I don't know about old lady, I thought you were the most beautiful Chemistry teacher that I ever had," said George. "And you are still beautiful Ms. LeFlore." He saw Candace walk up behind them and said, "Hi, how are you."

"Thank you George, that is so kind of you, even if you're just saying that." Janet said. "George this is my daughter-in-law Candace and the latest addition to our family, his name is Burton, but I think they are calling him Bridge."

"Hello Candace, very nice to meet you and little man there," said George.

"Hi," said Candace.

"Mrs. LeFlore I have been out in California working for the last few months, and I just got back into town not long ago," George said. "I heard Dr. LeFlore had passed away."

"Yes, he died back in October of last year," said Janet.

"You and Dr. LeFlore have always been two of my favorite people," George said. "Dr. LeFlore was my doctor and you were my favorite chemistry teacher."

"Dr. LeFlore and I were also very fond of you George," replied Janet.

"I had to stop by and give you my condolences Mrs. LeFlore, I'm so sorry to hear that Doc passed," said George.

"Yes, I am too," Janet said. "Very thoughtful of you to come by to see me."

"Anytime Ms. LeFlore," George said. "If there is anything I can do please let me know. I will be in town for the rest of the month before I return to work in California."

"You know Ms. LeFlore doesn't really know what she is talking about," Candace said as she pointed her finger to her head and twirled it at the temple. "She's not as astute as she used to be."

"What?" replied George with a frown.

"She's, u know," Candace said waving her fingers at her temple insinuating Mrs. LeFlore was crazy.

"What did you just say?" asked Ms. LeFlore.

"You heard me," said Candace with a chuckle.

"Candace I think you need to go back into the house," said Janet as Candace's cruel comments were extremely embarrassing to Janet.

"Mrs. LeFlore I got to run anyway," George replied. "I just wanted to make sure I came by to see you when I was in town, to let you know how sorry I was to hear about Dr. LeFlore."

"George it's always a pleasure to see you," Janet replied. "Feel

224

free to stop by anytime you're in town. I'm retired now, so most of the time, I'm here at home."

"OK you take care Mrs. LeFlore," said George as he hugged Janet goodbye.

"Bye George it was so nice to see you," replied Janet as they hugged goodbye.

When Janet returned inside, she took a seat in the living room for a moment. She was extremely angry that Candace had tried to embarrass her in front of her company and had furthermore, insinuated that she was crazy. They had only been back for a few days and Candace was up to it again. Janet's first mind was to go and confront Candace about her comments right then and there, but she decided that she was not going to allow Candace to know she had succeeded in making her angry. She thought that maybe she would mention it to Burton, but then Janet knew Candace would only tell Burton that she did not say any such thing.

Janet was furious. How could she stand there in her doorstep and make such a comment to someone she did not even know? Janet had loaned Burton over Twenty Thousand Dollars so that he could buy that house for her and the kids. She was doing everything she could to help Burton with Candace and his children. She showed absolutely no appreciation. How could she be so insensitive and rude toward her. How could she have stood there and completely disrespect her like that in front of company. If she would do it once and she allowed her to get away with it, surely knowing Candace she was going to try it again.

Janet thought to herself, she politely walked up and butted herself into a conversation that did not concern her, and then made those ridiculous comments about her. As Janet expected more visitors over the days to come, she wondered if this woman was going to try and embarrass her in front of all her company, insinuating that she was crazy. Janet knew one thing for sure, Candace was not going to get away with what she had done. She wanted to go and slap the shit out of her, but she knew Candace was holding the baby and she might hurt the baby. There had been many times in the past where Candace had said or done things and Janet just let it slide or she would let Beck deal with it. At least then she had her husband to bounce it around with. She missed Beck now more than ever, for so many years Beck had been her protector and defender. Now he was gone, and she felt that she did not have anyone to stick up for her. Ultimately if she brought it to Burton, it would put him on the spot. Candace would say Janet was trying to start confusion between them. She would try to get him to choose between the two of them.

Janet did not want to hurt Burton in any way; however, she knew she was not going to let Candace get away with what she had just done and said. Janet was going to make sure Candace knew in no uncertain terms, with Beck or without Beck, she was not going to be disrespected or talked about in any way. She was uncertain how she was going to do it, but she was going to confront her woman to woman about this incident and preferably it would not be in the presence of Burton or the other kids.

Another day or so went by, Janet mentioned what had happened to Burton, but she did not relate to him exactly what had happened or what had been said. She only told Burton that Candace had made some snide remarks toward her. She quickly downplayed the incident and told Burton not to worry about it. Clearly this was between Janet and Candace. She did not want Burton getting involved. Janet knew Candace would only try and twist it around to make herself the victim anyway. Besides this was between the two of them, Burton was not there, and he had not heard or witnessed anything. It was imperative that she handle this and make it perfectly clear to her daughter-in-law that she was not going to tolerate any disrespect from her.

Janet knew in her heart that Burton was still grieving his dad. She knew he was hurting just like she was, and he was trying hard to keep everything together for her, his children and Candace. She did not want to bother him with anything else or try and put him in a situation where he felt he was being asked to resolve this issue between them. Janet was going to resolve this herself. She would simply wait the appropriate moment to confront her about this.

Early the next morning Janet heard Candace in the kitchen fixing the babies bottle. The noise she was making in the kitchen awakened Janet. Janet could see Candace walking back and forth from the stove to the refrigerator. Janet also noticed she was not holding the baby in her arms. She was merely making preparation to feed the baby when he awoke, but it did not appear he had awakened yet. Burton was not awake, and neither were any of the other kids. This was the perfect opportunity to speak with her about the incident the day before. Janet sprung out of her bed and went to the bathroom and urinated. When she came out of the bathroom, Candace had left the kitchen and was on her way back upstairs. Janet ran quickly up the other stairway so she could catch her before she went back into the bedroom. As Janet reached the top of the stairs, she saw Candace at the top of the other stairway. She walked quickly down the hallway toward Candace before she even realized what was going on.

"Good morning Candace," said Janet.

"Hi," said Candace.

"Let me tell you something," Janet said. "Don't you ever try and disrespect me in my house again, you hear me."

"Mrs. LeFlore I've never disrespected you ever," said Candace.

"You call trying to insinuate that I'm crazy in front of my company," Janet said. "You don't think that's disrespectful?"

"I'd never disrespect you or anyone, Mrs. LeFlore," said Candace.

"Let me tell you something, Ms. Candace," Janet said. "You will respect me in my house or anywhere you might happen to be around me, or else I'm going to snatch that nappy hair right off your head. You'll find out just how crazy I really am, just try me. I'll beat the breaks off you, Candace."

"This isn't your house, it's Dr. LeFlore's house," said Candace.

"What did you say?" said Janet.

"Dr. LeFlore didn't really love you," Candace said. "Because if he did, he wouldn't have had children by other women."

"You don't know anything about my husband and I'm not about

227

to tolerate your mouth, not one more minute," Janet said. "You need to shut up if you have any remote idea what is good for you, because I'll show you better than I can tell you," she said.

"I think its disrespectful to all of us that you already have other men coming over here to see you before the dirt has even settled on Dr. LeFlore's grave," said Candace.

"Other men coming to see me," Janet said. "That was a former student of mine and one of Beck's patients. You're getting it mighty twisted young lady," replied Janet.

"If you ask me that's disrespectful," replied Candace. "Excuse me, you're crazy and I don't have any more time for this. I have children to take care of," said Candace as she started to walk away from Janet.

Janet was blocking the hallway. Candace walked around Janet and attempted to proceed to the bedroom. As she walked around Janet, Janet grabbed her by the back of her collar and snatched her to the floor before Candace even realized what had happened. She dragged Candace down the hallway toward the room where Burton was sleeping. Janet pushed open the door with one hand and dragged Candace with the other hand. Altogether she must have snatched her about fifteen feet along the floor. She saw Burton laying there in the bed fast asleep, holding his infant son in his arms. Janet pulled Candace on the floor around to the other side of the bed to where Burton was sleeping. Once she got to where she knew Burton could see them, she called him.

"Burton, Burton!" exclaimed Janet.

"What is it?" Burton said as he woke out of his deep sleep and lifted his head from the pillow and looked in their direction. Burton saw Janet standing there holding Candace by the collar of her shirt. Candace was on the floor behind Janet.

"Burton!" said Candace.

"What is it?" asked Burton.

"You better get this Bitch!" Janet said. "You better get this Bitch. She's messing with the wrong one." Janet let Candace's collar lose and walked out of the bedroom leaving Candace on the floor and

Burton sitting up in bed now looking on with a confused frown on his face.

"You're going to let your mom attack me," said Candace.

"What are you talking about?" Burton asked. "What's going on?"

"She's crazy," said Candace.

"Yea bitch you got one more time to come out of your mouth with that shit, and you're going to find out just how crazy I am," replied Janet.

"Mrs. LeFlore, I didn't do anything to you," Candace replied. "I didn't do anything to her Burton."

"You will respect me in my house or anywhere you see me," Janet said. "Or I'm going to snatch another hole in your ass."

"Please this is ridiculous," said Burton.

"I'm telling you right now, you better get that little dumb bitch in check or I will," said Janet."

Janet stormed out of the door and went downstairs. The commotion had awakened the baby. Candace got up off the floor and walked over to the side of the bed. Burton handed the baby to her. She went to look for the bottle she had prepared earlier for him. Burton was still laying there dumfounded about what had just occurred. He was not certain what had happened. All he knew was it appeared his mom had dragged Candace into his room. He wondered what Candace had done to make his mom so angry. Janet was clearly extremely upset and that was not like Janet. He was not sure if he had ever seen her so angry in his entire life. Janet was livid. He was not certain what she was talking about. He was sure; however, she meant whatever she was saying. He covered his head and tried to go back to sleep.

Burton asked Janet what had made her so mad at Candace. She indicated that Candace had embarrassed her in front of someone who had come by to visit and give their condolences. When he asked Candace, what had happened she denied any and all wrongdoing and acted as if Janet had tried to attack her for absolutely no reason. Burton knew Janet was in a very vulnerable state of mind at this juncture, and he knew that Candace had done something to antagonize her. Burton also knew it was likely Candace would continue to antagonize Janet. He knew then it was extremely important that he hurried to get his house in order so they could move. Although he did not want to leave Janet alone, it was time. She would have to start making the adjustments in her life that she needed to make. He would need to make the adjustments he needed to make in order to take care of his family. It was not fair to his mom to have Candace around the house antagonizing her during this time in her life.

Meanwhile, Lamont was still in town and was coming by daily to visit with Janet. Burton had also heard his cousin was going to some of the churches in the community asking that they give him money. A local pastor had approached Burton on the street one day and asked him if he had a cousin named Lamont LeFlore. When Burton acknowledged that he did have a cousin named Lamont, Pastor Tyson said Lamont had told him he was John LeFlore's grandson and that he had fallen on hard times. He requested the church give him financial assistance which he indicated they had given him. The preacher also said his church was not the only one Lamont had asked. Pastor Tyson indicated that to the best of his knowledge Lamont had received assistance from at least four of the six churches he knew for a fact he had asked for donations from. Pastor Tyson told Burton that he estimated Lamont had received approximately Four or Five Thousand Dollars from the respective churches.

Burton's son Breton told him that he was riding with Grandmother and Lamont after school and they had gone to McDonald's. Breton said Lamont approached some woman at the checkout counter and started talking with her. According to Burton's son, after a brief conversation with the lady, she purchased Lamont lunch and they went and sat at a table in the restaurant and ate together. Breton related this story to his dad about the same time Pastor Tyson had told him about the money Lamont had received from the local churches.

Knowing his cousin, Burton did not find any of this hard to believe. He just kept feeling like Lamont ultimately wanted to set his mom up for some type of con or fraud. Lamont was a con man to his heart and there was no way he could make himself feel comfortable with Lamont continuing to want to hang around Janet. Janet was such a trusting person. Janet found it hard to think or believe that anyone was out to deceive her or take advantage of her. Janet truly wanted to believe that everyone was honest and trustworthy like her.

The following night Janet received a phone call from a homeless shelter downtown. The man on the phone asked to speak with Janet when Burton answered the phone. Burton asked who was calling and the man stated he was from the Rescue Mission. He told Burton that he had Mrs. LeFlore's son there who stated he had nowhere to go for the night because she had put him out, and would not allow him to stay at home with her. Burton asked what the man's name was, and the voice on the other end of the phone said his name was Lamont LeFlore. As if Burton was surprised. He found it unbelievable that Lamont had gone to a homeless shelter and had them call Janet with that bullshit. There had been many times over the course of his life, when Burton had thought his father to be an asshole with little understanding. He had witnessed some instances in the past where his dad had dealt rather harshly with Lamont. Burton told the man his mother was not available and hung up the telephone.

"Who was that Baby?" asked Janet.

"It was someone from the Rescue Mission," said Burton.

"The Rescue Mission," Janet said. "What did he want?"

"He said he was calling because your son was down there and had nowhere to stay or anywhere to go because you had put him out and wouldn't allow him to come home," said Burton.

"What son is he talking about," Janet said. "You're my son and you're right here."

"He's talking about Lamont," said Burton.

"Lamont!" Janet exclaimed. "Lamont is at a homeless shelter and he told them I put him out?"

"Yes, that is exactly what I'm saying," replied Burton.

"Oh, my goodness," Janet asked. "Why would he tell a lie like that?"

"Because he's a con," Burton said. "Can't you see Lamont is out to con everyone he comes in contact with. I know he is trying to con you if he hasn't already."

"I know I can't find my driver's license, my bank card and one of my credit cards," said Janet.

"So, Lamont stole your bank card and a credit card?" asked Burton.

"I'm not sure it was him, Burton," Janet said. "I called and neither my bank card nor credit card had any unusual charges made on the accounts. I told them to notify me if there were any charges made to the cards."

"Good. Well maybe he'll try and use them, and they'll arrest his ass," Burton said "I guess they will finally get him for the money he stole from Grandma Teah. Mom nobody got your cards but him."

"Burton all I said was I can't find my cards," Janet said. "Let's not jump to any conclusions yet. If he has the cards and he tries to charge anything on them, they will pick it up right away since they have been alerted to look for any suspicious activity on the cards."

"You just don't get it do you Mom," said Burton.

"He's your cousin," replied Janet.

"Mom tell me the truth," Burton said. "Have you given Lamont any money since he has been down here?"

"I gave him Five Hundred Dollars," said Janet. "Total I have probably given him about Six Hundred Dollars."

"Are you serious," said Burton.

"Yes, I gave him Five Hundred Dollars," said Janet.

"Why is this the first time you mentioned it to me Mom," said Burton.

"Because I knew you would be upset about it. Burton, it's just a few hundred dollars," Janet said. "That's not going to make or break me. I gave it to him, and I don't mind him having it."

"Now your credit cards are missing, and you got people calling from homeless shelters," Burton said. "Lamont is going to mess around and make me hurt him."

"Baby there is nothing wrong with showing some compassion

toward people sometimes," Janet said. "He's family."

"If he was family, he wouldn't be around here causing unnecessary problems for you when you have enough going on in your life right now." Burton said, "Mom from what I hear, he's gotten several thousand dollars from some local churches, so please don't give him any more money, or you'll never be able to get rid of him."

"Whaaaaaat!" exclaimed Janet.

"Yes, you heard correctly," Burton said. "I heard from Reverend Tyson he's been to several churches in the area begging and hit them all up for money and most of them gave it to him."

The next day Lamont drove his car to Janet's house and parked it out front at the little driveway in the front yard. He indicated to Janet and Burton that his vehicle had broken down and needed to be repaired. He asked Burton if it would be alright for him to park it there until he was able to get it fixed. Janet said it was alright, so Burton had no choice but to agree reluctantly. As long as Lamont understood he still was not welcome to stay at the house with Janet. However, at this point there was no room for him anyway with Burton, Candace and Janet's grandchildren there with her.

The situation with his cousin Lamont was starting to become a bit of a nightmare for Burton. At every turn and every juncture here was Lamont with some different angle at taking advantage of his mother's kindness and generosity. He did not trust Lamont one bit and started to fear what Lamont might be waiting to orchestrate if he got the opportunity. He was convinced that Lamont was the one who had stolen her identification and credit cards. Burton started to suspect that Lamont might have been attempting to steal Janet's identity. As far-fetched as it sounded, he did not put anything past him.

Burton asked himself, what would his dad do? He did not have to search long or hard for the answer to that question. He knew full well what Beck would do in the same or similar circumstance. As a matter of fact, he knew his dad would not have waited nearly as long to nip Lamont's mess in the bud. Deep down inside, Burton felt his

Dad would have been disappointed to even know he had allowed him to come in the first place. As much as he did not want to do it, he was going to have to take some serious steps to get rid of him once and for all.

Janet soon told Burton she was unable to find her lipstick and few other items of makeup she had in her purse. She had also mentioned having misplaced another credit card. Burton was unconcerned for the most part about the lipstick and makeup as figured his mom had just misplaced her lipstick and the other personal items from her purse that she claimed she could not find. However, the fact that she said she was missing another credit card was cause for concern.

Burton asked his boys if they had seen any of Grandma's stuff. Breton and Bryceton denied having seen any of her belongings. Burton then asked Breaghan who was only three years old at the time. Breaghan was only talking a little bit, but he was walking and already into everything. Breaghan looked at his dad very innocently as he appeared to understand his dad's questions but did not know how to answer. Burton repeated the question to Breaghan who continued to look at him very innocently. Burton was not sure what was going on in his son's mind. He was not sure if he understood what he was asking, even though he appeared to understand, he did not answer.

They were in the kitchen. Breaghan walked toward the dining room and looked into the room. He turned around and walked back toward his dad and held out his hand. Burton took Breaghan's hand. He was starting to wonder if he might be on to something. Breaghan never said a word as he held his dad's hand and led him toward the dining room. He followed his son but was uncertain what he wanted. Once in the dining room, Breaghan took him over to the corner of the room. In between two shelves, was an antique footrest that was placed against the wall. Breaghan looked up at Burton and then down at the footrest. Burton asked Breaghan again if he knew where Grandma's stuff was. Breaghan reached over and opened the footrest. Inside the footrest was a box compartment. When Breaghan opened the footrest, Burton could see Janet's license, credit cards and makeup inside.

At that point, he realized his son had taken the items and placed them very neatly inside of the footrest. Burton was somewhat relieved to have found the items Janet was missing. He called Janet into the dining room, where she now saw her things neatly placed in the footrest. Everything she claimed to be missing was there. Her driver's license, her credit cards and her lipstick and makeup had all been placed in the footrest. There was no doubt that Breaghan had placed them in there. After having a laugh about it with his mother, he removed the items and handed them to her. Burton took notice to the fact, that Breaghan did not move the items and leave them sitting around. He put them all into the same place and had them neatly organized and put safely away. Breaghan was a precocious and intelligent child who never stopped fascinating Burton.

Janet was relieved to have her identification and credit cards back as she suspected Lamont had taken them too. Similarly, Burton had a load off his mind now that he knew Lamont had not taken his mom's stuff. Burton thought it was good for him, that he did not take Janet's cards and identification. He was sorry for having accused him of any wrongdoing; however, nothing changed the fact that he was going to have to get rid of his cousin. Lamont's continued presence was counterproductive, and he had become nothing more than an unwanted intermeddler. As far as Burton was concerned, the call from the Rescue Mission trying to make his mother feel guilty about him not having a place to stay was the last straw. It was time for him to go home or back to where he had come or wherever he was going because Burton was not going to have him causing Janet any unnecessary stress and confusion.

The next day Lamont came by the house to see Janet. Burton was there and decided to talk with him about some of the things he had been hearing as well as the call from the Rescue Mission. He felt bad that he had accused him wrongly of taking Janet's identification and credit cards, but none the less he was going to have to ease up on his mom with his shenanigans. When he arrived at the house, Burton saw this as a good opportunity to talk with him.

"Lamont why did you have somebody from the Rescue Mission call Moms last night?" asked Burton.

"That wasn't intentional Burton," Lamont said. "I went down there because I needed somewhere to stay for the night, and they asked if I had any relatives in town that I could stay with. I didn't know they were going to call Aunt Janet."

"But obviously you gave them her phone number, and as we discussed before, it's not like she is the only relative or person you know in Mobile who might let you stay with them," according to Burton.

"Lamont you have been nothing but welcome here," Janet said. "You stayed with me for almost two months and I didn't put you out."

"Burton said I had to leave," replied Lamont.

"Yes, Lamont you had to leave," Burton said. "Who comes to someone's house under the pretext of attending a funeral and stays for almost two months. Who does that Lamont?"

"Hey, I apologize it was a misunderstanding," Lamont said. "Aunt Janet I'm sorry they contacted you last night. I didn't ask them to."

"Lamont, my mom is going through enough right now without all of this unnecessary bullshit going on concerning you," said Burton.

"I want to move down here, and I should have some arrangements for a pad very soon," said Lamont.

"If you want to move down here nobody is trying to stop you," Burton said. "There is a whole city out there, do your thing but that doesn't have to involve my mom."

"Lamont, I have tried to help you and you know it," said Janet.

"Aunt Janet, I promise you, I will pay you back," replied Lamont.

"Reverend Tyson said you're going around to churches in town asking for money," Burton said. "Lamont, the LeFlores are proud, hardworking people, they are not beggars."

"Burton I don't know why he would bring that to you, but truthfully that is personal," Lamont said. "It doesn't concern you."

"It doesn't concern me Lamont and there's a whole lot of things that don't concern me or Moms," Burton continued. "That we don't want to be concerned with especially at a time like this. You feel me."

"Sure," replied Lamont. "I'm on dialysis. I have to dialyze a minimum or three times a week. I can't work."

"You didn't work before you went on dialysis," Burton interjected. "There is no way you can't tell me you couldn't do some light work for a few nights a week like down at Bill's club and he could pay you under the table," he said. "But you haven't even called him.

Later that night Burton looked outside of his window into the front yard. He could see Lamont's car parked in the driveway to the left side of the house. From the window there appeared to be a light on in the car or some object in the vehicle. Burton could not tell what it was from his window, so he decided to go outside and take a closer look. Burton found a flashlight in the drawer downstairs and proceeded out the back door. He walked around the house to the front yard where the car was parked. As he approached the car, he could tell there was no light on in the vehicle. However, there did appear to be an unknown object inside the car. Burton walked up to the window on the driver's side of the car and he saw what appeared to be Lamont sleeping on the front seat of his car. He shined the flashlight into the car to verify that it was in fact his cousin. Burton was somewhat angered to find his cousin sleeping outside in the car because he knew if Janet found out she would feel sorry for him and invite him to stay at her house again.

Burton knew it would only be a matter of days before he and his kids moved into their new house, and he was not about to have Lamont moving back in the house with his mom. Burton wondered why all of this was going on now, in the wake of his father's death. Finally, he came to the realization that it was going to continue until he manned up. No more Mr. Nice guy, cousin or no cousin, family or no family this dude had to go, plain and simple. Lamont knew his aunt was emotionally vulnerable, and he knew her to be a kind and generous person. He had every intention of praying on her for everything he could get. Now he had devised a scheme to park his car in the yard and sleep there until she invited him back into the house to stay. Who knows what he had concocted in his mind to try and get over on Janet? Burton thought about opening the door, pulling him out of the car and just trying to beat the crap out of him. Then Burton thought he would go back inside, call the police and tell them someone was sleeping in a car parked in their front yard.

Burton decided not to call the police or to try and do bodily injury to his cousin. He then shined the flashlight into his face to awaken him. He stood there outside of the window for about a minute with the flashlight shining in his face before he stirred and woke up. Burton could tell he was a little alarmed when he woke up with all of this light shining in his face. Lamont eventually realized it was Burton standing outside of his car with a flashlight.

"Hey, would you mind getting that light out of my face," said Lamont.

"Dude what are you doing?" asked Burton.

"I'm trying to get some sleep," replied Lamont.

"Why are you sleeping out here in the front yard in your car," said Burton.

"Where else do you suggest I sleep," said Lamont.

"Practically anywhere you like except here," said Burton. "Why are you trying to put my mom through this shit man? She doesn't need this."

"I don't see where you have any big law firm on Royal Street," said Lamont.

"Say what, what did you say?" asked Burton.

"I said I don't see where you have any big law firm on Royal Street in Downtown Mobile," Lamont said. "You're not balling, and you don't have a Million-dollar law practice on Royal Street."

"Perhaps I'm not and no I don't have a law office on Royal Street," Burton said. "But what the fuck does that have to do with anything?"

"At least your father left you something," Lamont said. "He left you well off; John, my dad didn't leave me shit. None of us, me,

Chris or Butch. John didn't leave us shit."

"Maybe he didn't leave you shit because he knew you would just coke it up, and snort it all up your fucking nose," Burton replied.

"Uncle Walker cared enough about you to leave you well off," said Lamont.

"For your information, my father didn't leave me shit either," Burton said. "What he did or did not leave me is none of your business," he said. "So, I'm still trying to figure out what the fuck you're talking about."

"You know exactly what I'm talking about," replied Lamont.

"Lamont you're not going to be around here putting my mom through unnecessary changes," Burton said. "She's been through enough. So, this is what I'm going to need you to do."

"Yea and what do you need me to do?" asked Lamont.

"I'm going to need you to have this car out of her front yard no later than Friday of this week," Burton said. "If the car isn't out of the yard by Friday, I am going to have it impounded."

"I told you it's not working, and I need to get it fixed," replied Lamont.

"That's cool and you certainly can't get it fixed with it sitting out here in the front yard," replied Burton.

"Alright I guess I can get it done by Friday," said Lamont.

"Fixed or not," Burton said. "It needs to be moved by Friday. If you keep fucking with my mom, there are going to be some real consequences."

"Aunt Janet is my aunt, she is my peeps too," Lamont said. "I haven't been doing anything but hanging out and trying to keep her company to keep her mind off Uncle Walker having passed."

"That's cool, just know that I need you to have this car out of here no later than Friday, take care," said Burton.

Burton turned around and walked away from the car. He meant every bit of what he said. His cousin was being ridiculous, and it was just time for him to leave. Burton felt that Janet needed to be protected from him, because in Burton's mind, he was trying everything he could to play on his mom's sympathy and emotions.

239

Now he realized why Beck had dealt so harshly with him in the past. Lamont could be a nice person at times, but he was just plain trifling. If he had a home in Georgia somewhere, how could he just drop everything and leave. Burton didn't know and he did not care. He had to go.

For weeks now, Burton had been doing renovation work at his new house on Oak Knoll. He had planned for the work to have been completed much earlier. He had hired Henry Rhodes, the handy man that his dad had used for so many years to work on the property. Burton had asked him to paint four bedrooms; however, it seemed that every day Candace would go by and ask him to do something different. Instead of painting the rooms like he was supposed to do, he would do what Candace had asked instead of what he had been hired to do.

Several weeks had gone by and a lot of things had been done, except what Burton had hired him to do. Furthermore, what he had done was botched for the most part. At the end of the week, he would expect Burton to pay him for the week, even though he had made very little progress toward the job he had originally been hired to do. For a few weeks, Burton had reluctantly gone along with this, because he wanted to allow his wife to have some input into what was going on with the work to the house. However, Burton quickly started to realize that Rhodes was taking advantage of the situation and milking him for money.

Burton was gearing up for his new business venture, with his real estate company and he thought and expected that Rhodes was going to be an integral part of that operation. Rhodes had been working for his family for many years. While doing work on his new home, Rhodes had asked Burton to loan him money to purchase a new truck. Burton figured it would be no problem, since he was planning to be working with Rhodes for some time now as he built his business. Burton loaned Rhodes Three Thousand Five Hundred Dollars so he could purchase a new truck. Burton was also paying him several hundred dollars a week for the work he was doing at their house.

Approximately six weeks had gone by and Rhodes was still dragging out the work, insisting he had done a lot of work per Candace's request even though he had not made any substantial progress toward completing the four rooms. Eventually, Burton got fed up. Burton had been fed up. When Friday rolled around, Burton asked if he had completed the rooms. Rhodes said he would have it done by the end of the following week. Burton told Rhodes that he would pay him when he finished the rooms. Rhodes became angry stating that he needed his money. Burton indicated that he now understood why his dad would get into it with Rhodes sometimes about various jobs that he did for him. During the course of the argument Rhodes indicated that he resented working for Burton because he was much older than Burton and had always looked at Burton as a child. It was hard for him to respect Burton as a man, and he resented working for someone who was so much younger than him. Although he had no problem borrowing money from Burton to buy himself a new truck.

Rhodes and Burton argued for a considerable amount of time out front of the house. It became increasingly evident that Rhodes was just playing Candace against him and milking them for as much money as he could get. He knew full well what he was doing and finally during the verbal altercation between them, he had said he did not want to work for Burton. So, it became obvious to Burton that Rhodes was not going to play any role whatsoever in his real estate business. Burton payed Rhodes some money and fired him on the spot stating there was no reason in returning to work at his house on Monday. Although, parting with Rhodes was bittersweet. He had been working for his family for many years. For the sake of posterity, Burton really wanted to keep Rhodes on as he moved full force into his new business. However, the sentiments voiced during their disagreement were clear as day and there was no way Burton would consider continuing to work with this man from this point. Burton also planned to make sure Rhodes would not do any more work for his mother either.

CHAPTER TEN

Janet found herself now all alone in her huge house, as Burton and his family had now moved into their new home around the corner. This is the moment of truth she had tried so hard to avoid for the last few months since Beck had passed. The instance where she would discover herself at home forlorn and confined by the solitary walls that housed her being, with nothing but the memories of the life she had once shared with her husband Beck. The silence in her house was so loud it was almost deafening.

She wondered what she would now do with herself since she was a retired widow. For the majority of her life, two of the most important things that kept her going were her marriage to Beck and work. Now she was retired, and her husband was dead. Burton had been a loving and devoted son. He had stuck closely by her side for the last few months and helped her considerably, but he had his own family to take care of. She could no longer monopolize all his time and attention. Janet felt useless and like she had no real purpose in life anymore.

She struggled to try and redefine herself as she sought to find a new sense of self-esteem and meaning for her life. A part of her felt that her life had ended when Beck died. Beck had been her everything ever since she was a teenager. She had known no man but him for close to Sixty years. Certainly, she was not about to remarry at her age. Who would want to marry her anyway at the ripe old age of Seventy-Three?

Anyone who even pretended to want her would surely have some type of ulterior motive. She would never find the tender sincerity and love she had once shared with Beck, with another man. Sure, there had been days in her life with Beck that she would like to forget or wished had never happened. However, all in all, she was thankful for her life with Beck. Beck was her soul mate and she felt blessed to have been able to share her life with a man like Beck who she had a common vision with and who she respected and admired so deeply. Janet would not have traded their lives together for anything in the world, and she was not about to entertain the idea of having someone else in her life at this point.

So, who was she now, besides a lonely old lady? She still had her sisters, but most of them were busy with their own husbands and families. When the depression she had been dreading for some time, started to set in, she felt like she did not want to live anymore. However, she was afraid to die. The melancholy seemed to move in like a huge dark rain cloud that had been looming in the distance for the longest time.

Now the gloom and grayness had managed to locate itself over her personal space and become a raging storm. Her life seemed like it had come to a standstill. Janet felt despondent and her spirits reached an all-time low. Janet tried to find something to be happy about since all she could grasp was unhappiness and despair. She prayed this feeling she had inside would not last until the day she took her last breath and said her final goodbye.

Janet struggled to recognize a sense of self because she no longer knew or recognized herself. She wondered exactly who she was at this point. She felt so isolated and forsaken. She could not overcome a sense of abandonment, even though she knew her precious Beck would never abandon her in life. It seemed like she did not have a friend in the world. Janet cried and cried and cried now that she was alone. These were her private tears. The tears she did not want anyone to know about except God. She prayed to God to give her strength to face the days to come as she knew it would not be easy. The same day Burton and his family moved into the massive house, his in-laws showed up. Literally no sooner than they had moved whatever little furniture they had into the house from their other house and out of storage, Candace's mother, father and one of her sisters arrived. Burton and his family had not spent one night in the house before they got there. This would have been the first night in their house. It was late in the evening when they arrived. Candace ushered them in and told them to put their things in the master bedroom. Although Burton was happy to see her parents, it seemed like they would have at least waited for a day or two for them to get settled before they showed up. Burton had just purchased a brand-new bed for the master bedroom they had not even slept in yet. Not to mention the bedroom itself.

He decided not to say anything or raise any objection to his in-laws sleeping in their new bedroom and brand-new bed before they had a chance to sleep there. However, he was not happy about it. Later that night Burton decided to go and visit with his mom for a minute before he went to bed. Since they had not put any blinds up to the windows in the bedroom yet, Burton passed by the window to his bedroom on his way out and saw them about to go to sleep in his new bed. It seemed to Burton that his newly purchased bed that was intended to be private for him and his wife had now become public. He did not mind her family coming to visit as he understood they were curious and excited about the new house. He just thought they should have had at least a brief minute to get settled in before they welcomed any company. After visiting briefly with his mom, he returned home and made a pallet for himself on the living room floor and went to sleep alone.

That night Janet struggled to maintain her composure as she continued to feel so sad and alone. This was the first night she had spent by herself in the house since Beck had passed. She laid down in bed on the side of the bed where Beck used to sleep. Janet tried to smell him on the sheets as she nestled her head in the pillow, eyes puffy and red from having cried most of the evening. She was sniffling and she wiped her nose. Janet took a deep breath and tried to just lay there for a minute and not think about anything.

She tried to make her mind go totally blank since she could not seem to think about anything but Beck and how she was going to go forward from here without him. Janet did not have any financial concerns. She was not worried about money or how she was going to pay her bills. She wondered how she was going to live without the relationship and companionship of the man she had been married to for all these years.

She and Beck had an alarm system in their house. Beck had always been very adamant about their security. He had an array of devices installed around their house to detect anyone and anything that should not be there or might possibly cause them a threat. Usually, Beck and Janet would always turn the alarm system on before going to bed. Tonight, Janet started to turn the alarm on, and then she stopped and decided not to. She thought to herself, she would be terrified if the alarm went off in the middle of the night and it was a false alarm.

As far as anyone coming into the house to harm her, she was not certain if she even cared anymore. Subliminally she wondered if Beck's spirit was still in the house and if his spirit would provide her with any protection and comfort. Surely God would look out for her as she would be sleeping in her huge house alone for many nights to come. She was used to the house and was not afraid to be there by herself. The only thing she really feared right now was her own thoughts and feelings. She was not worried about anybody, more so she was concerned about what was going on inside her own mind, mostly the grief, sorrow and depression she was experiencing.

Janet sipped her champagne as she tried to drift off to sleep. Laying there on Beck's side of the bed brought her what little comfort she had decided it was going to give. It is like you tell yourself there is something you can do to make yourself feel a little better and just accept in your heart it will, so you can have some way to pacify yourself. Once again she felt the tears welling up inside of her eyes as she no longer had any reason to hold them back. She hoped that after she finished crying it might make her feel better. Her jaw was hurting her again. The pain was enormous. She wondered in comparison what hurt worst; her jaw or the sadness in her heart. She decided to take a pain pill. After all, this would help her sleep better through the night. After taking the pill and a few more sips of her champagne she drifted off to sleep.

The next morning for Janet was pretty much like the day before. She awakened having rested well. She prepared herself some coffee and a small breakfast of two croissants and jelly. Her jaw was still hurting some and she thought about taking another pain pill but decided against it. Janet took a few bites out of her croissant, but she still did not have much of an appetite. Her back was hurting, and she had a pain in her side. She could not understand why. Janet felt like she was breaking down physically. She wondered if she had simply become old and unattractive. Janet felt like she was hurting everywhere. She was hurting emotionally and physically. Janet sat there at her kitchen table by herself sipping her coffee and staring into space. She would have liked to have seen Leassie, but it was the weekend so Leassie did not come to work that day. Janet sat there quietly absorbed in her thoughts for over an hour before her sister called and interrupted her silence.

"How are you doing sister?" said Anna.

"A little lonely, but I'm doing," Janet replied. "Burton and the kids moved into their new house yesterday."

"You bought Burton and Candace a house?" said Anna.

"I gave them the money for the down payment," Janet said. "He said he would pay me back, but I told him not to worry about it. I just hope they like the new house." She said, "with the new baby they needed the extra space, and it's a beautiful house."

"Well, well," said Ann.

"He and the boys are right around the corner from me," said Janet.

"That's nice," Anna said. "I'm sure you're happy to have them back in Mobile,"

"I guess if they had stayed in Wilmington, I might have considered moving back," Janet said. "I'm not sure how that would have worked after I've been here most of my adult life."

"So, what is he doing now?" Anna asked. "Is he going to practice Law?"

"He didn't tell you?" Janet said. "Burton has founded a new business. He is going into the real estate business. He is going to use Beck's old office, and he has gone full steam ahead since the first of the year."

"The real estate business," said Anna.

"Yes, he didn't tell you," Janet said. "That's all he's been talking about."

"I heard him say something about real estate while we were in Mobile for the funeral," Anna said. "I assumed he was talking about renting out you and Beck's houses."

"Yes, he is going to be handling our properties," Janet said. "Amazingly it's only been a few months and he has already gotten some pretty nice listings. I'm starting to see his signs all over town."

"Oh really, that is wonderful," replied Anna.

"Burton is such a blessing from God," Janet said. "He's also been very helpful and supportive of me here lately, and he's been handling pretty much everything pertaining to Becks estate."

"You're just going to let him sell all your property?" said Anna.

"I hope not, but I trust his judgment," Janet said. "At the end of the day, it's his anyway. One of these days I'll be gone, and it will belong to him anyway so who cares really."

"That's your baby," said Anna.

"Yes, he is," Janet said. "And how is your baby, Bobby Beck?"

"He's fine," said Anna. "Me and Mike are planning to go to Connecticut to visit him soon."

Burton had spent the entire Saturday there with his family and his in-laws. He was busy entertaining them and getting things organized around the house. However, his mom was heavy on his mind all day as he knew this was her first day alone in the house without anyone there to keep her company. Burton knew she was lonely and so as the day went on, he contacted her. Burton indicated that Candace's parents were there visiting, and he invited her over to the house to visit with him and Candace's family. He hoped that visiting with them might lift Janet's spirits.

A few hours later in the evening, Janet managed to get herself together. She took a bath, put on some clothes and powdered her face. She drove around the corner to Burton's house. As she turned down Oak Knoll and made the curve toward their house, she saw the large house sitting back off the street. She parked out front and turned off her car. She exited the vehicle and walked up the long walkway to the front door of the house. She approached the over-sized front doors and rang the doorbell. Burton heard the bell and left the table where he was talking with Candace's parents and her sister to answer the door. He was excited to welcome Janet to their new home.

"Hi Baby," said Janet.

"Hi Mom, it's so nice to see you," Burton said. "Welcome to our new house."

"Who is that Burton?" said Candace.

"It's my mom," replied Burton.

"Your mom," replied Candace.

"Yea my mom," Burton said. "Come on in Mom."

"Are Candace's parents here?" asked Janet.

Janet started to step inside. Before Janet could get inside of the door, Candace had jumped up from the table and ran to the door and blocked Janet from coming into the house. She shoved Burton to the side and blocked the doorway.

"Mrs. LeFlore you're not welcome in my house," said Candace.

"Excuse me," Burton said. "This is our house and my mother is always welcome any time."

"No, she's not," said Candace.

"Really says who?" asked Burton.

"Says me," Candace replied.

"Mom, never mind her," Burton said. "Please come in."

"No Burton maybe I shouldn't," Janet said. "I don't want to cause any confusion in your household."

"Well that is exactly what you're doing," Candace said. "I would appreciate it if you would go back to your car and leave."

"Candace you better watch your mouth," said Burton.

"I don't want her here. She's not welcome," said Candace.

"Burton I better go," Janet said as she turned and started to walk back to her car.

As Janet started to walk back to her car, Candace pushed past Burton and followed Janet into the yard as if she was going to try and fight Janet. Her parents and sister heard the commotion from where they were seated in the dining room. Although it is not likely that Candace was going to assault Janet in any way because Janet would have probably dusted her from one end of the yard to the other. Candace did behave in a threatening manner toward her as though she were trying to provoke or intimidate her. Burton went out into the yard to make sure there was no type of physical confrontation between the two of them. Candace's sister Lydia came to the door and called her. Her parents never came to the door to see what was going on.

"Candace!" Lydia said. "Hi, Mrs. LeFlore!"

"If you have any idea what is good for you, you will back up off me," Janet said. "Hi, Lydia, nice to see you. Please tell your mom and dad I said hello."

"Candace!" Lydia said. "Mrs. LeFlore don't leave."

"No, she's leaving," said Candace.

"Candace if you don't want me here then that's fine with me," Janet said. "After all it's your house."

"Candace, get your ass away from my mom," said Burton.

"Burton' I'm leaving," Janet said. "I know where I'm not wanted.

"Candace come here!" exclaimed her sister Lydia.

"Candace come here, what are you doing!" demanded her dad.

Janet continued to her car as Burton followed. Candace's father came outside and grabbed her by the arm pulling her back inside of the house. Burton made sure Janet made it to the car. Before Janet got into the car, he gave her a hug and helped her to take her seat inside the car. Janet sat down in her car and Burton closed her car door. He indicated to her that he was going to get his car and would meet her at her house in a few minutes. As Janet drove off, Burton headed up the walkway back inside of the house. To say the least, Burton was furious. First and foremost, Candace had disrespected him to the utmost. Certainly, he was aware of the tension that had existed between Candace and Janet for the last few weeks since they got back to Mobile. He had spent a considerable amount of time and energy trying to quell the static between them. However, for Candace to behave that way toward Janet on her visit to their new home was inexcusable.

Burton walked back into the house where he saw Candace's parents still seated at their new beautiful glass dining room table. They appeared to be somewhat upset and agitated themselves. Her sister Lydia was standing near the wall at the end of the table, and Candace stood there attempting to play the victim as usual. It was her modus operandi to start mess and try to play the role of the victim. Burton was enraged. He was so angry that he knew it would be best for him to leave the house immediately before he did or said something he would later regret. There was no point in trying to argue about it because it would only escalate into something he was not prepared to deal with at that point.

He looked around at those people and wondered to himself how they could have the audacity to show up at his house before he and his family had a chance to spend the first night in the house. Yet Burton had welcomed them and been polite and tried to be a perfect gentleman toward all of them. Burton was so angry about the way Candace had behaved toward his mother, he started to go and get all her parent's stuff and throw it out the door. However, he realized he was a rational human being, and that two wrongs were not going to make a right. One principal Janet had always taught him was that two wrongs did not make a right.

Burton would have to exercise the extreme degree of self-control that he had learned over the years in dealing with this woman he had been married to for close to twenty years. After all, this was his house. He bought it, he begged Janet for the down payment, and he signed the loan documents pledging that he would be responsible for the monthly payments. Candace nor any of her folks had put up or loaned a single dime. Candace had even refused to sign the mortgage document. How dare she treat his mom like that, especially when she must have been at her lowest possible denominator in life.

Right about now, Burton was enraged, and he knew he would need to get away from there before he said or did something drastic. There was no way he could continue to sit around and look at Candace or his in-laws for one more minute after what had just happened. Anything he said from that point was going to be inhospitable and anything he did from that point was going to be unbecoming of his character. He started to get his things and leave; however, he could not bear to walk out of their new house on practically the second night they were there. Burton knew he was about to become that man that he never in life wanted to be. So, he grabbed his keys and left the house immediately. He drove straight to Janet's house to talk with her for a little while and make sure she was alright.

Burton found Janet there at her house crying. Burton

tried to comfort her and calm her down. Janet was heartbroken. She had so willingly given Burton the money to help with the purchase of the house. She did not want any praise or accolades for having helped Burton to purchase the house. Janet was simply hurt that Candace had been so rude to her. She was not at her strongest point psychologically and had been caught totally off guard by her daughter-in-law's actions toward her that night.

"Mom, I'm sorry about what happened," said Burton.

"How could she?" Janet asked. "How could your wife treat me like that?"

"I don't know what to say," said Burton.

"Does she know I helped you buy that house?" Janet asked as she cried.

"Yes, she knows," Burton said. "She's just a fuckin bitch."

"I love your babies so much," Janet said. "I love my grandchildren. She doesn't want me to see the kids," she said. "I guess she's never going to bring them over here to see me."

"Mom if she doesn't bring them to see you," Burton replied. "I will."

"She was so rude to me and mean to me while you guys were here," Janet said. "What have I ever done to her? Why does she dislike me so much?"

"Well you did drag her down the hall Mom," Burton said. "And you said you were going to snatcher her another asshole."

"This started before then Burton," Janet said. "She's not going to disrespect me, I'm sorry."

"Mom her parents show up the day we move into the house," Burton said. "I just bought a brand-new bed for the master bedroom. They're sleeping in my bedroom and my bed before I even had a chance to sleep in it myself."

"If Candace doesn't want me in your house and she doesn't want me to come to your house," Janet said. "Then fine, you don't ever have to worry about me darkening your doorstep again."

"Mom you are always welcome in any house where I live," Burton said. "Please don't say that."

"Not according to Candace I'm not, and that is your wife," said Janet.

"Did I want to see them the same day we moved into the house, No I didn't," Burton said. "But I welcomed them, and I've been nice to them ever since they got here, you see what I'm saying. How she could turn around and act like that right there in front of her parents and her sister," Burton said. "I have a hard time explaining her, she's crazy and her parents stand by and look stupid because they can't even do anything with her."

"Burton will you promise me you'll bring my grandbabies around to see me," said Janet as she wiped the tears from her eyes.

"Mom will you please stop crying," said Burton.

"Because I'm not coming around there anymore, I mean that," said Janet. "Promise me you will bring my grandkids to see me, I'll watch them for you if you ever need someone to babysit."

"Yes, you are," Burton said. "Yes, you are coming around there and you are always welcome in my home regardless of what she said tonight. And yes, we need someone to babysit sometime. I'm sorry that happened, and I can't offer any explanation for what she said Mom, but you are always welcome in my home. She hasn't paid the first fucking bill up in there," he said as he gave his Mom a big hug. .

The next morning was Sunday. Janet got up early and decided she would go to church. She took a bath and powdered her face and put on her lipstick. She found one of her white blouses and her white pants suit and headed about a mile from her house to Good Shepherd Church. It was a cool and brisk morning in March, as springtime was about to begin. This morning she had a lot on her mind and a lot of things she wanted to pray about. Outside of still grieving over the loss of Beck, she was now very hurt and upset about the incident that had occurred the night before with

Burton's wife at their new house. She wondered if Candace was going to try and prevent her from seeing her grandchildren. This worried her because she had hoped this would be her chance to devote much of her time being a good grandmother. She got into her car and drove about a mile or so to the church. She arrived about five minutes late. She quietly entered the chapel and took a seat in the back pew where she and Beck used to sit. She sat there and opened her Prayer Book and Hymnal and followed along with the service.

Janet decided she would start attending church more regularly than she had previously. She did not have much else to do with her time now. She was retired and a widow. Her soul and heart were heavy. She needed to find a way to ease the weight of the burdens she was carrying. Janet hoped that church would be a way to help her come out of her depression. She wanted to connect with the Lord and find peace in his loving kindness. Now that Beck was gone she started to think more about her own mortality. She realized she was getting older and that her days on this earth might be numbered as well. Janet wanted to find her strength and her will to go on, if for no other reason than to be there for her son Burton and her beautiful grandchildren. As she sat there listening to the pastor delivering the sermon, she thought about her mother-in-law Teah, who had been a dedicated member of the church.

Janet thought about how much Teah had loved Good Shepherd Church and had always sat on the same back pew every Sunday where she was now seated. For a moment Janet could almost feel Teah's presence there in the church. She thought about the relationship she and Teah had shared over the years. She had always tried to be kind and respectful to her mother and father-in-law. She loved John and Teah. She always felt they had loved her and treated her just like their own daughter. She had tried to be kind to Beck's mother. Janet had even devoted herself to helping Beck care for Teah in her later years. Janet did not feel Burton would be able to depend on his wife Candace to help take care of her in the event she needed any care during her later years. She hoped she would not need any care as she grew old; however, she was getting old and her later years were quickly approaching. Janet said a prayer asking God to help her work through the tension between her and her daughter-in-law, so hopefully, they would have a better relationship in the future.

Janet sat there listening, standing and kneeling as the church service progressed. However, it seemed like her mind kept wandering. She tried to stay focused on the service, but her mind continued to wander. The choir sang a song from the hymn and Janet hummed along. She was not exactly certain what the words were. As the service neared communion, the collection plate was passed around. Janet pulled out her checkbook and wrote a check for One Thousand Dollars. She placed the offering into the collection plate. She had greatly appreciated the church conducting Beck's funeral service. This was the first time she had been back to church since Beck's funeral. She wanted to give something back to the church since they had been so helpful to her during their time of need.

The collection plate was taken up to the pulpit and soon the members of the Church were ushered up for communion. Janet approached the altar and kneeled as she took Communion. She glanced over to the place where Beck's casket was placed during his funeral. She wondered to herself, how long it would be before her casket would sit right there in the same place when she died. She could not help but feel she was already dead, still walking around in her shell of a body.

She did not want to be dead yet. She missed her husband with all her soul, but she was not ready to be dead. She was not ready to die, and she would somehow have to find a way to overcome her feelings of being dead emotionally. She wanted to live. She wanted to be alive and to feel alive again, she thought. Janet finished communion and went back to her seat. The organist played a tune on the church organ as the priest passed out communion to the other parishioners. Janet knelt and said a prayer for Beck, Champ, Mamma, Poppa, Teah, and John. She also prayed for her sister El, her brother AB and her sister Evangeline who had died when they were young children. The Church sang its final Hymn, and everyone went to the fellowship room.

Members of the church welcomed Janet back. They all hugged her and asked her how she had been doing. They asked her to make sure and try to start coming to church every Sunday or as often as she could. They also promised her the church would always be her family. All the love and support was good for Janet. She was so happy she had gotten up and decided to attend this Sunday. She also had plans to start attending every Sunday if she could. Janet had to try and make a transition back into the real world and into the remainder of her life. Good Shepherd had been her church ever since Teah invited her to attend when she first moved to Mobile with Beck. Even though Janet had not been raised as an Episcopalian, she attended St. Augustine's College, which was an Episcopal institution. She met Beck at St. Augustine's. Beck was already an Episcopalian. Janet joined the faith during college.

Over the years she and Beck did attend church; however, they had not always attended as regularly as they should. She did not attend as regularly as she would have liked to, but as of today, she had resolved to start attending with more frequency. After all, it seemed like a pretty good idea to pray and pray to the good Lord to lift this feeling of abject despair away from her. As of today, Janet was making a pledge to become an active member of the church. She left the fellowship hall and decided to ride out to the cemetery to visit with Beck. She headed to her car and went to the cemetery.

Janet drove into iron gates of Magnolia Cemetery and turned down the road leading to their cemetery plot. She got out of the car and approached Beck's barren uncovered grave. There was no tombstone or cemetery marker on or over the ground to designate where he was buried. She only knew he was buried next to her son Walker Junior. She decided she would work on getting his grave marker so that he could have something to mark his final resting place. Yes, he had gone on and left her, but he still needed her. She stood there in the graveyard looking down onto her husband's grave thinking about what she would put on his tombstone.

She would have to tell the people at the monument company what she wanted to put on Beck's headstone, and she would need to consult with Burton to see if there was anything he wanted to be said on the stone. She and Burton had already ordered the stone, but they had not communicated with them about what they wanted to go on the stone. She would need to call and get to work on it this week. Since all the stones in their cemetery plot where eight feet long and there was space for considerable wording, Janet wanted to say something beautiful and befitting about her husband Beck. She would need to call and see if the large piece of marble had arrived. There were so many things she needed to do in the upcoming week.

Janet felt as if she was trapped in the doorway between life and death. Standing there in the cemetery where her husband and their family were buried, in the same plot where she would probably soon be entombed. As with every human being from the day they are born into this world, we are all existing between the entrance of life and the exit of eternity. Her husband Beck used to say, 'Maybe death isn't so bad, I've never seen anyone fighting and screaming to get back here.' Beck was a doctor and he had seen many people die over the course of his life and career as a physician. His philosophy was relatively accurate. Janet had to agree with him on one thing, you never did see anyone kicking and screaming to get back here. Maybe death was not so bad. The only problem was, no matter how good death might be, life was so wonderful, and life is so worth cherishing and appreciating every moment. The death of her husband only helped to reiterate on the collateral fact that she would soon be joining him and there was only a little time left to live out whatever life she was going to have.

After spending a few more minutes at Beck's graveside she decided to go home. On her way to the house, she stopped by the grocery store and picked up a few items. Then she went to McDonald's to get a cheeseburger and some fries since she did not plan to cook during the evening. She turned left on Springhill Avenue and then right onto Loiselle Street as she headed toward her house. Janet turned left down Oak Knoll, she wanted to stop by and see Burton and the kids, but she was reluctant after what had happened last night. She decided to put everything, every aspect of her life into God's hands. She had prayed and she would continue to pray; however, she was not going to go to Burton's house today. She wondered what she would do for the rest of the afternoon when she got home. She thought the day was a day of rejuvenation, recollection, prayer, and rebirth. She started feeling a sense of peace within.

The following day we find Janet seated in the office of Attorney Phil Leslie. Janet had made an appointment with him because she wanted to draw up a new will. She and Beck had done a Will together several years ago. Beck's Last Will and Testament left everything to Janet and Janet's previous will left everything to Beck. These wills were drawn up while both of them were still living. Janet never really liked the idea of not including her son in her will; however, she and Beck had discussed it. Beck was so adamant that he did not want to risk Burton's wife Candace getting anything from him if he died, they decided that is how they would both draft the documents they intended to execute simultaneously. At the time Beck drafted his second and last will he was already suffering from cancer. They both knew there was a strong likelihood that Beck would predecease Janet. However, now Beck was gone, and she wanted to do another Will leaving everything to Burton.

"Mrs. LeFlore, Mr. Leslie will see you now," said the receptionist.

"Thank you," Janet said as she entered Mr. Leslie's office.

"Mrs. LeFlore, how are you?" said Mr. Leslie.

"Please just call me Janet," Janet replied. "I'm fine, how are you today?"

"Pretty good," Mr. Leslie said. "How is Burton? Is he still up in North Carolina, or where was he?"

"Wilmington," said Janet.

"Aren't you from North Carolina?" asked Mr. Leslie.

"Yes, yes I'm from Wilmington," Janet said. "Wilmington, North Carolina."

"I thought I remembered you or Dr. LeFlore telling me you were from somewhere in North Carolina," Mr. Leslie said. "Burton may have told me."

"Burton was teaching business law there at the University of North Carolina," Janet said. "But thank goodness he and his family have moved back here to Mobile."

"That's good," Mr. Leslie said. "I haven't talked to him in a while. He will usually come by and see me occasionally or give me a call."

"He is doing good, Mr. Leslie," said Janet. "He and his wife had a new baby. They moved back home to Mobile and bought a house around the corner from here."

"Janet it's my understanding based on our phone conversation that you want to revise your Last Will and Testament," said Mr. Leslie.

"That's what I want to do," replied Janet.

"You indicated you wanted to leave everything to your son Burton," said Mr. Leslie.

According to Janet, "Yes I want to leave everything to Burton and then to my grandchildren in the event that he predeceases me," said Janet.

"I've drafted a preliminary document for you to review," Mr. Leslie said as he handed the document to Janet. "I have it here in the computer so we can make any changes you deem fit. Basically, it states what you indicated to me over the phone."

"I want to leave everything I have, or may have to my only living son Burton LeFlore," said Janet.

"Take a look over what I have here and if everything is

alright with you we can sign it, have it witness and notarized," said the Attorney.

"Let me see it," said Janet as she picked up the Will that Mr. Leslie had propounded.

"If this is satisfactory then I can get someone in here to witness your signature," Mr. Leslie said. "The will says you are leaving everything to your son and your grandchildren as contingent beneficiaries," said Mr. Leslie.

"Give me a second to read over it," Janet said. "Then we'll go ahead and get it witnessed."

In about an hour, Janet left the attorney's office with her new will signed and witnessed. She felt good to know that she was making preparation for the upcoming years of her life. This was the first step. She decided to go straight to Burton's office and give him the will. She wanted Burton to have a copy of the will and to know that she had now drafted something transferring her assets to him in the event she passed away. She pulled into the parking lot of Burton's office. Janet knocked on his door and found him there working at his desk.

"Hi Mom," said Burton.

"Hey Baby, how are you?" Janet replied. "I have something I want to discuss with you."

"I had something I wanted to tell you too," Burton said. "First of all, I'm very sorry about what happened last weekend. I feel like what Candace did was inexcusable and I'm so sorry Mom."

"I have prayed about it, Burton, and it's like I told you last weekend, if she doesn't want me to come to your house then I won't," said Janet.

"Mom please stop saying that," Burton replied.

"How are her parents?" Janet said. "Are they still here?"

"Not sure how they are doing, and I really don't care," Burton said. "I didn't have a lot to say to them yesterday, but they did try and talk with her about how she acted toward you."

"Anyway, I wanted to discuss something with you," said Janet.

"Mom you will never guess what?" said Burton.

"What?" asked Janet.

"Candace says that she's pregnant again," said Burton.

"Candace is pregnant again!" Janet exclaimed. "You mean to tell me you guys are expecting another baby. That was fast, seeing as Bridge is only three months old."

"That is about all that came out of yesterday's conversation," Burton said. "I find it hard to see how we keep having babies and our relationship seems to be getting worse and worse."

"Burton you have got to do whatever you can to keep your marriage and your family together," said Janet.

"I'm trying Mom, but she's ridiculous and I don't know how much longer I'm going to be able to continue to deal with her," Burton said. "How does she have the audacity to even try to pull a stunt like she did last weekend."

"Another baby on the way," Janet said. "Do you think she will have a girl this time or another boy?"

"I don't know," Burton said. "I'm still trying to get over the shock at this point and wondering if she is actually pregnant or just trying to use that as an excuse to try and justify her absurd behavior."

"If she is expecting, congratulations on baby number five," said Janet.

"Whatever, if she's pregnant certainly I'm happy, but like I said Mom the relationship between us doesn't seem to be getting any better," Burton said. "I thought maybe when we moved into the new house it would be a good change for us, but I'm starting to wonder now if anything has changed at all. It just seems like we keep having more and more children. Meanwhile, the spiritual and emotional divide between us is getting greater and greater."

"Burton your children are wonderful, and they are nothing but a blessing from God," replied Janet.

"I know," Burton replied. "Anyway, what did you want to talk to me about?"

"I had an appointment with Attorney Leslie earlier today," Janet said as she took the will out of her purse and handed it to Burton.

"What's this?" asked Burton. "A will, I already have a copy of Daddies will."

"No, it's not Daddies Will," Janet said. "It's my will. I had Mr. Leslie draft a new will for me. I would like for you to read it if you have a minute."

"Sure," he said as he took the document out of the envelope that it was encased in.

"In the event, I pass away," explained Janet. "I want to leave everything I have to you as my beneficiary and to your children as my alternate beneficiaries, in the event something was to happen to you before I die."

"Mom, I really appreciate this," Burton replied. "It seems to me there's been enough death and more than enough conversation about it. I don't want anything from you Mom. I want you alive and happy and here with me. I've lost my brother. I've lost my dad. I don't know what I would do if anything happened to you Mom."

"As we both know, death is just a reality of life Burton," Janet said. "I want to have my affairs in order when that day should come, and as I have already said to you, I want you to take over the management of all of my and Beck's property and you can keep all the revenue and income from the rent."

"Thank you, so far almost everything is rented except 1358," Burton replied. "We have got to make some repairs to the house and hopefully get somebody in there within the next month or two."

"You handle it and you manage it however you want," Janet said. "I trust you, besides, it's yours anyway."

"You don't realize how much it means to me to hear you say you trust me," Burton said. "Thank you for putting your confidence in me. I promise you, Mom, I won't let you down."

"I know you won't," replied Janet.

"Everything in your will seems to be as you indicated," stated Burton as he continued to read through the document his mother had handed him.

"I want you to put it somewhere, where you will always be able to find it if need be, and also remember Mr. Leslie should have a copy as well in his files," said Janet.

"I want you to know that I love you, son," said Janet.

"I love you too, Mom," replied Burton. "Thank you, I have to admit. It kind of hurt my feelings to find out Dad did not include me in his will."

"Burton, don't take it the wrong way. Your dad told me to be sure and help you if you needed it," Janet said. "He had some issues with your wife and that is why he drafted his will the way he did. Candace was not one of your dad's favorite people and to be truthful with you, it wasn't easy for me to go into Leslie's office today and do this after how she talked to me on Saturday. But it's what I wanted to do and what I've been planning to do ever since Beck passed."

"Thank you, Mom," said Burton.

"As far as your marriage goes, I can't tell you what you should do," Janet said. "Maybe you and Candace should start attending church more often and seek some spiritual counseling," said Janet.

"I don't think she wants to go to church," Burton said. "She seems to have a problem with everything. Last summer before we left Wilmington, I invited Aunt Ann, Julia, and Bethany over to the house along with some other family members during their family reunion. I brought some hors d' oeuvres for them to eat, and she threw the food out in the back yard. Luckily it was wrapped in paper and I was able to salvage most of it." He said, "I care about her but she's crazy as a loon and sometimes it takes all of the discipline and self-control I have to keep from going off on her."

"I hope and pray you will work your way through it, Burton, one way or another," Janet said. "I do believe you love your family, and you think you may be expecting another baby, what a blessing."

CHAPTER ELEVEN

In April of 2004, Janet visited with her Accountant in order to prepare her tax return. She had a 10 o'clock appointment with him. Janet gathered her tax information together as she stepped into Mr. Hubbard's office. His secretary greeted her as she took a seat briefly to wait while he completed his consultation with the client before her. It was a warm spring day in the sunny south. Janet wore a comfortable cotton blouse with her white pants and sandals. Janet carried her file under her arm with all the information she thought he would need to prepare her taxes. Janet approached this meeting with some trepidation as she felt a little apprehensive about filing her returns. Last year in 2003, it was reported that she owed in excess of Twenty-Five Thousand Dollars in taxes.

Janet was experiencing a sense of uneasiness as she waited for him to call her into his office. She hoped and prayed that he would not try and tell her that she owed some type of ridiculous amount of money. She was a retired schoolteacher. She and her husband had worked hard all their lives and paid their share of taxes to the Federal Government. When Janet filed her tax return last year, the IRS had been attempting to collect from her for the remainder of the year and she kept trying to explain to them that there was no way she could pay them what they claimed she owed. She and Beck had some investments and beyond her investments and his retirement which she received, she was basically living off her retirement and social security.

Beck was earning the lion's share of the money that financed their lifestyle before his death. They never owed more than a Thousand or Fifteen Hundred Dollars. Usually, they were getting a return in the mail. Now suddenly, since Beck was dead her accountant started saying that she had no deductions. How is it that she had become a widow basically living off her retirement and social security and had no deductions. She had much less money to live on now that her husband was dead, but the IRS was saying that she owed more money in taxes than ever before. It boggled her mind. Janet could not understand how when she started living on less money, then her tax returns started indicating she owed more money.

She stepped into Hubbard's office, he pleasantly greeted her as she gave him her information. He started plugging her finances into his computer. She sat there trying to be jovial and polite as he punched the numbers onto his computerized tax forms. The two of them exchanged casual conversation as he worked on her tax return. Mr. Hubbard was a comedic and pleasant person for an accountant. He did not fall in the category of being extremely boring as most people envision and imagine accountants to be. Charles was personable and was somewhat entertaining as he usually required his clients to sit and watch him as he prepared their tax returns. Janet and Beck had discovered him many years ago when he was a struggling young professional with few clients. They both liked him, and they had been using his services for over twenty years now.

Although Charles was charming and funny, cracking jokes and talking with Janet during her appointment with him; Janet remained quiet because she was hoping with all her heart, he was not going to complete her return and say something like what he had said the year before. She appreciated Charles' conversation; however, she anxiously awaited the end of the dog and pony show. She was patiently waiting for him to get to the last line of her return and tell her how much she owed to the Internal Revenue Service in the form of taxes. Janet was on pins and needles. He asked her if she had made any contributions to her church or any charitable organizations since according to her accountant those were the only type of deductions she could possibly have to claim on her tax return.

"Janet your grand total today is $31,000.00," said Hubbard.

"How could I possibly owe the IRS $31,000.00?!" exclaimed Janet.

"The problem is Janet," Hubbard said. "You don't have any deductions. I plugged in all of your charitable contributions to the church and that is about all you have to deduct."

"I'm just a retired teacher," Janet said. "I'm living off of my retirement and social security for the most part and the money from Beck's life insurance isn't supposed to be taxable."

"Well you cashed in a few of your investments and those are taxable," replied Hubbard.

"How am I going to pay the IRS $31,000?" Janet asked. "Beck and I worked our entire lives and we paid our taxes. I for one have been working and paying taxes for almost 60 years. Doesn't that count for something?"

"How many times have you heard the saying," Hubbard said. "There are two things in life that no one can avoid and that is death and taxes."

"That's so unfair," Janet said. "So, if you add the Twenty-Something Thousand, I am supposed to owe from last year, it's close to $50,000.00. I can't pay the IRS $50,000.00 that will take every dime I have."

"Janet you are a wealthy old lady," said Hubbard.

"I'm not that damn wealthy," Janet replied. "Charles you must have made a mistake. Charles, you must recheck your numbers."

"Janet I can check over this return but, unless you have some additional information to give me that might offset some of your taxable earnings," Hubbard said. "I doubt if there is going to be much difference in the outcome."

"Here I am in my old age and the IRS is going to take everything I have," said Janet. "Oooohhh, this is so unfair, this is like a bad dream."

"There are instances where you might be able to negotiate with the IRS to pay a lesser amount," Hubbard replied. "You might have to sell some property or liquidate some stock or something."

"It's getting late," Janet said. "I'd better go. How much do I owe you?"

"One Hundred and Fifty Dollars," Hubbard replied.

Janet wrote the accountant a check for One Hundred and Fifty Dollars. He handed her the Tax Return and her other paperwork.

Hubbard asked her if she wanted to file her return electronically. Janet told him that she was not ready for him to file that return. She said she wanted him to double check the return and give her a call tomorrow. He agreed that he would double check it and he gave her a copy of her state and federal return with an envelope addressed to the respective departments so Janet could mail the return. Janet took the return and the other information she had brought with her and told the accountant goodbye. Hubbard escorted her to the door and promised he would check over the return and give her a call. She thanked him and walked out to her car.

Her grandson Breton had been outside waiting in the car for her. Very often Breton would come by the house after school and Janet would allow him to drive her. She had taught him how to drive over the last year. She and her oldest grandson were very close. They were both Capricorns. His birthday was on Christmas and her birthday was the day after Christmas. She enjoyed having him accompany her places and he usually enjoyed it as well because she would let him drive. She had promised him that she was going to buy him a set of speakers for the car that Burton had said he could have; however, Burton had not allowed him to start driving the car yet. The place that sold the car audio system was not far from the accountant's office. After leaving Hubbard's they drove by the speaker shop so that she and Breton could look at speakers for his car. Truthfully Janet was so disturbed after she left the meeting with the accountant she just wanted to go home and did not feel much like buying speakers anymore, but she did not want to disappoint her grandson.

After going to the speaker shop, she went to drop Breton off at the house. Bryceton and Breaghan where outside in the front yard playing. They ran to the car and greeted Janet and Breton as they pulled up to the front of the house. Breton got out and Janet came around onto the other side of the car to get into the driver's seat. Breaghan and Bryceton ran out into the street and around the car. Janet gave them a big hug. Janet reached in her purse and gave them some Jolly Ranchers that she had just purchased from the gas station on their way home. Bryceton and Breaghan happily took the candy and hugged their grandmother again. Breton went inside while Janet stood outside and talked with the younger boys for a moment.

Usually on Sundays, after Janet would leave church, she would ride by the house and see if the boys were outside. If they were outside playing, she would stop and talk with them for a moment. There was still some strain between her and Candace. Although, she had been around to the house on numerous occasions since Candace had so rudely told her she was not welcome. She still did not visit that often. Sometimes she would come by and visit with Burton while Candace was not there. On many occasions, she would ride by their house and see if the children where outside, if not, she would keep going. Occasionally, Candace would bring the kids by for her to babysit.

Janet went on to her house as she tried to figure out what she was going to do about this rather exorbitant amount of money she was supposed to owe to the Internal Revenue Service. Just thinking about it made her jaw start to hurt as she moped around her kitchen trying to figure out what she was going to have for dinner. Janet decided she needed to discuss this with Burton. She called him. He was still at the office working when she contacted him. Janet asked him if he would stop by the house a little later when he got a minute. Burton assured her that he would come by as soon as he could. About an hour later Burton arrived at the house.

"Burton," Janet said. "I had a meeting today with Charles to file my taxes."

"How did it go?" asked Burton.

"Have you filed your taxes yet?" asked Janet.

"No not yet," Burton said. "I need to make an appointment with Charles myself, but I think I'm going to request an extension and get with him after tax season."

"He said that I owed over Thirty Thousand Dollars in taxes," said Janet.

"Thirty Thousand Dollars," Burton said. "Are you serious."

"Yes, that is what he said," Janet replied. "And if you add the

Twenty-Something Thousand from last year, they are going to claim I owe over Fifty Thousand Dollars in Taxes to the IRS."

"What!" Burton exclaimed. "How could you owe the IRS that much money?"

"I don't know," Janet said. "I don't know. I don't understand how I could possibly owe that much money."

"Do you want me to call Charles and ask him?" asked Burton.

"I don't know what to do," Janet said. "What am I going to do."

"Mom well just have to get to the bottom of this somehow," said Burton.

"Do you think they will try and take my home?" Janet cried. "All my life I've worked, me and your father. We always paid our share of taxes. We had more money and paid less tax and now I have less money and I'm retired; how do I owe more tax now than I ever did in my life." Janet said, "It doesn't make sense. How could this happen?"

"I agree with you Mom that makes absolutely no sense," Burton replied.

"So you live your entire life, work your fingers to the bone and then when your time comes to slow down and live off of what you think you earned, it seems the IRS steps in and decides they want to take it all. Just take whatever you thought you might have had to live on for the rest of your days."

A few weeks later, Burton went out of town for a few days. Janet was with her Grandson Breton that evening. She had picked him up from school and he had been driving her around most of the afternoon. Burton had told Breton he could not drive his car yet because he did not have any insurance on the vehicle. However, since Breton had his new speakers in the car, he had grown tired of sitting in the driveway listening to his music. For the most part, Breton obeyed his dad and did not drive the car anywhere. With his new speakers now installed and his dad out of town, he could not resist the temptation to take a drive in the car. He only had his driver's permit though and he could not legally drive unless there was another licensed driver in the vehicle. Breton begged Janet to go for a ride with him in the Trooper. At first, Janet said they should not drive the car since Burton had told him not to. Breton begged and begged until finally, Janet agreed to take a ride with him in his car.

The two of them went by the house on Oak Knoll. Janet and Breton swapped vehicles and got into the Trooper to take a ride. Janet rode in the passenger seat as Breton drove. Breton started to turn the volume up high on his speakers, but Janet told him that she could not handle the music so loud. Breton politely turned the volume back down for his grandmother. The two of them turned onto Spring Hill Avenue and drove several blocks beneath the majestic oaks that line the street toward downtown. Breton made a right turn on Catherine Street and drove toward Government Street. Breton approached the light on Government Street. He stopped and was sitting there in the car with Janet at the corner of Government Street and Catherine Street. Suddenly, the two of them looked up and could see the lights of a vehicle that appeared to be heading for them as it came across one lane in front of some other cars that were also driving in the same direction. Before they knew it, the car had struck the Trooper which was parked at the light. The vehicle was traveling at a relatively high rate of speed and knocked the Trooper with Janet and Breton in the vehicle onto the curb.

After the car ran into them, it stopped for a moment. The driver of the other vehicle backed up and sped off down the street. There was a substantial amount of damage to the car. The two of them struggled to regain their composure as it became evident they both were still alive. Janet had hit her head on the passenger side window, and she felt like she had dislocated her shoulder. Breton was a little shaken up but for the most part, he was fine. Both had their seat belts on. They sat there and helplessly watched the car that had hit them speed away from the scene of the accident. Other drivers who had witnessed the accident immediately called the police. The accident occurred in front of a grocery store and people who were in the parking lot ran over to see if they were alright. They struggled to get the doors open and were eventually able to exit the wrecked car. The police arrived. Breton was terrified as he stood there looking at his mangled car. All he could think was that his dad was going to kill him.

One of the people who witnessed the accident came over and said they had written down the license plate of the other car involved. The police officer took Breton's driver's permit and Janet's license and began making their report of the accident. It was obvious to the officers and everyone that saw what happened that the other vehicle was at fault. There was practically nothing Breton could have done to have avoided the accident. Janet was very protective of her grandson as they talked with the police officers. She wanted to make sure they understood, he was a pretty good driver and had done nothing to cause the accident.

The officers agreed that it did not appear the young driver was at fault. They asked about the insurance on the car. Janet told them the insurance card was not in the car. Breton indicated there was no insurance on the vehicle and that was why his dad had told him not to drive the car. After the officers concluded their report and called a tow truck to get the vehicle. Janet and Breton indicated they did not have a way to get home. The officer that worked the scene said that he would give them a ride. They got into his car and he transported them back to Janet's house.

"My dad's going to kill me," said Breton.

"Don't worry Breton," Janet said. "We'll just have to explain to him what happened and I'm sure when we tell him the whole story, he will just be happy that we're alright."

"That's right son," the officer said. "You and your grandmother were lucky. You guys could have been seriously hurt or even killed in that accident."

"My shoulder feels like it might be fractured," Janet said.

"Grandmother are you hurt?" asked Breton.

"Ms. LeFlore, do you want me to take you to a hospital or call paramedics to come to your house?" asked the officer.

"No, it's probably OK," Janet said. "I just want to get home now. I'll see how it feels in the morning."

"In my line of work," the officer said. "I've seen a lot of

accidents and I still say you guys were lucky."

"Yea so now I survived the accident only for my dad to kill me," Breton said. "He is going to be so mad, and the car is probably totaled."

"Everything is going to be alright, Breton," Janet said. "A car is a material thing and material things can always be replaced. Human life is something that can never be replaced. That's why I always tell you driving is a very serious thing."

"I agree with your grandmother," the officer replied. "Anytime you get behind the wheel of a car you got to be careful and abide by the law. Sometimes, just like tonight, you can be stopped at a light and somebody run into your car."

"That should be a lesson, you should always exercise extreme care when driving and understand that even when you exercise the utmost caution something can still happen," said Janet.

"That's about the size of it," said the officer.

"Breton, we'll get the car fixed one way or another," said Janet.

"My dad's not going to fix the car," Breton said. "He already told me he wasn't going to fix the car if I wrecked it.

"What did I say, Breton," Janet said. "We'll get the car fixed even if I have to pay for it out of my pocket. I agreed to ride with you in the car and we both knew your dad told you not to drive the car." She continued, "Right about now we need to be thankful that no one was hurt in that accident, but if they don't total it, I'll repair the car. If they do total it, we'll buy you another car."

"Will you Grandma?" said Breton.

"Yes," Janet said. "I promise you. We'll just have to call them tomorrow and see how much they estimate the damage to be and go from there."

"You'll talk to my dad?" asked Breton.

"Yes, I'll talk to him," said Janet. "You can make a left here at the corner. My house is right down the street here."

"Yes Mam," said the officer.

"Can you give us the name and the phone number of the place where they towed the car?" asked Janet.

"Yes Mam," the officer said. "I have it right here."

"We're right down here at the end of the street," said Janet.

"Grandma we forgot we left your car over at our house," said Breton.

"That's alright," Janet said. "When we get home, you'll just have to call your mom or walk back to the house and get the car. I need to get home right now. I'm an old woman and I've had enough excitement for one day. Please just drop me off right here."

"Yes Mam," the officer said as Janet and Breton got out of his car. "Here's the number."

"Thank you so much, Mr. Officer," Janet said. "We greatly appreciate you bringing us home."

It was now the Summer of 2004 as Janet went to visit with her sister's in Wilmington. They were all planning to stay at the family homestead at 1013 South 12th Street. Everyone had decided to meet and spend some family time together as they planned a birthday party for Mary Lilly. It was the first time Janet had been back to Wilmington since she had been there with Burton for the birth of his fourth son. Janet arrived at the Airport in Wilmington to be met by her sisters Bethany, Ann and Julia. Janet was happy to see them. She had not seen them since Beck had passed away almost three years ago.

Janet was glad to be back in her hometown as she always loved traveling to Wilmington. She had missed seeing her sisters, even though she talked with them frequently on the telephone. She was also looking forward to seeing her godmother Mary Lilly Lofton. They were all planning to have a 100th Birthday party for her. Yes, she was turning 100 and it was possible she was already a little older than 100 since she did not have a birth certificate. The only record she had of her birth was an inscription written in the front of a Bible. However, at this point, it was believed that she was to turn 100 and they had all decided to throw her a party.

Janet still felt a little angry as she pulled up to the house in her sister's Mercedes. She thought about how she and Burton's family had to stay at the beach for those few weeks before he moved back to Mobile and how upset she had been when they would not allow Burton to stay in the house temporarily; however, at this point, Janet was no longer on the warpath about it.

Janet had the capacity to forgive, and she loved her sisters dearly. She was going to try and put it behind her. Burton and his family were now back in Mobile and living in their own house. Janet had spent a lot of lonely days between then and now. She just wanted to have fun with her sisters and her godmother.

At this point, she was more focused on taking this opportunity to do something special for a person who had done so many special things for her during her life. She and Mary Lilly had always been close. Mary Lilly had always been a dear godmother and friend to Janet throughout the many years since Janet was a baby. Certainly, she was not going to get her sister's full help and support if she went around the entire time mad and lamenting about the past. She felt like she was in a better place with her sisters now and certainly Burton and his family were in a better place. So now it was time to plan something nice for Mary Lilly.

As soon as she got to the family homestead and settled into the house. She decided to walk across the street to Mary Lilly's and visit with her for a little while. The party was supposed to be a surprise for her, and she hoped that none of her big-mouthed sisters had spilled the beans about what they were planning. She crossed the street and entered the gate to her yard. There she found her elderly godmother who said she was waiting for the rain to stop so she could walk to the grocery store and buy a few items to cook for her dinner. Janet said that she should not worry about cooking any dinner this evening and that she wanted her to come and have dinner with her and the sisters at 1013. Janet told her she was not sure what they were having, but whatever they had she was welcome to share. Mary Lilly accepted the invitation. Janet came inside and sat and talked with her for a spell before they returned across the street to see what her sisters had prepared for dinner.

That evening after dinner, they all walked Mary Lilly across the street to her house. They returned to their house, changed into their pajamas and turned on the television. They pulled out a bottle of wine and poured a few glasses as they sat around talking and making plans for Mary Lilly's party. By now it was dark outside as the evening progressed.

"We can set up the tables and chairs outside in the back yard," said Anna.

"Julia, will you make some of your chicken salad?" Bethany asked. "You make the best chicken salad. If you do the chicken salad, I will make some finger sandwiches," she said.

"You got a deal, Bethany, I'll make the chicken salad," said Julia.

"I'll call Harris Teeter in the morning and order her a cake," Janet said. "Also, I went by Dillard's before I left Mobile and bought this blouse for Mary Lilly," she said. "I thought she would like it. Hope it fits. Isn't it pretty?"

"Oh yes that's nice, I'm sure she'll love that," Anna said. "I found a watch on sale at Saks and decided to get that for her."

"I bought her a pair of house shoes," said Bethany.

"I found this eyeglass chain, you know one of those little chains that you attach to your eyeglasses so when you take them off your face you can let them hang around your neck," Julia said. "I thought she would like that since she's always saying she has to look for her glasses."

"Can you believe, our second mother is a Hundred Years old?" said Janet.

"Isn't that amazing, a Hundred Years old and her mind is just as sharp as a whistle," said Ann.

"And she's probably in better health than all of us put together," said Julia.

"You know actually, she may be as old as One Hundred and Four," said Bethany.

"I think it's closer to One Hundred and Two," replied Janet.

"For all practical purposes she is going to be One Hundred, that's what we're going to put on her cake," said Anna.

"If we each put up about Forty Dollars apiece, we should have enough money to get everything we need for the party," said

Bethany.

"No need for that, I'll pay for what we need," Janet replied. "Here's Two Hundred Dollars, that should be enough to get what we need, don't you think."

"If you put up the money Jeannie, then I guess we'll have to do most of the work," replied Julia.

"So, Jeannie's putting up Two Hundred, then it's a done deal," said Anna.

"Sounds good to me Jeannie," said Bethany.

"Tomorrow we'll get the cake and other items we need," Janet responded. "And we'll prepare all of the food."

"We need to ask a few of the neighbors to come, and celebrate with us," said Julia.

"I'm going to fix myself another glass of wine," Anna said. "Would anyone like another glass?"

"Ann, why don't you refresh my glass also sister," said Bethany.

"Lets shoot for about 2 o'clock on Friday," Janet said.

"2 o'clock on Friday sounds like as good a time as any," replied Julia.

"Is everyone in agreement at 2 o'clock on Friday?" Anna asked Janet.

"That should give us more than enough time to get everything in order and invite a few of the neighbors," said Bethany. "2 o'clock it is."

"Sounds like we got a plan," Janet said. "Now pour me another glass of that wine."

"Which brings us to you Jeannie," Anna said as she refreshed Janet's glass. "How have you been doing sister?"

"I'm fine, I miss Beck a lot," Janet said. "When I'm home, I get very lonely sometimes. I still have pain in my jaw, but other than that I'm doing pretty good."

"It certainly is understandable that you still miss Walker," said Julia.

"Certainly, you still miss Walker," Anna stated. "We've just been a little concerned about you."

"Really, and why is that?" asked Janet.

"First of all, you said you weren't certain if you could find your way around the airport to your connecting flight," Anna said. "When we made your reservation, we had to request an escort to get you from one flight to the other."

"Atlanta is a huge airport, have you been through there since they built that new airport?" asked Janet.

"How are you holding up mentally, Janet?" Bethany asked. "You said you still miss Walker a lot. Have you been experiencing any depression?"

"Occasionally," Janet replied.

"Have you been to see a doctor about it?" asked Anna.

"No, I don't need to see a doctor," Janet said. "I'm not taking any Antidepressants. This is something that I've been working through myself, and I will continue to work through it. It's not like I'm the only woman on earth who ever lost her husband."

"No, you're not the first woman who ever lost her husband," Anna said. "That's why we think, it's something more than just your missing Beck."

"Who exactly is we, and what exactly do you think?" asked Janet sarcastically.

"We, meaning me, Julia, Peter, Carol, and Bethany," Anna said. "And medical professionals in general."

"I greatly appreciate your concern," Janet said. "And your so-called medical professionals."

"It just concerned us that you seem to be getting a little forgetful," said Julia.

"Yes, I'm getting a little forgetful as I grow older," Janet said. "I used to be able to remember everything, but I'm almost as old as Mary Lilly now so if you ask me, I'm allowed to forget something every once in a while," she continued. "It's no cause for alarm and it certainly isn't going to be the end of the world."

"Jeannie, we think you might want to go and see a doctor," Anna replied. "Perhaps you should see a neurologist and let him check you out."

"Maybe there's one here in Wilmington that you can visit while we're here," said Bethany.

"Maybe we can call and see if we can get you an appointment," said Julia.

"If I were to go and see a neurologist, it would be for this pain in my jaw, and I've already seen several about this pain. So far it hasn't done a damn bit of good," said Janet.

"We're not talking about your jaw," Anna replied. "We're talking about you being a little disoriented at times and a little forgetful."

"I have no plans on seeing any doctor while I'm here in Wilmington," Janet said. "So, you can kindly mind your own business. How about that Anna, how about you and the others mind your own business? Because I'm doing just fine."

"We're just a little worried about you Jeannie," said Bethany.

"Nothing but love sister," said Julia.

"That's all," said Ann.

"I appreciate your concern, but you need to worry about your own asses," Janet replied. "I'm doing great and I'm just taking life and living life one day to the next. I suggest you do the same."

The next two days they all worked together to do what they needed to do to have the party for Mary Lilly. They got the cake and a few groceries for the event. They prepared the food. They had a guy who lived down the street come and cut the grass so the yard would look nice. They also put together the decorations and invited some of the neighbors. Working together it did not take them long to prepare the food. By Friday everything was ready to surprise the 100-year-old birthday girl.

Mary Lilly was pleasantly surprised. Almost the entire neighborhood attended. They sang happy birthday. They played music, danced, laughed and ate. They took pictures. Some of the neighbors even brought extra dishes which was good, because they had a few more people turn up than they had expected. Overall the party was a lot of fun for everyone and Mary Lilly had an incredible time.

Later that evening following the party Janet grew tired. She decided to take a nap. It was unusual for Janet to take naps; however, today was an exception. Janet had gotten up early and worked diligently with her sisters to get everything ready. She had also had a few glasses of champagne during the party and she was pooped. She decided to lay down for a little while to get her energy back.

Anna, Bethany, and Julia were tired as well as they sat around on the sofa watching a movie. Bethany and Julia were both sitting on the sofa half asleep while the movie played. Ann was also falling asleep as she sat there basically with one eye closed and the other open trying to watch television. The telephone rang and Anna answered it. It was Burton on the line.

"Hello," said Anna.

"Hi Aunt Julia," said Burton.

"No this is Aunt Ann," Anna said. "Is this, Burton?"

"Oh, hi Aunt Ann," Burton said. "Yes, this is Burton. How is everything going?"

"Fine, we had a birthday party for Mary Lilly today," said Anna.

"How did it turn out?" asked Burton.

"I think she enjoyed it," said Ann.

"How old is she now?" Burton asked.

"We celebrated her One Hundredth Birthday today," replied Anna.

"She is a little older than that isn't she?" asked Burton.

"For all practical purposes she's One Hundred today," replied Anna.

"That's nice," Burton said. "I'm sure she enjoyed it."

"Yes, I think she did," Ann said. "We're all worn out right about now."

"I was trying to reach my mom," Burton said. "Is she around anywhere?"

"She's back there in the bedroom taking a nap right now," said Anna.

"A nap," replied Burton.

"Burton there is something I need to talk with you about," said Anna.

"About what?" asked Burton.

"It's concerning your mother," said Ann.

"Is she alright?" Burton asked. "What is it."

"I can't talk right now," Anna said. "I'm watching a movie. I'll call you later."

Burton hung up the phone with Anna. He was somewhat worried now. First of all, it was unusual for his mom to be taking a nap since she rarely took naps. He wondered if she was feeling ill. He did not appreciate her sister arousing his attention by stating that she wanted to discuss something with him about Janet, and then not telling him what she was talking about before abruptly ending the conversation. On top of that, she sounded like she had an attitude about it.

For several minutes Burton sat there staring at the telephone wanting to call her back and ask her to tell him what the hell she was talking about. Burton was already worried about his Mom for many reasons. He had wanted Janet to take this trip to Wilmington because he thought it would do her good to spend some time with her sisters. However, he thought it to be very rude of Ann to make such a statement and then hang up.

Burton tried hard to get it off his mind, but he was now very irritated and wondered what was going on for her to say she needed to talk with him about his mother in such a flippant manner. He did not like the way it sounded. Burton hoped his mom would call him back soon because he thought he would discuss it with Janet.

Anna had opened a can of worms and not had the decency to tell him what it was about. He tried to get it off his mind and divert his attention to something else. About an hour or so later, his phone rang. He noticed the number was from the house in North Carolina. He answered it not knowing if it was his mother or her sister.

"Hello," said Burton as he answered the telephone.

"Hi Baby," Janet said. "You called me?"

"Hey Mom," Burton replied. "Yea I called you, but they said you were asleep."

"Yea I was tired, so I took a little nap," said Janet.

"Is everything alright?" Burton asked. "Are you OK?"

"Yes, I'm alright," said Janet.

"That's good," said Burton.

"We were up late last night," Janet stated. "And we had a birthday party for Mary Lilly today."

"I know about the party," Burton said. "You sure everything is alright?"

"Yes," Janet said. "Why do you ask?"

"Aunt Ann said she had something she wanted to discuss with me concerning you," Burton replied. "Do you have any idea what she's talking about?"

"She said she wanted to talk with you about something concerning me?" asked Janet.

"Yea," replied Burton.

"I don't know, I have no idea," said Janet.

"I called to talk with you," Burton said. "She answered the phone and said, she wanted to talk to me about you, and then she said she would call me back because she was watching a movie."

"I would like to know what the hell she wants to talk with you about too!" Janet exclaimed. "Perhaps we should ask her!" She said, "Hey Ann, exactly what the hell do you want to talk with my son about regarding me?"

"Mom," said Burton.

"He said that you told him you wanted to discuss something with him about me," Janet said. "What would you want to discuss with him about me?"

"I told Burton I would call him back," Anna said. "He wasn't supposed to tell you."

"He wasn't supposed to tell me what?" asked Janet.

"Nothing," replied Anna.

"It must have been something," Janet said. "You said it. How do you think you're going to talk to my son about me behind my back and he's not going to tell me! Let me call you back."

As Janet hung up the phone Burton could tell that his mother had become very irritated and agitated. The urgency of her voice as she rebuffed her sister immediately gained his attention. Burton could hear the hurt, disappointment, and anger she felt with each word she spoke. Apparently, what he had conveyed to Janet, had incensed her and he was not sure why. Burton had indicated to his mom what her sister Ann had said, but he had not said anything that he thought would fuel her fire. Her voice sounded like a quiet plea and a shrill in the same breath. He could hear Janet becoming aggressive and argumentative toward Anna. He could hear Anna becoming defensive and saying something derogatory about him in the background. Burton could tell that a serious confrontation was about to arise between his mother and Ann. Janet was pissed.

"What exactly do you want to talk with Burton about anyway?" asked Janet.

"Burton wasn't supposed to tell you," said Anna.

"He wasn't supposed to tell me what?" Janet replied. "Are you two in on this too? Julia? Bethany?"

"Janet, calm down," said Julia.

"Jeannie, what are you talking about?" Bethany asked. "I doze off for a second and now what?"

"I spoke with him about something private," Anna said. "He wasn't supposed to go and tell you."

"You want to talk to him about how I'm becoming a little forgetful," Janet said. "You want to talk with him about how I said I was afraid to go through the airport by myself. You think he doesn't already know that? What are you going to do Ann, you're going to fix it? Huh, you're going to fix it! Is that what you're going to do? I'm a lonely widow and I'm growing older. When did it become a crime to grow old?"

"He wasn't supposed to say anything to you about our conversation," said Anna.

"You think you're going to talk to my son about me behind my back and he's not going to tell me," Janet said. "Is that what you think? You think you're going to tell my son; he should put me in a Nursing home or some shit like that?"

"Janet!" said Bethany.

"Don't you 'Janet' me," yelled Janet.

"Please Jeannie," said Julia.

"You've forgotten, all of you have forgotten, how hard Mamma and Poppa struggled to make ends meet taking care of us. But they were determined that we were all going to have a good life and they stood defiant in the face of all the struggles they endured. You've forgotten the tears that Mamma cried some nights while she rocked us to sleep not knowing where she and Poppa would get money for food, clothes or shoes to put on our feet, and those same tears were the strength that renewed our commitment to face tomorrow. And even though sometimes there was barely enough to feed one, ten of us ate!" Janet continued, "We surrounded each other. We nurtured each other and we stood hand in hand in the face of adversity and being poor. We loved each other," Janet said. "We didn't have much coming up, but there was always so much love, laughter, happiness and singing in our home. We loved each other with an intensity that breathed life into all of us each and every day. I don't know what has happened to you, I don't know what has happened to this family."

"Jeannie, we're still the same family," said Julia.

"That's right, Jeannie! We're still the same family and there's still nothing but love between us," said Bethany.

"No, you're not," said Janet. "No, this is not the same family. I'm looking at you right now and I feel like you're a woman I don't even know." Janet continued, "I feel like I'm looking at a woman I don't even want to know. Much less my own sister. My sister!"

"What would make you say such a thing?" asked Ann.

"You think calling my son and talking to him behind my back about me is love?" Janet asked. "Call him! Call Burton and let's all hear what you have to tell him about me."

"I'm tired now and I was watching a television program before he caused all of this confusion," said Ann.

"Burton didn't cause any confusion," Janet said. "Bitch, you caused the confusion. You messy bitch," according to Janet. "You caused the confusion."

"Janet please calm down," said Julia.

"We've all had a long day," Bethany said. "I think we should just calm down and get us a got damn glass of wine and stop all this arguing."

"We should think about what the Bible says," Julia replied.

"Julia this has nothing to do with the Bible," said Anna.

"Sister, how can we all be reading from the same Bible yet skipping over the most important words," said Janet.

"It was love that trumped all the evils in the world," said Bethany.

"There is enough love in this room, between us sisters," Julia said. "To get beyond this argument."

"Yes, it's so petty," said Bethany.

"I'm not petty," replied Anna.

"Yes, you are," Janet said. "Big foot heffer."

"I'm no heffer," said Ann.

"Can we stop with the arguing and name calling," Bethany said. "Can we please."

"Rest assured whatever I have to say about you," Janet said. "I'm woman enough to say it to your face. Dumb heffer."

"I'm not going to have you calling me names," said Anna.

"I'm not going to have you," said Janet.

"We were having such a good time, until a few minutes ago," said Julia.

"Yes, we were," said Bethany.

"I'll tell you what," Janet said. "You better watch what you say to my son about me behind my back," Janet said. "Because if I don't like what you said, it's going to be hell to pay. Don't think Burton is going to keep any conversation that you have with him a secret from me."

"I haven't said one word to Burton about you," said Anna.

"And you better not," said Janet.

"Janet, I don't think she meant any harm," said Julia.

"I didn't," said Anna.

"Can we just stop this and get some rest," said Bethany.

"Our family used to be so full of love," Janet said as she cried out and stormed down the hallway.

Janet felt that she had become disjointed and misaligned with her sister. It seemed to her they were both pushing their buggies down the aisle of a store and refused to greet each other with a simple smile or a cordial hello. It is uncertain what caused the controversial words Janet had said to her sister, but it certainly had caused her to become angered and to weep and to bow her head. To that end, Janet appeared to be lost in a puddle of tears about whatever had moved her to feel how she felt. Janet was overcome with a sense of anxiety and fear. She hoped she was not losing her mind.

Janet had so much looked forward to seeing her sisters and visiting with them in Wilmington. She had been willing to forgive and forget about them not wanting Burton and his family to stay in the house a few years back. She had willingly agreed to come and vacation with them at 1013. She had been anticipating with much joy the prospect of giving her godmother Mary Lilly a birthday party to commemorate her reaching the Hundred Year mark in her life. She had been so lonely and sad over the last few years. Although Janet talked with all of them frequently, Janet missed her sisters. She missed seeing them and being around them. Now here she was arguing with Anna.

She was older than Anna, Bethany, Carol, Peter, and Julia. As a matter of fact, her brother Warren was one year younger than her, which left her absolutely the oldest. Warren was reportedly suffering from Alzheimer's. Warren had heart surgery a few years ago and he never was the same after his surgery; however, his doctor's and everyone said he was now suffering from Alzheimer's.

Janet could not believe how they acted as though they were looking down their noses at her, especially Ann. She knew she was somewhat forgetful, and this bothered her and disturbed her. Although, Janet hoped and prayed it was just minor forgetfulness due to old age and not Alzheimer's. She did not understand it and she did not know what to do about it. Janet thought about Mary Lilly who was over One Hundred Years Old. Mary Lilly's mind was so sharp. She did not seem to forget anything even at her age. Mary Lilly was also still a very attractive woman at One Hundred. Mary

Lilly remembered everything at her ripe old age just like she used to be able to do.

Janet was not sure how to characterize what was going on with her, but she was not going to allow Ann or anyone else to put her into a box. She was still in control of her life, and she was still aware of everything going on in and around her. She was not going to apologize to Anna for accosting her. She felt Ann was wrong and she did not appreciate her trying to undermine her in the eyes of her child. Even though she had hoped for better, she was not surprised at how Ann was acting. She and Anna had been so close over the years, but here lately it seemed that she and her sister were becoming increasingly at odds.

Anna always wanted to try and control everything. Janet was certain that she was not going to allow her sister Ann to control any aspect of her life. Janet was most definitely not going to let Ann try and influence her son in any way about her health, condition or well-being. During her brief period of paranoia, she hoped and prayed Burton would not allow himself to be sucked in by any of her lies or misrepresentations. She had grown to become somewhat distrustful of Anna in the last few years.

She wished that Beck had been there with her, or at least she could have picked up the phone and called Beck. She may not have even wanted to tell him what had just transpired. If only she could just hear his voice. Janet searched her mind to find her husband's voice. She needed and wanted to just hear his voice. It seemed that her family was starting to turn on her just like his family had turned on him. Of course, when Beck's brother and sister started to change their tune toward him, she thought to herself that her sisters and brothers would never sink so low. Janet believed that her family was better than that. She thought the love they had for one another would endure, beyond any land, any property, any house or any money they might possibly obtain.

Janet had truly hoped and prayed that her family would rise above the greed and avarice she had witnessed with her husband and his siblings. Beck had tried to warn her before he died, but she did not want to listen. Janet did not want to hear or entertain the idea that she would encounter anything like what her husband Beck had gone through. She wanted to internalize a thought deep down in her heart that her relatives were better. Janet stayed in her room for the rest of the night. Her sister's Julia and Bethany kissed her goodnight. Anna did not go back into her room that night.

As soon as she realized the coast was clear and Janet was not around, Anna called Burton on the telephone. She dialed the telephone hoping that Janet would not hear her and come back into the den.

"Hello," said Burton.

"I said something to you in confidence," Anna said in a very disappointed and indignant tone of voice.

"What do you want to talk with me about anyway?" asked Burton.

"I want to talk with you about your mother!" said Anna.

"What about my mother?" asked Burton.

"You weren't supposed to go back and tell her," said Ann.

"I don't know what you would possibly want to talk with me about concerning my mother," Burton said. "Anything that you would feel the need to discuss with me about my mom, more than likely I'm going to discuss it with her. Why wouldn't I," he continued. "Since when do you and I have confidential conversations about my Mother."

"I'll talk with you later," Ann replied. "We'll take this up at a later time."

"If you have something you want to talk to me about," Burton said. "I would greatly appreciate if you would go ahead and say what it is you want to say."

"I'm going to finish watching my movie now," Anna answered. "I need to go," she said as she abruptly ended the conversation and hung up the telephone.

Burton hung up the phone and once again sat there puzzled and wondering what she wanted to talk with him about and why she kept acting so secretive. He had also heard his mother going off on her earlier that evening when he mentioned that Anna said she wanted to talk with him about something. He could not understand why his mom had become so upset and similarly, he could not fathom why his aunt was acting strange. However, Burton knew his mother's sister well enough to know that she must have been up to some of her shit as usual. He decided he was not going to continue to worry about it. He had spoken with Janet and she said she was doing fine. His mom had gotten on Ann's case, so he decided enough was enough for one evening.

The next day Janet awoke and went into the kitchen to fix herself a cup of coffee. Bethany, Anna, and Julia also got up about the same time. Everyone was cordial and greeted one another. Janet begrudgingly said hello to her sister Ann who responded in a similar manner. Janet did not have a lot to say to her sisters other than to comment on what a beautiful morning it was. She drank her coffee and quietly finished her toast and sausage as she listened to her sisters chitter chatter. She decided she would go over to Mary Lilly's house and talk with her. Last night's argument with Anna still had her feeling some type of way. She got dressed and headed across the street to Mary Lilly's house. She did not invite anyone to come with her or say where she was going.

"Where is Janet going?" asked Julia.

"Maybe she just went outside," said Bethany.

"Do you see how combative she became last night, that's a clear indicator," said Anna.

"She did get angry," Bethany said. "I thought she was going to try and fight you for a minute."

"Why would Burton tell her what I had said to him?" asked Ann.

"Burton is her son," Bethany said. "How would you expect him not to tell her."

"Do you think we can convince her to see a neurologist while we're here?" asked Anna.

"Jeannie said she wasn't going to see any doctors while she was here," said Bethany.

"Besides, don't you have to be referred to a neurologist by a primary care doctor?" said Julia.

"We probably need to make plans to go to Mobile as soon as we can," said Ann.

Meanwhile, Janet had made it over to Mary Lilly's house and was seated on her front porch with Mary Lilly. Mary Lilly was truly like a second mother to Janet and all her sisters and brothers. However, Mary Lilly was Janet's godmother. Mary Lilly had been a part of Janet's life ever since she was a baby. She had always loved Janet just like she was her own daughter. The two of them were very close. They had become closer over the years since Janet's real mother Mable had passed away. They were both seated in two large rocking chairs that Mary Lilly had on her porch.

"Janet that was so sweet of y'all to throw me that birthday party," Mary Lilly said. "I want you to know I really appreciated that. You all really made me feel special."

"Mary Lilly you are special to me and to all of us," Janet said. "Did you like the blouse?"

"Yes, it's beautiful," replied Mary Lilly.

"That's nice," Janet said. "Mary Lilly you're so blessed to have aged as gracefully as you have."

"One thing about growing old Jane is you have to do it one day at a time," Mary Lilly said. "I'm thankful for every day the good Lord has allowed me to open my eyes and live another day. Thankful to still have my mind and my health. Wish I could say the same for my teeth. Dentures, hallelujah."

"I never really thought about growing old or getting old until after Beck passed," Janet said. "Truthfully sometimes the thought of it's a little scary."

"There is nothing to fear," Mary Lilly said. "We have two choices in life, and that is to grow old or to die young."

"I'm certainly not ready to die even though I feel like a piece of my life ended when Beck died," according to Janet.

"I know losing your husband has been difficult for you Jane," Mary Lilly replied. "Sometimes we just have to try and accept the things we can't change. With each passing day, you should feel stronger and more able to deal with your loss."

"It seems like I can't remember as well as I used to, my jaw hurts so much sometimes I want to scream," Janet said. "I used to be able to remember everything. Ann, Bethany, and Julia tell me they are concerned about me. They said they think I should see a neurologist."

"Jane do you think you need to see a doctor?" asked Mary Lilly.

"For what," Janet replied. "I feel just fine."

"Then if you don't feel like you need to see a Doctor then end of discussion," Mary Lilly said. "There's no one in charge of your life except you and God."

"I got into an argument with Ann because she told Burton that she wants to talk with him about me," Janet said. "The nerve of her."

"Janet you know how Ann can be sometimes," Mary Lilly said. "I'm sure she means well. Just remember you're in control of your life."

"She is definitely a control freak," Janet replied. "She's going to mess around and get her block knocked off if she keeps messing with me. She's not going to control me."

"Janet your younger sisters have always looked up to you," Mary Lilly said. "You seem to forget sometimes. You were the apple of Angle and Mable's eyes." She continued, "They loved all of their children, but you Janet. You were always something special."

"Thank you, Mary Millie," said Janet.

"They have always admired you and always wanted to be like you. Now they see you going through a rough time in your life, and it probably scares them. Don't you let any of that bother you. You just keep on living and loving life and keep loving your sisters and praying to that man upstairs," said Mary Lilly.

"Seems to me that is about the same thing Mamma would say right about now," replied Janet.

"Mable was my best friend," according to Mary Lilly. "God didn't bless me to have a wonderful husband and ten beautiful children, but he did bless me to know and have an opportunity to love you and all of your brothers and sisters just like you were mine." She said, "You and all of your brothers and sister are the closest thing to family I have. You are my family."

"God blessed us with you," Janet said. "You have always been a tremendous blessing in my life, Mary Lilly."

"My little Jane," Mary Lilly replied. "You were the most adorable baby. When you were born, I loved you so much. I used to think sometimes that you were my baby. I even thought about stealing you," she grinned a playful toothless grin. "Running away with you and raising you like you were my own. But I knew Mable would find me one way or another," she said as she chuckled. "You're the closest thing I have to a daughter in this world Janet, and I'm so thankful to have you in my life. I'm so thankful my friend Mable shared you with me."

"And you are like my second mom Mary Lilly," Janet replied. "Blessed to have you in my life," she said as she gave her godmother a hug.

"Janet, growing old isn't easy," Mary Lilly said. "You think it was easy for me to get to be past one hundred?" She said, "As old as I am, and the last I heard you still can't never get out of it alive. Unless maybe you're talking about some of that everlasting life, they promise you in the Bible."

"I love my sisters," Janet said. "But I'm not going to let them run my life, not then, not now, not ever!"

"Janet you're their big sister," Mary Lilly said. "You have always been their ray of hope. You have always showed them understanding, compassion, and love. I know how much you have done for all of them over the years. You have always been there for them when they needed you."

A few days later Janet returned to Mobile. Burton picked her up from the Airport. Burton was waiting for her at the baggage claim area. Janet was glad to be back home and to see her son. As Janet's bag came around the carousel, Burton picked it up and escorted Janet to the car. It was a warm afternoon in Mobile. Burton was glad that he was going in the opposite direction from the rush hour traffic. Burton had been a little worried about his mom ever since the argument with Anna and she had never called him back to elaborate on what she had said she wanted to discuss with him.

"Did you have a good time?" asked Burton.

"Yes, it was nice," Janet said. "We threw a nice party for Mary Lilly and I think she appreciated it."

"What was that all about between you and Aunt Ann?" asked Burton.

"Ann can kiss my bony ass," replied Janet.

"That's all good, but you are still not explaining to me what all that screaming, and yelling was about after I told you she said she wanted to talk with me about you," said Burton.

"Burton you know if she had something to say to you," Janet said. "Then she should be ready, willing and able to say it to me."

"I don't understand why she acted as if she had something to confide in me and legitimately thought I wouldn't say anything to you about it," Burton said. "Like, when do me and her have secrets to keep about you."

"Then I guess you know exactly what all the commotion was about," said Janet.

"Yes, but Mom that is out of character for you," Burton replied.

"Sister or no sister, she needs to act like she has some respect," said Janet.

"Respect about what?" asked Burton.

"You're joking right?" asked Janet.

"I didn't like the way she stepped to me," said Burton.

"I don't like it either," Janet said. "For all these many years, me and Ann were so close, I feel like my sister has turned on me. She seems to be against me in every way."

"Why do you say that?" Burton asked.

"When she and her husband didn't have a car," Janet said. "I gave her my car. When she wanted to come to

Wilmington for the holidays with Bobby, who do you think sent her plane tickets so she could join us, when we would usually drive." Janet said. "And let's not begin to talk about how much money I've loaned or basically given to her over the years because she has never paid me back." According to Janet, "When her husband was beating her ass every day when he couldn't pass his medical boards, who told her and Bobby Beck to come and stay with us. They stayed with us all summer and guess what? He finally passed. Do you remember that?"

"Mom I probably don't know everything," said Burton.

"And Julia," Janet said. "When Julia was going to Shaw College, Poppa said he could afford the tuition, but he could not afford the room and board." Janet said, "I told Poppa that she could come to Atlanta and stay with me and Beck. She applied and was accepted to Spelman College and she came and lived with me, Beck and Champ for the next three years. She seems to have forgotten. Have you forgotten?"

"I know you have done so much for your family," said Burton.

"You don't know the half of it," replied Janet.

"Mom I know what you've done for them," Burton said. "Don't think I don't know."

"You may know part of it," said Janet.

"Mom, I have only been here with you, since I've been here with you," said Burton.

"Your being here with me has been one of the greatest parts of my life Burton," Janet said. "Love you, Baby."

"Love you too," replied Burton.

Later that year in September the news and weather stations started broadcasting that a Hurricane had entered the Gulf of Mexico. According to the news, the Hurricane would make landfall in the Mobile area within the next two days. People along the Gulf Coast started rushing to the store to purchase provisions as others prepared to evacuate the area. The news called the Hurricane Ivan, and they followed its path through the warm waters of the Gulf of Mexico as it got closer and closer to the Mobile area. All over town, you could see people outside boarding up their homes. There were long lines at local stores as people flooded in to buy water, candles and other food items.

As the Hurricane got closer to Mobile and the weather stations started to report that Ivan would indeed hit the Port City, Burton's wife and children prepared to evacuate the city. Burton did not want to evacuate with them and decided to stay behind. Candace did not grow up on the Gulf Coast and she was afraid to be in the city when the Hurricane arrived. Burton, on the other hand, had been there through numerous Hurricanes. He did not want his family to leave; however, he decided it would be best to let them go. If anything did happen, he did not want it on his conscience that he had insisted they stay. Burton made some hotel reservations for them at a hotel in Atlanta. He loaded his family into the car and watched them drive off. He then started to make preparations for himself to weather out the storm.

Janet spoke with Burton about the Hurricane. Janet had no plans to evacuate either. Janet had grown up in a coastal town and had lived in Mobile for many years. Janet had survived numerous Hurricanes during the course of her life. She like Burton did not think it was necessary to evacuate. However, Burton did not want his mother to be alone in the house by herself. The two of them decided it would be best for him to come to her house or for her to go to his house during the storm. After some consideration, Burton decided they should weather the storm at his house. He urged Janet to pack a bag and get ready to come over to his house, so neither one of them would be at home alone during the Hurricane.

As the Hurricane got closer, Burton went to the house to get Janet. He helped Janet to secure her house to the best of their ability before leaving to go around the corner to his home. Janet came inside and settled into one of the kids' bedrooms. She and Burton sat in the den watching the news as Burton prepared something for them to eat. The two of them watched attentively as Doppler radar tracked the storm

294

and tried to predict with more certainty where they thought the eye of the storm would be. Janet and Burton had a little bite to eat as they sat together and talked.

Janet and Burton were somewhat anxious about the storm, but they were not afraid or extremely worried. This was par for the course for them. They had followed their usual Hurricane routine and they were ready to brace themselves for the storm. They were starting to feel that sense of foreboding and trepidation that comes before a storm. A few hours later the rain started and not long afterward came the heavy winds. It was not long before they were without power. Burton lit some candles in the house and played some music on his battery-powered radio. The two of them sat there in the security of the house as the storm raged outside.

Hurricanes can be a very spiritual experience if you are in a location where you feel safe from flooding and other carnage caused by the high winds and rain. They could hear and feel the winds roaring outside as the rain beat hard against the roof of the house. Janet and her son were quiet and calm as they patiently waited for the storm to run its course. At this point, there were not certain how long it would take. It was about Midnight and the eye of the storm was still out in the Gulf of Mexico.

They were now only at the outer bands of the storm as it slowly and deliberately made landfall along the Gulf Coast. Janet felt safe and secure there with her son Burton. Calmed by the candlelight and the sound of the rain she enjoyed this time alone with her son as they stood watching the storm.

"Wow, it's raining so hard outside," said Janet.

"Do you see that?" Burton asked. "Do you see how those trees are just rocking in the wind."

"Yes, I see it," said Janet.

"Looks like the water in the creek is getting higher and higher by the minute," said Burton.

"Hear those branches snapping," said Janet.

"Yea," replied Burton.

"Do you notice whenever a branch breaks nearby," Janet said. "You can smell the sap from the trees. Do you smell it?"

"I never noticed," said Burton.

"You don't smell it?" asked Janet.

"What does it smell like?" asked Burton.

"Like tree sap," said Janet. "You know how tree sap smells don't you."

"Yep," replied Burton.

"Did you hear that?" Janet asked. "Did you hear that limb pop nearby?"

"I heard it," Burton responded.

"Just breathe in, smell," Janet said. "Do you smell it?"

"Yea, I do smell the odor of tree sap," Burton said. "So that's what that is, like every time a limb breaks you can smell the sap."

"I tell you what," Janet said. "I'm not going to stand out here on this porch much longer. I'm going inside. Why don't you come back inside Burton?"

"I'll be in, in a minute," said Burton.

"I'm getting a little sleepy," Janet said. "That glass of champagne got me. I think I'm going to go and lay down."

"OK," said Burton.

"The phone is ringing," said Janet.

"Will you answer it," Burton said. "I don't know who would be calling this time of night."

"Hello," Janet said as she picked up the phone. "Oh, sure Candace, hold one second, I'll get him." Janet placed the phone down and called her son, "Burton! Candace is on the phone."

"OK, I'm coming," replied Burton.

Burton left the front porch where he was standing and closed the door. He went inside to answer the phone. Janet went into the bedroom to lay down. Burton was on the phone with his wife Candace for a moment. She had just called to see if he was alright. Burton assured her that everything was fine. Burton hung up the telephone and went into the bedroom to check on his mom. Janet had laid down and made herself comfortable. Burton returned to the front porch where he had been standing outside watching the storm. He noticed a large branch had fallen on his front porch almost exactly where he had been standing earlier before the phone rang. He was glad that he had not been standing there when the branch fell. Burton continued to stand on the porch observing as the winds and rain continued to get stronger and more intense.

Suddenly Burton smelled the strong and overwhelming scent of tree sap. Although, he could not see, nor had he heard any limbs break. He smelled the sap though and he stood there thinking about what his mom had said to him a few minutes earlier about the smell of tree sap when a limb broke nearby. Janet walked into the foyer area near the front door where Burton was standing. She told him to come into the house. She told him that he needed to come to the back part of the house because she needed to show him something. Burton and Janet walked down the hallway past the room where she was sleeping to the back of the house where the master bedroom was located. Burton discovered a tree had fallen and hit his house. There was damage in several places and water was seeping into the house.

The damage was luckily confined to one part of the house. Even though there was little Burton and Janet could do at that point about the damage, they were still relatively safe in the house. Burton closed the doors to his room. Janet went back to bed and Burton went back into the den area. The rain and gale force wind continued all night long as the eye of the storm made landfall during the wee hours of the morning. Janet tossed and turned most of the night, but she did manage to get a little sleep.

Even though the tree had hit the house, she still felt relatively safe there with her son. She worried about her house, hoping that she would not arrive home tomorrow and find some unexpected damage. She quietly said a prayer to herself asking God to protect her and Burton and deliver them safely through this storm. Janet thanked God for her son and the fact that she was not alone at home in a dark house with no power. She prayed there would be no damage to her house caused by Ivan. She got up again to use the bathroom and to check on Burton. Afterward, she returned to bed and laid there listening to the torrential downpour outside as she dozed off to sleep again.

The next morning after the rain stopped, eventually the heavy gray clouds cleared, and the sun revealed itself. Burton was able to go outside and assess the damage to his house. Janet and Burton then went around to her house. Although there were a lot of branches and twigs in the yard, there was no damage to her house. Janet was approached by two young men who asked her if she needed help cleaning her yard. She told them that she would agree to hire them to help her get up all the debris and tree limbs from the yard. Janet and Burton spent the entire day cleaning up debris from their yards. Burton later hired the same two guys to come over to his house to help him cut the tree up that had fallen on his house and help him remove debris from his yard. The guys helped him at his house the next day. The following day Burton discovered one of his windows had been broken and his kids Play Station had been stolen.

Burton's family returned and life went on as usual. The city quickly recovered and transitioned back into the everyday ordinary lifestyle of this quaint and pristine southern town along the Mobile Bay. After a few days, you would not even know a Hurricane had ever passed through there. The power was restored to the city after about three days. People in Mobile are quite accustomed to heavy rains and it does not take long for the city and the community to get up and remove all the tree limbs that usually accompany a storm like Ivan. Usually, after about two to four weeks everything is back to normal. Burton received a check from FEMA for the tree damage to his roof and he had to make a claim on his insurance to get the roof repaired.

Janet's brother, Peter, contacted her to see if she was alright following the storm. Janet indicated to Peter that she was fine, and all was well. Peter invited her to come to Hampton, Virginia to visit with him. After giving it some thought, she decided she would accept his invitation and travel to Hampton to see her brother and the rest of her family in Virginia. Her brother Warren also lived in Hampton and her sister Carol. In addition, Janet has several nieces and nephews who lived there as well. Janet told Peter to call the airline and make her a reservation.

She indicated to him that she would need to request assistance through the airport because sometimes flying caused her equilibrium to be off. She said to give her the information and she would pay for the flight and travel there in a few weeks. She also had relatives in nearby Richmond. Janet came from a huge family and she had a lot of relatives. Many of them live and reside in Virginia. After her encounter with Ann, Julia and Bethany last summer she thought it would be a great idea to see the rest of her family. Recently she had been feeling a bit disgruntled about her family. This trip to Hampton would be a great opportunity to visit all the ones who had not been involved in Anna's mess from last summer. Janet was so happy that Peter had invited her to come and visit with him for a few days. She immediately began preparing to travel there. After all, she was retired and she was bored, there was nothing keeping her from going.

November arrived and Janet traveled to Hampton, Virginia to visit with her people. The air was frigid and crisp when her plane touched down in Hampton. She arrived at the airport in Virginia and Peter was there to pick her up. She was so glad to see her baby brother. It had been a while since she had seen her brother Warren and her sister Carol. She had not seen Warren and Carol since Beck's funeral. She was excited to be there and looked forward to spending time with Peter and all of them. Three years had passed since she lost her husband. The last few years had not been easy for her. She had grieved and been lonely and felt the pain of desperation and heartache.

However, Janet refused to allow herself to feel victimized by her circumstances. God had blessed her with another day to wake up and to live and to be herself. She had a golden opportunity to continue to seek and find happiness in this life. Janet was starting to feel like a person again. She was tired of licking her wounds. She wanted to live and relish whatever peace and joy she might have in this world for the remainder of her life.

The flight had caused Janet's equilibrium to be off, and she had requested a wheelchair to get her off the flight and out of the gate to the baggage claim area. Her brother Peter helped her into his car. Although, by the time they got to Peter's house she was feeling a little better and was able to walk inside on her own. Peter helped her with her bags as they went into the house. Janet's brother Peter was a widower who lived alone in a quaint two-story home located in a middle-class neighborhood in Hampton. Peter's wife Portia had passed away about five years prior. Peter has two children who also lived in the Hampton area. Janet had always had a soft spot in her heart for her youngest brother. She frequently commented on the fact that Burton looked very much like her brother Peter.

Janet and Peter had a bite to eat and sat in his den talking for the remainder of the evening. Janet expressed to him that she was eager to go and visit with her brother Warren and her sister Carol tomorrow. She was eager to see everyone. She had several family members in the area. Janet intended to make her rounds and see everyone as soon as she could. It was nice to be there with her brother; Janet would have some company for the next few days and she did not feel alone.

She also knew there would be no petty mess with Peter, like the experience she had earlier during the summer when she visited with Anna, Julia and Bethany in Wilmington. Peter was a kindhearted person who got along with everyone for the most part. He wanted to keep the peace and was known throughout the family as being one of the siblings who was always levelheaded.

Over the last few years, Janet had spent so much time alone. She was tired of being lonely. Janet looked forward to having so many of her family members around her while she was in Hampton. She finally felt like she was starting to do some of the things she wanted to do during her retirement. Janet planned to stay with her brother in Hampton for about two weeks. She and Peter had an enjoyable time talking and catching up that evening. Janet also contacted her brother Warren and his wife to let them know she had arrived and would be by there to see them as soon as she could. In addition, she spoke with her sister Carol and her daughter Cheryl, as well as her other nieces who lived in the area. Peter usually went to bed early so that night they both went to bed at about 11 o'clock which was still actually late for Peter. Janet was tired from the trip. She hoped she would not feel like she was off balance when she woke up in the morning.

The next morning Janet woke up well rested and feeling refreshed. She felt better and no longer felt like she was going to lose her balance like she had during her flight yesterday and directly following the flight. Peter's daughter Raina came over to the house with her babies and fixed them breakfast.

They all sat down and ate Pancakes with Maple Syrup, Bacon and Grits and her usual cup of coffee. Janet enjoyed talking with her niece and playing with her adorable babies. She was eager to see the rest of her family. After breakfast was over Janet helped Raina wash the dishes and she put on her clothes.

The remainder of the day she and Peter spent visiting with Warren at his house and her sister Carol at her house. Janet's brother Warren had been suffering from Alzheimer's. He was still relatively alert and recognized her, but she noticed marked differences in his condition since the last time she saw him. When Warren first started developing signs of the disease a few years ago, his daughter's Patsy and Rita along with his son Benny, basically went to war with his siblings over land that had been given to their father and jointly owned with the others.

They got Power of Attorney over his affairs and started to challenge his siblings on everything that he jointly owned. Warren had been given half of the family farm because he had dropped out of high school back in the 1930's and moved to the country and started managing his father's farm when he was barely a teenager. The remaining one half of their land in Brunswick County, North Carolina was split between the other eight children. There were a few siblings who had never been happy about this arrangement.

They were equally disgruntled when Warren's children took control of his affairs and started demanding their share of their dad's assets. They began by requesting that the farm be divided. For over twenty years since Mable died the entire family held title to the property as Tenants in Common. The thought of dividing out Warren's one-half share ruffled some feathers, to say the least. For the last few years, there had been an ongoing battle and feud between Warren's children and the others. The issue did not bother Janet as much as some of the others. The thing that bothered Janet the most was how she perceived her sister's as behaving after she allowed them to share in the family homestead. Janet had not become very consumed and caught up in what had been going on between Warren's kids and the family. Mostly their venom was directed at Anna, Julia, and Bethany.

For many years her brother Warren had been the other strong beacon of light in the family. Originally Warren and Janet had been given the family homestead by their mother Mable when she died. The reasoning behind Janet and Warren being given the family homestead was that Janet had put up a substantial amount of money and Warren provided a substantial amount of labor and money to get the house built. Warren had lived on and managed the family farm for several years before he entered the Army. When he followed his older brother A.B. to Hampton as an adult, he worked in the building trades as a contractor. Warren had been an avid hunter and fisherman for most of his life. However, now he was aging and in need of care. Warren and Janet were also born one year apart. Janet was a year older than Warren. The two of them had been very close growing up since they were so close in age. The two of them also had a similar ethic and philosophy when it came to their family.

Although Janet and Warren were not the oldest in the family, they had always been the leaders in the family. Both had been successful. Janet had obtained a master's degree and had a lucrative career as a chemist and teacher. Although Warren had dropped out of high school, he had done very well for himself. Over the years Janet and Warren had been the children that their parent's Angle and Mable could always depend on. They had been the sister and brother their other siblings could usually call on when they needed help or guidance.

Janet sat there with her ailing brother as it occurred to her that she was older than him. They were both getting up in age; however, her brother was more broken down physically. His mind was not as alert and keen as it used to be. Although her brother Warren was not the educated man that her husband Beck was, he was a very intelligent and knowledgeable man. Janet had the utmost respect, admiration, and love for Warren.

Warren was noticeably happy to see Janet. Janet knew that she would have to spend as much time as she could with Warren while she was in Hampton. She was also looking forward to seeing his children. She planned to make it perfectly clear to them she had no problem with giving them their share of the family farm which was left to Warren when their mom passed. Later that evening Janet went to visit her sister Carol and her niece Cheryl.

Peter said he needed to go home for a while and dropped Janet off at Carol's house. He said he would come back to pick her up in a few hours. After leaving Janet at Carol's, he returned to his house only to see on his caller ID that his sister Ann had called him about twenty times while he had been gone. Wondering if there was a problem, he contacted Anna who answered the phone on the first ring.

"Peter," said Anna.

"Hey Ann," Peter said. "I saw where you called me on

the caller ID, so I was returning your call. You alright?"

"Yes, everything is good," Anna said. "And you?"

"I've been over at Warren's house with Janet most of the day, and she wanted to go by and visit with Carol, so I took her over there so she could visit with them."

"How's Warren?" asked Anna.

"He's about the same," Peter replied. "I think he was glad to see Janet today."

"And what about Janet?" asked Anna.

"She's doing alright," Peter said. "She said her equilibrium was off yesterday when she got here. She asked them to transport her in a wheelchair, but by the time she got to the house she was able to walk alright."

"No, Peter, I'm already aware of the fact that she can't find her way around the airport anymore," Anna replied. "I mean you must realize that Janet is regressing, and Burton is no help to her whatsoever."

"Regressing?" Peter asked. "What are you talking about Ann?"

"She's regressing," Anna said. "She's getting worse, like Warren. Peter, surely you're not in denial about Janet."

"Denial," Peter said. "What would I be in denial about?"

"Denial about Janet," said Ann.

"Janet is doing fine," said Peter.

"No, she's not!" replied Ann. "She is not doing fine."

"Well she seems fine to me," Peter said. "I think it's doing her some good to be here around family. She said she still missed Walker and she had been lonely."

"Walker has been dead for three years now," said Ann. "This has nothing to do with her missing Walker and being lonely."

"Losing a spouse is not easy," Peter said. "I've been through it."

"Walker has been dead for three years now," replied Anna.

"That's what she told me, Ann," according to Peter.

"It doesn't matter what she told you," Anna said. "When she was in Wilmington with us a few months ago Janet was combative and disagreeable about everything."

"Well she's been having a nice time since she's been here," said Peter.

"We need to try and get her to a doctor," Anna said. "Me and Julia are thinking about going to Mobile sometime soon so that we can get her to a doctor down there."

"Maybe she should go and see a doctor," Peter said. "Now that you mention it, I have an appointment with my doctor tomorrow that I forgot about."

"Peter this is serious," said Anna.

"This pain that I have in my sciatic nerve is serious," said Peter.

"Peter, if you had observed what we observed in Wilmington, you would understand what I'm talking about," Anna continued. "Maybe you should talk to Julia or Bethany. Maybe they can help you to understand what I'm trying to tell you."

"Janet is right here with me," Peter said. "I can make my own observations and it appears to me that she's doing well. Sure, she is getting up in age, but we're all getting up in age. None of us are spring chickens you know."

"Peter this is more than old age," replied Ann.

"Have you talked with Burton?" asked Peter.

"Yes, I've tried to talk with him," said Anna.

"What did he say?" asked Peter.

"Burton doesn't care about his mother," Anna said. "I tried to talk to him, but he wouldn't listen."

"I think he cares about Janet," said Peter.

"No, he doesn't," Anna said. "We tried to talk with him in confidence last summer and he went right back and told her."

"Janet has been through a lot these last few years with Walker being sick and then passing," Peter said. "She seems like she's just trying to get her life back on course. It's not easy losing a spouse that you have been married to almost all of your life." Peter continued, "I know because I've been through it myself when Portia died."

"She hasn't been through anything out of the ordinary," Anna said. "Janet is showing signs of having Alzheimer's and dementia just like Warren."

"Well, Ann if she does get Alzheimer's then I'll still love her just like I always have, like I love Warren and the rest of you, just like I hope y'all would love me," Peter said. "And for the most part, she seems fine to me."

"You're missing the big picture here Peter," Anna said. "You have to promise me you will not discuss what I'm saying to you with Janet or Burton."

"No, I'm not going to discuss it with her," Peter said. "Especially if you say it's going to get her upset. I'm just trying to enjoy having my sister here with me for a few days."

"Peter promise me," Anna said. "You mustn't say anything to her about our conversation."

"I need to go up here and take my medicine, and then I got to drive back over to Carol's house to pick up Janet in a minute," Peter said. "It's practically my bedtime."

"If you can't take my word for it talk with Julia," Anna said. "Or talk with Bethany. Maybe they can help you understand."

"Well like I said, I'm getting tired," Peter continued. "I need to go up here and take my medicine and then I got to go and get Janet from Carol's house." He said, "We'll talk."

"You mustn't say anything to her about what I told you," said Ann.

"Don't worry," Peter said. "We'll talk."

Janet was at her sister Carol's house visiting with her and her daughter Cheryl when Peter arrived to pick her up. She was glad that Peter had arrived because she was ready to go back to his house and relax a little. She had been out and about all day, having spent most of the day with Warren and the remainder of the day with Carol. Cheryl asked Janet if she would give her some money and Janet gave her a

Hundred Dollars before she and Peter left to go back over to his house.

The next few days there in Hampton were wonderful for Janet. Practically every morning Peter's daughter would come over and fix them breakfast and then she would play with Raina's babies. Her other nieces Rosalind, Patsy and Rita and her nephew Benny also came over to Peter's to visit with her while she was in town. Janet spent a lot of time over at her brother Warren's house talking with his wife Bercinia and Warren as she had promised herself, she would do. She spent the remainder of her time with her sister Carol and her niece Cheryl. Usually, in the evenings she would go back to her brother Peter's house and sit around watching television and talking with him. Overall her visit was wonderful and turned out to be just what she had been needing. She decided to stay in Hampton for a few more days.

"Peter have you seen my purse around here anywhere?" asked Janet.

"No, I haven't seen it," Peter said. "You had it when we came into the house."

"You sure I had it when we got to the house?" asked Janet.

"I'm positive," Peter said. "You had it in your hand. It must be around here somewhere."

"I've been looking around for it and I don't see it anywhere," said Janet.

"Have you tried to backtrack your steps," Peter said.

"I'm sure it's around here," Janet said. "I just forgot where I put it."

"Sometimes I walk into a room to get something and forgot what the hell I went in there to get," said Paul.

"I know what you mean," Janet said. "Don't even get me started. I used to be able to remember everything. Everything, but now, hmm."

"Did you check upstairs in your room?" asked Peter.

"No, I didn't check up there," Janet said. "I did go upstairs didn't I?"

"Yes, Janet you went upstairs as soon as we walked in the door," said Peter.

"I did go upstairs, you're right it might be up there," said Janet as she walked up the steps.

"Do you see it?" said Peter.

"I'm looking," replied Janet. "Nope, I don't see it up here."

"I know you had it in your hand," Peter said. "It's got to be here in the house somewhere."

"Peter I've looked all over," Janet said. "I don't see it anywhere. Let me look in the bathroom."

"Yea maybe you left it in the bathroom," said Peter. "I'll look around down here."

"It's not in here either," Janet replied.

"Where was the last place you had it?" asked Peter.

"I don't remember," Janet replied in a slightly panicked voice.

"Here it is, Janet," Peter said. "It's in the living room, here on the table."

"Thank God, thank goodness, I didn't lose my purse." Janet continued, "Peter I want to tell you that I've had a wonderful visit here with you," Janet said. "I hope I'm not imposing too much."

"You're not imposing on me Janet," Peter said. "I have loved having you."

"This was just what I've been needing," Janet said. "I've been going through bouts of depression. Seems like I've been spending so much time alone these last three years since Beck passed," Janet said. "A year ago, Leassie retired and now I don't even have a housekeeper anymore. It's nice to be around family. I miss you guys so much sometimes."

"Janet one thing is for sure," Peter said. "I'm your brother and I'll always be there for you."

"I know you will," said Janet. "And haven't I always been there for you?"

"Yes, you have," Peter said. "You have been there for all of us. I remember when everyone started getting television sets and we didn't have a TV. We didn't have no TV."

According to Peter, "Everybody in the neighborhood had a television but us. And you bought the first television we got. That still ranks with being one of the most exciting days of my life."

"Mamma and Poppa were from a different era," Janet said. "They didn't know anything about any televisions back then. I remember all of you guys kept saying we don't have a television and Mamma and Poppa said they couldn't afford one. They probably could have afforded it but, it wasn't a priority for them."

"Janet you have done so much for so many of us in this family," said Peter.

"We all have Peter," Janet said. "You have done a lot for us in this family too. Like you helped Cabbie and Cheryl get that house. And it's a nice house. Such a blessing." Janet continued, "It's not so much in doing," Janet said. "You just hope people will be appreciative sometimes."

"Well to this day, I still appreciated you buying us that television," Peter said. "You talk about making a difference in my life. Boy, I felt like we had finally come up back then."

"Peter you're funny," replied Janet.

"You're laughing but I'm serious," replied Peter.

"Thank goodness I found my purse," Janet said. "My jaw is hurting me. I guess I'm going to go to bed."

"Janet I also want to tell you I appreciate you loaning me that Five Thousand Dollars last year," Peter said. "I'm going to pay you back too."

"I would appreciate it," Janet replied.

"Janet I'm going to pay you back," Peter said. "I promise you."

"Peter you don't have to repay me," Janet said. "That is a gift from me to you."

"Janet, I try to be a man of my word," Peter said. "You know they say; you always have to make sure you keep your word because there might come a day when you have nothing but your word."

"Your word has always been good with me Peter," said Janet.

"I mean that Janet," said Peter.

"I'm so tired," Janet said. "My jaw is hurting. It's been a long day. Glad I found my purse. Would you mind fixing me a small glass of champagne." Janet said, "Peter when you stopped drinking that was the best thing you could have done."

"Who are you telling," said Peter as he went into the refrigerator and retrieved the champagne.

"I'm not trying to be mean but, you were a real idiot when you drank," said Janet.

"Proud to let you know I'm over 25 years clean and sober," said Peter.

"Peter, I want you to promise me something," Janet said. 'You promise me that no matter what, you know how much I love you baby brother."

"I love you too," said Peter.

"Have you ever heard that song that says, 'Don't Believe the Hype?' "My grandson Breton likes to play that song on his new speakers that I brought him." She said, "He likes to turn those speakers up and it makes my damn jaw start throbbing. But have you ever heard 'Don't Believe the Hype?"

"No, I don't believe I've ever heard that," Peter said.

"That is what I suggest you do," Janet said. "Don't Believe the Hype."

"What hype?" asked Peter.

"Whatever hype you might be thinking about and not wanting to tell me," said Janet.

"Janet if there is anything you want to talk with me about," Peter said. "Feel free to talk to me."

"I'm talking with you now," Janet said. "You hear me talking to you, don't you?"

"I hear you," replied Peter.

"Pay attention," Janet said. "Please pay close attention to what I am saying to you, 'Don't believe the hype."

"Public Enemy, they're a rap group," Peter replied. "They sing that don't they?"

"Yes. Public Enemy," Janet said. "Don't Believe the Mutha Fuckin Hype."

"Never heard it," Peter said.

"Google it," Janet said. "You have a computer, don't you? That's what all these kids say today. Google it, Peter. Where is your computer?"

"I have a computer," replied Peter.

"Don't Believe the Hype," said Janet.

"I'll look it up," Peter replied. "

"Do that," Janet said. "Please do that for me. Promise me, Peter, you will do that for me. Will you do that, 'Don't Believe the Hype."

"I will ask Allan," said Peter.

"Peter, I have so much enjoyed my stay here with you," Janet continued. "I need to be getting home. Can you call the airline in the morning, or call with me and book me a flight back to Mobile? I really need to be getting home."

"You've been one of the greatest blessings to me and our entire family and I want you to know this," said Peter.

I am going to bed." According to Janet, "I have to be heading back home in a day or two."

CHAPTER TWELVE

In January of 2005, Janet is at home in Mobile with her grandchildren Bryceton, Breaghan, Bridge and Breck-Brook. The kids were playing in the Den and watching television. Candace had dropped them off after school like she usually did, and she had gone off somewhere. Janet did not expect her back until right about their bedtime. However, Janet did not mind, she looked forward to every moment she could spend with her grandchildren. Today Janet did not have anything for them to eat, so she called and ordered some Pizza. The boys were happy to hear this since they were all starving. Bryceton was now ten years old and in the Fifth Grade. Breaghan was six years old and in the First Grade. Bridge and Brook were both attending Pre-Kindergarten.

"Grandma Janet," Breaghan said. "Bryceton keeps hitting me."

"Bryceton, don't hit your brother," said Janet.

"I didn't hit him," Bryceton laughed. "I didn't do anything to him."

"Yes, you did," said Breaghan.

"Bryceton you should be doing your homework," Janet said. "Leave Breaghan alone. And Breaghan where is your homework?"

"I did it before I left school in study hall," said Breaghan.

"Are you telling Grandmother the truth," Janet said. "You don't have any homework left to do?"

"Grandma I promise, I did all of my homework," said Breaghan.

"Grandma, I'm hungry," said Brook.

"Yea Grandma I'm hungry too," Bridge said. "Is the Pizza still coming?"

"I ordered it," Janet said. "Hopefully it won't be long."

"Bryceton, I'm watching TV now," Breaghan said. "Don't hit me again or I'm going to punch you."

"There will be no hitting and no punching whatsoever," Janet said. "Do both of you understand."

"Grandmother, he started it," said Breaghan.

"Grandma Janet I swear I didn't do anything," Bryceton said. "And if he punches me, I am going to clobber him."

"There will be no hitting and no punching," Janet repeated. "Do both of you understand."

"Where's my dad?" asked Bridge.

"Can we call him?" asked Brooke.

"Sure, we can call him," said Janet.

"I'll call him," Breaghan said as he ran around his little brothers toward the phone. "I know his cell phone number." Breaghan picked up the telephone and dialed his dad's number.

"Grandma after they call my dad," Bryceton said. "Will you call and see how much longer it'll be before the pizza gets here?"

"Daddy," said Breaghan as his two other brothers crowded around the telephone.

"Hey, Dad," said Brooke.

"Let me talk to him," Bridge said. "Dad."

"Hi guys, how was school today?" asked Burton.

"Daddy the doorbell is ringing," said Breaghan.

"That must be the pizza," said Bridge.

"Dad I think the pizza man is here," Breaghan said. "We'll call you back. OK."

"Let's see if this is the pizza delivery person at the door," Janet said.

"That's him, Grandma," said Brooke.

"One minute sir," Breaghan said. "My Grandma is trying to find the key. Just wait right there."

Janet and the boys ate their Pizza together. After eating the boys settled down some and continued to watch television in the den. Bryceton completed his homework and stretched out on the sofa. The other boys were also starting to assume reclined positions on the sofa as well. She could tell they were all getting a little tired. Janet kept a vigilant eye on them as she continued to piddle around the kitchen.

She wondered if Burton was going to be coming by the house to see the boys for a little while. Janet had not seen Burton all day. As she was just about to call him, the telephone rang. Janet answered the telephone thinking that it might be Burton or Candace. However, it was her sister Julia.

"Janet," said Julia.

"Yes, this is Janet," Janet said. "Is this my sister Julia."

"Yes, it is," Julia said. "This is your sister Julia."

"Well hello there," said Janet.

"Just calling to check on you," Julia said. "It has been a few weeks since we last talked."

"Thank you for checking on me," said Janet.

"What are you doing?" said Julia.

"I've got my grandchildren, Bryceton, Breaghan, Bridge and Brooke," said Janet.

"That's so nice," Julia said. "You have quite a hand full."

"Julia, I know you don't have any grandchildren of your own yet," Janet said. "You're welcome to borrow mine any time."

"I'll keep that in mind sister," said Julia.

"I'm sure you'll bring them back with the quickness," said Janet.

"I'm sure they're good kids," replied Julia.

"Burton's children are so adorable," said Janet.

"I bet they are," Julia said. "I bet they have grown so much since the last time I saw them."

"They're growing like a weed," Janet said. "I never thought Burton would have ended up with five children, and not a single girl, all boys."

"Maybe I'll have some grandchildren of my own one day," Julia said. "But it doesn't look like it'll be anytime soon."

"I suggest you try it sometime," said Janet.

"You sure do have the kids a lot," Julia said.

"I look forward to having them around as much as I can," said Janet.

"Almost every time I call, you have the boys. Candace must be working," said Julia.

"No, she's not working, at least not that I know of," Janet said. "She usually comes by and leaves them here with me after they get out of school and that's fine with me."

"Don't let her take advantage of you, Jeannie," said Julia.

"Call it what you want," Janet said. "I'm retired, I'm not doing anything. There is nothing I would rather do than spend time with these wonderful blessings."

"Me and Ann were thinking about coming down there sometime soon," said Julia.

"Come anytime," Janet said. "I would love to see you and Ann."

"Are you sure you'll have time for us?" Julia asked. "Seems like you have your hands full with your grandchildren."

"Of course, I will have time for you and Ann," Janet said. "All I have is time."

"We were going to see if we could get Bethany to come too," Julia said. "But I'm not sure if she will be able to make it, but me and Ann are definitely coming," according to Julia.

"When do you plan to come?" Janet asked.

"We plan to come about April or May," Julia said.

Candace arrived to pick up the boys. Janet concluded her conversation with Julia as she went to help them organize their things before they left. Janet gave them all a hug and a kiss as they went out to the car where their mom was waiting for them. The boys told Janet goodnight as they departed her house. Janet took a moment to reflect on her talk with Julia about her and Ann coming to visit her. She thought back to last summer and some of the things Anna had said to her. Janet loved her sister Ann and Julia dearly, but she was not going to tolerate her coming down there with that same mess she was talking about the previous summer.

Janet went into her room and changed into her night clothes. The boys had worn her out and she was tired. She thought about how much she enjoyed spending time with them and how she appreciated their company. After changing her clothes, she went into the den to turn off the television and see if there was anything she needed to straighten up. The boys had not left the den in a mess this evening like they sometimes did. She poured herself a glass of wine and took it to bed with her.

The next morning David came by with his girlfriend Shakina. David wanted to ask Mrs. LeFlore if there was any work she needed to be done. David was a middle-aged man who had befriended Janet several years back. Very often he would do odd jobs for Janet around her house in exchange for payment. For some reason, Janet was very fond of David. David would always do whatever he could to help Mrs. LeFlore. Janet had a huge yard and there was always some work in her yard like cutting her grass or trimming the hedges or other things around the house she might have needed to be done. She sat and talked with David and Shakina for a minute over coffee. Janet told David that she would like for him to blow all the leaves off the driveway and sidewalk.

She told him that she would pay him Twenty Dollars. David agreed and they continued to talk and drink coffee. David finished his coffee and he and Shakina went outside. Janet gave him Twenty Dollars before he went outside to start the job. He got the blower out of Janet's garage and started to blow the leaves off the driveway like she had asked.

It was not long before David had finished blowing off the sidewalks and the driveway. He went and knocked on the door and asked if there was anything else she needed to be done before he and Shakina left. Janet indicated that the driveway and walkways looked much better. She gave David another Twenty Dollar bill. David realized she had handed him another Twenty. He reminded Mrs. LeFlore that she had already paid him Twenty Dollars. Janet paused for a moment, embarrassed that she had forgotten she had already given him Twenty Dollars. Janet told David it was alright, and to take the Forty Dollars. David accepted the money and returned to his car where Shakina was waiting.

"So how much she give you?" said Shakina.

"Damn babe why you all up in my grill about my money?" asked David.

"Because she gave you the money before you got them leaves up," Shakina said. "I saw her give you some more money when you went up to the door."

"You're a real nosy mutha fucker," David said. "She forgot she had given me the Twenty already and she gave me another Twenty. I told her she had already paid me. She said I could keep it."

"David, you is so stupid," said Shakina. "Don't you realize that woman got that... She got that ahhh."

"Mrs. LeFlore is a nice lady and she's been a blessing to me," David said. "She had been like a mother to me."

"She got that ahhh," Shakina said. "What they call that shit them old people be getting?"

"Alzheimer's," said David.

"Yea, yea that's it," Shakina responded. "Alzheimer's. You could be getting mad money from her."

"Mrs. LeFlore has been a friend to me," David said. "This not the first time she did that."

Later that day Candace arrived again with the children and dropped them off at Janet's doorstep. Janet was happy to see her boys again. Breaghan, Bryceton, Brooke, and Bridge entered the house one by one. Today the kids were acting rowdy and unruly. Janet admonished them and told them they would need to modify their behavior. The children persisted in being bad and acting up. Janet told them she was going to call their Dad if they did not stop. Bryceton, Breaghan, Bridge, and Brooke continued to be disrespectful and unmanageable. Bryceton and Breaghan threw an orange at Janet hitting her in the side. Janet once again threatened to call their dad and they do not appear to be worried in the least and continue with the behavior. Janet grabbed the telephone and called Burton.

"Burton you need to talk with your children," said Janet.

"What's wrong mom?" asked Burton.

"I've got your dad on the phone," Janet said. "I just want to let you know."

"Hello," said Burton.

"Yes Burton, I think you need to talk with the boys," said Janet.

"What's the problem mom?" asked Burton.

"Burton, I'm not going to keep calling you," Janet said. "You need to talk to these boys. They are misbehaving and I am not having it."

"Can you put them on the phone," said Burton.

"Your dad is on the phone," Janet responded. "He wants to talk with all of you."

"Tell them to come to the phone," said Burton.

"Your dad said he wants to talk with each of you right now!" exclaimed Janet.

"Hey Dad," said Breaghan and the other boys.

"What's the problem?" asked Burton.

"Janet's being mean," said Breaghan.

"They hit me with a piece of fruit," said Janet.

"Is that true?" Burton said. "Let me tell you guys something, I'm busy right now and if I have to stop what I'm doing and come over there and deal with this, it's going to be hell to pay."

"We didn't do anything Dad," said Bryceton.

"Yea," said Brooke.

"Burton I'm going to hang up this phone now," Janet said. "Don't let me have to call you again."

"Grandma why did you call our dad?" said Bridge.

"I'm going to call him again if you guys don't behave," Janet said. "Now you need to go down in the den and behave or. Don't let me have to call your dad again."

"Call him," said Bryceton.

"And that is exactly what I'm going to do," said Janet.

It was not long before another piece of fruit came flying over the banister and hit Janet in the arm. Janet was not sure which one threw this piece of fruit, but she was livid. Janet scolded all the boys again as she tried to figure out which one had thrown the fruit at her. She was angry and the kids seemed relentless in challenging her today. She was equally determined to stop them and return the peace that had existed in her home previous to their arrival.

Janet could not understand why her grandchildren were acting so defiant and mean toward her. She was determined she was going to nip this situation in the bud. She told the children she was about to call their dad. The children appeared to be completely unmoved by her threats and continued to misbehave. Janet picked up the telephone and dialed Burton's number again. The phone rang. Eventually, Burton answered. Janet informed him that the kids were still being bad, and she needed him to come over to her house immediately. Burton was noticeably angered that his mom had called him again about the same thing since he was busy at work. Janet put the phone on speaker so the boys could hear that he was coming to the house.

"Burton you need to come here right now!" said Janet.

"Mom I'll be there in a little while," Burton said. "I'm tied up right now."

"Burton, I need you to get here immediately," said Janet.

"You say you're tied up," Janet said. "I can think of four little boys who are about to get tied up with some extension cord if you don't get yourself over here. They're on speakerphone, they can hear you."

"Alright Mom," Burton said. "I told you guys if I had to leave work and come over there to deal with this, I'm going to beat your butts."

"I suggest you get here as soon as you can," said Janet.

"I'm coming," said Burton.

Janet hung up the telephone and instructed them that their dad was on the way to the house. At this point, they all realized they were about to get in trouble. The room got quiet as the kids sat there silently wondering what their dad might do when he arrived. They were also greatly looking forward to seeing him. Janet was fuming and she hoped that Burton would not be too hard on the kids. However, she was beyond reproach. The boys had been extremely disrespectful, and she thought it would be best to let her son handle the situation with his kids. However, it was good because she finally had their attention. It was not long before Burton arrived at the house.

She explained to Burton that the children had been mean and disrespectful to her. She told Burton the boys had thrown a piece of fruit at her. Janet was angry and she wanted Burton to discipline his children. Bryceteon, Breaghan, Bridge, and Brooke all sat very quietly now in the den. None of them said a word once Burton arrived. Janet was noticeably excited and upset. Burton noticed that Janet had urinated on herself. Burton took his mom aside and indicated that he noticed she needed to calm down and go into her bedroom and changer her pants. Burton was not sure After speaking with Janet, Burton calmly walked into the den where the boys were seated. He turned the television off and pulled up a chair in front of them.

"So, can I ask you guys a question?" Burton said. "Why would you throw something at your grandmother?"

"She, she, she," replied Brooke.

"Let me stop you there," Burton said. "Absolutely unacceptable. Under no circumstance should you ever do anything like that. This lady is your grandmother and you shouldn't ever do anything to her or anyone that might hurt them."

"We didn't try to hurt Grandmother or anybody," said Bridge.

"Well exactly what were you planning to do?" asked Burton.

"We were just playing," said Breaghan.

"No, because unless you are doing something like playing sports or something like that it's not appropriate to throw anything at somebody," Burton said. "You might hurt them and Bryceton you are old enough to know better."

"I didn't do anything," said Bryceton.

"Yes, you did," said Janet.

"No, I didn't Grandmother," Bryceton said. "Did you see me throw anything? I didn't do anything, and I don't feel like I should get in trouble for something I didn't do."

"Me either," said Breaghan.

"So, nobody did anything, right?" said Burton.

"So, you guys are going to try and tell your dad a big fat lie," said Janet.

"Mom you called me, now let me handle this," Burton said. "You will obey your grandmother and there will be no throwing anything at your grandmother. Do you understand?"

"Do you understand Bryceton?" asked Burton.

"Yes Dad," said Bryceton.

"Do you understand Breaghan?" asked Burton.

"Yes Dad," said Breaghan.

"Do you understand Bridge?"

"Yes Dad," said Bridge.

"Do you understand Brooke?" asked Burton.

"Yes Dad," said Brooke.

"Now apologize to your grandmother," said Burton.

"Sorry Grandma," they all said in unison.

"Apology accepted," said Janet.

"There are going to be some serious consequences if I hear something like this happened again," Burton said. "I mean that. Do you understand?"

"Yes, we understand," they replied again in unison.

Burton noticed that Janet still had not gone back into her room and washed up, changed her pants or her underwear. He did not want to say anything about it to her in front of the children; although, they probably had already noticed it. He did not want to embarrass Janet. He quietly pulled her to the side once again and indicated to her that she needed to go into her room and change her clothes. He took her into the bedroom and went back out and shut the door to give her some privacy. Janet did change her clothes. She gave herself a sponge bath and put on her nightgown, housecoat, and slippers. Burton had managed to get the children to calm down.

Janet emerged from her room with a look of renewed spirit on her face as though she were ready to take on the next challenge whatever it might be. He decided he would have them go upstairs and take their bath while he waited for Janet to get her clothes changed. Burton thought maybe the boys needed to take a bath anyway. While he was there at the house with them, it was as good a time as any. Burton went back into the den and marched all of them upstairs to bathe.

Burton completed having bath time with the kids and they all returned downstairs. Candace still had not arrived to pick them up. Burton had to go back to his office to finish some work. As the boys returned to the den area and resumed watching television, he reminded them, there would be no more bad behavior. They seemed to be more settled down and less hyper. Janet was satisfied that Burton had managed to diffuse the situation which had been brewing previously between her and the kids. She had also calmed down considerably. Burton felt it was now safe for him to go back to work. Burton hugged his kids and hugged Janet. He told Janet and the boys goodbye and headed to his car.

While driving back to the office, Burton thought about his mom having urinated on herself. Over the telephone and when he had arrived at the house, Janet was distressed and agitated. He wondered if the boys' behavior had stressed her to the point where she had simply had an accident. On the other hand, he wondered if she was becoming incontinent. He had never noticed, or had it ever appeared that Janet had any accidents previously. He pondered on whether Janet might need to start wearing those absorbent underwear for adults with incontinent issues. He concluded that maybe the kids' behavior had caused her to have an accident.

After all, people do occasionally have spills. Burton decided he would not jump to any conclusions either way and he would just have to monitor the situation and see if it happened again. To his knowledge, it had not happened before now, unless she had been hiding it from him. He thought it was probably safe to assume it was an accident and not something that had been ongoing. He was glad that he had been able to effectively manage the situation between Janet and the boys. Now he could finish his work in peace.

On the other hand, Burton was having a bit of a problem himself. He was starting to feel like his marriage was falling apart. For some time now, Candace had been showing very little interest in the children or Burton. She would pick them up from school and take them straight to Janet's house after school and would not come to pick them up until several hours later. Sometimes on the weekend, she would be out late with little explanation as to where she had been. She had printed up some business cards and was saying that she was in the music business. Although, whatever she called herself doing she was not generating any money for the family. Even though she was not working, she spent very little time if any doing anything to make a nice home for Burton and the kids.

About a year ago, Burton had come home about 1:00 am, only to find the kids at home by themselves. She had left all the younger boys there with their oldest son Breton. She had not bothered to call Burton or say anything to him about going out. Burton was shocked to find her not at home. However, he had been working all day and had a few drinks. He was exhausted and went to bed not long after checking on the children to make sure they were alright. Burton figured Candace would be back relatively soon. He thought to himself she probably had just run off to grab something from the pharmacy or maybe the grocery store.

The next morning Burton was awakened by his kids as they started stirring around. He noticed that Candace still had not arrived home. He asked his younger boys if they knew where their mom was, and they said they did not know. He asked his older son if he knew where his mom was, and he stated that some guy had been calling the house. He suggested that Burton hit call return on the telephone. Burton went to the phone and dialed star sixty-seven and it started to ring an unknown number. A few seconds later a man answered the phone.

Burton asked the man if he could speak with Candace. The man sounded startled that Burton had called his telephone. Burton exchanged some words with the person on the other end and the conversation ended quickly as the man hung up the telephone. Burton called the telephone number again but there was no answer. A few minutes later, Candace's pewter colored Yukon pulled into the driveway. Burton angrily asked her where she had been. She did not provide much of an answer. She came inside, dressed the younger kids and took them out to the car and drove off. Burton was furious and hurt. Burton felt that Candace had blatantly cheated on him as if she did not have a care in the world.

Recently, he had found some letters that Candace had written to the same guy. The letters were made out to a California addressed. Candace had started staying out to all hours of the night on a regular basis. By now Burton had learned the so-called man Candace had been with that night was a Twenty-Five-year-old struggling musician who played in some defunct rock band. The guy was originally from Mobile, but he lived in California and traveled to Mobile occasionally to visit his family there.

Burton had been so absorbed with his work, running his business and raising his young men he did not have a lot of time to waste pondering on what had happened over a year ago. The relationship between Burton and Candace had been somewhat strained, but Burton was so absorbed in his work. In many ways, he had disconnected himself emotionally from his wife.

He did not spend a lot of time worrying about what she was doing away from home so much even though she was not employed. For the most part, Candace got on Burton's nerves. A lot of the time he was happy she was gone, and he had time to spend with his children without the constant bickering that went on between them. However, now he had found several letters addressed to Brann and it was obvious to Burton that Candace had continued to maintain a relationship with this same person. Burton was no fool, he thoroughly believed Candace had slept with him that night she left the kids and did not return until the next morning. Of course, now he was confronted by these letters his wife had written to this guy basically stating that she loved him.

The next letter Burton found was addressed to him, and it said to pick up the Yukon at the train station. The correspondence did not state where she was going. All it said was that she was going out of town and he should get the Yukon from the Amtrak parking lot so he could take the kids to school. Burton called her cell phone but got no answer. He then asked Janet if she would ride with him to pick up the car. On their way to the train station, Burton indicated to his mom that Candace had gone out of town.

He asked her if she would come and stay with them for a few days to help him with the kids while Candace was gone. Janet said that she would love to come and help him with the boys for a few days. As Burton and Janet neared the train station, he could see his car parked there in the parking lot just as she said. It was almost like a mystery show where now they had found the car. The only question remaining was where was Candace.

There was no doubt in Burton's mind that Candace had gone to California where Brann lived. She would say she went to Los Angeles to visit her friend Laila from college; however, Los Angeles, California is also where Brann lived. Burton called Amtrak and tried to see if he could get them to verify that she had a ticket and where she might have been traveling. He told them he had found his wife's vehicle in the parking lot and he was not certain if he should file a missing person report or not. Burton indicated that he needed for them to verify whether his wife Candace had a train ticket and where she might be going. Eventually, Amtrak verified she had a ticket to Los Angeles. He tried to contact her again by phone but again he got no answer.

At this point, there was nothing he could do but get his car and go to pick his children up from school since it was almost time for them to be coming home. Janet went to her house and packed a bag so she could go to Burton's house to help him with the boys. On the way home from school, Burton explained to the children their mom had gone out of town. Burton was devastated at the thought of Candace having left town to go and visit another man. Here he was finding love letters and now she had straight dipped on him and the kids.

Burton was struggling to try and wrap his mind around what was going on in his marriage. Just when things seemed to be going good in his business and he was doing well financially, it seemed his marriage was starting to disintegrate. Not only was Candace cheating on him and had been for some time, but she also did not seem to give a damn who she might have been hurting by her ongoing relationship with this guy. Certainly, it did not surprise Burton. Now he was finally giving Candace and the kids the type of lifestyle she always said she wanted; however, she was not reciprocating in any way. She refused to get a job to help contribute to their income and she was not doing much in the area of being a homemaker.

It was quickly coming to view in Burton's perspective there was much more going on between Candace and Brann than met the eye. A side of him wanted to try and keep his family together; however, a side of Burton felt he would make sure this was not going to turn out well for Candace. He was not certain what he was going to do, but there was no way he was going to continue to allow Candace to keep on blatantly pursuing a relationship with another man with such a lack of disregard for how it could impact her family. He wondered if leaving her and filing for divorce would be the only solution.

Burton, Bridge, Breaghan, Brooke, and Bryceton all arrived back at their house with Janet. Janet busied herself straightening up. Burton got the kids clothes together for the next day and sat them down at the table to eat their dinner which he had purchased at Morrisons. Janet wondered where Candace had gone, but Burton did not tell her he suspected Candace had gone out of town because she was having an affair. He was embarrassed to tell Janet the truth about what he suspected or what he knew to be a fact.

It was Mardi Gras in Mobile. Burton always enjoyed Mardi Gras and loved to take his children to the Mardi Gras parades. As soon as the kids finished eating their dinner, Burton asked them if they wanted to go to the parade. Burton told them to go and put on their coats and get a bag for their candy and toys. The boys put on their jackets and indicated to their dad they were ready to go to the parade. Burton asked Janet if she wanted to go, and she said she would stay and continue to straighten up the house until they returned. Burton drove downtown with his boys. They parked the car and walked to a spot where they would wait for the parade to come by. It was not long before the parade began.

There were a lot of people out to see the parade that night as Burton stood there with his children watching ornately decorated floats ridden by masked riders wearing costumes. Each float was followed by one of the high school bands in the area. There were also people riding horseback as well and wagons carrying bands playing music. As the floats passed by, people in the crowd held up their hands and hollered at the masked riders to throw them some candy, necklaces or moon pies. Burton kept his family close to him during the Parade and told the boys not to wander off or leave the spot where they were standing.

As Janet stayed there at the house cleaning up the kitchen, she wondered to herself what was going on with Burton and his wife. It seemed to her that Candace basically did what she wanted with little regard for Burton or her children. The house was a mess, and she thought to herself that she could not understand how any woman, especially one who was not working, could allow her house to get so messy. She felt sorry for Burton and the boys. Janet could not help but feel that her son deserved better. She knew what a kind and giving person Burton was. Janet knew how much Burton loved his family and how hard he worked to provide for them.

She did not want to be judgmental and Janet felt uncomfortable saying anything to Burton about it. Janet wondered why her son would not discuss his feelings with her about the situation. She greatly enjoyed having her grandchildren with her almost every day, but she could not help but wonder what Candace could be doing away from them all the time. She was a woman herself and certainly no fool. It did not take a rocket scientist to see that Candace took the kids to school in the morning and had the entire day to herself. Then she would pick them up from school in the afternoon, bring them to her house and have the entire evening to herself. From the looks of the house, she certainly was not spending much time taking care of her home.

Janet worked diligently for the next hour and a half while Burton and the kids were gone to the parade to get the house in order. She hoped she could have the place relatively clean by the time they got back from the parade. She decided that if Burton did not say anything to her, she would keep her mouth shut and do whatever she could to help Burton and his family. At this point, she just wanted to be a part of his family. She was still hurt by the fact that Candace had tried to exclude her from their home a few years back. She had been so afraid Candace was going to try and prevent her from being a part of the children's lives. Janet felt it would be best for her not to interfere or attempt to intervene. Whenever Burton was ready to talk with her about his feelings he would. She knew deep down in her heart that Burton was not totally happy with the way Candace was conducting herself, even if he did not discuss it with her.

Janet did admire the fact that Burton appeared to be trying to put his children first and whatever problems he may have been experiencing with his wife second. She felt this was a definite sign of maturity on his part. She saw her son truly coming into his manhood and she admired the man he had become. She was thankful for the joy and companionship she felt from her grandchildren. Having lived many years and been married for most of her life, she knew either one of two things was going to happen. Either Burton and Candace would work out their problems or they would end up divorcing. It was clearly obvious to anyone watching what was going on, things could not continue the way they had been. Janet decided she would play her position and focus on being the best grandmother she could be to those adorable boys she loved so much and pray about the rest.

The next few days while Candace was gone turned out to be relatively enjoyable for Janet, Burton and the kids. Janet remained there with them for the entire time. She stepped in and tried to do everything she could to help Burton with his children and the house while Candace was gone. As the Mardi Gras season progressed the kids got a few days out of school. Burton loaded Janet and the kids into the car, and they went downtown to the Mardi Gras Parades and festivities. Janet was hanging out with Burton and his children during the festivities.

Although Janet was not a native Mobilian, she liked Mardi Gras. While standing there on one of the parade routes with Burton, Bryceton, Breaghan, Bridge, and Brooke, Janet wished her husband Beck could have been there with them. She started to recollect on the very first time she had ever attended Mardi Gras with Beck over Fifty years ago. Janet could remember just like it was yesterday, listening to Beck try and describe to her what Mardi Gras in Mobile was like when they were at St. Augustine's College.

She was just a teenager from North Carolina who had no idea what Mardi Gras was. Janet had heard of Mardi Gras in New Orleans. However, Beck who was from Mobile told her Mardi Gras originated in his hometown. She had barely heard of Mardi Gras and would listen to Beck's stories about Mardi Gras with amazement. She thought back to the first time she attended a parade with Beck and how odd she thought it was to see this man who she so respected and admired scuffling in the street for candy and trinkets being thrown from people riding the floats.

It seemed strange to her witnessing this event in the beginning, how the float riders where like God's in the sky bestowing blessings on the masses of people who had assembled there on the street. It was almost like a sort of ritual to her unlike any she had ever seen. Here she was almost Sixty years later, still standing on the streets of Mobile, Alabama at the parade. How it seemed the time and the years had flown by so quickly. The man who had brought her here was now gone. However now she was there with their handsome son and four beautiful grandchildren. Life in Mobile had been pretty good for her and she felt blessed to still be there for another parade at Mardi Gras with her family.

Suddenly Janet was popped in the head by a moon pie thrown from a passing float. It startled her as she looked up at the float and could see one of the masked riders about to throw a set of beads to the crowd. Janet reached her hands in the air and waved at the man riding the float. He noticed her in the crowd and threw her the set of beads which she caught. Janet looked over at her son and four grandchildren standing there with her at the Parade. She saw her grandchildren hustling to pick up the candy, beads and moon pies on the ground accompanied by her son Burton. She figured she might as well get some of that stuff and put it in her bag too. Janet did not plan to go home from the parade empty-handed. After all, she was not a novice anymore like she had been when the first came to the Mobile Mardi Gras with her soon to be husband Beck. Janet had gained some experience at this thing over the years and she was ready to do what they do.

Janet had fun attending Mardi Gras and babysitting the children for Burton over the next few days. During the day they would attend parades and the sunny Mobile weather was absolutely wonderful. It was starting to feel like springtime even though it was the middle of February. It appeared to her the boys were having an enjoyable time also and she was glad it was not cold so she did not worry they would catch a cold. Janet also watched the children for Burton a few evenings because he wanted to attend some Mardi Gras balls. When Burton dawned his black tuxedo with tails and his white tie he looked as if he would be the most handsome man at the ball. Burton was starting to look more and more like his dad. When Burton would leave to attend the Mardi Gras ball, she and the kids would watch television and play board games until they got sleepy. On Skinny Monday and Fat Tuesday, Burton, Janet, and the kids attended two parades that passed by Burton's office on Lexington Avenue. She and the kids had a great time as carnival season started to wind down and their vacation was over.

As the parades, parties, balls, and festivities came to an end everyone was worn out. The children would be going back to school on the upcoming Wednesday. The past week had been very nice; however, Candace still had not returned home. Burton had not mentioned anything about having talked with her either. Janet sensed that Burton was still upset about Candace having gone out of town; however, he had not said much about it over the last few days. The only thing he mentioned to Janet was that he had spoken with Candace's parent's and they indicated they thought she had used her Christmas money from them to go to California.

Candace did not arrive back in Mobile until the following Saturday. She waltzed in the door accompanied by her mother Louise. She arrived about midday on the following Saturday after Mardi Gras. Candace had been gone almost a week and a half. Janet had remained there with Burton and her grandchildren the entire time. Burton did not say much to Candace when she arrived. He was not going to cause a scene before Janet, Louise, and the kids. He was relieved that she had finally returned and still angry she had left.

Burton maintained his composure and did not argue with Candace. He simply asked Janet if she was ready to go back home. Janet indicated she was and said it would only take her a few minutes to get her things together. Janet packed her belongings, listening closely to see if an argument was going to break out between Burton and Candace. She hoped they would not argue, even though she knew Burton was upset about the situation. Janet tried to hurry and pack her things as to further avoid any chances that an argument would ensue between the two of them.

The atmosphere in the house at this point was tense. Burton tried with all his might not to do what he really wanted to do, which was probably slap the shit out of Candace. He stood there watching her silently as she parked her suitcase by the chair in the den and greeted the boys. Burton hoped his mother would hurry up because he felt the need to get away from there as soon as he could. He needed to get away from there and think through this. He knew full well that Candace had gone to see Brann and there was no way she was going to lie to him or make him believe she went to LA for any other reason. Burton was starting to dislike Candace with such a passion, he almost wished she would get all her stuff and get on that train and go back to Los Angeles for good.

Janet emerged from the hallway with her things and said to Burton she was ready for him to take her home. Janet made her way to the back door, past Candace's mother Louise. Janet looked at Louise who had a cheap and stupid expression on her face. The two of them barely said goodbye as Janet walked past Louise. Janet wondered to herself if this woman even took time to try and talk with or reason with her daughter in any way about what she might need to be doing to keep her marriage and family together. She was glad Burton had not made a scene when Candace arrived. Janet left accompanied by Burton who gave her a ride back to her house around the corner.

When they arrived back at her house, Janet waited to see if Burton had anything to say to her about Candace having gone to Los Angeles. Janet knew nothing about the guy Burton suspected she had gone to see in California. Janet asked Burton if he would help her with her bag and go into the house with her to make sure everything was alright. She was unworried about the house being alright. Janet wanted Burton to come inside with her for a minute to see if he would open up to her about his feelings regarding his wife.

Burton came inside and took Janet's bag into her bedroom. He gave the house a quick inspection and thanked Janet for helping him take care of the children while Candace had been gone. Burton hugged his mom. Janet looked at Burton affectionately and said she was glad to have been able to help. She indicated she had enjoyed her stay at his house with him and the kids. She asked him if everything was OK, and he did not reply. Burton simply shrugged his shoulders and hugged her.

CHAPTER THIRTEEN

Springtime had arrived early in Mobile this year. The Azaleas and the Dogwoods were in full bloom. It was pleasantly warm, and the sky was clear, sunny and blue on this picturesque April day. Janet went to the airport to pick up her sisters Anna and Julia. She was there waiting for them when they arrived. Anna and Julia were all smiles as they approached Janet at the airport hugging and kissing her. They got their suitcases and exited the airport into the parking area.

"Oh Lord," Janet said. "Where did I park the car?"

"You don't remember where you parked the car?" asked Anna.

"Hold on now it's got to be out here somewhere," Janet said. "This happens to be a big parking lot."

"Janet, did you drive all the way out here by yourself?" asked Julia.

"Yes of course I did," said Janet.

"Why didn't Burton ride out here with you?" asked Anna.

"He's at work and I didn't want to bother him," Janet said. "I don't have any problem driving to the airport to pick you guys up. I'm here aren't I?"

"Janet do you have any idea where you parked the car?" asked Anna.

"Excuse me, Ann. Give me just a second and I'll figure it out," said Janet.

"Do you still have that White Cadillac Deville that you had when we were here for Walker's funeral?" asked Julia.

"Yes," Janet said. "I think I parked it over there where it says arriving flights."

"We'll just have to look for it," said Anna.

"There it is," Janet said. "There's my car right there."

"Where," asked Julia.

"I hope you see it because this suitcase is heavy," said Anna.

"There it is," Janet said. "Come on let's go."

"Janet why don't you let me drive?" asked Anna.

"Yea Janet why don't you let Ann drive," said Julia.

"Sure whatever," Janet said. "But I just want to let you and you know, I don't need either of you or anyone else to drive me anywhere. I can drive myself just fine."

"Jeannie we're not trying to argue with you," said Julia.

"Give me the key so we can put our suitcases in the trunk," said Anna.

"How was your flight?" asked Janet.

"Beautiful blue skies all the way from Virginia," said Julia.

"And happy to see you sister," said Anna.

"It's nice to see you as well," Janet said. "It's been a while since either of you has come to visit me."

"Here we are," said Anna with a big fake smile from one end of her mouth to the other.

"Here we are indeed," said Julia.

"Why don't we grab a quick bite to eat," Julia said. "I'm a little hungry. We couldn't get anything but peanuts and pretzels on the plane."

"Do we need to stop and buy anything from the grocery store on our way to the house?" asked Anna.

"Let's be on our way," Janet said. "It's getting close to 3:30 and Candace may be coming by the house to drop the kids off. I need to be there when she gets there."

"Is Candace working now?" asked Julia.

"Then why do you need to be there at 3:30 for her to drop the kids off?" asked Anna.

"I don't know," Janet said. "I just need to be there when she drops my grandbabies off."

"Janet you're retired, and you said Candace isn't working," Anna said. "So why does she drop her kids off every day after she gets them out of school?"

"Surely this is your time to be you," Julia continued. "Practically every time we talk with you, you say you're watching those children."

"Those are my babies," Janet said. "I don't mind."

"Jeannie you mustn't let Candace take advantage of you," Anna said. "It would be different if she were working but she's not even working."

"You shouldn't be watching their children so much," said Julia.

"I'm blessed to have them," Janet said. "And I don't mind watching them. Just like you said, I'm retired now, and I can do what I want to do. There's nothing else I would prefer to do than be with my adorable grandbabies." Janet continued, "I can't wait for you to see them. They have grown so much since the last time both of you were here."

"We can't wait to see them either," Anna said. "I thought maybe we could have some us time, some sister time, some we time while we're here."

"I did too Jeannie," said Julia.

"We're going to have some sister time," Janet replied. "What makes you think we're not going to have any sister time?"

"I mean without those bad kids there the entire time we're here," said Anna.

"My grandkids are not bad," Janet said. "I mean they act up every once and a while like any other kids, but there are not bad by any stretch of the imagination. They're very well mannered, courteous and respectful."

"I'm sure they are Jeannie," Julia said. "We just wanted to share a little sister to sister time with you while we're here."

"We can share some sister to sister time," Janet said. "Do me a favor and stop making unfair assumptions about my grandchildren, and I think we will have a much more enjoyable time while you all are here."

"We'll surely keep that in mind," said Julia.

"Jeannie you need a break from those kids," Anna said. "I guarantee you. We will not be home by 3:30 today. We have to go grab a few items from the grocery store and we are going to stop somewhere and have a little bite to eat."

"I'm starving," Julia said. "I haven't had anything to eat all day."

"I have food at the house if you're hungry," Janet said. "But if you guys would prefer to eat out this afternoon, we can do that. I just didn't want to miss the boys if they came by today."

"I'm sure Candace will understand," said Anna.

"How's Burton?" asked Julia.

"He's fine," said Janet. "He's been working a lot."

"So how does Burton feel about Candace pushing their children off on you all the time?" asked Anna.

"Let me say this one more time," Janet said. "I have grandchildren, I love them, and I cherish every moment I get to spend with them. If you intend to have some good sister to sister time with me, you both need to understand this first and foremost."

"Julia and I would like to ask you if we can go to see a neurologist while we are here," said Anna.

"Yes, Jeannie we've been a little worried about you," said Julia.

"Why do you want me to see a doctor so bad?" Janet said. "I don't need to see no damn doctor."

"Better safe than sorry," Anna said. "Is what I always say."

"Talk with Burton about it," Janet said. "If he thinks it's a good idea then I'll go."

"Why would we need to talk with Burton about it?" asked Anna.

"Because he's my son," Janet said. "If I go and see a doctor, he should know about it."

Janet, Anna, and Julia spent the remainder of the afternoon in the streets. Anna was driving and she made sure they took their time and did not get back to the house until well after dark. Janet was glad to be with her sisters, but she missed having been there to see the boys if they had come by to see her today. Not long after they arrived at Janet's house, Burton showed up with the boys.

Apparently, when Candace could not find Janet, she dropped them off at Burton's office. Burton had taken them to get something to eat and had spent the evening with them. He dropped by Janet's house to see his aunts. He wanted his children to meet his Mom's sisters since they were so much younger the last time, they saw them. Breton, Bryceton, and Breaghan might have remembered them; however, the younger two had never met them before. He stayed for a few minutes with the boys and said hello to his mom's sisters.

"Burton your children are adorable," said Julia.

"Thank you, Aunt Julia," Burton said. "I'm pretty sure Bryceton and Breaghan remember you, but I don't believe Bridge and Brooke have ever met you."

"Bridge and Brooke are the two baby boys," said Julia.

"Yes, Bridge and Brooke are the youngest, and I don't think you guys have been here since they were born," replied Burton.

"Hey, hey, hey, Burton," Anna said. "The boys have grown so much since the last time we saw them."

"That's what kids do," Burton said. "They grow. How was your trip?"

"We arrived this afternoon and did some running around with Janet," Anna said. "We're just getting here to the house."

"I'm a little bushed myself," Julia said. "But we had good weather and no delays or cancellations on the way."

"We're not going to stay long," Burton said. "I just wanted to come by and say hello to you guys and make sure you made it in safely," Burton said. "How long are you guys going to be in town?"

"We'll be here for a week," said Julia.

"We really made this trip because we're a little concerned about Janet," Anna said. "Burton, would it be alright with you if we took Janet to see the doctor while we're here?"

"A doctor?" Burton asked. "What for?"

"When you get to be our age, and of course your mother is a little older than us," Anna said. "Sometimes it does the body good to have a checkup every once in a while."

"She hasn't been complaining about anything other than her jaw hurting occasionally," Burton said. "And she's already been to numerous doctors about that."

"We thought it would be something helpful we could do while we're here," said Julia.

"I guess it wouldn't do her any harm to go to the doctor," said Burton.

"Who is her doctor?" asked Anna.

"Actually, she has two," Burton said. "Dr. Hunte and Dr. Bell."

"Which one does she usually go to see?" asked Julia.

"I prefer Hunte, but Bell is right around the corner," said Burton.

"Around the corner where?" asked Anna.

"Right around the corner and down the street about one block," said Burton.

"I think I've heard her mention Dr. Bell before," said Julia.

"I'm sure you have," Burton said. "Bell and Hunte were friends and colleagues of my dad's."

"Why do you say you prefer Hunte over Belle?" asked Julia.

"One or two things he did when he treated my dad when he was sick," Burton said. "Made me think he wasn't that bright."

"And you say Bell is right around the corner," said Anna.

Burton concluded his visit with Anna and Julia. He called the boys and told them to come on. Burton marched his four children out of the door, and they continued towards their house. Meanwhile back at Janet's house, Anna and Julia discussed their plans to call Dr. Bell in the morning in order to try and set up an appointment to see if they could get Bell to refer them to a neurologist. They also talked about trying to find an attorney. However, they were not sure who they could call. Anna stated they would need to contact a lawyer so they could discuss with them what they might need to do in order to get control of Janet and her assets.

The fact of the matter was Anna and Julia had not come to Mobile simply to visit and exchange pleasantries with Janet and the family. Julia and Anna came to Mobile with an agenda which was to get Janet to a doctor, preferably a neurologist who could make a diagnosis. They then planned to get the medical documentation and present it to a lawyer. Their idea was to try and prove Janet had Alzheimer's and suffered from Dementia. They were not exactly sure how they were going to prove their allegations, but they had visited this bridge before when Warren started to show symptoms of aging, regression and memory loss. His children got POA over his affairs and started making life difficult for them. They were not certain exactly how it worked legally. They had discussions about the topic before when they had consulted an Attorney about Warren and his children.

The next morning, Anna and Julia called Dr. Bells office at 8:00 am to try and set up an appointment. The answering service answered the phone and they left a message. However, about an hour later when they had not heard from the doctor they called again. This time they got an answer from Dr. Bell's receptionist. Anna indicated to the receptionist they would like to make an appointment to see the doctor today. Ms. Bosley said she could fit them in this afternoon since it was Mrs. LeFlore. Anna told the lady she could come over and bring her sister as soon as she had a chance to finish her coffee and put on her clothes. They all had a quick bite to eat and a cup of coffee. They urged Janet to get her clothes as they went upstairs to get dressed. Anna and Julia would have to work fast since they had a lot to do in a short period of time.

They got into Janet's car with Anna driving and drove around the corner as Burton had said to try and find Dr. Bell's office. On their way to Bell's office, as they made the curb along Stanton Road, they noticed a billboard advertising the services of two local female attorneys. They decided they would contact the lawyers in the advertisement and see if they could get some advice and possibly some representation. Janet rode with her sister's Julia and Anna to the doctor's office as Janet pointed it out on the left-hand side. They pulled into Dr. Bell's parking lot and made their way inside of his office. Janet sat there in the waiting room with her sister's. She looked at them and looked around the waiting room. She looked back at her sisters and over at the receptionist desk. Janet asked her sisters why they had brought her to see a Doctor when there was nothing wrong with her. The two of them implored upon her they were just bringing her in for a routine checkup. Janet told them she did not see any reason why she would need a check-up when she was feeling perfectly fine.

Anna asked Julia to sit there with Janet and wait for the doctor. She said she would be right back. She took Janet's car and drove back down the street so she could write down the name and telephone number of the attorneys whose names appeared on the billboard. Anna retraced her path back to the advertisement and got the information. As soon as they got finished with the doctor's visit at Bell's office she planned to go back to the house and call to see if she could get an appointment to see these lawyers about Janet. Anna quickly returned to the doctor's office after writing down the names and number of the advertisement. Now she would try and figure out how she was going to convince Dr. Bell that her sister Janet needed to be referred to a neurologist.

They were not waiting long before Janet was called to the back into the examination room. Julia and Anna accompanied her inside as the nurse sat Janet down and took her blood pressure. Janet remained seated on the exam table, stood just outside of the door and Julia remained in the exam room with Janet. Anna wanted to try and catch the doctor before he went in to see Janet, so she could explain to him what her objectives were prior to him entering the room to talk with Janet.

Finally, Ann saw Dr. Bell approaching the examination room where Janet had been waiting. She did not want to stop him while he might have been passing by on his way to another room. She waited until he walked up to the door, stood there for a moment and looked her in the eye as if to say why are you blocking the doorway to where my patient is waiting.

"Dr. Bell I don't know if you remember me, I believe we met a few years ago when Walker died," Ann said. "I'm Janet's sister Anna."

"Yes, yes I remember meeting you," Dr. Bell said. "How is Mrs. LeFlore?"

"That's why we're here," Anna said in a condescending manner. "Has she been in to see you at all lately?"

"No, it's been about a year or so since I last saw her in my office," replied Bell.

"We're a little worried about her," Anna said. "We feel that she might need to go and see a neurologist who might be able to run some tests on her. Unless of course, you could order the tests."

"Why do you think she needs to see a neurologist?" asked Dr. Bell.

"Janet herself asked me to talk with you about this," Anna said. "It's not just us."

"Oh OK," said Bell.

"It's her memory, her behavior and a lot of other alarming telltale signs that make us think she may be suffering from Alzheimer's," said Anna.

"Certainly, it wouldn't hurt to refer her to a neurologist and let him run some tests on her," said Bell.

"Now you're talking," Anna said. "That is what we wanted to hear."

"Let me speak with Mrs. LeFlore for a minute and then I will see about making the referral," Dr. Bell said as he stepped past into the exam room where Janet was waiting. "Mrs. LeFlore, how are you, my dear?"

"I'm doing fine Bell," Janet said. "Here with my sisters today because they said they thought I should have a check-up." Janet continued, "Can't say anything is ailing me, but my jaw once in a while."

"You're still having pain in your jaw?" asked Dr. Bell.

"Yes, but other than the pain in my jaw," according to Janet. "I'm doing well as can be."

"Do you want to go and see another neurologist about it?" asked Dr. Bell.

"I have already been to several neurologists," Janet said. "I'm not going to let them cut the nerve in my face and I do take the pain killers sometimes, but I can't take them during the day because I need to function, and I can't function on the pain medication."

"Are you sleeping well at night?" Dr. Bell asked. "How about your memory?"

"She doesn't seem to be able to remember a thing, isn't that right Ann?" said Julia.

"The reason we're here," said Anna.

"Please excuse me, Julia," Janet responded. "Excuse me, Ann. I really appreciate my sister's concern, but I can speak for myself." Janet continued, "My memory is not as good as it once was. I once could remember everything," Janet said. "Now I can at least remember what I need to remember."

"Well I'm going to refer you to Dr. Kasmia and let him run some tests on you," said Dr. Bell.

"What is his name?" said Ann.

"Did you say Kas, what was that?" said Julia.

"Kasmia," Dr. Bell said. "Dr. Kasmia, his office is at Mobile Medical and Diagnostic," said Bell.

First thing the next morning Anna and Julia got up and dressed and went to visit the Attorney they had contacted the day before. David dropped by to say hello to Mrs. LeFlore and see if she had any work, she wanted him to do. Anna and Julia were glad to see David since they thought he could keep her occupied while they went to talk with the attorney. The two of them quickly looked around to see if they could recognize anything along the line of work for David. Anna suggested the walkway needed to be swept off and the yard needed cutting. David said he would get right to work and asked Mrs. LeFlore if he could have a cup of coffee before he started. Janet poured David a cup of coffee. Anna and

Julia told Janet they were going to run to the store and pick up a few groceries. They urged Janet to stay there with David and get ready for her appointment with the neurologist because they would be ready to take her as soon as they returned from the store.

Janet urged them to go ahead and she would stay and have a cup of coffee with David. She said she would be ready when they returned from the store. Hurriedly Julia and Anna took her keys and rushed out the door. Janet took another sip of the morning coffee and chatted with David while the sisters departed. Anna and Julia made their way to the attorney's office.

It was not long before they found her office and parked. They entered the law office met with the receptionist and took a seat. A few minutes later the secretary told them to step into Ms. Victoria Smoots office. Meanwhile, Janet and David finished their coffee and she opened the garage so David could get the lawnmower out to cut the grass. Victoria Smoots welcomed them and asked them to take a seat so they could talk.

"Ms. Smoots, we're here in the strictest confidence," Anna said. "We're worried about our sister Janet," said Anna.

"Janet LeFlore?" asked Ms. Smoots.

"Yes, our sister Janet LeFlore," said Julia.

"Ms. LeFlore taught me chemistry at Bishop State," said Ms. Smootts.

"She did," said Anna.

"Yes Mrs. LeFlore was my chemistry teacher many years ago," Victoria Smoots said. "Never really cared much for chemistry though."

"We contacted you because we need to know what we can do to help our sister and keep her son from taking everything she has," said Anna.

"What's the problem?" asked Smoots.

"Our sister is in need of help," said Julia.

"What kind of help?" asked Smoots.

"She can no longer manage her bank account and her bills," Anna said. "Her son is no help to her, and he and his family are taking all of her money."

"We don't know what to do, or what legal steps we need to take in order to prevent this from happening," said Julia.

"Are you wanting to seek Guardianship or Conservatorship of Mrs. LeFlore or her assets?" asked Smoots.

"Guardianship?" asked Julia.

"Yes, that is exactly what we are seeking," said Anna.

"Yes, Guardianship and Conservatorship," Ms. Smoots said. "Are you trying to prove she is incapacitated?"

"Yes, she's incapacitated," said Anna.

"That's it, incapacitated," replied Julia.

"Do you have any medical documentation to this effect?" asked Smoots.

"We've spoken with her primary physician and we have an appointment with the neurologist later today," said Anna.

"The only problem is, HIPPA prevents you from accessing her medical records," Smoots said. "You can't prove anything without her medical records."

"You can't take our word for this?" asked Anna.

"No, I can't take your word," Victoria said. "You must have some documented medical evidence which proves what you're saying, or it will be a real uphill struggle."

"How can we get the documentation if we can't see her medical records?" asked Julia.

"Do you think she would willingly agree to give you access to her records?" asked Victoria.

"I don't think she would," said Anna.

"Janet isn't going to give us permission to share her medical information," said Julia.

"On second thought, yes she will," said Anna.

"If you're her healthcare proxy then you will automatically gain access to her medical records," Smoots said "

"How can we become her healthcare proxy?" asked Anna.

"The only way you can become her healthcare proxy is if she is willing to go to the hospital and request an Advanced Directive along with the proper forms and documentation and ask her if she is willing to sign it."

"She has an appointment with a neurologist later today," said Anna.

"Tell the neurologist you need to talk with someone about an Advanced Directive," said Smoots.

"Advanced Directives," said Julia.

"Yes, Advanced Directives," Smoots said. "If we have to subpoena the evidence it could be time-consuming and very costly. If your sister is truly in the need of help this will be the quickest and most cost-effective way to proceed."

"We have little time and even less money," said Anna.

"If you can get her to sign the Advanced Directives naming either one of you her healthcare proxy then we would have a much better case."

"We have an appointment with the other doctor this afternoon," Julia said. "I'm sure he can diagnose her and."

"And we can find out where we need to go to get the Advanced Directives," said Anna.

"You have my number," Smoots said. "If you want to retain me to represent you, I will need a Twenty-Five Hundred Dollar retainer along with whatever evidence you have indicating your sister and my former chemistry teacher Mrs. LeFlore is not capable of deciding or knowing what is in her best interest."

"She has absolutely no idea what is in her best interest," said Anna.

"This is what we've been trying to say all along," said Julia.

"The more evidence you have the better off you'll be," said Smoots.

"Can we count on you?" asked Anna.

"Surely," said Ms. Smoots.

"This is extremely important to us," said Julia.

"We need to know we can depend on you to help us," Anna said. "Otherwise we might need to go and talk to someone else. We'll only be here for a few more days."

"With an Advanced Directive, a letter from a physician, or any evidence you might be able to depose from any person who might have knowledge of the facts," Smoots said. "We would have something that would allow us to move forward."

"We met with her primary physician yesterday and we have an appointment with the neurologist today," said Julia.

"Once we talk with the neurologist, we can see about getting the Advanced Directives," said Anna.

"It would be a great help," said Victoria Smoots.

"We're working on it," Anna said. "We will give you a call in a day or two before we leave."

Later that day, Anna and Julia took their sister Janet to the Medical and Diagnostic Center to visit with the neurologist. Armed with the advice they had just received from the attorney they had a pretty good idea what they needed to do in order to start building their case for Guardianship and Conservatorship of Janet.

They entered the doctor's office with Janet relating to the Neurologist and his staff that they had brought their sister to see him because she had Alzheimer's and was no longer able to manage her finances. To the neurologist who had seen and heard this type of thing before, the way the sisters communicated to him about their sister immediately sent up a red flag. The sisters seemed to be legitimately more concerned about their sister's finances than they were about her health.

However, with Mrs. LeFlore's consent, he conducted some tests and ordered a CAT scan of her brain. While Janet went for the CAT scan and concluded her visit with Dr. Kasmia, Anna and Julia spoke with his nurse receptionist about where they could go to talk with someone about a Living Will with Advanced Directives. The nurse directed them to the Administrative office where they could obtain help with getting what they were seeking.

Janet was taken for her scan. Anna and Julia went to speak with the hospital administrator about what would be involved in getting a Living Will. The administrator told them it was a very simple form they could have their sister fill out if that is what she wanted to do. They told the administrator their sister had been bugging them about it and they were just trying to help her. Anna and Julia said Janet was undergoing some tests at the hospital and they would bring her by her office as soon as she was finished with her tests.

Following the visit, the doctor indicated it would be a few days before he would have the test results and he would notify Mrs. LeFlore of any findings. Anna and Julia implored upon the doctor that they also needed to know what his tests indicated about their sister. Dr. Kasmia informed them HIPPA prevented him from releasing any of Janet's information to them. Kasmia also stated to them Janet had said she had a son named Burton. He asked about her son and said perhaps if they had some concerns about Mrs.

LeFlore they might want to talk with her son. Anna and Julia had already arranged to meet with the hospital administrator so they felt no reason to deliberate further with Dr. Kasmia about Burton or how they would gain access to Janet's medical records. Finally, before leaving the doctor's office Julia and Anna asked the doctor if he planned to prescribe anything for their sister. The doctor indicated that he would have no problem prescribing some Naminda or Aricept for Mrs. LeFlore; however, he had spoken with her about it and she indicated she did not wish to be prescribed any medications at this time.

From Kasmia's office, Julia took Janet straight to the administrator's office to see if they could get her to sign the documents, they would need to fraudulently gain access to her medical records. Janet told them she was tired and ready to go home, but they insisted she go with them to talk with the administrator. Janet reluctantly went with them to the administrator's office. When they arrived, she had the paperwork ready per Julia and the administrator's request.

"Ms. Anderson, this is our sister Janet LeFlore," said Julia.

"Mrs. LeFlore please have a seat," Mrs. Anderson said. "Your sisters said you were interested in doing a Living Will with Advanced Directives?"

"No not really," Janet asked. "What is that and why do I need one?"

"It's just a document we would have on file here at the hospital stating what types of treatments you would want and don't want." She continued, "It lets us know how you would like to be cared for as you age, and who should make decisions for you if you can't make decisions for yourself."

"Certainly, that would be my son," Janet said. "I think I need to discuss this with Burton first."

"Burton is already aware of what you are doing," said Anna.

"He is?" asked Janet.

"Yes, we discussed it with him at length," said Julia.

"And what did he say?" asked Janet.

"He said, and we all agreed, this would be the best thing to do," said Anna.

"Burton is waiting for us to call him now and let him know that we've gotten this done," said Julia.

"In that case, we probably need to go ahead and do it." Janet said, "And what were you saying Ms.," Janet said. "What is your name again mam?"

"I'm Ms. Anderson," said Ms. Anderson.

"Yes Ms. Anderson," Janet said. "What else were you saying about the Living Will?"

"The Living Will is a sort of road map for doctors and case managers to use in managing your care and for you to name a healthcare proxy," said Ms. Anderson.

"What is a healthcare proxy?" asked Janet.

"A healthcare proxy is someone who can ensure that doctors carry out your medical decisions or who will make decisions on your behalf in the event you are not able to make them for yourself. You mentioned you had a son?" asked Anderson.

"Yes, I have a son," Janet said. "His name is Burton and certainly I would want him to serve as my proxy if I could not make decisions for myself," said Janet.

"You could name your son and you could name one or both of your sisters as your alternate," Ms. Anderson said. "The rest of the document focuses on life support treatments and medical procedures, devices or medications to keep you alive when your body might not be able to keep itself alive on its own." She continued, "In the event you were suffering from a terminal or progressive illness or in the event you were ill and unlikely to recover, or if you were in a coma or persistent vegetative state. What would you want done and or who would you want to make those decisions for you?"

"I have excellent insurance that I've worked a thousand years to pay for," Janet said. "And luckily at my age, I'm still in pretty good health."

"Why don't you all sit here and go over this and let me know if you have any questions as long as it's not legal advice or medical advice," said Ms. Anderson as she hands Janet the document.

"I can't find my glasses," Janet said. "I think I may have left my glasses at home. I don't see them in my purse."

"Here Janet I'll help you read this," Anna said. "It's a very simple form."

"Janet I would let you borrow my glasses, but I think I left mine at the house too," said Julia.

"I brought my glasses and I will help you read this," said Anna.

"Maybe I should take it home and read over it after I get my glasses," Janet said. "And discuss it with Burton."

"Janet we're only going to be here for a few days," said. "We're trying to help you get this done."

"Everyone knows as you get older it's important to have things like this done," Julia said. "Just in case."

"Let me see that," Janet said as she took the document and started to look over it. "I can hardly tell what this says."

"It's just a Living Will," Anna said. "Here's where you sign it on the back and there are several questions you have to initial on this page."

"What am I supposed to be initialing?" asked Janet.

"Come on Jeannie," said as she took the form from her. "I will go over it with you."

"Let me see if I can find my other pair of glasses in my purse," said Janet.

"I'll read it too you," said Anna as she took the form and wrote her name in as healthcare proxy.

Anna did not read the form to Janet. She gave the form to Janet and she started to read the first page even though she was having difficulty without her glasses. She gave her the pen and directed her to initial her name on the blank spaces. At the very beginning, the first paragraph stated that if she were terminally ill and her attending physician determined that she had an incurable terminal illness or injury which will lead to my death within six months or less. Janet clearly initialed the space which said, I Do want medically indicated life-sustaining treatment, even if it will not cure me and will only prolong my life. Anna stopped her as he saw her squinting over the paper to see without her glasses. Ann crossed out her initials and checked the box which said, I DO NOT want life-sustaining treatment which would not cure me, but which would only prolong the dying process.

By placing a small x mark by certain boxes, Anna coerced Janet to initial all of the blanks stating she did not want any life-sustaining treatment; she did not want any pain medication to be administered if it were only related to comfort measures and she further tricked her into initialing the box saying she did not want any water or food. Another one of the boxes Janet started to write her initials and Anna directed here to stop. The box which said if she was in a persistent vegetative state if, in the judgment of my attending physician and another physician, I am in a condition of persistent vegetative state, I DO NOT want artificially provided nutrition and hydration under the circumstances indicated below.

Janet read both responses and started to initial the response which said, only if withholding it or withdrawing it, in the judgment of my physician, would cause me undue pain. Ann marked out her initials and told her she had initialed the wrong box, pointing to the line where it said she would refuse any such care in the event she needed it, even if withholding or withdrawing it causes pain.

Near the end of the document was a space where Janet was asked to select a Healthcare Proxy. She wrote in her name as healthcare proxy and wrote Burton's name as a secondary. Janet pointed to the line where the healthcare proxy was designated. She said she wanted Burton to be her healthcare proxy and it appeared her name was listed as the healthcare proxy. Ann lied to her saying Burton had been listed as her healthcare proxy and she had been listed as the alternate. They turned to the back page where Janet signed her name. two witnesses from the hospital staff witnessed.

Now having had Janet sign this Living Will with Advanced Directives which amounted to nothing more than a death sentence for Janet in the event she would go to the Hospital and need medical care. Anna had prompted her to initial no to everything except having Anna as her healthcare proxy. Ann had craftily persuaded Janet to sign this document which was not in her best interest from a medical standpoint. Furthermore, in the event she was to go to the Hospital and her son needed to assist her in making any decisions on her behalf, he would not be able to do so because the Living Will named Anna as her proxy. All of this was done by Janet's sister's Julia and Anna without Burton's knowledge, even though they told

Janet in Ms. Anderson's office Burton was fully aware of what was going on.

Julia and Anna left the hospital that evening feeling like they had accomplished a lot during this day. They had consulted with an attorney who they planned to retain to represent them in their effort to obtain Guardianship and Conservatorship over their sister. They had taken Janet to a neurologist who they hoped would more than likely diagnose her as having dementia, Alzheimer's or both.

If nothing more, they had given him some false information he would ultimately include in his report. If all else failed, they could later turn around and argue the misinformation in the report was truthful, because it was contained in the report. In addition, they had been able to get Janet to execute the Living Will naming Anna her healthcare proxy. This would allow them to gain access to Janet's medical records so they could obtain whatever information they wanted about her and turn it over to their Attorney.

Janet left the hospital somewhat bewildered. On one hand, she was glad to have had an opportunity to speak with the doctor about some of the issues she had been experiencing with her memory. Janet was appreciative of the attention she was getting from her sister's and the concern they were showing for her. She felt their intentions were legitimate and well-intended. She wanted to bring Burton into the loop and let him know what was going on. Janet had a follow-up appointment with the neurologist in two weeks to discuss her results. She hoped Burton would be able to come with her to the follow up so the two of them could discuss everything fully, and Burton could be informed. Janet also wanted to make sure she discussed the document she had signed.

Conversely, she wondered why her sisters seemed so concerned with bringing her to a doctor anyway and talking to him and his staff about how, according to them, she was no longer able to manage her money. Janet wondered to herself how they figured she could not manage her finances. It was just like Julia and Anna to try and talk about her after all she had done for them over the years. Janet started looking forward to them going back home and minding their own business. She hoped Burton would come with her to the follow up with Kasmia. Later that evening Burton came by to visit with his mom and her sisters. He found them all relaxing at Janet's house. It was not long before Anna and Julia sequestered Burton in the den to try and have a discussion with him about Janet. They did not mention the Advanced Directives she signed.

"Burton, we wanted to let you know we took your Mom to the neurologist today," said Anna.

"Who is the neurologist?" asked Burton.

"His name is Dr. Kasmere," Julia said. "I think that's how he pronounces it."

"I think it's Kasmia," said Anna.

"And so, what did he say?" asked Burton.

"Burton, we believe your Mother has Alzheimer's," said Anna.

"Is that what the Doctor said?" asked Burton.

"She has a follow-up appointment in about a week," said Julia.

"We won't be here," said Anna.

"We wanted to ask if you would make sure she gets to that appointment," said Julia.

"Sure thing," Burton said. "Not a problem, what day is she supposed to go back for the follow-up?"

"I think it's the 12th of May," Anna said. "We'll double check the date and time and be sure we let you know before we leave."

"OK that's fine," said Burton.

"You probably should talk with him about putting her on some medication," Anna said. "There's a few medications that a lot of people who have Alzheimer's take. It's supposed to slow the progression of the disease."

"First of all, we're not certain if my mom has Alzheimer's," Burton said. "And you know how my mom is about taking medications. That would be her decision if, in fact, she had Alzheimer's."

"There are a couple of other things we wanted to talk with you about," said Julia.

"It seems Janet spends a lot of time watching your children," Anna said. "Do you really think your Mother can handle the constant responsibility of babysitting the kids?"

"My mom says she enjoys when the boys come over here," said Burton.

"It seems that Candace leaves your children over here a lot," Julia said. "Are you sure your mother is capable of taking care of them?"

"Yes, I think she is perfectly capable of taking care of them," Burton said. "They make her happy, why would I not want her to spend time with her grandkids."

"We just feel it might be a bit much for her," said Anna.

"Look, you're not going to come down here for a few days and change anybody's life," he said.

"Do you think Janet should still be driving?" asked Julia.

"She really shouldn't be driving," said Anna.

"I don't know where you guys are going with this," said Burton.

"We don't think it's safe for her to be driving," said Anna.

"Yea she could have an accident and die," said Julia.

"I'm a little concerned about her driving, but she had been driving for about sixty years," Burton said. "Anyone who gets behind the wheel of a car could have an accident and die."

"You're not getting what we're saying," said Anna.

"I get exactly what you're saying," Burton said. "I realize my mother is getting older, but I'm not going to go and snatch the car keys from her just because you said so."

"We don't want anything to happen to her," said Julia.

"Your mother isn't just getting older, she has Alzheimer's," said Anna.

"Well, we're just going to take life one day at a time," Burton said. "I'm her son and I'm here with her every day. You guys come down here for three days."

CHAPTER FOURTEEN

Julia and Anna concluded their business in Mobile and returned to Philadelphia and Richmond respectively. Janet had been glad to see her sisters and she was happy they had gone home. She looked forward to getting back into her routine of spending time with her grandchildren. She had only seen the boys briefly for most of the time her sisters had been there. Janet was also a little nervous about her follow up appointment with the neurologist. She wondered what he might determine by the tests he had run on her during the earlier visit.

Deep down inside Janet knew she was becoming increasingly forgetful. However, it surely appeared to Janet that her sisters were mighty eager to get her to the doctor, especially since she had no plans on agreeing to take any medication. She thought about the statements she heard them make to the doctor about her no longer being able to manage her checkbook. Janet really was uncertain as to what they were talking about since she knew she could manage her checkbook just fine.

It was no secret Burton and Candace were having problems in their marriage. Burton had found several letters Candace had written to some guy in Los Angeles, California. It was the same person she had traveled to Los Angeles to visit a few months ago. Now Burton had discovered several notes she had written to him expressing her deep love and affection for him. Burton was starting to feel like quite the cuckold. His wife was blatantly cheating on him and she did not seem to have a care in the world for his feelings or the sanctity of their marriage. The entire situation was coming to a head because Burton had, in many ways, reached an emotional end with Candace. The two of them had been through so much during their years as a married couple. There had been many separations and reconciliations. Burton and Candace's relationship had been consistently tumultuous.

However, Burton loved her, and his children and he had tried hard to keep his family together. Although, he was not going to be blatantly disrespected and betrayed. Candace was the mother of his five children. He could not understand how this Forty-something-year-old woman seemed willing to throw everything they had under the bus for this scumbag who was every bit of Twenty-Five years old.

He discovered not just one but several letters Candace had written to Brann. Burton sat there reading what she had written on the pages in her letters in disbelief. Candace was not working. Burton was the only one working and he was paying all the bills. For the most part, he came home and found the house in complete disarray. She rarely prepared a meal for him and the kids, if ever.

All she did was get the children up, make sure they were ready for school and drop them off. As soon as they got out of school, she took them over to Janet's house where she watched them practically until it was time for them to go to bed. From that point on she did nothing to bring any money into their household. She acted as if she had no duty or obligation whatsoever to do anything to make their house a home or to generate any money to contribute to their home. However, she had time to write another man love letter's expressing her deep feelings for him.

Burton was furious and felt emotionally wounded. Of course, over twenty years of being married to Candace had left him emotionally scarred inside. Every person who loves someone else wants to be able to connect with them spiritually and on an emotional level. The essence of the purest love for another person is emotional vulnerability. Every human being wants to be able to coexist peacefully with their partners feelings, statements, actions, sentiments, vibrations, sensibility, and sensuality. Burton had long shut Candace off from the emotionally trusting side of his psyche. He had ventured with her in the barren wasteland of spiritual separation and subrogation. The two of them rarely had sex anymore. The communication between them was mostly negative and not good for the children to hear.

However, they were still together and now Candace seemed to be on a crash course mission which was sure to be devastating to their relationship, and sadly Candace acted as if she could care less. She was proceeding with reckless abandon where Brann and their relationship was concerned. Candace seemed to have little regard for her family or her marriage to Burton. Burton thought about when he first met Candace and they were apart by a thousand miles or more when he was in Mobile and she was with her parents in her home of Grand Rapids, Michigan. The two of them would write letters to each other almost every day. Now over twenty years later they were together and had five children. She was writing another man fantasizing about how wonderful life would be with him like nothing they ever had together even mattered. He was reading her letters to Brann and you would have thought he and the kids did not even exist. It was starting to become a bit more than Burton could handle and it was certainly more than he was going to continue to tolerate.

Burton could not believe his eyes as he read her words on the pages to this man. Burton could not fathom the idea he had married Candace and dedicated his life to her at the tender age of Nineteen years old. At a time in most young men's life when marriage is the last thing on their mind. He had made the commitment and sacrifice of taking a wife at a young age while they were still in college. Their first child had been born a few weeks before they were married at her house in Grand Rapids by her father who was a judge. Burton had always thought and believed he and his wife would grow closer through their struggle. Even though Burton knew his life would have been much easier if he had remained single, he loved Candace and his son. He wanted to spend his life with her and create a family life for his son. However, sadly enough it did not seem as though they had grown closer at all. Unfortunately, it seemed as if they were growing further and further apart.

"My babies," Janet said as she greeted her grandchildren after Candace dropped them off at her house. "How are my handsome boys doing?"

"Fine Grandma Janet," said Breaghan.

"Can Grandma have a hug," said Janet as she hugged Breaghan.

"Hello Grandma," said Bryceton as he hugged her.

"Hey Granny," said Bridge as he walked in the door.

"Granny?" Janet jokingly said as she put her arms around Bridge. "Did you just call me Granny?"

"Yea Granny," said her youngest Grandson Breck Brook as he

walked inside and gave her a hug and kiss on the cheek.

"I missed not seeing you guys the last few days," said Janet.

"We missed you too Grandma," said Breaghan.

"Did you really miss Grandma, Janet?" asked Janet.

"Yes," said Breck Brooke.

"We missed you," said Bridge.

"Hey Granny, I'm hungry, what do you have to eat?" said Bryceton.

"Yea Grandma Janet I'm hungry too," said Breaghan.

"Grandma hasn't cooked dinner today, but we can go to McDonald's and get a cheeseburger," Janet said. "I'm hungry too."

"I want a cheeseburger," said Brooke.

"Yea me too," Bridge said. "Can we go get a cheeseburger."

"I like McDonald's," Breaghan said. "Can we order some French fries?

"Grandma you know I don't eat cheeseburgers," said Bryceton.

"Well they have other stuff besides cheeseburgers at McDonald's," said Janet.

"Can I get a chicken sandwich?" said Bryceton.

"Sure, you can," Janet said. "You can have whatever you want and, yes, we can get French fries."

Janet grabbed her purse and car keys. She and the kids piled into her car and they drove to the nearby McDonald's to get something to eat. They ordered their food at the drive-through. When their order was filled, she quickly drove back to the house where they all ate their dinner from McDonald's. Janet was glad to have her grandchildren back at the house with her. She relished the time she spent with them.

She had truly missed watching them during the few days her sisters had been there. After eating with the kids, she took her broom and went outside. Bryceton stayed inside to work on some homework in the den. Breaghan, Bridge and Brooke followed Janet outside. The boys had their football and they started passing the ball to each other in the back yard. Janet went out to the carport and started sweeping up the leaves. The boys played outside for a while and then they went back inside to watch television. Janet stayed outside on the carport with her broom sweeping until it got dark.

A few days later, Janet went with Burton to her follow up appointment with the neurologist. The neurologist said he would need a few days to get her test results back and had rescheduled her for a follow up so they could go over her results. Janet was appreciative that Burton had accompanied her to the Diagnostic and Medical Center for her doctor's visit. She hoped Dr. Kasmia would give her a clean bill of health and not try and put her on any medication. However, she had already decided she was not interested in taking any medication for Alzheimer's patients. At least her son was there with her now instead of her sisters. This way Burton would be fully informed of anything going on with her. Janet and Burton entered Dr. Kasmia's office and took a seat in the waiting room. The nurse receptionist indicated it would not be long before Dr. Kasmia would be able to see her. After Janet and Burton waited for a few minutes, she called them back to meet with the physician.

"Mrs. LeFlore, I have your test results back from the other day," said Kasmia.

"I hope everything is OK.," said Janet.

"Well yes, everything is alright, but it appears based on your CAT scan that you have suffered a few mini-strokes in your brain," Dr. Kasmia said. "It's not altogether uncommon for a person your age to experience something like this, and it could be attributed to some of the memory loss you described to me during your earlier visit when you presented with your sisters."

"A mini-stroke in her brain," Burton said. "What exactly is that?"

"It's commonly referred to as Microvascular Disease or Vascular Dementia," said Kasmia.

"So, I don't have Alzheimer's though?" asked Janet.

"Alzheimer's is characterized by changes in the brain," Dr. Kasmia said. "Vascular dementia is not Alzheimer's per-se, but in some instances, Vascular dementia and Alzheimer's can occur at the same time."

"Dr. Kasmia, do you think I might have Alzheimer's disease?" asked Janet.

"It's possible you could be in the early stages Mrs. LeFlore," Dr. Kasmia responded. "However, it could be an isolated incident of you having some mini-strokes."

"What exactly does all of this mean for my mom Dr. Kasmia?" asked Burton.

"We will just have to monitor it," Kasmia said. "I can set up an appointment for her to come back in six months. There are some medications that I can prescribe."

"What kind of medications?" asked Burton.

"There's Namenda and there's Aricept," Dr. Kasmia said. "These are medications used to treat Alzheimer's. It could slow the progression, or it could possibly stop her from having the mini-strokes."

"What do you think?" Burton asked. "Do you want to try taking the medication?"

"No, I don't," Janet said. "Dr. Kasmia I'm a chemist, and over the course of my career, I have worked to develop pharmaceuticals. I never liked the idea of being on a lot of medications unless I absolutely had to, and I don't feel like those are medications I need now."

"The same thing Mrs. LeFlore said before," according to Kasmia. "I will see you in six months."

The following day Janet went out to visit with her accountant so she could file her income taxes. Janet gave Mr. Hubbard all the information he needed to file her return. She nervously sat there as she waited for Mr. Hubbard to punch her numbers into his computer tax program. After about thirty minutes of inputting her information, he looked up from his keyboard at her and said she owed to the Internal Revenue Service. He asked Janet if she wanted to look over it and she took the tax return and glanced over it.

How could I possibly owe so much to the IRS she asked him. Hubbard stated that she had few exemptions or deductions to offset any of her income. As Janet sat there looking over the return, Mr. Hubbard indicated he could go ahead and e-file the return if it was alright with her. Janet said she did not want to file the return until he had a chance to review it again and explain to her how she could possibly owe what he was saying she owed.

Janet left Hubbard's office and drove back to her house. Janet wondered how she was ever going to pay the IRS. She thought she might want to discuss what Hubbard had said with Burton. However, when she arrived at her house, she did not call Burton to discuss the matter with him. Instead, she went inside and changed into her heavy cotton gown. She found her broom and went outside to the walkway. Janet was barefoot as she had not bothered to put on any shoes or slippers. She was going to sweep off the walkway while she waited for her grandchildren to come.

While she stood along the walkway leading to her house, she wondered how she would ever be able to pay the internal revenue service. It was a warm April afternoon in Mobile. The springtime Azaleas were in bloom displaying their beautiful flowering pedals. The Dogwood trees Janet had transported back to Mobile from Wilmington many years ago were also blossoming in the picture-perfect spring day. While Janet continued to sweep, she admired the flowers, hedges, and trees that were in bloom. Being outdoors on such a nice day was soothing to her. She started to feel more relaxed and less worried, less stressed.

Meanwhile, Burton had found more letters written by his wife to Brann. By now Burton had come across close to ten letters written by Candace addressed to Brann. Only now the letters were stating that she was pregnant with his child. Burton sat there reading her words as he started to cry. A few tears streamed down his cheeks as he continued to read. He was absolutely flabbergasted. He could not believe what he was reading with his own eyes. Here his wife and the mother of his five children was stating in her own words she was pregnant with another man's baby. This was only a few months after her visit with him in Los Angeles.

She was leaving these letters around as if she could care less if he found them either. However, since finding the first few letters, he looked in her car. Inside the car was where he found more current correspondence suggesting she was pregnant with his child. It was becoming increasingly evident to Burton that this situation was going to get ugly. He pondered in his mind how he was going to handle this information. As a married man with five children already, he knew legally he was the father of number six in the event she was to have another child. At this point, Burton and

Candace's sex life had dwindled to nothing. So, Burton knew there was no chance she could be pregnant with his child. What was he to do? Their relationship had been extremely strained, and it was obviously getting worse.

Burton decided he would contact this guy and have a word with him about what he had been reading in the letters written and address to him. He had obtained his phone number off a piece of paper he had found in Candace's car. He decided to call Brann and let him know that in no uncertain terms if Candace was pregnant with his child, he was going to make sure he would have to take care of his responsibility. He wanted to see exactly what his perspective was on the current developments Candace was alleging. Burton felt he had no choice but to confront this individual about what he knew full well was going on. Burton found his telephone number and called him. The phone rang a few times and Brann answered.

"Is this Brann," said Burton.

"Yes," said Brann.

"This is Mr. LeFlore," Burton said. "The reason why I'm contacting you today is that it has come to my attention that my wife is pregnant with your child. I just want to let you know, if she is going to have your child, I'm going to make sure you're going to have to man up and take care of your responsibility where your child is concerned."

A few seconds after Burton concluded his statement Brann hung up the telephone. Burton was furious and here this little punk bitch had hung up the telephone just as he had guessed he would do. Burton was about ready to go to California and confront him in person, but he realized that would only be something done out of anger and spite. This was only something Burton had known about for some time coming to a head. He dialed his phone number again. This time the phone rang but no answer. Burton hung up, placed his cell phone on his desk and leaned back in his chair as he contemplated. Suddenly his cell phone rang. He reached down to pick up the phone. He looked at the display window and noticed it was Candace on the phone. He thought it was ironic he was receiving a phone call from Candace right after he had just contacted Brann.

"Burton, why did you call him?" Candace asked. "Why are you trying to ruin my happiness."

"I'm sorry I would never want to ruin your happiness," Burton said. "I needed to let him know that if you guys are having a kid, he is going to need to take care of his responsibility. because I'm certainly not going to."

"Why are you trying to ruin my happiness," said Candace.

"Your happiness huh," said Burton.

"Why would you call him?" asked Candace. "Why would you try and interfere in my life like that."

"You're the one who's married and having a baby by another man," Burton replied. "I guess you do have an awful lot going on in your life right now and believe me, I would certainly not want to interfere, and fuck you by the way." As he hung up on Candace, he saw another call coming in from a number that appeared to be Brann.

"This is Mr. LeFlore," said Burton.

"Hey Burton, this is Brann," said Brann.

"I pretty much said what I had to say to you during our earlier conversation," Burton said. "If she is pregnant with your child, I'm going to see to it you take care of your responsibility."

"Are you sure it couldn't be yours?" asked Brann.

"I'm pretty damn sure it's not mine because I'm not fucking her," Burton replied. "Apparently you are though."

"She must have got a condom out of the garbage can that I had used to fuck another girl and impregnated herself with it," Brann said. "We've never been together like that."

"You can tell it to the judge dude," Burton said. "That's your problem, not mine. I'll tell you what, you can have her. I'll put her back on the train and send her back to you, and you guys can work it out."

"Candace is stalking me, she calls me ten times a day and she keeps sending me all these letters," Brann said. "I only date models, not fat two hundred fifty-pound women with four and five kids."

"I don't know what you're going to do man," Burton said. "But I do know what you're not going to do." Burton continued, "You're not going to bring a child into the world and not take care of it. No woman is going to say she's pregnant with someone's child unless they had sex with that person," Burton said. "Or she wouldn't come out her mouth with something like that. Whatever is going on between the two of you is between you. I'm letting you know. You're going to take care of your child."

Burton was in a total state of disbelief. He had just had a conversation with another man about whether his wife was pregnant with a child he knew was not his. And in the meantime, his wife had been immediately informed about their conversation. She subsequently calls Burton and leaves him utterly astonished by stating he was interfering in her happiness. Burton felt there was no way he could remain there in the house with her. Given the current information before him, there was no way he could bear to walk around and live in the same house with her as though they were husband and wife.

Burton felt totally betrayed by Candace. There was no way he could even bear to look at her with the thought she might be carrying some other man's child. Certainly, she could not legitimately even claim to be pregnant by someone she had not had sexual relations with. As he struggled to wrap his mind around what was going on, he became full of the impression that he needed to get his things and move immediately out of the home they shared together.

Burton was not sure how long he was going to be staying there with Janet, but he was certain he would not be going home anytime soon. He would be staying there with Janet long enough to figure out if Candace was expecting a baby. However, even if she was not expecting, it did not seem to Burton like he had any plans on trying to reconcile with her. As far as Burton was concerned, she was his wife, and here she was acting and behaving as if she could care less about him or their family. Perhaps the time had come for her to get some letters. Like some letters from an attorney who said he was asking for a divorce. Even though Burton and Candace had separated numerous times before and got back together, somehow Burton felt this was the end of the road for the two of them.

He settled in at Janet's house. Sad about what had been transpiring between him and his wife and being away from his children, he attempted to adjust to being at his Mother's house. One thing was certain, there was no way he was going back home with

Candace potentially pregnant with a child that was not his. No matter what he would have to do what he needed in order to make himself comfortable staying there with Janet. This was his only revenge, his only way of letting Candace know he had had enough. This was the only way he had to try and make her understand she had made her choices and would now have to live with them.

After a few days at Janet's house, Burton started to realize that some things were going on around there that he had not been totally aware of previously. One thing he realized was there were a lot of bill collectors calling the house constantly. Janet had money and she was not struggling financially, so Burton found it difficult to understand why so many so-called creditors were calling the house. A while ago, Janet had put her lights and water on automatic draft; however, it seemed that most of her bills that were not on automatic draft were not being paid.

Burton remembered a conversation he had with his oldest son Breton, who had been staying with Janet the previous summer, when Breton told him several bill collectors were calling the house. Breton stated to his dad that practically every time the phone rang it was a bill collector on the line. However, it appeared most of the collection calls were from people trying to collect money for magazines Janet had ordered. Janet was receiving about twenty different magazines a month. She was not reading any of these magazines that came to her house on a regular basis. Burton wondered why his Mom had ordered so many magazines. He was aware of agencies out there who prayed on elderly people and Burton wondered if some of these companies were praying on Janet. She had so many magazines coming to the house, there is no way she could have possibly read all of them. Many of the magazines sat unopened on the counter still in the plastic wrapper. Burton started answering the telephone for Janet and telling them she wanted to cancel her subscription. Slowly but surely, the phone calls started to decrease in frequency.

Janet had a credit card company calling her about paying a credit card bill even though she did not have a card in her possession from this company. Most of what she was supposed to owe them was interest and late fees and service charges. She had never made a charge on the alleged card and did not have the card anywhere in her purse or around the house. Burton asked the company to review their records and indicate when the last charge was made on the card. The company said there had never been any charge made to the credit card by his mom; although, they were calling her daily to attempt to collect money from Janet.

Burton also did not realize how often David came by asking his mom for work. Although Burton had known for a long time that David did odd jobs for Janet. When he moved in with her, he was not aware of how frequently he imposed upon her. It became evident to Burton that David may have been taking advantage of Janet. As Burton started to come to grips with the issue surrounding Janet and her reported memory loss, along with the way she was managing her finances, it was highly possible that David was fully aware of the situation with Janet. Although Burton had no actual evidence to prove his assertion, he was certain David might be exploiting opportunities to milk her for more than the menial jobs he did were worth. Since there seemed to be numerous instances when Janet would simply find a job for David to do because she believed he must have needed the money and she wanted to help him.

Almost every day, David would come by the house. Sometimes he would come with his girlfriend and sometimes he would show up by himself. He would sit and drink a cup of coffee with Mrs. LeFlore and then start asking her if she had any work for him. There were a few instances where she might have legitimately had some chore for him to do; however, more often than not, she would ask him to do something like mop the kitchen floor and then turn around and give him way more than the job was worth. Somehow Burton started to strongly suspect that David might be getting money from Janet for a job, and then later in the evening before he left, telling her she had not paid him thereby getting paid twice for the same job. David did not have any regular employment, so Burton started wondering how he was surviving. It came to his attention that David could have been surviving off contributions and payments from Janet.

Burton was not certain David was cheating his mother out of money; however, there was a strong possibility. He decided he needs to get rid of David and stop him from coming by so often trying to create work for himself. As far as Burton was concerned, he needed to sever ties with David.

Burton realized this would not be altogether easy because Janet was very fond of David and had no problem finding work for him so he could make a few dollars. Similarly, Leassie was no longer able to work for Janet and had not been employed in the house for almost three years. He thought to himself, it was time to try and find a housekeeper and caretaker. There was a lady named Mavis he had spoken to about the job on a few occasions. Burton had met Mavis several years ago when she was working at the fish market. Although at this point, David had become one of the things Burton felt he should eliminate. One day Burton ran into David and his girlfriend as they arrived at the house.

"David," said Burton.

"Burt what's up," David said. "Is your mamma here?"

"Yea she's here," said Burton.

"How you been doing?" asked David.

"I've been fine," Burton said. "And you?"

"Pretty good," David replied.

"Can I talk to you for a minute," said Burton.

"Sure, what do you want to talk about?" asked David.

"I hear the State Dock's is hiring," Burton said. "They have a lot of skilled and unskilled jobs available. Those jobs pay Thirty and Forty dollars an hour and up as well as benefits. Have you ever thought about going down there and applying?"

"No," said David.

"Some of those jobs pay a real wage that you can support yourself and your kids and your women on," Burton said. "It pays much better than being my mom's maid."

"You're mom's maid?" said David.

"Yea, seems to me like you want to be my mom's maid, and I don't see how a grown man can support himself and his family on maid wages, especially when they've got good paying job with benefits at the Docks."

"What you say?" asked David.

"You heard me," Burton said. "Did I stutter?"

"Your mother Mrs. LeFlore is my dear friend," said David.

"I know and she's very fond of you as well David," Burton said. "It's just that she won't be needing you anymore."

"I'll just talk with Mrs. LeFlore about that," said David.

"No there is nothing to talk about," Burton said. "I said what I had to say. If you would like to come by and see her every once in a while that would be fine, but as far as you coming by here every day asking her to pay you for some kind of work that she really doesn't need to be done is not going to happen anymore."

"Damn Burt!" said David.

"You got an attitude?" Burton asked.

"Man, fuck you," said David.

"Fuck me!" Burton said. "Really! Hey, David, you need to bounce."

Burton and David parted company as David got into his car and backed out of the driveway. Burton was quite insulted by David's comments and demeanor toward him; although, it could have certainly been expected, seeing as Burton was terminating his hustle. Burton could see there were several things going on in Janet's life, and in her home that concerned him. One thing that was bothering him had been David. From that point on Burton had pretty much stopped David from coming around to the house asking Janet for work.

The long hot summer progressed. Burton had a condominium in New Orleans east in a complex called Chimneywood on Morrison Road near Interstate 10. Burton inherited the property from his brother Champ when he passed. Ever since Champ passed, he had the property rented out. Walker Junior had a much more valuable property on Marais Street in Treme' near the French Quarter, but Burton, Janet, and Beck felt pressured to sell the property after Champ died even though they should have held onto it for dear life.

The property belonged to Burton; however, there was a note on the house and there was not enough income to pay it. Burton was in law school and did not have the money to pay the note. Consequently, Beck and Janet struggled to pay the mortgage. None of them had any fond memories of this house since it was not long after Champ moved in the house, he took sick. They sold the house on Marais but kept his condo in New Orleans East. Everyone had fond memories of his condo and they had no problem keeping it rented. There was a mortgage on the condo. The balance on the mortgage was Twenty-Five Thousand Dollars. Burton had some cash available and he decided to pay off the mortgage with Bank of New Orleans. After all, he had a good tenant living there and once he paid off the mortgage, he would finally realize a profit from the rent.

Burton took the Twenty-Five Thousand Dollars and paid off his note with Bank of New Orleans. Even though he could have used that money elsewhere, Burton was glad he had paid off the mortgage on the property. About two weeks after he paid off the mortgage his tenant gave notice that she was moving. Shortly afterward she did, in fact, move out leaving Burton with an empty condominium. Burton traveled to New Orleans and decided he would invest some money in repairing the property so that he could get it rented to another tenant.

He took his maintenance man Julius and one other worker named Candy to help him do the repairs on the property. They stayed in New Orleans for several days working on the condominium. He cleaned the property, painted the entire unit, shampooed the carpet, and fixed a leak in the roof along with some other minor repairs. He was disappointed that his tenant had moved out on him right after he paid off the mortgage, and now he had to spend even more money to maintain the income stream from the property. He remained optimistic that he would be able to recoup his money within a few years. Now that he had done some work on the property and refurbished the condo, he planned to rent it out again at a higher price.

While in New Orleans he advertised his condo and interviewed a few prospective tenants. Burton finally found a young lady who was interested in renting the unit. She was on Section 8 and had a voucher for almost One Thousand Dollars for a three-bedroom house. The prospective tenant and her mother owned and operated an art store in New Orleans. She told Burton her mother owned the Art Store and she worked for her mother. Since Burton loves art and collects a great deal of it, he bargained with his new tenant Clarissa, to allow him to have several hundred dollars' worth of artwork from their art store and she would pay him the remainder of the deposit in cash. Burton selected some artwork that he wanted.

Some of the paintings were in her store and he also found a few pieces in a catalog that they promised to order for him, and have it delivered to their store for him to pick up upon arrival.

Overall Burton was feeling good about his new tenant and was greatly looking forward to all the new artwork Clarissa had given him and ordered for him. He was glad that he had gotten the mortgage out of the way even though he used just about all the cash he had on hand to pay it off. He would not be collecting the rent and paying the condo assessments and sending the rest to the Bank of New Orleans. By now he had just about finished the work and it would only be a few days before his tenant moved into the house. Burton was not worried about getting his rent because, Clarissa's housing assistance was pretty much guaranteed; although, he would still have to wait at least a month or possibly two months before he would receive the first payment. They concluded the work and Clarissa moved into the unit.

In addition to all the work Burton had done on his condo in New Orleans, Burton's oldest son Breton and his girlfriend Verina were planning to move to New Orleans in about a week and a half to start college at Xavier University. Burton had thought about letting them move into the condo, but decided it would be best if they stayed on campus when they first started school in New Orleans. Besides he wanted to recoup some of his money out of the property. Perhaps in a year or two if everything worked out for them in New Orleans, he could let them move into the condo after he had recouped some of what he had paid out on the mortgage. To say the least there was a lot going on. Now Burton was looking forward to Breton and Verina moving to New Orleans to start school in a few days and he was looking forward to the additional money he would be collecting from his property in New Orleans East. Burton was feeling good about New Orleans, not to mention he had partied some while he had been there. He had gotten his work done and had a nice time in the Big Easy. He returned to Mobile. He busied himself trying to help his son get ready for school.

A few more days went by and Breton and Verina moved to New Orleans to start school. About a day after they started school in New Orleans, news reports started to air stating there was a Hurricane moving into the Gulf of Mexico. Panic started to spread in most communities located on the Gulf since at first, they were not exactly certain where it would land. Another day went by and then news reports started to suggest the Hurricane which they called Katrina would likely make landfall somewhere along the Louisiana, Mississippi, Alabama or Northwest Florida. As the Hurricane gained strength and moved further through the Gulf of Mexico toward land, reports started to indicate that it would hit near New Orleans, the reports stated the Hurricane was very strong and would likely be a category four or five.

Many people along the Gulf Coast, particularly in the New Orleans area started to prepare themselves to evacuate. However, many tried and true residents of New Orleans decided not to evacuate. Burton's wife Candace got the kids in the car and said she was going to drive somewhere north of Jackson, Mississippi. Breton and Verina also drove to meet them. Burton who was now staying at Janet's house since he and Candace had separated, did not evacuate. He remained in Mobile at the house with Janet. He went and purchased a few necessities from the store like candles, water, snacks, and beer. He and Janet prepared to ride out the storm together at her house. Early in the morning on August 29, the horrific Hurricane called Katrina hit the Gulf Coast. When Katrina made landfall, it had a Category Four on the Hurricane barometer. Katrina brought winds of 100 to 140 miles an hour and covered close to four hundred miles along the Gulf of Mexico's coast. All the way from Pensacola, Florida to Lafayette and Baton Rouge, Louisiana experienced torrential rainfall and heavy winds. However, New Orleans caught the brunt of the storm. A few hours into the storm effect, the city known for a drink called Hurricane started to flood as the levees along Lake Pontchartrain were breached and water started to flow into the city. New Orleans flooded as the waters rose to levels of eight feet in some areas.

Meanwhile, in Mobile where Janet and Burton were, they had periodic rain and a few gusts of heavy wind. Mobile did undergo a mild hurricane effect. Mobile had some minor flooding and a few felled tree limbs, but Katrina seemed more like a tropical storm than the catastrophic monster which it turned out to be for the city of New Orleans. Janet and Burton lost power for a few hours; however, by midday, the power had been restored. Janet and Burton were able to go outside after the storm to assess the damage to the yard and it was minimal. However, when Burton went around to his house on Oak Knoll, he discovered another tree had fallen into the roof in the same area where the tree had fallen during Hurricane Ivan.

It was not long before Janet and Burton started to watch the news which was now showing images of Hurricane-ravaged New Orleans covered with water. Janet and Burton watched as areal camera footage of New Orleans showed people standing on top of their houses along with bodies floating in the flood waters. Janet and Burton could not believe they were witnessing such carnage following the storm. It was not long before CNN verified the fact that New Orleans East which is closest to Lake Pontchartrain was completely submerged in water. Burton and Janet surmised it was reasonably certain his condominium in New Orleans East was flooded. He had not spoken with his tenant and was not certain if they evacuated or not. Burton and Janet said a prayer for New Orleans as they continued to watch the news stories about the devastation in New Orleans and Mississippi. Bay St. Louis, Gulf Port and Biloxi, Mississippi were also severely damaged by Katrina. The death toll in Mississippi was very high and there was a considerable amount of damage. The Gulf Coast stood in a state of emergency and it seemed the federal government was dragging their feet with desperately needed assistance.

CHAPTER FIFTEEN

March of 2006 brought another bad wind as Anna, Julia, Bethany, and Peter arrived in Mobile to visit Janet. The morale along the Gulf Coast was still relatively low following Hurricane Katrina. Burton had now been separated from his wife for almost a year now, and the tension between him and Candace was just as thick as ever. He was still staying at the house with Janet. Now here his aunts and uncle had arrived. Burton had just recently hired a lady to come into the house and do some cleaning and to cook some meals for Janet. The new housekeeper named Mavis, worked hard that day with two of her family members to clean the entire house so it would be presentable for Julia, Bethany, Anna and Peter.

Janet was elated to see her sisters, and she was especially delighted to see her brother Peter. Peter had never been to Mobile before. He had never been to visit and had not come to Mobile for Beck's funeral. Burton was glad to see them, but he felt bombarded by them since he still had not discussed with everyone the fact that he and Candace were separated. Burton was certain Janet had probably mentioned it here and there, but he had not discussed it with anyone and felt somewhat uncomfortable revealing much of what was going on in his life to his mother's siblings.

Burton was also becoming increasingly aware that his mother was slipping a little. Janet was definitely not as astute as she had always been. Janet was becoming increasingly forgetful. However, she was still managing her finances, driving and still in control of her life for the most part. Burton was giving her some assistance with some things. Besides hiring the housekeeper, he was not trying to run Janet's house. Burton was laying his head there, going to work and spending time with his kids in the evenings and weekends.

Janet's sister's and her brother had arrived to continue their agenda of retaining an attorney and gathering medical evidence as well as whatever additional evidence they could put together to seek control over Janet and her finances. Janet received a comfortable retirement check and was also collecting social security. Janet had significant real estate holdings in North Carolina and Mobile. She also had some investments which made her financially comfortable. Her sister Ann had convinced all the siblings to come down to Mobile this time. The only two who did not come were Warren and Carol. Warren had Alzheimer's and Carol refused to have anything to do with their plan.

However, Peter, Bethany and Julia went along with Anna and agreed to meet with the attorney they wanted to retain. They also agreed to pool their money to pay the lawyer for her services. The evening they arrived at the house, Janet, Anna, Bethany, Julia, and Peter all sat around and talked with Burton for a while before going to bed.

"Champ's old condo on Morrison was almost completely underwater," Burton said. "The entire first floor was underwater."

"Was there anyone living there?" asked Bethany.

"Yes, the lady who had just rented the apartment evacuated with her family and she is still in Missouri now," according to Burton. "I invested a lot of money in renovating that apartment after the last tenant moved out. I had a mortgage on the condo which I paid off, and this lady had only been living there about two weeks before Hurricane Katrina hit. I didn't even get the first month's rent. All that money invested and no return. She has called me several times over the last few months to ask me if I'm going to repair the property."

"What are you planning on doing?" asked Peter.

"I don't know yet," Burton said. "I'm going to wait a little while and see if things stabilize in New Orleans. Breton and his girlfriend had to finish the semester at Springhill College," said Burton.

"They're back in New Orleans at Xavier now," said Burton.

"How does Breton like Xavier?" asked Anna.

"He said he is majoring in Biology and wants to go to medical school," said Burton.

"He's still dating the same girl?" asked Julia.

"Yes, he's still dating Verina," said Janet. "Her name is Verina. He's crazy about Verina, and she is majoring in chemistry."

"That's nice," Julia replied.

"You wouldn't even recognize New Orleans now," Burton said. "Breton couldn't even get into his dorm room until late October, but they were just able to return in January."

"How are the baby boys?" asked Peter.

"They're doing good," said Burton.

"I bet they're getting on up there," said Peter.

"They're getting bigger by the day," Burton said. "You'll see em soon. I don't know if they have ever met you, Uncle Peter. You weren't down here for dad's funeral."

"Burton, I have back pain real bad," Peter said. "It's hard for me to travel."

"It's good to see you made it this time," Burton said. "The first time you've ever been to Mobile huh?"

"First time, first time," Janet said. "My baby brother finally came to visit me." She reached across the table and hugged her brother.

"Well there's a first time for everything," replied Peter.

"There sure is," said Burton.

"Burton would you mind reaching in the refrigerator and handing me that bottle of Barefoot," said Anna.

"Sure," said Burton.

"Yes, the bottle of Barefoot right there," Anna said. "Thank you," as Burton handed her the bottle of wine.

"Jeannie how have you been doing?" asked Bethany.

"Yes, Jeannie how have you been sister?" asked Julia.

"I'm fine for an old lady," Janet said. "Enjoying my wonderful grandchildren and loving retirement, and by the way, it's so nice for you all to come and see me. I really appreciate that."

"Sister would you mind passing that bottle of Barefoot over here when you get finished with it," said Bethany.

"That's good," Julia said. "We've all been thinking about you, Janet."

"Yes, we've been thinking about you Jeannie," said Bethany.

"I appreciate you," Janet replied. "I've been thinking about you guys too."

"Burton, are you staying here with your mom now?" asked Anna.

"I've been staying here for the last few months," Burton responded. "Candace and I are separated."

"Get out of here," said Anna.

"Yea we have been separated," said Burton.

"What's going on with you and Candace?" Bethany asked. "Excuse me, I apologize if it's none of my business just say so."

"I've been staying here for the last few months," Burton said. "Candace and I are separated. It's pretty self-explanatory right now."

"I hope you all can work things out Burton," said Julia.

"I don't know if that's going to happen," said Burton.

"Burton you and Candace have been together for a long time and you have five children," Janet said. "I hope you guys can save your marriage."

"I appreciate that Mom," Burton said. "I'm not so optimistic about it right now."

The next morning as Burton left for work. Anna, Peter, Julia, and Bethany tried to distract Janet and Mavis. Mavis was cleaning the kitchen, so Bethany asked her to come upstairs and help her wash the bathtub. Anna and Julia contacted the attorney's office while Peter walked outside in the yard with Janet. They wanted to let Ms. Smoots know they had arrived in town and wanted to meet with her. They scheduled an appointment for the following day which was a Thursday at 11:00 am. Bethany prepared some grits and some Conecuh sausage and told Mavis to just relax. Of course, this was fine with Mavis as they all sat and ate grits, sausage and honeydew melon for breakfast. Smoots had been waiting to hear from them and she was ready for their meeting.

Peter stayed back at the house with Janet and Mavis while Anna, Bethany and Julia went to consult with Ms. Smoots. They crowded into Smoots office and sat down with her at her desk. They gave her four checks for Five Hundred Dollars apiece to cover her Two Thousand Dollar retainer as they started to discuss the alternative facts the sisters were going to attempt to allege in court Victoria explained to them the legal parameters they needed to recognize as they embarked on this court action which they anticipated bringing against their sister Janet, her son and her estate.

"We have Two Thousand Dollars to retain you," Anna said. "That's Five hundred apiece."

"How is Mrs. LeFlore doing?" asked Victoria. Smoots.

"She is not doing well," said Anna.

"Her condition seems to be getting worse and worse," said Julia.

"We're here to try and get help sorting through all of this," Bethany said. "Do you think you'll be able to help us?"

"Most certainly," replied Victoria. "I have reviewed the letter from Dr. Kasmia."

"What do we do from here?" asked Anna.

"We file our petition in Probate Court," said Victoria.

"How long will that take?" asked Julia.

"We can file it and then give Mrs. LeFlore and her son time to respond," Victoria said. "Or we can file it as an emergency petition. If we file it as an emergency petition it would be more compelling."

"What do you mean?" asked Anna.

"If we serve them, then Mrs. LeFlore and her son have time to get legal counsel and defend against this lawsuit you're filing," Victoria Smoots said. "If you file it as an emergency petition then it is much more compelling to the court. We can get a lot of things done a lot quicker, like freezing her accounts and getting an accounting of her assets, etc."

"Then we need to file an emergency," said Julia.

"Yes, exactly what we need to file," replied Anna.

"How do we do that?" asked Bethany.

"We show up to court and inform the judge an emergency exists," said Smoots.

"They're going to serve some papers," Smoots said. "Let me know where you want the papers served and we can get the ball rolling. You have paid me my retainer. I'm ready to get to work for you. How do you want to handle this?"

"How can we do the emergency?" said Anna.

"We go to the Probate courthouse and request a hearing with Judge Davis," said Smoots.

"That's it?" asked Anna.

"Yes and no," said Smoots.

"What is the yes and what is the no?" asked Bethany.

"This is a court proceeding," Smoots said. "You got one party represented and ultimately if you intend to pursue your case the other party has a right to representation. I've asked around and people at the bank say Janet is handling her business and no one has anything bad to say about her son. We'll also need a letter or some type of evidence stating that Mrs. LeFlore is incapacitated and not able to take care of herself," said Smoots.

"That should be no problem," Anna said. "We can ask Dr. Bell."

"Whatever evidence you submit needs to be able to stand up in court if you want to prevail," said Smoots.

"We're all here and we're ready to try and get our sister Janet the help she needs," said Bethany.

"Just represent us and tell us what we have to do from this point," said Julia.

"I'm telling you now," said Smoots.

"We've paid you and we are ready to move forward," Anna said. "Our sister's condition is progressing, and her son and his family are taking advantage of her. We don't know what to do to protect our sister."

"We can protect your sister from her son," Smoots said. "You will simply have to give the legal system a chance to work."

"I certainly hope so," Anna responded. "He and his children and his wife have been praying on her for some time now and it has to stop."

"Do you have the evaluation done by the neurologist from last year?" asked Victoria. "It will be hard to move forward without any sort of written medical evaluation from a physician."

"Yes, we do have the evaluation from the neurologist," Anna said. "We have access to all of Janet's medical records at the hospital now."

"We'll try and make an appointment with Bell to see if we can get another letter for you," said Julia.

"It's clearly what you need at this point," Victoria said. "This is a copy of my representation agreement. I would appreciate it if you would review it and sign it."

"Everything appears to be in order," Bethany said. "I'll sign it."

"I can't sign it quickly enough," said Anna.

"Where do I sign?" Julia asked. "Our brother Peter is also here, and we will get him to sign it too."

"Please review my representation agreement thoroughly before you sign, because I have a feeling that we are going to be deep in the trenches with this one," said Smoots.

"Ms. Smoots my sister is suffering from Alzheimer's and her son and his family are abusing her," Ann said. "This case is as plain and simple as a case can get."

"No case is plain and simple as it seems," said Smoots.

"We assure you," Julia said. "We're only trying to do what is in the best interest of our sister Janet."

"And we need your help," said Bethany.

"I'm here to give you all of the help you need," said Smoots.

"I'm so afraid for Janet," said Anna.

"Why do you say you are afraid for her?" asked Smoots.

"Because her son and his wife and children are praying on her, taking advantage of her," said Anna.

"Evidence is the substance of any case that will compel any judge or a jury to rule one way or another," said Victoria.

"We have some evidence for you," said Julia.

"My sister needs our help," said Bethany.

"We're here to help her," Anna said. "Please, we need to move forward as soon as you can."

"I can get all of the paperwork done to move forward," Smoots said. "Just let me know how you plan to proceed with this. Either we serve Mrs. LeFlore and her son, then give them a chance to respond; or we hit them with an emergency proceeding," Victoria said. "The emergency proceedings are much more compelling to the court and they cover a lot more ground in much less time. You need to try and get control of her assets and direct the course of these upcoming proceedings. Time is of the essence. Your sister's life and her well-being are at stake," said Victoria.

"When you said we cover more ground with the emergency proceeding what do you mean by that?" asked Bethany.

"It means we can go into court and have all of her assets frozen immediately and get the Probate Judge to enter a protective order for Mrs. LeFlore and hopefully get her out of a bad situation quicker," Victoria Smoots said. "Are any of you planning to take Mrs. LeFlore with you to get her away from her son?"

"No, no we're not going to take her with us, not right now," said Anna.

"What are your plans?" asked Smoots. "Do you think it would be better for her to go into a nursing home?"

"We're afraid her son is going to put her in a nursing home, and we don't want her in a nursing home," Anna said. "If we could get control of her money, assets and rental property then we could easily set it up for her to be cared for her in her home."

"Alright well think about how you want to pursue this case and let me know," said Smoots.

"Thank you, Ms. Smoots," Julia said. "We'll be here for a few more days."

"We'll think about it and give you a call tomorrow," said Anna as she Bethany and Julia exited the attorney's office.

Later that evening, they sat around the house trying to figure out what would be the best way to go about bringing their case in court. Janet had gone outside, and she was sweeping the carport. None of them went outside with Janet. Peter, Julia, Bethany, and Anna discussed what Attorney Smoots had said with Peter.

"Look at her out there sweeping the carport like she's in a whole different world," said Anna.

"Ann, if Jeannie wants to sweep the carport, then it's her carport and she is going to sweep it," said Bethany.

"We need to decide how we're going to handle this," said Julia.

"Based on what the lawyer was saying," Anna said. "It would be best to do the emergency."

"But how are we going to do that with Burton here?" asked Julia.

"You know I'm not even sure if this is the right thing to do," Peter said. "Maybe we should just talk with Burton and explain to him that he needs to start taking care of his damn mother."

"Don't you think we've tried to talk with Burton," Anna said. "This is our only alternative."

"He's here with her at the house now," said Peter.

"Have you seen the sheets on Janet's bed," Anna said. "They're filthy."

"I haven't seen her sheets, isn't that why he hired the lady, what's her name?" asked Peter.

"Mavis," said Bethany.

"Yea Mavis, she is supposed to clean the house for Janet," Peter said. "Janet has had a housekeeper for a long time. And she's here with her now."

"No telling how long that is going to last before he goes back to Candace and moves back in with his family," said Julia.

"He probably isn't even staying here," Anna said. "He probably just came over here because he heard we were coming."

"No, I think he is staying here now," Bethany said. "Janet has mentioned it to me on several occasions over the last few months."

"She's mentioned it to me too," Peter said. "We can avoid all this court stuff and paying this lawyer all this money and we just stress upon Burton what he needs to be doing."

"He knows what he needs to be doing," Anna said. "He's not doing it and he's not going to do it. He could care less about Janet."

"You do what you're gonna do," said Peter.

"We need to get a letter from one of Janet's doctors besides the one we have from the neurologist," said Anna.

"Thought you said the doctor around the corner could give us another letter?" asked Julia.

"We'll have to call his office and make an appointment," said Bethany.

Burton pulled into the back yard. Janet was standing there sweeping the carport. Burton asked Janet where her company was and she said they were in the house. He hugged Janet and asked her to come inside and rest for a minute. Although Janet wanted to continue sweeping for a while longer, she agreed to go in the house with Burton. Janet and Burton strolled down the walkway leading to the back porch. Burton and Janet entered the house. Bethany, Peter, Ann and Julia were all seated around the island bar in the middle of Janet's kitchen. Burton was greeted with a host of smiles, grins, and hellos. Burton brought Janet over to the table and urged her to take a seat. However, she was thirsty and went into the refrigerator and poured herself a glass of Pepsi.

"I'm going up to Wilmington pretty soon," said Burton.

"Really? When are you going to Wilmington?" asked Anna.

"Probably in the next month or two," Burton said. "Those people I rented Mary Lillie's house to aren't working out. They're not paying their rent. I'm getting them out of there and then me and Julius are going to do some work on the house and try and get it rented again."

"In a month or two?" said Julia.

"Yea I'm going to have to go up there pretty soon," said Burton.

"I didn't know you had her house rented?" asked Bethany.

"I've had it rented ever since Mary Lilly passed away," Burton said. "But so far the last two tenants I had in there didn't pay. That's why I need to go up there."

"It's hard trying to manage property when you're not living nearby," said Peter.

"That's true," replied Burton.

"Wilmington is beautiful this time of year," said Julia.

"You'll have to be sure and let us know when you go," Anna said. "We might want to ride down and meet you there."

"No problem," said Burton.

"Jeannie you should be tired," Bethany said. "You have been out there in the yard working for a couple of hours."

"I'm fine, just getting some exercise," Janet said. "I enjoy being out in my yard. It's relaxing."

"Jeannie, are you hungry?" asked Julia.

"Yes. I wouldn't mind having a bite to eat," said Janet.

"I'll fix you a plate Jeannie," said Bethany as she started to get Janet's food. "Burton do you want some?"

"I already had something to eat with the kids," Burton said. "I'm not hungry right now."

"How are the kids?" asked Julia.

"They're fine," Burton said. "They'll probably be over here a little later."

"I hope they'll come by," said Janet as she sat there nibbling at the food Bethany had just handed her.

"Janet you sure do love those grandchildren of yours," said Peter.

"I don't have much to look forward to at this point in my life," Janet said. "I love them so much. They're just as sweet as they can be," jokingly Janet continued, "Most of the time!"

"I'd better be going," Burton said as he started to head for the door. "I need to get back to the office and finish my work. I'll see you guys a little later."

Little did Burton know as he left the house, he had answered his aunt's question and helped them to solve their dilemma. Armed with the information that Burton was planning to leave town and go to North Carolina soon, they could wait until he left and then come back to Mobile and file their petition as an emergency in Probate Court. They could contact their attorney tomorrow and let her know they wanted to file it as an emergency, but they would need to return and do it later. Now all they had to do was wait for Burton to make his trip to Wilmington. Anna's mind was busy at work. She would make sure Bethany, Julia, and Peter were on the same page at the earliest possible opportunity. They all sat there with Janet while she finished her dinner.

The next day Anna contacted Victoria Smoots and told her they had decided they would pursue the case in Probate Court as an emergency petition instead of having Janet and Burton served and given a court date to be heard. Ms. Smoots asked if she wanted to try to get on the docket before they left town. Anna explained to the attorney she would have to wait for a month or two and then return to Mobile to do it. She did not explain to Ms. Smoots that she wanted to wait until Burton went out of town.

Ms. Smoots was told she would need to get some of Janet's financial information together for her. She would need to know where Janet had bank accounts and where she might have had any investment accounts. Smoots explained she would need this information to give to the court to have her assets frozen and seized. Anna promised Smoots she would get that information together for her as soon as possible. She hung up the phone with the Attorney and immediately went into Janet's room and started snooping around in her papers.

A little later that day, Anna suggested to Janet they needed a couple of dollars to buy some groceries for the house. She asked Janet if she had been to the bank lately. She knew Janet made frequent trips to the bank. Even though Janet was retired she still went to the bank almost every day. She urged Janet to come and ride with her to the bank so they could get some money.

Janet grabbed her purse. They went in Janet's car to two different banks. She followed Janet into the bank. Everyone knew Janet at the bank and the clerks were kind and attentive to her. While Janet conducted her business at the teller window, Anna approached the bank manager and requested information regarding the bank's phone number and address. Julia and Bethany stayed at the house and continued to go through some of Janet's papers to see what they could find. After Janet finished making her bank rounds, they went to the grocery store to buy a few things for the house. Anna questioned Janet repeatedly about where she had accounts and even asked her about some of her other investments. Janet answered Anna's questions very freely and candidly. Janet is an extremely trusting person and had no problem discussing her accounts and money with her sister.

Sadly enough, Janet was slipping mentally, and she needed her sister and brother's love and support. Although, Janet did not need any help from them whatsoever financially. What her sisters were planning was misguided, cruel and totally uncalled for. They were there in Mobile visiting with her and she was happy to have them. However, all they were doing the entire visit was plotting to bring a lawsuit against Janet and her son for control of her assets. They were trying to gather whatever evidence they could find. They intended to allege she was mentally incompetent and did not know what was in her best interest.

Mainly their case was going to be directed at Burton. They understood their lawsuit hinged on Janet's competency because naturally if it was established that she suffered from Alzheimer's, the next question would be who was going to make decisions for or manage her finances in the event she was unable to do so. Janet and Burton were extremely close. Burton was a loving, dutiful and attentive son. Surely, she would say she wanted Burton to make important decisions for her. The gist of the case would be to prove that Burton was not a good person and would not care for his mother. Therefore, the court would need to put them in control of everything.

Janet and Burton had no idea they were sleeping with the enemy. They were entertaining family sitting around eating and drinking with these people who had misaligned intentions. Janet did not have a clue as to what they were up to. Although Burton had every reason to be highly suspicious about his Aunt's frequent visits to Mobile. Burton legitimately thought his mother's sisters were visiting because they wanted to spend time with her and were concerned about her in the right way. He had no idea what was going on with his mother's folks, even though the writing was all over the wall. Burton needed to step up the level of care and attention to his mother and her affairs, but he was slowly but surely easing his way into it. Burton was aware of his mother's digression, but he was not totally accepting of the idea that she was suffering from Alzheimer's.

When their brother Warren first started fading, they were advised by an Attorney when his children sought power of attorney over his affairs that they should have petitioned the court for conservatorship or guardianship of their brother's assets. Warren's children Patsy, Rita and Benny had been a real pain in their ass since they took control over Warren's business. Although Burton had taken no steps to gain power of attorney over his mother or to challenge them on any of their jointly owned property. They had learned something, and they wanted to try it before Burton managed to get himself in gear. Their intentions, motivations, and actions were so severely disconnected from any shred of moral or rational interpretation. Their sister Janet needed their compassion and understanding, not their utter contempt and disdain. Certainly not what they were contemporaneously planning and orchestrating while coming to visit as a fair weathered family to gain control over Janet's money.

Burton came by and picked up his Uncle Peter one morning. The two of them rode around and went down to Burton's real estate office. They then drove downtown so Burton could check his post office box. Burton and Peter admired the construction of the new Retirement Systems of Alabama high rise which was being built in Mobile. Despite the damage caused by Hurricane Katrina, the construction of the new RSA tower had never missed a beat. The new skyscraper in the heart of Mobile was under construction and it was quite a sight to see as it stood amid the city scenery in its pure grandeur and ostentation.

Burton wanted to drive his uncle by his house on Oak Knoll to show him where he lived. As Burton and Peter drove down Oak Knoll Circle, Burton saw Candace pulling out of the driveway in the Yukon. She passed him and his uncle as she drove out of the cul de sac. She frowned at Burton as she passed him and did not even speak to him. Burton was certain his Uncle Peter had witnessed Candace drive right past and not even acknowledge him. As Burton was desperately trying to piece together the puzzle of his life with his wife and family, he had no idea what was brewing in the wings with his mom's people.

In an effort to prove to Peter that they had tried to talk with Burton, Anna and Julia staged another so-called intervention with Burton. They were planning to leave on the following Sunday, so the Saturday before they left, they waited for Burton to come home. They asked him to come into the den so they could have a private conversation with him. Anna, Julia, and Bethany sequestered Burton in the den to talk with him for Peter's benefit. Here they had hired an attorney and they were going to seek Guardianship and Conservatorship over Janet. They had every intention of making him into the villain of the day. They were going to lie on him, smear his name and denigrate his character. The real question would be why they were placating Burton with their rhetoric about Janet. Burton was living with Janet in the same city and for the last few months, he had been living there with her at the house. Just like they had told Peter earlier they were through talking with Burton. The only reason they ever spoke with him in the first place was to see how much cooperation they could get from him in their scheme without him knowing what was going on.

"Burton, we'll be leaving tomorrow, and we wanted to speak with you about Janet before we left," said Anna.

"What do you want to talk about?" asked Burton.

"We're still worried about your mom," said Julia.

"I think it's wonderful you have been coming to visit her and spending time with her, because at the end of the day that is what family is about," Burton said. "She doesn't seem like the same person since my dad's been gone."

"We understand this but," Anna said. "The doctor suggested she take some medications and she still isn't taking any."

"She said she didn't want to take it," said Burton.

"Why not?" asked Julia.

"I don't know, she's never liked taking medications," Burton said. "She won't even take pain killers to help with the pain she has in her jaw."

"If the doctor recommended it, why wouldn't you encourage her to take it?" asked Anna.

"If she doesn't want to take it then she doesn't want to take it," Burton interjected. "I agree with her I am the same way. We don't believe in, or like taking medication unless it's absolutely necessary and here we are not dealing with a medical necessity. Why would I encourage her to take something she clearly said she didn't want to take? That makes no sense."

"And she's still driving after we told you last time she shouldn't be driving," said Anna.

"I'm here with my mom every day and I'm not going to snatch her car keys and everything else away from her just because you say so," Burton replied. "I'm concerned about her driving but that's something she and I are going to deal with in our own time, not because you came down here for two or three days and said so."

"It doesn't seem like you're listening to what we're trying to say to you," said Julia.

"Your mother's sheets are filthy," Anna said. "Have you seen her sheets. How could you let her sleep on dirty sheets?"

"She told me she didn't want to change the sheets because those were the lasts sheets that Dad had slept on," Burton said. "But I've hired some help to come in and clean the house and I'll have her change the sheets. The sheets do need to be cleaned, but if someone tells you I don't want to change the sheets because they were the last sheets my husband slept on, then what am I supposed to do. If you were so concerned about her sheets being dirty last time you were here, why didn't you change them?"

"You could change them, Burton," said Bethany.

"My Mom is perfectly capable of changing her own sheets if that is what she wanted to do," said Burton.

"Janet has always prided herself in her appearance," Julia said. "Her appearance has always meant so much to her and it seems like lately, she had not been looking like herself."

"She's getting a little older Aunt Julia," Burton replied.

"Her ADT security system is no longer being monitored," Anna said. "Are you aware of that?"

"Yes, I asked her several years ago, not long after my dad passed, why she wasn't turning on the alarm at night when she went to bed," Burton said. "She said she didn't want the alarm on because sometimes there were false alarms. She felt like it would horrify her if the alarm went off while she was sleeping. That was something she did a long time ago."

"What about all of the bill collectors that are calling?" asked Julia.

"They aren't calling anymore," Burton said. "I've made an effort to get most of that cleared up. You see all of these magazines. She's ordered a lot of magazines and most of those bill collectors are the companies who sold her those magazines."

"It's not just magazine companies," Anna said. "The last time we were here the cable company came out to turn off the cable and I had to pay them," said Anna.

"You had to pay them," Burton said. "Or you paid them with her money?"

"I wrote them a check on Janet's account," replied Anna.

"So why are you saying you had to pay them?" Burton said. "My mom is perfectly capable of paying her bills without any help from you Aunt Ann."

"Janet needs help paying her bills," said Anna.

"Yes, and I have my own bills to pay," Burton said. "But I'm starting to help her with her bills too."

"Burton we just want you to take care of your mother if she needs it," said Peter.

"That's all we want Burton," Bethany said. "That's all we want."

"My mom has been through a lot these last few years," Burton said. "She's getting older. I know she is getting old. You act as if I'm not aware that my mother is getting older. My dad was getting older and he just died a few years ago. You guys are getting old. I'm getting old. We're getting older. Mom is 80 years old. You act as if you expect her to be the same woman she was when she was 30 or when she was a young girl growing up in Grandma and Granddaddy's house in Wilmington when you were kids or something. Maybe that scares you to see your sister growing old, but it doesn't scare me. I'm just happy to still have her here with me. My mom always said to me, 'we have but two choices in life, to grow old or die young.' "

"We're not just talking about growing old here," said Anna.

"Then what are you talking about?" asked Burton. "The only thing you can do for her is to be her sister and show her love and kindness. I know for a fact that's all she's ever shown any of you."

"Jeannie is very special to us Burton," said Bethany.

"Janet has been a good sister to all of us," Peter said. "And I know she has been a good mother to you."

"Yes, she has," Burton said. "But I'm not talking about her in the past tense, because she's still a good mother and a good sister. Another thing I don't think you realize is that she constantly talks about how much she misses my dad."

"Burton your mother doesn't miss your father!" Anna said. "Your father has been dead for five years now. She doesn't miss him! Janet has Alzheimer's! She has Alzheimer's and you're in denial. You need to accept that your mother has Alzheimer's"

"She may have Alzheimer's, she may not have Alzheimer's," Burton said. "We're going to take life one step at a time."

"Ann, who are you to speak about my heart or how I feel," Janet said. "Do you know my heart? Do you know what makes me sad or what makes me happy? Do you know the loneliness that I have experienced since Beck passed? How can you sit there and say to my son that I don't miss my husband? How do you know what I miss or don't miss? If your husband was gone, could I speak on how you felt about it? How would you even know if I missed my dead dog? I still miss Mamma and Poppa! I miss A.B. and El and our sister Evangeline. How do you know what I feel in my soul?" Janet continued, "I miss Beck with every fiber of my life, every day of my life. He was my husband for over Fifty years. Tell me what do you know about that? I loved my husband. I will miss him until the day they lay my body down next to his and I go to join him in heaven. If you want to talk about you then fine, but I suggest you leave talking about me and how I feel to me."

Burton abruptly ended the conversation. He had been watching Janet looming around in the background listening to every word that was being said. Anna, Julia, Bethany, and Peter said they wanted to have a private conversation, but they all seemed to be talking with no regard for Janet who was walking around very quietly listening to every word being said. Basically, at this point, Janet had said all that needed to be said. Anna did not immediately reply to Janet's statements. Julia, Bethany, and Peter were silent. Nobody said a word as Burton got up and left the table where they had been seated and approached Janet to circumvent any tension that might have been developing in the room as his mom weighed in on their conversation.

Janet and Burton dropped Peter, Julia, Bethany, and Anna off at the airport the next day. They returned home and life for Janet resumed back to normal. Janet liked all of the attention and the visits she had been receiving from her sisters. Now her brother Peter had come to Mobile for the first time to see her. Neither Burton nor Janet had a clue they had retained an attorney and were trying to breach her doctor-patient confidentiality to wrongfully attempt to use her medical records against her to gain control of her money and assets.

Janet and Burton both thought her siblings were sincere and meant well. Although Burton resented the way they always seemed critical of Janet and him. They had such a condescending attitude. They were his mother's family, and he saw his Mom becoming more vulnerable around them. Janet had always been very giving and forgiving but they all knew not to fuck with her. Everyone in her family showed her the utmost respect. He did not know how to interpret the situation. All of his life, Janet had always been very much in control when it came to her family, especially her sisters.

Mavis the new housekeeper had started coming regularly Monday through Friday. Mavis was dependable and arrived at work on time. She prepared meals for Janet and did light housekeeping for her. Burton did direct her to change the sheets on Janet's bed which she did. Those sheets were dirty as they could be. Janet had not washed them in almost five years.

A few weeks went by and it was now springtime in sunny Mobile, Alabama. For several days straight the weather was simply stunning. Crisp blue skies amid the blossoming and flourishing flora of lower Alabama. The type of days when the temperature is perfect, and everything was green and in bloom as the splendor of springtime resonated in the air. The beauty of the sunny southern weather was mesmerizing. Janet was drawn to her yard. All her Azalea bushes were blossoming their precious watermelon red and white petals.

She loved being outdoors in her beautiful and spacious area outside of her massive home. She got her broom and went outside to sweep the leaves off the walkway. Janet stayed outside for several hours sweeping all of the leaves off the pathway leading to her back door. As Janet swept, she felt almost as though she were in a trance. The spring weather was captivating. Janet knew it was about time for her grandchildren to get out of school.

She hoped Candace would bring them by the house. Perhaps they would enjoy playing in the yard while she swept the driveway. Mavis came to the door and asked Janet to come inside and take a phone call. She put down her broom and went inside to answer the telephone. Mavis said it was the kids' school on the phone. The school contacted Janet and asked if she would come and pick the boys up since they claimed Candace had not yet presented herself to pick up the children.

Janet told the school there was no reason to contact Burton because he was at work. She said she would be more than happy to come to get the boys from school. She immediately changed her clothes, got her purse and keys. Janet jumped into her car and drove down Stanton Road toward Springhill Avenue. She made a right onto Springhill and proceeded to Interstate 65. The boys' school was located on Azalea Road. Janet exited Interstate 65 onto Airport Boulevard and proceeded to Azalea Road where she made a left turn on Azalea Road. She drove down Azalea toward the school as she did not want the boys to wait there for her too long. She hurried as much as she could. As she drove to the boys' school, she thought she would take them to get something to eat on their way back home.

She was not exactly certain where the school was, but she had the address and knew it was on Azalea Road; however, the school sat back off the road a considerable distance. Hurriedly Janet drove down Azalea Road looking for the school so she could pick up the children. She looked on both sides of the street, but she did not see the school anywhere. She continued to drive down Azalea but still did not see the school. Before she knew it, she had driven all of the way down to Cottage Hill Road. She had been to the boys' school before and she felt she had passed the school, but she was not sure where she was.

She saw an elementary school on the corner of Azalea Road and Cottage Hill, she remembered how she would drop Burton off there when he was a youth for tutoring. Janet also saw a CVS Drugstore to her left. She made a turn into the parking lot of the school and looked for the kids. Janet was certain the boys would be outside waiting for her when she arrived. She drove around the school parking lot and did not see the boys anywhere. Janet was suddenly severely confused. She drove across the street to the CVS parking lot and parked.

Now that she was inside the parking lot it seemed she lost all her bearings. She wanted to pick up the boys from school but was uncertain where the boys were or where the school was located. She wanted to return home, but she was not sure exactly how to get back to her house. Janet sat there for a few minutes and pondered on her current situation. She figured it would be best to call Burton. She tried to use her cell phone but was unable to reach him because she could not remember his phone number.

Janet started to panic and feel frantic, anxious and nervous as she tried to figure out how she could pick up the boys and get back to her house. A car pulled up next to her. Janet approached the driver of the car and told her she was unable to find her grandchildren and she was trying to pick them up from school. Janet further stated to the lady she was not sure how to get back to her house. The lady recognized Mrs. LeFlore because she had taken chemistry from her. She immediately went over to Mrs. LeFlore and brought Janet into the drugstore with her and asked the receptionist to call the police.

Janet stood there at the checkout counter as the clerk called the police. Janet wondered to herself why they were calling the police and not her son. The lady asked Janet if she was alright, and she stated she would like for them to contact her son Burton. A few minutes went by and an officer responded to the scene. Janet met with the officer and indicated to him she needed to find her grandchildren and she wanted to get home but was not sure how to get there.

"I'm Janet O. LeFlore and I'm looking or my grandchildren. They're in school and I need to pick them up, but I can't find the school," said Janet.

"Mam do you have your driver's license?" asked the officer.

"Yes, give me a minute," Janet said as she retrieved her purse. "I'll get it for you."

"This is Mrs. LeFlore," Monique said. "She used to teach chemistry at Bishop State. She said she's not sure how to get home and she wants to contact her son."

"Do you have your son's phone number?" asked the officer.

"Mrs., LeFlore do you have his number?" asked Monique.

"Yes, I do," Janet said. "I have to find it."

"I will be more than happy to contact him if you have a number where I can reach him," said the Officer.

"His number is 378-6590," Janet said. "I think that's it."

"Will you please call him and see if you can get him to come get her?" asked Monique.

"I'm dialing his number now," said the officer.

"I need to pick up my grandbabies," said Janet.

"Mrs. LeFlore we are just going to try and see if we can get your son out here to pick you up right now," said Monique.

"You're calling Burton," Janet said. "Yes, please call Burton."

"Mr. LeFlore this is Officer Marcella," the police said. "I am here with your mother Mrs. LeFlore. She asked me to call you."

"Is everything alright?" asked Burton.

"Well yes," Officer Marcella said. "Your mother needs you to come and get her. We are at the CVS at Azalea Road and Cottage Hill. How long do you think it would take you to get here?" he asked.

"Give me twenty minutes and I'll be there," Burton replied.

A few minutes went by and Burton arrived at the CVS on Cottage Hill and Azalea Road. The school had also contacted Burton when Janet did not show up. Burton went by the school to see if his children were still there, apparently, Candace had finally come and picked them up. He continued out Azalea Road in an attempt to retrieve his mom. Burton pulled into the CVS parking lot and saw Janet's car there parked next to the police cruiser. Janet saw him as he entered the parking lot. She waved at him as he approached her and Officer Marcella.

Janet stood there leaning against her car. She was relieved to see Burton coming. She was totally confused and disoriented. Janet was glad the kind policeman had not tried to put her in jail. She felt alone and insecure as she saw her son approaching. Janet hoped that now Burton was here, everything should be alright. She would be able to find her way home now and hopefully get to her grandchildren because they might be waiting for her to pick them up from school.

"Are you Mr. LeFlore, her son?" asked Officer Marcella.

"Yes," replied Burton.

"Burton," said Janet.

"This is your mom?" asked Marcella.

"Yes, this is my mom," Burton said. "Her name is Janet LeFlore."

"I've been here with her for the last few minutes. She said she doesn't think she can make it home," Officer Marcella said. "She needs some assistance, are you able to see to it she gets home safe?"

"What's the problem?" asked Burton.

"I got lost and I don't know where I am," Janet said. "Where are we?"

"Right now, we're at the CVS on Azalea and Cottage Hill," Burton said. "The kids' school is down the street. Across the street is a school where you used to drop me off every morning for summer camp."

"I looked all over for their school and couldn't find it anywhere," said Janet.

"You just passed it about a mile and a half back that way," Burton said. "Haven't you been to their school before?"

"Yes, I've been to their school once or twice before," Janet said. "I thought I remembered where it was, but I couldn't find it and I got lost."

"Can you assist her in getting home?" asked the officer.

"Of course," Burton said in total shock. "Yes, I'll take her home."

"Do you need to call someone to drive her car or do you want me to call a tow truck?" asked Officer Marcella.

"No that won't be necessary," Burton said. "Mom, get in the car. Let's go home."

"I need to go to the school and get Breaghan, Bryceton, Bridge, and Brooke," said Janet.

"I went by the school and they left already," Burton said. "Candace must have picked them up."

"Are you sure she should drive sir?" asked officer Marcella.

"She can drive," Burton replied. "She drove all the way out here. She said she doesn't know her way home. It's fine. She can follow me to the house. I will get her home. Mom, get in the car and follow me."

"I'll be right behind you Baby," said Janet.

"Just get in the car and follow me," said Burton.

"Alright," said Janet.

"Thank you, officer. She'll be fine," Burton said. "She can drive. I'll make sure she gets home."

"Thank you so much for helping me," said Janet.

"No problem Mrs. LeFlore," Officer Marcella said. "I just want to make sure you get back safely. Glad your son is here now."

"Yes sir, I can take it from here," said Burton.

"Come on Mom do you think you can make it?" asked Burton.

"I'll be right behind you," said Janet.

Janet followed Burton back down Azalea Road toward Airport Boulevard. To avoid getting on the expressway, he took McGregor Street back on the way back to her house and turned onto Springhill Avenue. He monitored Janet through his rearview mirror. She appeared to be handling the car and was able to follow him as they drove through the city back toward the house. A few miles later Janet and Burton were turning onto her street and approaching the driveway. By now it was almost dark. Burton decided he would talk with his mom about whether or not it would be safe for her to continue driving when they got back to the house. He was not exactly sure how to go about having this conversation with her because he thought she might become defensive. They pulled into her yard and parked their cars. Burton went over and opened the door for Janet as she turned off the car and collected her purse. He escorted her into the house.

"Mom I think we need to talk," Burton said. "Most importantly I'm glad you're alright and home. I'm trying to understand what happened back there. I can't help but be concerned about whether or not you should continue driving."

"Burton I truthfully can't explain it," Janet said. "One minute I was trying to find the kids school and the next minute I felt lost and I had no idea where I was."

"We can't let that happen again Mom," said Burton.

"Baby, don't worry," Janet responded. "Maybe I'll have to stop driving. That was a terrifying experience."

"Mom I want you to give me the keys to the car," replied Burton.

"Here," she said as she handed Burton the keys.

"I can drive you or maybe if Mavis's license is good, she can drive you around some," said Burton.

"I don't want to drive anymore," Janet said as she rubbed her forehead. "You won't get a fight out of me about that. I don't want to ever feel like I did sitting out there in that parking lot again. I felt so helpless, lost, alone and afraid. I don't ever want to feel like that ever again."

"You don't have to be alone," Burton replied. "And you can still get around, we just have to make some adjustments."

"They say you may forget what someone said to you, and you may forget what someone did to you, but you will never forget how they made you feel," Janet continued. "I would say this situation is analogous. I forget things sometimes, but I'll never forget how it felt sitting there in that parking lot not knowing if I could find my way home. Thank you for coming to get me, Baby."

"Mom, you don't have to thank me for anything," said Burton.

"I don't know what I would do without you Burton," said Janet as she struggled to fight back her tears.

"I'm your son," Burton said. "As long as there is blood flowing through my veins, I will always be here for you."

"Thank you, Burton," Janet said. "I don't know what to say."

"You don't have to say anything," Burton said. "Just assure me that you won't get behind the wheel of your car again."

"I promise Burton," Janet said. "I'm done driving. I gave you the keys and I give you my word."

"Then this is a start," Burton responded. "We have an understanding about the car."

"Yes," said Janet noticeably rattled and upset as she agreed to Burton's request that she not drive anymore.

"Alright then if we are both in agreement that you'll let someone else drive you if you need to go somewhere," Burton said. "Then I think we have made some headway in this conversation between us. This is only for your safety and well-being."

"I said I don't want to drive anymore," Janet said. "How many times do you want me to repeat myself. It's not easy growing old. I won't drive. I'll let someone else drive me."

Afterward, Burton told Mavis she could drive Mrs. LeFlore around to do her errands or if she just wanted to get out of the house. Mavis started driving Janet and she did not show any interest or desire to drive anywhere from that point on. Burton was starting to see more and more signs that Janet was suffering from diminished capacity and dementia. Although he knew he was justified in requesting she not drive anymore, he was surprised that she so willingly and graciously agreed. He had heard stories of families with a parent, spouse or loved one who suffered from Alzheimer's who strongly resisted any prohibitions on their right to operate a motor vehicle.

Burton was increasingly aware that Janet was becoming more and more forgetful. She was slowly slipping mentally as she grew into her early Eighties. It was also becoming increasingly evident to him that he would need to step up his effort with regard to her personal affairs. Over and over again he was starting to witness and experience the strong, brilliant, beautiful, vibrant woman he had always known as his mother becoming more withdrawn and less in touch with the real world. It was hard for him to deal with and difficult for him to accept the changes Janet was undergoing in her life.

A few weeks went by, as Burton prepared to travel to Wilmington with Julius to deal with his nonpaying tenants. He had finally managed to get them to move by filing an Eviction in New Hanover County. The tenants went ahead and vacated as soon as he filed the eviction. He was glad of this because he was not sure if he would have been able to make it there for their court date. Luckily his tenants were professional rent dodgers and they already knew enough about the game to understand they had to move when he filed their eviction. Mary Lilly's house was now vacant, and he needed to get up there for a few days to do some work on the property and find a new tenant.

He and Julius traveled to Wilmington to handle their business. They got there and immediately started work on the house. Burton had to put the two of them up in a hotel and finance the repairs, so he had no time to waste. He and Julius needed to get in there and do what they had to do and get out of there. As soon as Anna and Julia found out Burton had made his trip to Wilmington, they got their ducks in a row and made plane reservations to fly to Mobile. The cost of their tickets was extremely high since they had to make their airline reservations on such short notice. However, they paid the airfare in excess of One Thousand Dollars to get to Mobile quick, fast and in a hurry.

Mother's Day was soon approaching. Burton was inundated with thoughts of his mom as he and Julius worked on the house. Burton was there in her hometown of Wilmington working on the street where she grew up as a child. There was a lady who was living across the street, who had indicated she was preparing to move out of her house and wanted to know if she could rent Mary Lilly's house at 1006 S. 12th Street. Burton had taken the woman's application and it appeared she would be a suitable tenant with enough income to pay the rent. The only problem with this lady was she had five children. She had three boys and two girls.

The house was technically a two-bedroom house even though there was perhaps another room in the house she could use as a bedroom. Burton felt this lady would pay the rent, but he was concerned her kids would likely result in a lot of wear and tear on the house. However, at this point, the last two tenants he rented the house to had not paid him, and he was desperate to get a paying tenant into the house so it would not sit vacantly and fall victim to vandals and vagrants.

The prospective tenant had an adorable young daughter who looked almost just like Janet when she was a child. This young lady bore a striking resemblance to Janet in photographs he had seen of her when she was young. Burton even told the lady her daughter looked a lot like his mom. She also played outside a lot and was a tomboy like everyone told him Janet had been as a youngster.

Burton decided he would rent the house to them. So now all he had to do was finish the work so he could get back to Mobile.

"Mom I'm standing outside of Mary Lilly's house on the porch and the weather is simply beautiful here today," said Burton.

"How much longer do you think it will take you to finish the work on the house?" asked Janet.

"A few more days and I'll be finished," Burton said. "I think I've found a new tenant for the house."

"That's good," Janet said. "How much are you renting the house for?"

"Seven Hundred Fifty Dollars a month," said Burton.

"You think you can get that much for the house?" asked Janet.

"Sure," Burton replied. "The rents here in Wilmington are much higher than in Mobile."

"Who's the new tenant?" asked Janet.

"Her name is Denise," Burton said. "And you know what?"

"What?" asked Janet.

"She has a little daughter who reminds me so much of you," Burton said. "She looks just like you looked when you were her age. It's so surreal being here in your hometown, standing on Mary Lilly's porch on the street where you grew up watching this young lady skateboarding up and down the street. Even though I know they didn't have skateboards when you were growing up."

"No, they didn't have skateboards when I was growing up," said Janet.

"It's weird," Burton said. "It's almost like I'm looking at you when you were a child. Sometimes I wish I had a daughter."

"So far you're five boys for five boys not a girl in the bunch," said Janet.

"Maybe one day, I'll have a daughter," said Burton.

"I would like to know what you're trying to do to straighten things out with your wife?" asked Janet.

"Mom I don't think Candace and I are going to be able to straighten things out this time," Burton said. "As much as I hate to say it, I'm at the end of my rope with Candace and I know we have five children together, and I would like to see it work, but I don't think it is going to happen."

"You need to straighten out your life before you think about having any more children," Janet responded. "I don't want to see you and Candace divorce."

"It's fairly certain that's what is about to be happening soon Mom," Burton replied. "I don't see us reconciling this time and its only inevitable that we are going to be getting a divorce."

"Whatever you do Burton," Janet said. "Don't forget your children must come first and foremost before any and all petty differences you may have with Candace."

"Mom I'm putting my children first," Burton said. "I believe I'm doing just that."

"The most important thing you can do is put your children first," said Janet.

"I've been with Candace for over Twenty years Mom, and this is not easy for me," said Burton.

"I'm expecting Candace to bring the boys by here in a little while," Janet said. "How long do you think it'll be before you get back to Mobile?"

"A few more days and I'll be home," said Burton.

"By the way," Janet said. "Julia and Bethany are on their way down here."

"Again," said Burton.

"They said they'll be here tomorrow," Janet said. "Will you be back by then?"

"No, I probably won't be back until Saturday or Sunday. I need to finish the work on this house and then I need to get it rented."

"OK Baby but will you hurry and come home," said Janet.

"They sure are making a lot of trips to Mobile," Burton said. "It's nice that your sisters are reaching out to you and trying to spend more time with you."

"They said they want to go to Biloxi to the Casino while they are down here, and I need some money to buy some food for them while they're here."

"I'll call Steve and ask him to send you a check out of your investment account," said Burton.

"That will be fine," Janet said. "Ask him to send me a Thousand Dollars, that will give me enough to buy some groceries and take them to Biloxi."

"I'll call him and tell him to send you the money," Burton said. "And I will see you in a few days."

"I'll see you at the end of this week," Janet said. "I love you, Baby."

"I love you too Mom," said Burton.

"Call me tomorrow," said Janet.

"Alright, I'll talk with you then," said Burton.

Janet hung up the phone with Burton. She was surprised and disdained by her son's lack of perception and understanding. As much as she loved her sisters and wanted to see them all of the time, even Janet who insisted that she be allowed to survive and exist in her perpetual bubble of incorruptible, naivete and unwillingness to admit any wrongdoing or ill intentions in any person who might be around her or in her presence. Even Janet wondered to herself why Burton was not suspicious of her sisters' actions. These heifers had not been to visit her so much in all of the years of her life in Mobile. She could not understand why Burton who was always suspicious of everything and everyone, had not said anything about all of these visits by her sisters in such a short period of time. Not to mention all of the conversations about her and her so-called condition. However, Burton had a lot going on at the time with his business, his failing marriage, his children, additional various and sundry matters, his mother and everything else going on in his life.

She felt uneasy knowing Burton would not be there when her sisters arrived in Mobile. Janet wondered what they would do now they knew Burton was out of town. Old or not, Janet knew they were up to something. After all, game certainly recognizes game. Janet recognized and saw the game going down within her family and with her sisters. Of course, even though she knew it was pervasive within her personal space, she decided not to acknowledge it and trust Anna, Bethany and Julia. After all, they were her sisters. She had not heard much from her sister Carol though.

That night Janet went to bed looking forward to seeing her sisters. Although she felt a bit of anxiety about their visit. She tossed and turned all night. It seemed odd to her they wanted to rush to Mobile as soon as they found out Burton had gone to Wilmington to work on the house. She would have felt much better if Burton had been there. Janet tried to dream of Beck and how he always made her feel strong and invincible. However now she felt vulnerable and alone. She wanted so much to believe her sisters were honest, but they always seemed to be nitpicking and critical of everything about her and her life. Janet hoped Burton would hurry up and make his way back home. She went to the kitchen and poured herself a glass of champagne and went back to bed. Finally, after taking a few sips of her glass she drifted off to sleep.

The following day Anna, Bethany, and Julia arrived in Mobile. They rented a car at the airport which they never did. As soon as they got into town, before going to Janet's house they visited with Victoria Smoots and told her they were in Mobile and wanted to file the emergency petition on their sister's behalf. The attorney reiterated to them the fact that their complaint and petition would be more provoking to the court if they had some type of written documentation from one of Janet's doctors stating that Janet was incapacitated, unable to take care of herself and in need of help and assistance. Victoria Smoots told them she would prepare the petition and try to get it set for the next Probate Court docket for the judge to hear. All they would need now would be a letter from one of Janet's physicians. Anna, Julia and Bethany decided to go and speak with Dr. Bell about writing the letter. They would have to try and figure out a way to convince him to comply without Janet knowing.

Anna decided when they got to Janet's house, she would hand write a letter, which they could then take to Dr. Bell and request he transcribe it onto his letterhead. Anna had seen people come into her husband Mike's office on occasion with something they had written out asking the doctor to make their words his words. She had borrowed some plain white paper from Ms. Smoot's office. Now she only had to figure out what to say in the letter. As soon as she arrived at the house with Julia and Bethany, she went upstairs into the room where she planned to sleep and started drafting the letter. She sat on the side of the bed and drafted her letter on the nightstand. Bethany and Julia stayed downstairs and chatted with Janet as they brought their bags into the house. Ann tried to come up with something quickly so hopefully, they could get it over to

Dr. Bell's office before he closed. Anna drafted the following letter:

"Mrs. Janet O. LeFlore is my patient who suffers from Alzheimer's Disease (dementia), and it is getting progressively worse. She is unable to live alone and take care of herself and her responsibilities. It is my opinion within a reasonable degree of medical certainty that she needs someone with her 24 hours a day, that she should not drive a car or babysit her grandchildren alone. At this point in her disease, she could be a danger to herself and others. If you have any questions, please contact my office." She signed her name Anna Lane at the bottom of the letter and put Janet's phone number above her signature.

She rushed downstairs where Janet, Bethany, and Julia were talking. Anna rushed by them and out to the car to retrieve her suitcase from the trunk. She also placed the letter inside of the car trunk so Janet would not find it while they were riding over to the Doctor's office. She got Janet along with Bethany and Julia and escorted them out to the car. Janet asked where they were going? Julia explained to her they were going to see Dr. Bell.

Janet told them she did not know why they needed to see Dr. Bell because there was nothing wrong with her. They ignored her as they drove around the corner to his office. You would have thought Ann was rushing Janet to the emergency room as fast as she was driving. A few seconds later they were pulling into Bell's parking lot. Dr. Bell had several patients sitting there in the waiting room when they arrived. burst into his door pulling Janet by the arm followed by Bethany and Julia. She sat Janet down in one of the chairs and approached the reception desk.

"I'm Ms. Lane and I'm here with Dr. LeFlore's widow, Mrs. LeFlore, we need to see Dr. Bell," Ann said. "I realize we don't have an appointment, but we really must talk to him, it will only take a minute."

"Pretty please," said Julia.

"We have an emergency of sorts with our sister Mrs. LeFlore and we need to see if there is any way he can help us to help her," said Anna.

"Dr. Bell is in with a patient right now, but I will talk with him and let him know you're here," said Pam the receptionist.

"We know she doesn't have an appointment and he has a pretty full waiting room right now," Ann said. "There is no need for him to see her as a patient today, we just want to ask if he will write a letter for us and we only have two days to be here, if there is any way he could write it for us this afternoon so we can get our sister some immediate help," as Anna rambled on and on at the reception desk Dr. Bell came walking by. She waved at Dr. Bell grinning from ear to ear. "Dr. Bell how are you, remember me, I'm Janet LeFlore's sister."

"Yes, of course, I remember you," said Dr. Bell.

"Dr. Bell you're just the man we want to see," said Julia.

"We know you are extremely busy, but could we speak with you for a quick second?" said Anna.

"Sure, come on in," said Dr. Bell as he looked over and waved at Mrs. LeFlore sitting there.

"Dr. Bell we're trying to get some assistance for our sister Janet, and we would like to ask you if you would type this letter for us?" asked Anna.

"Janet has Alzheimer's," said Julia.

"Dr. Kasmia diagnosed her last year," Anna said. "We have the report if you want to see it."

"We just need you to write a letter for us," said Julia.

"Her condition is getting worse and we are trying to get her some help," said Anna.

"And only have a few days here in Mobile," said Julia.

"Sure, I will write a letter," Dr. Bell said. "Who do you want to address it to?"

"You can just address it to whom it may concern," Ann said. "I have the letter right here. All you have to do is have one of your girls type it for us."

"Is there any possible way we could have it back by in the morning," said Julia.

"Yes, we need it in the morning," said Anna.

"Tomorrow is Wednesday and I'll be out of the office," Dr. Bell said. "My son is graduating from medical school on Thursday and I'll be going out of town for the graduation."

"Oh my goodness. That's wonderful," said Anna.

403

"Congratulations, I know you must be the proud poppa," said Julia.

"What medical school?" asked Anna.

"John's Hopkins," said Dr. Bell.

"John's Hopkins!" Anna exclaimed. "Very impressive."

"Thank you, I'll have Pam type it up for you right now," Dr. Bell said. "That way I can sign it and you can take it with you. Why don't you have a seat in the waiting room, and I'll get that done for you right now."

"Thank you so much, Dr. Bell," said Anna.

"Yes, God bless you and congratulations on your son's graduation from medical school," said Julia.

"Thank you," Dr. Bell said. "Have a seat in the waiting room and she will get this ready for you."

"How is Burton doing?" Dr. Bell replied. "He knows about all of this?"

"He is doing well," said Anna.

"Oh yes," said Julia.

"He knows," said Anna.

"Yes, he is," said Julia.

"He is the one who asked us to come over here and talk with you," Anna said. "The only thing is he is out of town right now."

"No problem. Just have a seat and I can have it ready for you momentarily," said Dr. Bell.

Anna and Julia returned to the waiting room and sat down next to Bethany and Janet. Bethany, Julia, and Anna where high profile in the waiting room as they sat there coddling and placating their sister Janet. Everyone in Mobile knew Mrs. LeFlore. All of the patients in the waiting room knew who she was. One of the patients even came over and spoke to her. He said that he had been a former patient of her husband Dr. LeFlore. Another patient had studied chemistry under Janet at Bishop State and she was so happy to see Mrs. LeFlore. Dr. Bell came out and spoke to Mrs. LeFlore again as she sat there surrounded by her sisters.

He did not, however, ask Janet to come back into his office or one of his examining rooms to discuss the letter he was about to sign. Bell made no attempt to examine or evaluate Mrs. LeFlore. There was a lot going on with him, and he assumed that since Mrs.

LeFlore was there present and surrounded by her sisters that she was aware of whatever it was they were trying to do. Pam his receptionist finished the letter, he signed it, gave it to Anna, Bethany, and Julia. The sisters left the doctor's office with Janet in tow. When they arrived back at Janet's house, they called Victoria Smoots and told her they had the letter and they were ready to move forward with their court petition.